Iamblichus *De Anima*

PHILOSOPHIA ANTIQUA
A Series of Studies on
Ancient Philosophy

Founded by J. H. Waszink† and W. J. Verdentus†

Edited by
J. Mansfeld
D. T. Runia
J. C. M. Van Winden

Volume 42
John F. Finamore and John M. Dillon
Iamblichus *De Anima*

Iamblichus *De Anima*
Text, Translation, and Commentary

BY

John F. Finamore
John M. Dillon

Society of Biblical Literature
Atlanta

IAMBLICHUS *DE ANIMA*

Library of Congress Cataloging-in-Publication Data

Iamblichus, ca. 250–ca. 330.
  [De anima. English & Greek]
  Iamblichus De anima / text, translation, and commentary by John F. Finamore and
John M. Dillon.
    p. cm. — (Philosophia antiqua ; v. 42)
  Originally published: Leiden ; Boston, MA : Brill, 2002.
  Includes bibliographical references and index.
  ISBN 978-1-58983-468-2 (pbk. : alk. paper)
  1. Soul. 2. Iamblichus, ca. 250–ca. 330. De anima. I. Finamore, John F., 1951– II.
Dillon, John M. III. Title.
  B669.D42E5 2010
  128'.1—dc22

                       2009053322

Printed in the United States of America
on acid-free paper

For Susan and Jean

. . . οὐ μὲν γὰρ τοῦ γε κρεῖσσον καὶ ἄρειον,
ἢ ὅθ' ὁμοφρονέοντε νοήμασιν οἶκον ἔχητον
ἀνὴρ ἠδὲ γυνή.

TABLE OF CONTENTS

Preface ix

Introduction 1

Greek Text and English translation of the *De Anima*.................. 26

Commentary to the *De Anima*.. 76

Greek Text and English translation of Pseudo-Simplicius and
  Priscianus 229

Commentary to Pseudo-Simplicius and Priscianus 252

Bibliography 279

Index Locorum... 286

Index Nominum.. 296

Index Rerum 299

PREFACE

The genesis of this edition goes back to the early 1970's, when John Dillon composed a preliminary draft of a text and translation of the surviving portions of Iamblichus' *De Anima*, in the wake of his edition of the fragments of his commentaries on the Platonic dialogues.[1] This project, however, went no further at the time, and it was not till many years later, in 1986, that Dillon decided to revive it by inviting John Finamore, who had recently published a monograph on Iamblichus' theory of the "vehicle" of the soul,[2] which had involved close study of Iamblichus' *De Anima,* among other texts, to join him in putting out a proper edition, with commentary, of what remains of this interesting work. Intensive and continuous work on the project was postponed until 1995 after the co-authors had completed other projects of their own. This present edition is the result of that pleasant cooperation.

Iamblichus' *De Anima* survives only in the pages of John of Stobi's *Eclogae,* where it makes up a considerable portion of John's chapter *On the Soul.* John is interested in the work, however, primarily from a doxographic point of view, so that what we have is mainly a survey and critique of previous opinions. On the other hand, Iamblichus' own doctrinal position does become apparent at various points, particularly in the context of the criticism of his immediate predecessors, Plotinus, Amelius and Porphyry, and, since most topics proper to a discussion of the nature and powers of the soul are covered, it may be that we do in fact have a large part of the work. The idiosyncrasy of Iamblichus' position, however, only becomes plain when one takes into consideration certain passages from the later commentary of Pseudo-Simplicius on Aristotle's *De Anima* and from Priscianus' *Metaphrasis in Theophrastum.* We have included those as an appendix to this edition.

Iamblichus comes, of course, near the end of a long line of philosophers who have composed treatises on the soul, or on some aspect of it, and he is himself plainly cognizant of that tradition.

---

[1] *Iamblichi Chalcidensis in Platonis Dialogos Commentariorum Fragmenta,* Leiden: Brill, 1973.

[2] *Iamblichus and the Theory of the Vehicle of the Soul,* Chico: Scholars Press, 1985.

Beginning in the Old Academy, both of Plato's immediate successors Speusippus and Xenocrates wrote treatises *On the Soul* (Xenocrates in two books), though we have no idea of their contents--except, no doubt, that they incorporated their respective definitions of the soul, both recorded by Iamblichus. Then, of course, there is the surviving treatise by Aristotle, which forms an essential part of all later discussion, whether one agreed with his doctrine or not. Theophrastus also contributed treatises *On the Soul* and *On Sense-Perception,* the latter of which survives, while a summary of the former is preserved in the *Metaphrasis* of Priscianus. The early Stoics also wrote on the subject, notably Zeno and Chrysippus, presenting a doctrine of a unitary soul (though divided into eight parts), distinct from the body--unlike Aristotle's theory--but interpenetrating it, and composed of material *pneuma.* Their doctrine of a unitary soul was disputed by the later Stoic Posidonius, who wrote a treatise *On the Soul* in at least three books, and who reintroduced from Platonism the concept of an irrational as well as of rational soul (for which he is commended by Galen, in his treatise *On the Doctrines of Hippocrates and Plato*).

Among later Platonists, Plutarch composed a treatise *On the Soul* of which only a few fragments survive, but his treatise *On the Creation of the Soul in the Timaeus* is preserved, and is of great interest, not only for its presentation of his own position, but for its information on the theories of his predecessors, such as Xenocrates and Crantor. Of other Middle Platonists, we know of a specific treatise *On the Soul* only from the second-century Platonist Severus, though others, such as Atticus and Numenius, certainly had views on the subject of which we have record, and they all make an appearance in Iamblichus' work. The work of the later Aristotelian Alexander of Aphrodisias *On the Soul* was also influential, particularly on Plotinus, though Iamblichus has no occasion to mention him by name.

As for Iamblichus' immediate predecessors, Plotinus does not, of course, compose treatises in the traditional scholastic manner, but various of his tractates, notably *Ennead* 4.3-5, *Problems of the Soul,* 4.7, *On the Immortality of the Soul,* and 4.8, *On the Descent of the Soul into Bodies,* are of importance for Iamblichus (though his references to Plotinus are actually rather non-specific and confused, as we shall see). Of any relevant treatise by Amelius we know nothing, but from Porphyry we know of treatises *On the Soul* and *On the Powers of the Soul,* fragments of the former of which are preserved by Eusebius, of the latter by John of Stobi.

Iamblichus' treatise, therefore, comes at the end of a very long tradition, of which he is the heir, and to some extent the recorder, and we must be grateful to John of Stobi for preserving even as much as he did of it.

The authors wish to thank the previous and current graduate students at the University of Iowa who worked on typing and proofing various sections of the text, especially the Greek text: Lisa Hughes, Svetla Slaveva-Griffin, Gwen Gruber, and Keely Lake. Dr. Finamore expresses his thanks to the Iowa Humanities Council, whose assistance allowed him to travel to Dublin in April 2000 to meet with Dr. Dillon and discuss the project.

The two authors divided the work of the translation and commentary between them. Although different sections were the primary responsibility of one of the authors, both authors read and commented on the sections of the other. In April 2000, the two authors met in Dublin to go over and correct the *De Anima* sections. The appendix was completed and reviewed by mail and e-mail. The final result is a truly collaborative project.

The following is the breakdown of the primary responsibility for the sections of the *De Anima* and the appendix on the Pseudo-Simplicius and Priscianus:

Sections	Primary Translator/Commentator
1-9	Dillon
10-16	Finamore
17-24	Dillon
25-38	Finamore
39-53	Finamore
Appendix	Finamore

John M. Dillon and John F. Finamore

INTRODUCTION

I. *Iamblichus: Life and Works*[1]

Of Iamblichus' life, despite the biographical sketch of the late fourth century sophist Eunapius of Sardis, in his *Lives of the Philosophers and Sophists*,[2] little of substance is known. Reading between the lines of Eunapius, however, and helped by pieces of information from elsewhere, reasonable conjecture can produce probable data.

Eunapius reports (*VS* 457) that Iamblichus was born in Chalcis "in Coele (Syria)." After Septimius Severus' division of the Syrian command in 194 C.E., this refers, not to southern, but to northern Syria, and so the Chalcis in question must be Chalcis ad Belum, modern Qinnesrin, a strategically important town to the east of the Orontes valley, on the road from Beroea (Aleppo) to Apamea, and from Antioch to the East.[3] The date of his birth is uncertain, but the tendency in recent scholarship has been to put it much earlier than the traditional date of c.265 C.E. Alan Cameron, in "The Date of Iamblichus' Birth,"[4] bases his conclusions on the assumption that the Iamblichus whose son Ariston is mentioned by Porphyry (*VPlot. 9*) as having married a lady disciple of Plotinus, Amphicleia, is our Iamblichus. This assumption seems reasonable, since Porphyry expects his readers to know who this Iamblichus is, and there is no other Iamblichus in this period and milieu. Porphyry's language is ambiguous, but to gain a credible chronology, one assumes that Ariston married Amphicleia some time after Plotinus' death, and probably not long before 301 C.E., when Porphyry composed the

---

[1] For a fuller version of the account given here, see J. Dillon, "Iamblichus of Chalcis" in *ANRW* II 36:2 (1987), 868-909, itself a revised version of the introduction to his edition of the fragments of Iamblichus' commentaries on the Platonic dialogues, *Iamblichi Chalcidensis in Platonis Dialogos Commentariorum Fragmenta*, Leiden, 1973.

[2] Editions: W.C. Wright, Loeb Classical Library (with Philostratus, *Lives of the Sophists*), Cambridge, 1921; G. Giangrande, *Eunapii Vitae Sophistarum*, Rome, 1956 (page numbering from Boissonade's edition, Paris, 1822).

[3] J. Vanderspoel, "Themistios and the Origin of Iamblichos," *Hermes* 116 (1988), 125-33, has presented an interesting argument in favour of the Chalcis in Lebanon (mod. Anjar), but not so persuasive as to induce me to change my view.

[4] *Hermes* 96 (1969), 374-6.

Life. Even so, and accepting that Ariston was much younger than Amphicleia, one cannot postulate a date for Iamblichus' birth later than 240 C.E. Iamblichus was not, then, much younger than Porphyry himself (born in 232), which perhaps explains the rather uneasy pupil-teacher relationship they appear to have enjoyed.

According to Eunapius, Iamblichus was "of illustrious birth, and belonged to the well-to-do and fortunate classes" (*VS* 457). It is remarkable that this Semitic name[5] was preserved by a distinguished family in this region, when so many of the well-to-do had long since taken on Greek and Roman names. But there were, in fact, ancestors of whom the family could be proud, if the philosopher Damascius may be believed. At the beginning of his *Life of Isidore*,[6] he reports that Iamblichus was descended from the royal line of the priest-kings of Emesa. Sampsigeramus, the first of these potentates to appear in history, won independence from the Seleucids in the 60's B.C.E., and was in the entourage of Antony at the Battle of Actium. He left a son Iamblichus to carry on the line, and the names "Sampsigeramus" and "Iamblichus" alternate in the dynasty until the end of the first century C.E., when they were dispossessed by Domitian. Inscriptional evidence, however, shows the family still dominant well into the second century.[7]

How or why a branch of the family got to Chalcis by the third century is not clear, but it may have been the result of a dynastic marriage, since Iamblichus' other distinguished ancestor mentioned by Damascius is Monimus (Arabic *Mun'eim*). This is not an uncommon name in the area, but the identity of the Monimus in question may be concealed in an entry by Stephanus of Byzantium (s.v. *Chalcis*), which reads: "*Chalcis*: fourth, a city in Syria, founded by Monicus the Arab." Monicus is a name not found elsewhere, and may well be a slip (either by Stephanus himself or a later scribe) for 'Monimus.' This would give Iamblichus an ancestor of suitable distinction, none other than the founder of his city.[8] What may have

---

[5] The original form of Iamblichus' name is Syriac or Aramaic: *yamliku,* a third person singular indicative or jussive of the root *MLK,* with *El* understood, meaning "he (sc. El) is king", or "May he (El) rule!".

[6] Ed. C. Zintzen, Hildesheim, 1967, 2; and now P. Athanassiadi, *Damascius, The Philosophical History* (Athens, 1999).

[7] *Inscriptions grecques et latines de la Syrie* V, 2212-7. Cf. also John Malalas, *Chron.* 296.

[8] Unless in fact the reference is to the *god* Monimos, attested by Iamblichus himself (*ap.* Julian, *Hymn to King Helios,* 150CD) worshipped at Emesa in association with the sun god. The royal family may conceivably have traced their ancestry to

happened is that a daughter of the former royal house of Emesa married into the leading family of Chalcis, and one of her sons was called after his maternal grandfather.

There is no doubt, at any rate, that Iamblichus was of good family. Such an ancestry may have influenced his intellectual formation. His tendency as a philosopher, manifested in various ways, is always to connect Platonic doctrine with more ancient wisdom (preferably, but not necessarily, of a Chaldaean variety), and within Platonism itself it is he who, more than any other, is the author of the ramified hierarchy of levels of being (many identified with traditional gods and minor divinities) which is a feature of the later Athenian Platonism of Syrianus and Proclus. With Iamblichus and his advocacy of theurgy as a necessary complement to theology, Platonism also becomes more explicitly a religion. Before his time, the mystery imagery so popular with Platonist philosophers (going back to Plato himself) was, so far as can be seen, just that--imagery. With Iamblichus, there is an earnest emphasis on ritual, enabling the Emperor Julian to found his church on this rather shaky rock.

The mid-third century was a profoundly disturbed time to be growing up in Syria. In 256 C.E., in Iamblichus' early youth, the Persian King Shapur broke through the Roman defenses around Chalcis (the so-called *limes* of Chalcis), and pillaged the whole north of Syria, including Antioch (Malalas, *Chron.* 295-6). It is not known how Iamblichus' family weathered the onslaught. Being prominent figures, especially if they were pro-Roman, they may well have withdrawn before it and sought refuge temporarily on the coast.

At this point, the problem arises of who Iamblichus' teachers in philosophy were. Eunapius writes of a certain Anatolius, μετὰ Πορφύριον τὰ δεύτερα φερόμενος (*VS* 457). This phrase in earlier times simply means "take second place to"[9] but a parallel in Photius[10] suggests that for Eunapius the phrase meant "was successor to." If this is so, it poses a problem. It has been suggested[11] that Iamblichus' teacher is identical with the Anatolius who was a teacher of Peripatetic philosophy in Alexandria in the 260's and later (in 274) consecrated bishop of Laodicea in Syria. This suggestion, however, comes up against grave difficulties: chronology requires that

---

this deity, identified with planet Mercury.
[9] e.g. in Herodotus, 8. 104.
[10] *Bibl.* 181 = Damascius, *V. Isid.* 319, 14 Zintzen.
[11] Dillon, 1987, 866-7.

Iamblichus was a student no later than the 270's, so that it must be concluded that we have to do here with another Anatolius (the dedicatee of Porphyry's *Homeric Questions* (Ὁμηρικὰ ζητήματα), and so probably a student of his) who represented in some way Porphyry during his absence (perhaps still in Sicily?). This, however, assumes a situation for which there is no evidence, namely that Porphyry established a school in Rome between his visits to Sicily, or that Plotinus had founded a school of which Porphyry was the titular head even in his absence in Sicily. Another possibility, of course, is that Eunapius is profoundly confused, but that conclusion seems to be a counsel of despair.

When Porphyry returned from Sicily to Rome is not clear. Eusebius, writing sometime after his death (c. 305 C.E.), describes him (*HE VI* 19,2) as "he who was in our time established in Sicily" (ὁ καθ᾽ ἡμᾶς ἐν Σικελίᾳ καταστάς) which suggests a considerable stay. J. Bidez,[12] however, takes this as referring only to the publication of Porphyry's work *Against the Christians*. Porphyry refers to himself as having returned to Rome at *Plot.* 2, but when that happened he does not indicate. That he returned by the early 280's, however, is a proposition with which few would disagree, and if Iamblichus studied with him, it would have occurred in this period. The only (more or less) direct evidence of their association is the dedication to Iamblichus of Porphyry's work *On the maxim "Know Thyself."*[13]

What the relationship between the two may have been cannot be determined. In later life Iamblichus was repeatedly, and often sharply, critical of his master's philosophical positions. This can be seen in his *Timaeus Commentary,* where, of thirty-two fragments in which Porphyry is mentioned, twenty-five are critical, only seven signifying agreement. The same position is evident also in the commentary on Aristotle's *Categories,* as preserved by Simplicius, but there Simplicius reports that Iamblichus based his own commentary on that of Porphyry[14] (something also likely for his *Timaeus Commentary*), so that such statistics given previously are misleading.

[12] *Vie de Porphyre* (Ghent and Leipzig, 1913) 103 note 1.
[13] Unless account be taken of Iamblichus' assertion in the *De Anima* (375.24-25) that he had 'heard' Porphyry propound a certain doctrine. The verb *akouô* with the genitive came to be used in peculiar ways in later Greek, however, denoting acquaintance at various removes, so that one cannot put full trust in this testimony. There is no real reason, on the other hand, to doubt that Iamblichus and Porphyry were personally acquainted.
[14] *In Cat.* 2, 9ff. Kalbfleisch.

However, the *De Mysteriis* is a point-by-point refutation of Porphyry's *Letter to Anebo* (which, in turn, was an attack on theurgy probably aimed at Iamblichus), and Iamblichus' references to Porphyry in the *De Anima* are generally less than reverent. No doubt, also, Iamblichus' lost work *On Statues* had much to say in refutation of Porphyry's work of the same name.

There is no need, however, to conclude that Iamblichus learned nothing from Porphyry, or that they parted on bad terms. The refutation of one's predecessors was a necessary part of staying afloat in the scholarly world, then as now, and Iamblichus was enough of an original mind to have many modifications and elaborations to introduce into Porphyry's relatively simple metaphysical scheme. Also contact with Plotinus was a personal experience for Porphyry, which it was not for Iamblichus. This has some bearing, along with the considerations of ancestry mentioned earlier, on Iamblichus' enthusiasm for theurgy, an enthusiasm of Porphyry himself in his youth, which was something direct contact with Plotinus tended to suppress. When Porphyry wrote his *Letter to Anebo,* he was actually providing a recantation of his earlier beliefs, as expressed in the *Philosophy from Oracles.*

Even as it is not known when or where[15] Iamblichus studied with Porphyry, so it is not known when he left him, returned to Syria and founded his own school. From the fact that he returned to Syria, rather than staying on as successor to Porphyry (he was, after all, his most distinguished pupil), one might conclude that there was tension between them. But Iamblichus by the 290's would already be, if our chronology is correct, a man of middle age, and it is natural enough that he should want to set up on his own. Porphyry, after all, did not die until after 305 at the earliest, and probably Iamblichus departed long before that.

For Iamblichus' activity on his return to Syria one is dependent on Eunapius' account, which, with all its fantastic anecdotes, is claimed by its author to rest on an oral tradition descending to him from Iamblichus' senior pupil Aedesius, via his own revered master Chrysanthius. Unfortunately, Eunapius is vague on details of prime importance. Where, for example, did Iamblichus establish his school? The evidence seems to be in favor of Apamea, rather than his native Chalcis. This is not surprising: Apamea had been a distinguished

---

[15] It is conceivable, after all, that he went to study with him in Lilybaeum.

center of philosophy for well over a century (at least), and was the home town, and probably base, of the distinguished second century Neopythagorean Numenius. It was also the place to which Plotinus' senior pupil Amelius retired in the 260's, no doubt because of admiration for Numenius. Amelius was dead by the time Porphyry wrote his *Commentary on the Timaeus* (probably in the 290's), but he left his library and possessions to his adopted son Hostilianus Hesychius, who presumably continued to reside in Apamea.

Once established in Apamea,[16] Iamblichus seems to have acquired support from a prominent local citizen, Sopater, and in Eunapius' account (*VS* 458-9), he is portrayed as being in possession of a number of suburban villas (προάστεια) and a considerable group of followers. There are glimpses of him in the midst of his disciples, discoursing and fielding questions, disputing with rival philosophers, and leading school excursions to the hot springs at Gadara. Iamblichus had strong Pythagorean sympathies, inherited from Numenius and Nicomachus of Gerasa, and one would like to know how far his treatise *On the Pythagorean Way of Life* reflects life in his own school. Probably not very closely, in such matters as community of property or long periods of silence, or we would have heard about it from Eunapius. More likely the school of Iamblichus was like any contemporary philosophic school in the Platonist tradition, a group of students living with or round their teacher, meeting with him daily, and probably dining with him, pursuing a set course of reading and study in the works of Aristotle and Plato, and holding disputations on set topics.

Possibly Iamblichus' ten volumes on Pythagoreanism, entitled collectively *A Compendium of Pythagorean Doctrine*, constituted an introductory course for his school. It is plain that there was study of at least some Aristotle, the logical works (Iamblichus, as we have seen, wrote a copious commentary on the *Categories*, heavily dependent on that of Porphyry, but with transcendental interpretations of his own), the *De Anima*, and perhaps parts of the *Metaphysics*, followed by the study of Plato. For Plato, Iamblichus, building on earlier, Middle

---

[16] There is some conflicting evidence, from Malalas (*Chron.* XII 312, 11-12), indicating that Iamblichus was established with a school at Daphne, near Antioch, in the reigns of Maxentius and Galerius (305-312 C.E.), and Malalas says that he continued teaching there until his death. Malalas, despite his limitations, is not entirely unreliable on matters affecting his home area, so it is possible that Iamblichus spent some time in Daphne; there is no doubt, however, that Apamea was his main base.

Platonic systems of instruction (such as described in Albinus' *Eisagôgê*), prescribed a definite number and order of dialogues to be studied. In the *Anonymous Prolegomena to Platonic Philosophy*[17] ch. 26, there is a course of ten dialogues attributed originally to Iamblichus, starting with the *Alcibiades I*, and continuing with *Gorgias, Phaedo, Cratylus, Theaetetus, Sophist, Statesman, Phaedrus, Symposium* and *Philebus*, leading to the two main dialogues of Platonic philosophy, the *Timaeus* and the *Parmenides*, the former "physical," the latter "theological." Of these, there are fragments or evidence of commentaries by Iamblichus on the *Alcibiades, Phaedo, Sophist, Phaedrus, Philebus, Timaeus*, and *Parmenides*, the most extensive (preserved in Proclus' commentary on the same dialogue) being those on the *Timaeus*. It is surprising not to find any mention in this sequence of either the *Republic* or the *Laws*. They were probably regarded as too long, and in the main too political, to be suitable for study as wholes, but there is indication that sections such as *Republic* 6, 7, and 10, and *Laws* 10, received due attention.

Formal exegesis then, played a significant part in the curriculum of the school, but notice must also be taken of the reputation which Iamblichus acquired in later times (mainly because of the excesses of such *epigoni* as Maximus of Ephesus, the teacher of Julian in the 350's) for magical practices. He probably used the *Chaldaean Oracles* in lectures, since he composed a vast commentary (in at least 28 books) on the *Oracles*. There is only one story related by Eunapius in which Iamblichus is said to have performed a magical act, and that was during the above-mentioned visit of the school to the hot springs at Gadara. Iamblichus, in response to insistent requests, conjured up two spirits in the form of boys, identified as Eros and Anteros, from two adjacent springs (*VS* 459). On another occasion, however (*VS* 458), he is recorded as dismissing with a laugh rumors that during prayer he was accustomed to rise ten cubits into the air, and that his body and clothing took on a golden hue. Nevertheless, his championing of theurgy (which is really only magic with a philosophical underpinning), presented at length in the *De Mysteriis*, introduced a new element into Platonism, which was to continue even up to the Renaissance. Partly this was a response to a Christian emphasis on the miracle-working holy man. It might have happened without Iamblichus, but certain elements in his background perhaps disposed him

---

[17] Ed. L. G. Westerink (Amsterdam, 1962).

to making Platonism into more of a religion than had hitherto been the case.

The details of Iamblichus' philosophical system are not relevant to the present work, which concerns only the soul, not Iamblichus' complete metaphysical hierarchy. We will discuss Iamblichus' psychology below.

Iamblichus seems to have lived in Apamea until the early 320's. A terminus is found in Sopater's departure for Constantinople to try his luck with imperial politics in 326/7, by which time his revered master was certainly dead. A most interesting testimony to Iamblichus' status in the 320's is provided by the letters included among the works of the Emperor Julian.[18] These were composed by an admirer of Iamblichus between the years 315 and 320, who was then attached to the staff of the Emperor Licinius. This person cannot be identified,[19] but Eunapius (*VS* 458) gives the names of various disciples, Aedesius and Eustathius (who was Iamblichus' successor) from Cappadocia, and Theodorus (presumably Theodorus of Asine) and Euphrasius from mainland Greece. Besides these it is possible to identify Dexippus, author of a surviving commentary on Aristotle's *Categories,* and Hierius, master of the theurgist Maximus of Ephesus. To some of these there is a record of letters on philosophical subjects by Iamblichus (Sopater, Dexippus and Eustathius, at least). One is even tempted to wonder whether the recipient of a letter *On Ruling,* a certain Dyscolius (perhaps identical with a governor of Syria around 323)[20] may not be the mysterious correspondent mentioned above. But even if that were known we would not really be much wiser.

A little more may be said on the rest of Iamblichus' known literary production. His *De Mysteriis,* more properly entitled *A Reply of the Priest Abammon to the Letter of Porphyry to Anebo, and the Solution of the Problems Raised Therein,* is a defense of theurgy against a series of skeptical questions raised by Porphyry. *On the Gods* was much used by Julian and probably served as a chief source for the surviving work of

---

[18] *Epp.* 181, 183-7 Bidez-Cumont (= 76-8, 75, 74, 79 Wright, *LCL*). How they fell into the hands of Julian, or came to be included among his works, is uncertain, but he was avid collector of Iamblichiana. On this person, see T.D. Barnes, "A Correspondent of Iamblichus," *GRBS* 19 (1978), 99-106, who sorts out the problems connected with him most lucidly.

[19] An intriguing possibility, not raised by Barnes, is that this person may have been none other than Julius Julianus, Julian's maternal grandfather, who had been praetorian prefect and virtual head of government under Licinius, and would to that extent fill the bill nicely.

[20] See Jones, *Prosopography of the Later Roman Empire,* I 275.

Sallustius *On the Gods and the World*. As for the *Compendium of Pythago-rean Doctrines*, it consisted of a sequence of ten works of which only the first four survive (and possibly the substance of a fifth in a curious compilation, *The Theology of Arithmetic*, which as it has been trans-mitted is largely a cento of passages from a lost work of Nicomachus of Gerasa (by the same title) and one of Anatolius, presumably Iamblichus' teacher, *On the Decad and the Numbers within it*). The remaining volumes are: the *Protrepticus*, or *Exhortation to Philosophy*, a work based on Aristotle's lost *Protrepticus*, but including large sections of Platonic dialogues, various *Pythagorica*, and an extract from the work of an unknown fifth century B.C.E. sophist, now known as the *Anonymus Iamblichi*; the work *On the General Principles of Mathematics (De Communi Mathematica Scientia)*, which is again a cento of previous works, borrowed without acknowledgement; *On the Pythagorean Way of Life*, an account of Pythagoras' life again gathered from others' works but with extended treatment also of Pythagorean doctrines and *bios* or "way of life;" and a commentary on the *Introduction to Arithmetic* of Nicomachus of Gerasa, which is somewhat more original, if only by virtue of its rather different nature. D. J. O Meara[21] has recently identified in later Byzantine sources some extracts from later volumes (such as Iamblichus planned) on Physics, Ethics, Music, Geometry and Astronomy, but it is plain that, if they existed, all would probably be compilations of previous doctrines. Even that, however, would be of value, as it doubtless was to Iamblichus' students, who were the primary intended audience of these works.

Respect for Iamblichus as a philosopher has increased in recent years, as his distinctive contribution to the doctrine of the later Athenian school of Neoplatonists becomes clearer. He is an influence of prime importance on Syrianus, and hence on Proclus, as both of them freely acknowledge. In this way he inaugurated a scholastic tradition of Platonism which, becoming more ramified in the works of such men as Damascius and Dionysius the Areopagite, descended to later Byzantine writers like Michael Psellus, and, through the translations of William of Moerbeke and, later, of Marsilio Ficino, to the West. Iamblichus' commentaries seem not to have long survived the closing of the Academy in 529 C.E. Damascius, Olympiodorus and Simplicius can all quote from them, as can Priscianus and John of Stobi from his *De Anima* (and John from his letters), but Psellus

---

[21] In *Pythagoras Revived,* Oxford, 1989.

and the Byzantine scholars after him were dependent for their references to his technical works on Proclus. Only Iamblichus' exoteric works, the *Pythagorean Sequence* and the *De Mysteriis,* survived into later Byzantine times, as they still do, to give a distorted and inadequate view of his achievement.

II. *The* De Anima

It is difficult to say with any precision when Iamblichus wrote and published his *De Anima.* The reason for producing the work, however, is very clear. Iamblichus has decided to set forth clearly and in no uncertain terms his own theory of the soul. Throughout the work, Iamblichus is at pains to maintain two basic "truths." First, in his theory of the soul he is following the true philosophical tradition that included not only Plato and Aristotle but also a whole host of ancient sources from the Egyptians and Chaldaeans through to Orpheus. Second, all philosophers since Aristotle have misconstrued this true psychology. The *De Anima,* therefore, is a polemical work aimed against a host of writers (Peripatetics, Stoics, Epicureans, Middle Platonists, and in particular his own immediate predecessors Plotinus, Amelius, and Porphyry) but one that aims to place in clear light Iamblichus' doctrine of the soul. Iamblichus took a similar approach in his *De Mysteriis,* starting each of his arguments with a quotation from Porphyry's *Letter to Anebo.* In the *De Anima,* however, Iamblichus' targets are more manifold and his message more focused.

How much of the *De Anima* survives? Our fragments from the work are all contained in the fifth-century compilation of John Stobaeus, who excerpted and collected passages from the writings of Greek writers and philosophers. Practically nothing is known of Stobaeus' life. Bishop Photius (9th Century) tells us that Stobaeus made his collection for the benefit of his own son Septimius.[22] After the time of Photius, Stobaeus' work was divided into two separate parts: the *Eclogae Physicae et Ethicae* (which had comprised the first two books of the original work) and the *Florilegium* (the final two books of the

---

[22]   Photius 167. For the background, see J. Mansfeld and D. T. Runia, *Aëtiana* (Leiden 1997) 196-197. For the educational uses of the text and the "bee metaphor implicit in the term ἀνθολόγιον," see 205-206.

collection).[23] Most of the passages from Iamblichus' *De Anima* come from the *Eclogae*.

Stobaeus preserves two long extracts from Iamblichus' treatise in the course of his chapter *On the Soul*[24] (1.362.23-385.10 and 454.10-458.21), two shorter segments (1.317.20-318.15 and 3.608.25-609.3, on intellect and memory, respectively), and two miscellaneous sentences of uncertain placement within the *De Anima* (2.6.9-11 and 2.207.15-17). This may represent the bulk of the work, although Stobaeus is really only concerned with its doxographic aspect. An outline of the *De Anima* as we have it will be useful:[25]

Section	Wachsmuth and Hense	Topic
1	1.362.24-363.10	Criticism of some Aristotelian terminology
2-9	1.363.11-367.9	Previous "incorrect" definitions of soul
10-13	1.367.10-370.13	General discussion of the powers of the soul
14	3.608.25-609.3	Discussion of individual powers: memory
15	1.317.20-318-15	Discussion of individual powers: intellect
16	1.370.14-372.2	Activities of the soul
17-24	1.372.3-375.28	Acts of the soul

---

[23] See Mansfeld and Runia (above, note 22) 196-198. The question of how Stobaues edited his work and its relation to earlier such anthologies is beyond the scope of the present work. For that topic, see Mansfeld and Runia's chapter on Stobaeus (196-271) and R. M. Piccione, "Caratterizzazione di lemmi nell' *Anthologion* di Giovanni Stobeo," *Rivista di Filologia e di Instruzione Classica*, 127 (1999) 139-175.

[24] Chapter 49, Περὶ Ψυχῆς, is the longest of the 60 chapters in volume 1 (318.16-472.2). This is fitting for a topic of universal concern for all philosophical schools. On the arrangement of Stobaeus' material and its relation to *Placita* literature, see Mansfeld and Runia (above, note 22) 213-217; for arrangement within chapters, 218-224. Although the arrangement of all of chapter 49 is beyond the scope of this work, it is worth noting the position of J. Mansfeld, "Doxography and Dialectic: The *Sitz im Leben* of the 'Placita,'" in *ANRW* 2.36.4 (1990) 3076, that "the account of Iamblichus, De anima ap. Stob. Ecl. Phys. I 49 . . . is still indebted to the themes, contents, and diaereses of the Plac." Mansfeld is concerned with only 363.11-367.9 (= sections 2-9), but his claim that these sections follow the *Placita* in discussing the soul in the categories of corporeal, then incorporeal, etc. is certainly correct. This ordering probably is Iamblichean rather than imposed on his text by Stobaeus.

[25] We have divided the surviving text into sections based on the divisions established by Festugière, but have added further divisions of our own. As a general rule, we have tried to divide the whole work into sections that treat a single topic and then assign to each of these sections a number for easy reference. This process became more difficult toward the end of the work, where Stobaeus' excerpting itself becomes more piecemeal.

25	1.376.1-377.10	The number of souls in existence
26-27	1.377.11-379.10	Descent of souls
28-33	1.379.11-382.16	Embodiment
34	1.382.17-24	Souls' association with the gods
35	1.382.25-383.14	What makes life valuable
36	1.383.15-384.18	Death
37	1.384.19-28	The fate of the soul after death
38	1.385.1-10	The substances intermediate between body and soul
39-46	1.454.10-457.6	The judgment, punishment, and purification of souls
47-53	1.457.7-458.21	The soul's ultimate reward
54-55	2.6.9-12, 2.207.15-18	Two short fragments of a general nature

Our extracts from Stobaeus seem to start very near to the beginning of Iamblichus' treatise, although Stobaeus, as we have said, is concerned primarily with the doxographic portions of it. It is possible that Iamblichus may have given some account of his own position before starting on his survey of previous opinions, but it is more probable that all that we are missing is some dedicatory and prefatory material. It would be more natural for Iamblichus, following the practice of Aristotle (and, of course, many later authorities), to introduce his own views *after* a survey of his predecessors.

The preface, however, probably contained some reference to Aristotle's treatment of the subject, since the reference to him at the beginning of our surviving extracts has a resumptive sound to it. It is agreed now[26] that there is no clear evidence that Iamblichus wrote a commentary on the *De Anima,* but there is no question that he regarded it as a seminal work, on which to base his own treatise.

In our commentary, we will suggest various possible places in the work where portions of Iamblichus' text have been lost to us, sometimes due to Stobaeus' editing and sometimes due to the physical ravages of time. For now, we will make just a few brief points. First, sections 14-15 (on memory and intellect) suggest that Iamblichus would have included discussions on the various individual powers of the soul. Extracts from the Pseudo-Simplicius' *In De Anima* and Priscianus' *Metaphrasis in Theophrastum*[27] show that Iamblichus discussed

---

[26] Cf. H.J. Blumenthal, "Simplicius(?) on the First Book of Aristotle's *De Anima*," in I. Hadot (ed.), *Simplicius: sa vie, son oeuvre, sa survie,* Berlin-New York, 1987, 91-112.

[27] We have collected, translated, and commented upon some of these in an

the powers of imagination (F and G) and some aspects of vision (H and I, which concern light and the transparent). It seems most likely, therefore, that Iamblichus would have discussed various powers of the soul, from the powers of each sense through to imagination, desire, and thought. It seems likely to us that some of the discussion of these powers in these treatises of the Pseudo-Simplicius and Priscianus is Iamblichean, but we have here dealt only with those texts in which Iamblichus is mentioned by name.

Second, the excerpts from the *De Anima* as we have them suggest a carefully organized plan. Iamblichus moves from the doctrines of Aristotle and others, to a discussion of the soul's essence, powers, acts, and activities, to a consideration of the soul's journey into and out of body, and finally to its post-corporeal reward. In relation to this plan, we can see that we have most of the important material.

Third, at times we are at the mercy of Stobaeus, who edits Iamblichus' prose to suit his own purposes.[28] Stobaeus' *Anthology* was written for the use of his son Septimius as he pursued the study of philosophy. Thus, Stobaeus shows more interest in passages that set out the multiple theories of various philosophers than those that would have highlighted Iamblichus' doctrine. Hence, we find more doxography than Iamblichean psychology, although the Iamblichean doctrine still comes through.

Iamblichus himself is not concerned with a thorough investigation of his predecessors' thoughts. This fact becomes most clear in the case of Plotinus, whose rich and textured philosophy of soul is often reduced to oversimplifications that seem to do no more than make Plotinus look wrong.[29] What interests Iamblichus is his own theory and its relation to Plato and what he sees as the ancient religious tradition. The result is a tendency to place his opponents in a single camp, the easier to argue against them. If that requires some dubious simplifying of their views, Iamblichus does not hesitate. Nonetheless, there is much here that is useful. Iamblichus preserves theories of his predecessors, especially of the Middle Platonists, that seem accurate. And even in the case of Plotinus, Iamblichus occasionally admits that matters are more complex than he is letting on.[30]

---

appendix to this work. We will discuss the possible identity of the Pseudo-Simplicius below in the Introduction.

[28] For Stobaeus' methods of organization, see Mansfeld and Runia (above, note 22) 204-209.

[29] See, for instance, sections 5, 6, 13, 17, 19, 23, 26, 46, and our notes *ad loc.*

[30] See section 6 and our notes.

Iamblichus seldom gives us his own opinion directly. He uses the first-person pronoun only rarely for giving his own view[31] and prefers to associate his beliefs directly with Plato[32] or "the ancients."[33] In section 7, when giving his doctrine about the soul, Iamblichus clearly highlights his view that the ancient Greek philosophers and the even more ancient religious authorities had held the true conception of things–and that he himself is squarely in their camp:

> It is these doctrines to which Plato himself and Pythagoras, and Aristotle, and all the ancients who have gained great and honorable names for wisdom, are completely committed, as one will find if he investigates their opinions with scientific rigor; as for myself, I will try to base this whole treatise, concerned as it is with truth, on these opinions.

As we have seen, this is part of his strategy: to show that he has reached back past the mistaken views of the Platonists, Peripatetics, and Stoics to the original font of all wisdom. Finally, Iamblichus uses a periphrasis with an optative to indicate obliquely his own opinions.[34]

A. *Iamblichus' Psychological Doctrine*

What is perhaps most surprising about the haphazard transmission of Iamblichus' *De Anima* is the undeniable fact that its most important doctrine was ignored by Stobaeus. Iamblichus hints at his unique doctrine of the soul in section 7. After stating that Numenius, Plotinus, Amelius, and Porphyry all more or less share the view that there are no differences between different classes of soul (in section 6), Iamblichus lays out his own doctrine:

---

[31] Although Iamblichus uses the first person nine times: in sections 1 (363.3), 4 (364.2), 7 (366.11), 20 (373.11), 24 (375.25), 29 (380.6), 31 (381.16), 40 (455.4), and 50 (458.12), in only four of these is he stating his own view on a matter of substance (sections 1, 7, 20, 29).

[32] Section 10 (where Plato is conjoined with Aristotle and then Pythagoras as holding the correct view); 13; possibly 15 (Οἱ δ᾽ ἀπὸ Πλάτωνος καὶ Πυθαγόρου); 16; 21; 22 (where Plato is again paired with Pythagoras); and 35.

[33] Sections 37, 40, 41, 42, 43, 44, 45, 47, 48, 50, 53. All but the first of these come from the final pages of the *De Anima*, 454.10-458.21, where Iamblichus is discussing the soul's posthumous fate, a topic of appropriate concern for earlier religious thinkers.

[34] Section 4, (ἄλλος ἄν τις καθαρώτερον αὐτὴν προστήσαιτο, 364.6-7); 13 (τάχα ἄν τις ἐπινοήσειε καινότερον, οὐκ ἀπιθάνως 370.12-13); 18 (γένοιτο δὲ κἂν ἄλλη δόξα οὐκ ἀπόβλητος, 372.15); 31 (γένοιτο δ᾽ ἂν καὶ ἄλλη τις δόξα οὐδέπω καὶ νῦν ῥηθεῖσα, 381.5-6).

The doctrine opposed to this, however, separates the Soul off, inasmuch as it has come about as following upon Intellect, representing a distinct level of being, and that aspect of it which is endowed with intellect is explained as being connected with the intellect certainly, but also as subsisting independently on its own, and it separates the soul also from all the superior classes of being, and assigns to it as the particular definition of its essence, either the middle term of divisible and indivisible beings <and of corporeal and in>corporeal being, or the totality of the universal reason-principles, or that which, after the ideas, is at the service of the work of creation, or that life which has life of itself, which proceeds from the Intelligible realm, or again the procession of the classes of real Being as a whole to an inferior substance.

The doctrine that the soul is the mean between two extremes, Intellect and Body, is an integral part of Iamblichus' theory of soul. Iamblichus carefully situates the human soul apart from the Intellect, from which (as in Plotinian philosophy) the soul emanates, and apart from the higher orders of soul, including the "superior classes" (daemons, heroes, pure souls). The human soul exists at its own level and acts as a mediator between these higher entities and things corporeal. The theory that soul is such a median entity, however, is not really new in Platonism. As much as Iamblichus tries to obscure that fact in section 6, the truth is that Plotinus and Porphyry share this doctrine with Iamblichus.

The full force of Iamblichus' innovatory thinking becomes clear only when we combine his statement in section 7 with three extracts from the Pseudo-Simplicius' *In De Anima*.[35] From these passages it becomes clear that Iamblichus held not only that the soul was a mean but also that, since the activities of the human soul differ when it intelligizes above and when it acts in a body, the very essence of the soul is double. The human soul is both Intellect-like and animal-like, but is neither permanently. The essence of the soul is double and at variance with itself. It is this conception of the soul that defines Iamblichus' unique psychological theory. Iamblichus thereby makes the soul a mean in the strongest sense possible, verging on a Heraclitean explanation of its duality. The soul is not in essence always intelligizing (or it would be Intellect), nor is it always involved in activities in Nature (or it would be animal soul). The soul therefore is both at once. This mediality is its permanent condition, not its intelligizing or its lower-order activities alone.

---

[35] Pseudo-Simplicius, *In De Anima* 5.38-6.17, 89.33-90.25 and 240.33-241.26, which appear as sections B, C, and D in the appendix. See our notes there.

The implications of this theory are far-reaching. If what it is to be a human soul necessarily involves two aspects, higher and lower, then the human soul must live two lives. It must engage in intellectual acts as well as in acts in Nature. Therefore, every human soul must descend into a body, or part of its essence would be unfulfilled, which is impossible. Further, in order to be fully human, the soul must ascend again, either after death or in this life through theurgy. In this way, theurgy takes on exceptional importance in Iamblichus' philosophy. It is not some adventitious magical adjunct that can be jettisoned from human life. Theurgy is a fully natural part of the human condition, inherent in Nature, existing for those wise enough to utilize it so that they may raise their souls to the highest aspect and fulfill their role as true mediatory entities.

B. *Pure Souls*

Besides this central doctrine of the soul as a mean, the *De Anima* presents other Iamblichean doctrines as well. The concepts of the descent of the soul and the different classes of human soul are closely bound together. In discussing the soul's descent (sections 26-27), Iamblichus argues (following Plato's *Timaeus*) that there is a certain necessity to the descent and the order through which the souls are brought to generation. The Demiurge sends all souls into the cosmos, and all souls follow a leader-god (one of the planets or stars) with its entourage of angels, daemons, and heroes. Within this descent there are clearly different sorts of human souls. Some are purified and, although sometimes existing in bodies, remain a cut above other mortals, able to re-connect with the supra-celestial Intellect and engage in pure intellection.[36]

This division allows Iamblichus to further differentiate reasons for human souls to descend. All souls must descend, but these pure souls do so purely and voluntarily, in keeping with divine ordinance. Lesser souls, however, may descend for further punishment for offences committed in previous lives. These descend unwillingly for punishment and correction.[37]

In section 29, Iamblichus makes a threefold division: (1) pure souls descend freely in order to make the world a better place.

---

[36] On the triple division of human souls, see G. Shaw, *Theurgy and the Soul* (University Park 1995) 143-147 and our notes to section 30, below.
[37] Cf. section 30.

Iamblichus probably has in mind such human souls as those that inhabited the bodies of Pythagoras and Plato. They live in this world of generation but are not of it. Their divine thoughts help us lesser mortals re-ascend and better our own lives. (2) Souls that require punishment are forced to descend and live a life designed to pay the penalty for past sins. (3) In between the two extremes, there is the soul which has made some progress in its past lives but has not yet achieved the status of pure soul. It descends in a partially free manner since it must still pay for its previous offences but it also is somewhat willing to make the descent since it will thereby improve its lot and work its way further upward toward the rank of pure soul.

The details of this remarkable doctrine will be discussed in the commentary, but here we may note the resemblance between Iamblichus' theory of the highest form of ascent and the Buddhist theory of *bodhisattvas*, enlightened souls who postpone their assumption of the highest phase of Buddhism in order to assist the spiritual process of the rest of the human race. Since Iamblichus was hardly acquainted with Buddhism, this is presumably a coincidence, but an interesting one. A difference is important as well. The *bodhisattvas* choose to help their fellow creatures; the highest human souls in the Iamblichean universe *must* descend and help. The similarity with the philosopher-rulers in Plato's *Republic* is clear. Like them, perhaps, the pure souls see no conflict between the desire to intelligize and the need to descend and help others, but the descent is necessary nonetheless (*Rep.* 540a-c).

C. *The Afterlife*

The last sections of the *De Anima* (39-53) offer Iamblichus' views on the soul's existence after its separation from the body at death. Just as a soul's previous existence determines its allotment in its descent and birth, so the sort of life the soul lived in the body will determine what happens to it after death. Following and interpreting Plato's eschatological myths, Iamblichus states that souls undergo judgment, punishment, and purification after death. Pure souls, however, are exempt from all three, since they are already pure. It is the lower two categories of human soul (those that have descended for punishment and correction, in various degrees) that are judged in Hades, punished, and thereby purified of the stains accumulated in their recent life.

Iamblichus raises several questions about the role of judgment, punishment, and purification. He contrasts the views of "the ancients" with those of "Platonists and Pythagoreans." It is the ancients, of course, who hold the correct opinions in each case. The judges and those responsible for punishing and purifying errant souls are divinities with ethereal bodies (the visible gods and superior classes) who do their judging in ethereal space, probably under the Moon.[38] The goal is, of course, the cleansing of the soul so that it may again ascend to the realm of Intellect (sections 41-43). Souls that are successfully purified rise to the sphere of the angels and assist the gods in administering the universe.[39]

Iamblichus takes care to point out that the ultimate union of soul with gods and Intellect does not mean that the soul becomes a god, but that it ascends to their sphere and unites with them while retaining its own identity.[40] This, of course, is in keeping with the soul's dual essence. It cannot become a god or Intellect without ceasing to be a soul, which it can never do. Thus, after the union with the gods and its time in the sphere of the angels, the soul must again descend and fulfill its other essential role of being human and living with a body.

III.   *The identity of the Pseudo-Simplicius*

We have mentioned above two works important for our understanding of some of Iamblichus' doctrines (including that of the soul itself) in the *De Anima*. These works are a commentary on Aristotle's *De Anima* that has come down to us under the name of Simplicius[41] and a paraphrase of Theophrastus by Priscianus.[42] Both of these authors refer to Iamblichus by name and claim to follow him in certain passages, which we have collected in the appendix.[43] These

---

[38]   See section 40 and notes.

[39]   See sections 47, 48, 52, and 53 along with our notes *ad loc.*

[40]   See section 50 and notes.

[41]   Pseudo-Simplicius, *Simplicii in Libros Aristotelis De Anima Commentaria*, in *Commentaria in Aristotelem Graeca*, vol. 11., ed. M. Hayduck, Berlin 1882.

[42]   Priscianus, *Metaphrasis in Theophrastum*, in *Commentaria in Aristotelem Graeca*. suppl. 1.2, ed. I. Bywater, Berlin 1886.

[43]   Although we suspect that much of both works is Iamblichean throughout, for the purposes of this study we have focused our attention only on passages in which Iamblichus is named, or, in the case of Passage I, where the material presented by the Pseudo-Simplicius closely parallels that of a passage by Priscianus

passages shed further light on the contents and the philosophy of Iamblichus' work on the soul. The identity of the author of the Aristotle commentary, however, remains controversial.

In an article published in 1972,[44] Steel and Boissier first set forth arguments to show that the author of the commentary on Aristotle's *De Anima*, which had come down to us under the name of Simplicius, was actually Priscianus. As one would expect, their thesis was not universally accepted.[45] I. Hadot argued that the work was in fact by Simplicius.[46] In different articles written at different times, Blumenthal first argued that the commentary was probably written by Simplicius[47] and then later that it was probably not written by Simplicius but was almost certainly not written by Priscianus.[48] In 1997, Steel reworked his thesis, adding more evidence for his view that the commentary was written by Priscianus.[49]

Let us state at the outset that we are in complete agreement with both Steel and Urmson that this work is not by Simplicius.[50] As Steel says, one need simply read another of Simplicius' commentaries and compare it to this commentary on the *De Anima*, and the reader will be immediately struck by the differences both in style and content. Whether the author is Priscianus or not, however, requires further investigation.

Steel presents the arguments for Priscianus' authorship of the commentary on Aristotle's *De Anima*.[51] These include:

(1) A reference to an "epitome" of Theophrastus in the *De Anima* commentary 136.29 (Steel 126, 127, and 136-137)

(viz., Passage H).

[44] C. Steel and F. Boissier, "Priscianus Lydus en de *in De Anima* van Pseudo(?)-Simplicius," *Tijdschrift voor filosofie* 34 (1972) 761-822.

[45] For an overview of the controversy, see Steel's introduction in Huby and Steel, 105-106 and Blumenthal in R. Sorabji, *Aristotle Transformed*, 324.

[46] I. Hadot, "The Life and Work of Simplicius in Arabic Sources," in R. Sorabji, *Aristotle Transformed*, 290-292. See also her response to Blumenthal's paper in Blumenthal and Lloyd, 94.

[47] H. J. Blumenthal, "The Psychology of (?) Simplicius' Commentary on the *De Anima*," in Blumenthal and Lloyd, 73-75 and 92-93 and in the 1988 addendum to "Neoplatonic Elements in the *De Anima* commentaries," in R. Sorabji, *Aristotle Transformed*, 324.

[48] H. J. Blumenthal, *Aristotle and Neoplatonism in Late Antiquity: Interpretations of the De Anima*, Ithaca (1996) 65-71.

[49] In the introduction to his translation of the commentary in Huby and Steel, 105-137.

[50] In Huby and Steel, 105 and J. O. Urmson, *Simplicius: On Aristotle's On The Soul 1.1-2.4.*, Ithaca (1995) 2-4.

[51] In Huby and Steel, 126-137.

(2) A comparison of the language in the commentary and the *Paraphrasis* (in sections on light and the transparent), which shows that they are indeed verbally very close (Steel 128-132)

(3) A shared discussion of the non-Aristotelian theory that darkness is an actuality (Steel 132-133)

(4) Similarities in the sections on imagination (Steel 133-134)

Steel's arguments are carefully developed and very strong. We agree that the correspondences in the Greek words and phrases in both the commentary and the *Paraphrasis* are too close to be accidental. Further, even where the vocabulary differs, there is a strong unity of doctrine between the two texts, as Steel says. In short, to our minds, Steel has proven that these two texts share a common point of view and common doctrines, as well as various details of terminology.

But do these common features prove common authorship? We do not think so. In the conclusion to his introduction, Steel provides alternative theories to explain the close connection between the two texts (134-135). Besides his own thesis (that the two works are by the same author, Priscianus), one other hypothesis, which Steel mentions and criticizes, deserves closer inspection, viz., that both authors are writing with their eyes on the same text, that of Iamblichus' *De Anima*.

Steel (135) brings three arguments against the claim that both authors are following Iamblichus:

(a) "[A]n accurate comparison of some parallel passages shows that the author of *in DA* was working with the text of [Priscianus] in front of him."

(b) Shared stylistic elements can be explained only on the hypothesis that the works were written by the same author.

(c) "[A]lthough both texts refer to Iamblichus, they never quote him literally."

Taking the last statement first, a comparison with, say, Proclus' references to Iamblichus in his *Timaeus* commentary will show that Neoplatonic interpreters did not always quote their predecessors accurately or admit when they were quoting them literally.[52] Proclus'

---

[52] Indeed, there are few such verbatim quotations in Iamblichus' *De Anima*, and even then they are (as are the correspondences between the two works of the Pseudo-Simplicius and Priscianus) quotations of no more than a word or two. Consider Iamblichus' reference to Plotinus, Empedocles, and Heraclitus on the reason for the soul's descent in section 23 (375.5-8W). Iamblichus quotes three Greek words (τῆς πρώτης ἑτερότητος,) accurately from Plotinus *Enn.* 5.1.1.5 (ἡ πρώτη ἑτερότης) but paraphrases Empedocles' words "I am a fugitive from god" (φυγὰς θεόθεν, Fr. 155.13) as "a [first] flight from god" (τῆς [πρώτης] ἀπὸ τοῦ θεοῦ φυγῆς).

method is not to give long, extended quotations from his principal sources (not even from the commentary of Iamblichus himself) but to entwine the thoughts of previous thinkers into his own. He refers to past philosophers by name at times (although at other times, they are relegated to a series of μέν . . . δέ clauses), but he does not tend toward verbatim quotations.[53] Thus, one finds the author's original ideas and, very probably, isolated words that occurred in the original. And this is just the sort of situation we have in texts of both the Pseudo-Simplicius and Priscianus. The fact that neither gives accurate quotations from Iamblichus is therefore not surprising, and certainly should not be used for evidence that they are the same person.[54]

Iamblichus goes on to cite Heraclitus' words, "the rest which consists in change" (τῆς ἐν τῷ μεταβάλλεσθαι ἀναπαύλης), but it is impossible to determine what the original version might have been. Heraclitus' fragment 84a (μεταβάλλον ἀνα-παύεται, "changing, it rests") derives from Plotinus *Enn.* 4.8.1 and is probably itself a paraphrase. Indeed, as we point out in our commentary to section 23, Iamblichus may be cribbing from Plotinus. We thus have a problem similar to the one we have with the Pseudo-Simplicius. Is Iamblichus citing (and further paraphrasing) the references to Heraclitus and Empedocles from Plotinus' text or (as seems more likely) is he citing the words of the two Presocratic philosophers from a text either identical with or similar to that used by Plotinus?

It should be pointed out here that Plotinus himself might have found these two quotations from Heraclitus and Empedocles placed side by side in his own sources. W. Burkert, "Plotin, Plutarch und die Platonisierende Interpretation von Heraklit und Empedokles," in J. Mansfeld and L. M. de Rijk (edd.), *Kephalaion: Studies in Greek Philosophy and its Continuation, Offered to Professor C. J. De Vogel* (Assen 1975) 137-146, compares Plotinus 4.8.1 with passages from Hierocles, Plutarch, and Clement and shows affinities in their comparisons of Heraclitus, Empedocles, and Plato. Burkert suggests a common source, who composed the cento just before Plutarch wrote. J. Mansfeld, "Heraclitus, Empedocles, and Others in a Middle Platonic Cento in Philo of Alexandria," *Vigiliae Christianae* 39 (1985) 131-156, rpt. in J. Mansfeld, *Studies in Later Greek Philosophy and Gnosticism* (London 1989), includes Philo in the list of writers making use of this earlier source, and therefore dates the source back to Alexandrian times (136). For Plotinus' use of this cento, see J. Mansfeld, *Heresiology in Context* (Leiden 1992) 300-302 and 306-307.

[53] On Proclus' method of referring to Iamblichus' lost commentary, see Dillon (1973) 57-60. Of 83 fragments from Proclus' commentary, only two (Fr. 34 and 64) may be verbatim quotations from Iamblichus. See Dillon (1973) 57, who adds "and even these may have been interfered with to some extent by Proclus."

[54] Of the remaining six fragments from Iamblichus' *In Timaeum* commentary, five are from Simplicius' *Physics* commentary (*In Tim.* Frr. 62, 63, 67, 68, and 90). All of these are extended quotations from Iamblichus' lost work, and all are introduced as such by Simplicius. The one remaining fragment (*In Tim.* 89) comes from the Pseudo-Simplicius' *In De An.* (133.31-35). This fragment is not a quotation but a paraphrase of Iamblichus' interpretation of Plato's theory of vision. We have therefore further proof that the methodology of Simplicius and the Pseudo-Simplicius differ, but we cannot identify the author from this evidence, except perhaps to say that he is an author prone to paraphrase rather than direct quotation. On the quotations of Iamblichus from Simplicius, see Dillon (1973) 60-63.

Steel's first two arguments (a and b, above) are also not persuasive. In two passages on the faculty of imagination (passages F and G in our edition), Steel thinks that the texts show that we have a single author and that the Pseudo-Simplicius "has made his commentary on DA with the *Metaphrasis* before his eyes." We argue in the commentary that the case is not so clear. Rather, the fact that the Pseudo-Simplicius (in Passage G) emphasizes the role of the pneumatic vehicle of the soul in imagination and asserts that the faculty of imagination can actually modify and improve a past image that it has received, while Priscianus does neither in Passage F, suggests not a single author referring to a previous commentary of his own but two separate authors using a common text and emphasizing different features of it.[55]

We conclude therefore that one should not affirm the identity of the two authors based upon the evidence Steel presents. Furthermore, there are passages in which the two authors are at variance. Huby points out two such occasions of dissonance. In her discussion of *In De An.* 135.25-136.2 and Priscianus *Metaphr.* 10.31-11.14, she shows that the two authors appear to disagree about whether light causes bright objects to be seen or rather renders them invisible.[56] She says that Priscianus in *Metaphr.* 31.32-33 appears to be arguing against a position held by the Pseudo-Simplicius at 240.8-10 (of the twofold intellect).[57] Steel himself admits that Priscianus and the Pseudo-Simplicius articulate different theories about the active and passive intellects.[58] He explains the difference by positing that the *Metaphrasis* presents an earlier view of Priscianus (in which he accepts Iamblichus' doctrine), while the *In De An.* represents a later return to a less Iamblichean position. "Nonetheless," Steel maintains,[59] the author of the *In De Anima* (whom he takes to be Priscianus) "was convinced that . . . he remained perfectly true to Iamblichus' thought."

---

[55] Similarly, Steel (132-133) points out that Priscianus in Passage H and the Pseudo-Simplicius in Passage I relate that darkness is itself an actuality, an unusual doctrine at variance with Aristotle's. Steel wishes to conclude that *since* the doctrine is heterodox, the two authors must be the same. We argue in the commentary that this same evidence can equally be accounted for if the two different authors held the same view, after finding it in the *De Anima* of Iamblichus.

[56] In Huby and Steel, 55 note 123. See our discussion in the commentary to Passage I.

[57] In Huby and Steel, 68 note 386. See our commentary to Passage E.

[58] In Huby and Steel, 134. See also Steel's *The Changing Self* (Brussels 1978) 153-154.

[59] In Huby and Steel, 134.

The fact remains, however, that there is a shift of doctrine between the two texts. No matter how similar the vocabulary of the two texts may be, no matter how important the figure of Iamblichus is for both, the doctrines clash. To our minds, this shift represents not a difference in the opinion of a single author over time, but two different authors making use of the same Iamblichean material, one (Priscianus) agreeing with Iamblichus and the other (the Pseudo-Simplicius) disagreeing.

We discuss other differences between the two texts in our commentary, but these are mainly differences in emphasis between the two authors, not outright doctrinal conflicts. Nevertheless, we think that these differences show that there were two authors following a common source, Iamblichus, but articulating different aspects of his doctrine.

Finally, there is the matter of the possible reference to Priscianus' *Metaphrasis* at *In De An.* 136.29: "I have defined these things[60] more clearly in my *Epitome* of Theophrastus' *Physics*" (καὶ σαφέστερον μοί ταὐτὰ ἐν τῇ ἐπιτομῇ τῶν Θεοφράστου Φυσικῶν διώρισται). There are, as Blumenthal pointed out,[61] two problems with the attribution. First, if Priscianus is not the author, then the reference is not to a work by Priscianus but to a now lost work by an unknown author. Second, the *Metaphrasis* seems to be a good deal more than the mere summary of Theophrastus' doctrines that the term "epitome" suggests. Steel[62] has replied that others have taken the term "epitome" too narrowly and that it may well include works as wide-ranging as the *Metaphrasis*. Steel suggests Themistius' *Paraphrases* of Aristotle and Galen's *Epitome* of the *Timaeus* (in an Arabic version) as examples of such *epitomai*. Although an interesting suggestion, it seems unlikely. The sorts of epitome that we have knowledge of, especially those said to be written by the original author, show that the common meaning of the term was a shorter summary of a larger work. Certainly, the epitome may have included some explanations of philosophical points (such as the theory of vision), but it would not have been as expansive as the *Metaphrasis*. Furthermore, and this seems to us to be the crucial

---

[60] "These things" refer to aspects of the theory of vision within the transparent medium. The author emphasizes that it is the colored object in the medium that stimulates vision, not the medium itself. Steel points out that Priscianus discusses this material in 8.1-15.5 of his *Metaphrasis*. See Huby and Steel, 127.

[61] Blumenthal (1996) 68-69. See also Huby's response to an earlier paper of Blumenthal in Blumenthal and Lloyd, 95.

[62] In Huby and Steel, 136-137.

point, if the doctrinal and linguistic arguments do not prove that the two works are those of a single author, then the reference to the epitome at 136.29 can prove nothing in itself.

IV. *Manuscripts, Editions, Translations*

The manuscript tradition of the work is relatively simple, there being only two mss. of primary importance.[63] Farnesinus (F), 14th century, is in the Museo Nazionale in Naples. Parisinus (P) is 15th-century and is in the Bibliothèque Nationale in Paris. We were able to obtain a photocopy of P from the Bibliothèque Nationale. F is the more accurate of the two manuscripts.[64] We could not, however, obtain a photocopy. On the basis of our consultation of P, it is plain that Wachsmuth's editing was not deficient in any way. We have reprinted Wachsmuth's text with a few changes, which we will list below. A third manuscript, Laurentianus (L) is Florentine and 14th century. It contains only parts of Stobaeus' text. Of Iamblichus' *De Anima*, only the two final short fragments (54 and 55) are in L, and thus it is not of prime importance for this study.[65]

We also were greatly benefited by Festugière's French translation and notes, contained in an appendix to the third volume of his *La Révélation d'Hermès Trismégiste*[66] Festugière's sensitive reading of Iamblichus' work has produced many instructive insights, of which we have taken advantage in our commentary. In addition, Festugière has produced many useful emendations of the text, many of which we have adopted. We discuss these matters in more detail in our commentary.

---

[63] On the two manuscripts, see Mansfeld and Runia (above, note 22) 198-199 and C. Wachsmuth, *Anthologii Libri Duo Priores Qui Inscribi Solent Eclogae Physicae et Ethicae*, Vol. 1 (Berlin 1884, 2nd ed. 1958) xxv-xxvii. Section 14 of the *De Anima* derives from Stobaeus' *Florilegium* (see above): O, Hense, *Anthologii Libri Duo Posteriores*, Vol. 3 (1894, 2nd ed. 1958). The manuscripts used there are S (Vienna, 11th century), M (Marcianus, 15th or 16th century), M^d (Escurialensis, 11th-12th century) and the 16th-century edition of Victor Trincavellus of Venice. For these, see Hense, vol. 3, vii , xxiii, and xxix.

[64] "F is of better quality and more complete than P," Mansfeld and Runia 198; "aemulo Parisino longe melior," Wachsmuth xxv.

[65] On this MS., see Mansfeld and Runia 199 and Wachsmuth xxviii-xxix. For a stemma with all three manuscripts, see Mansfeld and Runia 200.

[66] A.J. Festugière, *La Révélation d'Hermès Trismégiste*, Vol. 3 (Paris, 1953) 177-248.

V. *Emendations and Variations in the Greek Text of Iamblichus'* De Anima

A. *Iamblichus,* De Anima

Page	Wachsmuth	This edition
364.10	<ἐν> λόγοις περιεχούσιν	λόγους περιεχούσῃ
365.11-12	γένη αὐτῆς	ἐν αὐτῇ
366.9-10	ἐπιστασέως	ἐπιστήμης
366.23	ἀμέσους	μέσας
367.1	ἐντελέχειαν	ἐνδελέχειαν
367.7	ἐμψυχῶσθαι, αὐτῇ δὴ	ἐμψυχοῦσθαι, αὐτῇ δὲ
367.7-8	ὑπάρχειν	ὑπάρχον
367.21	τιθέασιν	προτιθέασιν
368.15	ἄλλα κατ᾽ ἄλλα	ἄλλα καὶ ἄλλα
318.5	[περὶ τοῦ νοῦ]	περὶ τοῦ νοῦ
370.4	καθ᾽ ἑκατέραν	καθ᾽ ἑτέραν ἑτέραν
371.19	ἀπολελυμέναι	ἀπολυόμεναι
371.19	[ἀπόλυτοι]	ἀπόλυτοι
373.6	<καί>	
374.2	αὐτῶν	αὐτῶν
374.3	θέλωσιν	ἔλωσιν
374.22	διαστασιάζουσιν	διαστάζουσιν
375.19	ἐπὶ	ἀπὸ
376.5	ἀνασχέοντες	ἀνασχόντες
376.9	διαλήψεως	ἀποδιαλήψεως
377.4	αὐτῷ	αὐτῷ
377.21	παρὰ	περὶ
380.28	ἄλλοτε ἄλλους	ἄλλοτε ἄλλως
380.19	[μήτρας]	μήτρας
382.3	ἀπολελύσθαι	ἀπολύεσθαι
382.7	ἐπικρατεῖ	< ἢ> ἐπικράτεια
384.6	ἀχράντως	ἀχρόνως
384.9	τὰ ζῷα	τῷ ζῴῳ
384.13	καθαπερεὶ	καθάπερ
454.5	τῆς ἀγγελίωδους	τοῦ ἀγγειώδους
457.9	ἰσαγγέλους	εἰς ἀγγέλους
457.25	ὑπερβαινούσας	ὑπερβαίνουσαν
458.1	οἰκείας	οἰκίας
458.1	πρόσθεν	πρὸς τῆς
458.7	προσεοίκασι	προσεικάζουσι
458.11	ἀχωρίστων	χωριστῶν

B. Pseudo-Simplicius, In De Anima

Page	Hayduck	This edition
241.12	αὐτήν	ἑαυτὴν

C. Priscianus, Metaphrasis in Theophrastum

Page	Bywater	This edition
23.15	ταῖς τῶν ἑτέρων δυνάμεσιν	τὰς τῶν ἑτέρων δυνάμεων

1 Ἀριστοτέλης μὲν οὖν τὰ μάλιστα δοκοῦντα τῇ ψυχῇ ὑπάρχειν εἰς τρία τὰ κυριώτατα γένη ἀναγαγών, κίνησίν τε καὶ γνῶσιν καὶ λεπτότητα οὐσίας, ἣν ἐνίοτε καὶ ἀσώματον ὑπόστασιν ἐπονομάζει, ἐς ταῦτα | τὰ τρία τὰς καθ᾽ ἕκαστα διωρισμένας ἐπαναφέρει δόξας, πέρας   5
τῶν ἀπείρων ἀνευρὼν οὕτω καὶ σαφῆ καὶ σύντομον περίληψιν. Ἐγὼ δὲ
ὁρῶ ἐν τούτοις τοῖς ὅροις πολὺ μὲν τὸ ὁμώνυμον καὶ συγκεχυμένον, (οὐ
γὰρ ὡσαύτως αἱ κατὰ μεταβολὴν καὶ αἱ κατὰ ζωὴν θεωροῦνται
κινήσεις, ἢ αἱ μορφωτικαὶ καὶ <αἱ> ἄμορφοι γνώσεις, ἢ αἱ τοῦ ἀέρος
καὶ αἱ τῶν καθ᾽ αὐτὰ ἀσωμάτων καθαρότητες τῆς οὐσίας,) πολὺ δὲ καὶ   10
τὸ ἀτελὲς αὐτῶν καὶ ἐνδεές· οὐ γὰρ ἔνεστι πάντα περιλαβεῖν τὰ γένη
τῶν δοξῶν ἐν τοῖς τρισὶ τούτοις ὅροις.
2 Τινὲς εἰς τὰς τῶν τεσσάρων στοιχείων ἀρχὰς τὴν οὐσίαν τῆς ψυχῆς
ἐπαναφέρουσιν. Εἶναι μὲν γὰρ τὰ πρῶτα σώματα ἄτομα πρὸ τῶν
τεσσάρων στοιχείων στοιχειωδέστερα· εἰλικρινῆ δ᾽ ὄντα καὶ πεπ-   15
ληρωμένα πάντη καθαρᾶς πρώτης οὐσίας μὴ δέχεσθαι μηδ᾽ ὁπωστιοῦν
εἰς αὐτὰ διαίρεσιν. Ταῦτα τοίνυν ἄπειρα ἔχειν σχήματα, ἓν δὲ αὐτῶν
εἶναι τὸ σφαιροειδές, ἀπὸ δὴ τῶν σφαιροειδῶν ἀτόμων εἶναι τὴν ψυχήν.
3 Ὡς δὲ τῶν Ἀριστοτελικῶν τινες ὑφηγοῦνται, εἶδός ἐστι τὸ περὶ τοῖς
σώμασιν, ἢ ποιότης ἁπλῆ ἀσώματος ἢ ποιότης οὐσιώδης τελεία· ἢ   20
παράκειται δόξῃ οὐ παραδοθεῖσα μέν, δυναμένη δὲ πιθανῶς λέγεσθαι
αἵρεσις, ἢ τὴν συνδρομὴν τῶν ὅλων ποιοτήτων καὶ τὸ ἓν αὐτῶν
κεφάλαιον, εἴτε τὸ ἐπιγιγνόμενον ἢ τὸ προϋπάρχον, τιθεμένη τὴν
ψυχήν.

362: 1 Lemma in FP deest. Ἰαμβλίχου ἐκ τοῦ περὶ ψυχῆς add. Wachs.
363: 5 ἑκάστους Usener. **7** ὁρῶν FP: corr. Canter. **8** καὶ αἱ F, ἢ (in καὶ corr.) αἱ P.
ἢ αἱ P², ἢ καὶ FP¹. **9** μορφωτικαὶ P¹. ἢ ἄμορφοι FP: καὶ <αἱ> ἄμορφοι Wachs. **10** ἢ αἱ
τῶν FP: καὶ αἱ τῶν Wachs. αὐτὰ F. **12** τῆς δόξης FP: τῶν δοξῶν Usener. **16** ὁπωστι-
νοῦν FP: corr. Usener. **17** αὐτὰ FP: corr. Heeren. **19** ἀτόμων F, αὐτῶν P. **20** ἐπὶ
τοῖς Meineke. **21** δόξα FP: corr. Usener. **22** ἤ τε συνδρομὴ FP: ἢ τὴν συνδρομὴν
Meineke, Heeren. **23** εἴτε τὸ F, ἤτε τὸ P. προϋπάρχοντι θεμένη P.

IAMBLICHUS, ON THE SOUL

I. *The Nature of the Soul*

1. Aristotle, then, after he has assembled the qualities that seem most particularly to pertain to the soul into the three main categories of motion, knowledge, and subtlety of essence, which he also terms sometimes incorporeal substance, relates to each of the three categories the opinions appropriate to them, thus discovering a limit for the boundless and a clear and concise means of defining the opinions. I see in these categories much that is ambiguous and confused (for motions in the category of change are not to be considered as identical with motions in the category of life, nor kinds of knowledge that involve imagination with those that transcend it, nor the sort of purity of essence proper to air with that of things essentially incorporeal), and much that is incomplete and inadequate (for it is not possible to take in all the varieties of opinion under these three categories).

Soul Composed of Atoms

2. Some trace back the essence of the soul to the first principles of the four elements. For the primal atomic bodies are more elemental even than the four elements; being unmixed and completely filled with pure primal essence, they do not receive in themselves any trace of division. These primal bodies possess an infinite number of forms, one among which is the spherical, and it is out of spherical atoms that, they say, the soul is constituted.

Soul the Form of Body

3. As some of the Aristotelians teach, the soul is form associated with bodies, or a simple incorporeal quality, or a perfect essential quality. Closely allied to this opinion there is a view, not handed down by tradition but plausibly derivable from it, which makes the soul the combination of all the qualities and the simple summation of them, whether arising as a result of them or existing prior to them.

364 4 Μετὰ δὴ ταῦτα τοὺς εἰς μαθηματικὴν οὐσίαν ἐντι|θέντας τὴν οὐσίαν
τῆς ψυχῆς καταλέγω διευκρινημένως. Ἔστι δὴ γένος ἕν τι αὐτῆς τὸ
σχῆμα, πέρας ὂν διαστάσεως, καὶ αὐτὴ <ἡ> διάστασις. Ἐν αὐτοῖς μὲν
οὖν τούτοις Σεβῆρος ὁ Πλατωνικὸς αὐτὴν ἀφωρίσατο, ἐν ἰδέᾳ δὲ τοῦ
πάντῃ διαστατοῦ Σπεύσιππος· ἐν αἰτίᾳ δὲ ἤτοι ἑνώσει τούτων ἄλλος ἄν   5
τις καθαρώτερον αὐτὴν προστήσαιτο τελεώτατα. Πάλιν τοίνυν ὁ
ἀριθμὸς ἐν ἑτέρῳ γένει κεῖται. Ἀλλὰ καὶ τοῦτον ἁπλῶς μὲν οὕτως
ἔνιοι τῶν Πυθαγορείων τῇ ψυχῇ συναρμόζουσιν· ὡς δ᾽ αὐτοκίνητον
Ξενοκράτης, ὡς δὲ λόγους περιεχούσῃ Μοδέρατος ὁ Πυθαγόρειος, ὡς
δὲ κριτικὸν κοσμουργοῦ θεοῦ ὄργανον Ἵππασος, ὁ ἀκουσματικὸς τῶν   10
Πυθαγορείων· ὡς δ᾽ Ἀριστοτέλης ἱστορεῖ, Πλάτων ἐκ τῆς τοῦ ἑνὸς ἰδέας
καὶ τοῦ πρώτου μήκους <καὶ πλάτους> καὶ βάθους αὐτὸ τὸ ζῷον
προϋποτιθέμενος καὶ τὸ μὲν ἓν νοῦν, τὴν δὲ δυάδα ἐπιστήμην, δόξαν δὲ
τὸν τοῦ ἐπιπέδου ἀριθμόν, τὸν δὲ τοῦ στερεοῦ [τὴν] αἴσθησιν
διοριζόμενος.   15
5 Ἔτι τοίνυν τὴν ἁρμονίαν ἴδωμεν, οὐ τὴν ἐν σώμασιν ἐνιδρυμένην,
ἀλλ᾽ ἥτις ἐστὶ μαθηματική. Ταύτην τοίνυν, ὡς μὲν ἁπλῶς εἰπεῖν, τὴν τὰ
διαφέροντα ὁπωσοῦν σύμμετρα καὶ προσήγορα ἀπεργαζομένην
ἀναφέρει εἰς τὴν ψυχὴν Μοδέρατος· τὴν δ᾽ ὡς ἐν οὐσίαις καὶ ζωαῖς καὶ
γενέσει πάντων μεσότητα καὶ σύνδεσιν ὁ Τίμαιος αὐτῇ ἀνατίθησι, τὴν   20
365 δ᾽ ὡς ἐν λόγοις τοῖς κατ᾽ | οὐσίαν προϋπάρχουσι Πλωτῖνος καὶ
Πορφύριος καὶ Ἀμέλιος παραδεδώκασι, τὴν δὲ συνδιαπλεκομένην τῷ
κόσμῳ καὶ ἀχώριστον τοῦ οὐρανοῦ πολλοὶ δή τινες τῶν Πλατωνικῶν
καὶ Πυθαγορείων προκρίνουσιν.

364:1 μαθηματικὴν ἰδέαν sugg. Wachs. **2** καταλέγω διευκρινημένως F, καταλέγωσιν
εὐκρινημένως P: καταλέγωμεν εὐκρινῶς Heeren. ἕν τι F, ἔτι P. **3** αὐτῇ in αὐτὴ corr.
P. <ἡ> add. Wachs. **4** οὖν om. F. αὐτὴν ἀφωρίσατο om. Heeren. δὲ om. P.
5 ἀδιαστάτου Ravaisson, Speus. pl. p. 40 male. Σπεύσιππος P², πεύσιππος FP¹. ἢ τῇ
FP: ἤτοι Usener. **6** καθαρωτέραν Heeren. αὐτῆς προστήσαιτο <τὴν> τελειότητα
sugg. Wachs. προσήσαιτο P. **8** συναρμόσουσιν P. **9** λόγους FP: <ἐν> λόγοις Usener
coll. v. 25. περιεχούσαν FP², περιέχουσα P¹: περιέχουσιν Usener, περιέχοντα (scil:
ἀριθμὸν) Heeren, περιέχουσαν <ψυχὴν> Diels-Kranz, περιεχούσῃ Festugière. **12.**
καὶ πλάτους om. FP: add. Heeren coll. Arist. τοῦτο ζωὴν FP: τὸ ζῷον Heeren.
13/14 δὲ τὴν τοῦ P. **14** τὴν del. Wachs. **17** ὅτις FP: corr. Canter. μαθηματικὴ F,
θαυμαστικὴ P: φανταστικὴ Canter mrg. ταύτης Meineke. **20** τούτων FP: πάντων
Usener.
365: 24 καὶ om. P.

Soul a Mathematical Essence

4. Next, I propose to list carefully those who relate the essence of the soul with mathematical essence. Of this the first kind is figure, which is the limit of extension, and extension itself. In these very terms it was defined by Severus the Platonist, while Speusippus defined it as "the form of the omni-dimensionally extended." One might, however, employing a purer definition, define it most perfectly as the cause, or rather the unity, prior to these two.

Number, again, constitutes a second kind [of mathematical essence], and indeed some of the Pythagoreans apply it to the soul simply as such; Xenocrates [applies it] as self-moved; Moderatus the Pythagorean, as comprising ratios; Hippasus the Pythagorean auditor, as being the instrument by which the god who creates the world measures. As Aristotle relates, Plato [constructs the soul] by premising that the Essential Living Being is made up of the idea of the one and of the primary length <and breadth> and depth, and defining the one as intellect, the dyad as scientific knowledge, the number of the plane, opinion, and sense-perception the number of the solid.

Soul an Attunement

5. Next, let us consider (the claim that soul is an) attunement, not the attunement inherent in bodies, but that which is mathematical. It is this attunement, to speak simply, that which renders symmetrical and agreeable those things which differ in any way, that Moderatus applies to the soul. Timaeus, on the other hand, refers attunement to the soul as being a mean and conjunction in beings and lives and the generation of all things, while Plotinus, Porphyry, and Amelius have taught that it is attunement as residing in essentially preexistent reason-principles; while many of the Platonists and Pythagoreans adjudge it to be the attunement which is interwoven with the cosmos and inseparable from the heaven.

6 Ἴθι δὴ οὖν ἐπὶ τὴν καθ᾿ αὐτὴν ἀσώματον οὐσίαν ἐπανίωμεν, διακρίνοντες καὶ ἐπ᾿ αὐτῆς ἐν τάξει τὰς περὶ ψυχῆς πάσας δόξας. Εἰσὶ δή τινες, οἳ πᾶσαν τὴν τοιαύτην οὐσίαν ὁμοιομερῆ καὶ τὴν αὐτὴν καὶ μίαν ἀποφαίνονται, ὡς καὶ ἐν ὁτῳοῦν αὐτῆς μέρει εἶναι τὰ ὅλα· οἵτινες καὶ ἐν τῇ μεριστῇ ψυχῇ τὸν νοητὸν κόσμον καὶ θεοὺς καὶ δαίμονας καὶ 5 τἀγαθὸν καὶ πάντα τὰ πρεσβύτερα ἐν αὐτῇ ἐνιδρύουσι καὶ ἐν πᾶσιν ὡσαύτως πάντα εἶναι ἀποφαίνονται, οἰκείως μέντοι κατὰ τὴν αὐτῶν οὐσίαν ἐν ἑκάστοις. Καὶ ταύτης τῆς δόξης ἀναμφισβητήτως μέν ἐστι Νουμήνιος, οὐ πάντη δὲ ὁμολογουμένως Πλωτῖνος, ἀστάτως δὲ ἐν αὐτῇ φέρεται Ἀμέλιος· Πορφύριος δὲ ἐνδοιάζει περὶ αὐτήν, πῇ μὲν 10 διατεταμένως αὐτῆς ἀφιστάμενος, πῇ δὲ συνακολουθῶν αὐτῇ, ὡς παραδοθείσῃ ἄνωθεν. Κατὰ δὴ ταύτην νοῦ καὶ θεῶν καὶ τῶν κρειττόνων γενῶν οὐδὲν ἡ ψυχὴ διενήνοχε κατά γε τὴν ὅλην οὐσίαν.

7 Ἀλλὰ μὴν ἥ γε πρὸς ταύτην ἀνθισταμένη δόξα χωρίζει μὲν τὴν ψυχήν, ὡς ἀπὸ νοῦ γενομένην δευτέραν καθ᾿ ἑτέραν ὑπόστασιν, τὸ δὲ 15 μετὰ νοῦ αὐτῆς ἐξηγεῖται ὡς ἐξηρτημένον ἀπὸ τοῦ νοῦ, μετὰ τοῦ κατ᾿ ἰδίαν ὑφεστηκέναι αὐτοτελῶς, χωρίζει δὲ αὐτὴν καὶ ἀπὸ τῶν κρειττόνων γενῶν ὅλων, ἴδιον δὲ αὐτῇ τῆς οὐσίας ὅρον ἀπονέμει ἤτοι **366** τὸ μέσον τῶν μεριστῶν καὶ ἀμερίστων | <τῶν τε σωματικῶν καὶ ἀ>σωμάτων γενῶν, ἢ τὸ πλήρωμα τῶν καθόλου λόγων, ἢ τὴν μετὰ τὰς 20 ἰδέας ὑπηρεσίαν τῆς δημιουργίας, ἢ ζωὴν παρ᾿ ἑαυτῆς ἔχουσαν τὸ ζῆν τὴν ἀπὸ τοῦ νοητοῦ προελθοῦσαν, ἢ τὴν αὖ τῶν γενῶν ὅλου τοῦ ὄντως ὄντος πρόοδον εἰς ὑποδεεστέραν οὐσίαν. Περὶ δὴ ταύτας τὰς δόξας ὅ τε Πλάτων αὐτὸς καὶ ὁ Πυθαγόρας, ὅ τε Ἀριστοτέλης καὶ ἀρχαῖοι πάντες, ὧν ὀνόματα μεγάλα ἐπὶ σοφίᾳ ὑμνεῖται, τελέως ἐπιστρέφονται, 25 εἴ τις αὐτῶν τὰς δόξας ἀνιχνεύοι μετ᾿ ἐπιστήμης· ἡμεῖς τε περὶ αὐτὰς τὴν μετ᾿ ἀληθείας πραγματείαν πᾶσαν πειρασόμεθα ἐνστήσασθαι.

365: 1 ἴθι P², ἴσθι FP¹. **3** δή om. P. **4** εντωουν (ἐν τῶουν F) αὐτῶν FP: corr. Heeren. **6** ἐν αὐτῇ FP: γένη αὐτῆς Usener. **8** ἑκάστ (supra τ sprscr. ς.) F. καὶ ταύτης P², κατὰ ταύτης FP¹. ἀναμφισβήτως FP: corr. Heeren. **10** φέρετα P. ἐν διάζει P. **11** διατεταγμένως FP: corr. Meineke. συνακολουθεῖν F. **13** γε om. Heeren. **16** μετὰ νοῦν F, μενοῦν P: corr. cod. Vatic. **17** μερίζει FP: χωρίζει Canter mrg.
366: 19/20 σωμάτων FP: <τῶν τε σωματικῶν καὶ ἀ>σωμάτων Usener. **20** ἢ τὴν FP: καὶ τὴν vulg., Canter. **22** προσελθουσῶν FP: corr. Usener. τῶν αὐτῶν γενῶν FP: τὴν αὖ τῶν γενῶν Usener. ante ὅλου add. ἢ Heeren. **23** ὄντος om. P. δὲ FP: δὴ Usener. **25** πᾶν P. μεγάλα F, μεγάλ P: μεγάλως Heeren. **26** ἐπιστήμης FP: ἐπιστάσεως Usener. ἡμεῖς δὲ Heeren. **27** τὴν om. Heeren.

Soul an Incorporeal Essence

6. Let us now ascend to the consideration of that substance which is of itself incorporeal, distinguishing in order all the opinions about the soul in relation to it also. There are some who maintain that such a substance as a whole is homogeneous and one and the same, such that all of it may be found in any part of it; and they place even in the individual soul the intelligible world, and gods and daemons and the Good and all the beings superior to it, and declare everything to be in each thing in the same way but in a manner appropriate to its essence. Numenius is unambiguously of this opinion, Plotinus not completely consistently, while Amelius is unstable in his allegiance to the opinion; as for Porphyry, he is in two minds on the subject, now dissociating himself violently from this view, now adopting it as a doctrine handed down from above. According to this doctrine, the soul differs in no way from intellect and the gods, and the superior classes of being, at least in respect to its substance in general.

7. The doctrine opposed to this, however, separates the Soul off, inasmuch as it has come about as following upon Intellect, representing a distinct level of being, and that aspect of it which is endowed with intellect is explained as being connected with the intellect certainly, but also as subsisting independently on its own, and it separates the soul also from all the superior classes of being, and assigns to it as the particular definition of its essence, either the middle term of divisible and indivisible beings <and of corporeal and in>corporeal being, or the totality of the universal reason-principles, or that which, after the ideas, is at the service of the work of creation, or that life which has life of itself, which proceeds from the Intelligible realm, or again the procession of the classes of real Being as a whole to an inferior substance. It is these doctrines to which Plato himself and Pythagoras, and Aristotle, and all the ancients who have gained great and honorable names for wisdom, are completely committed, as one will find if he investigates their opinions with scientific rigor; as for myself, I will try to base this whole treatise, concerned as it is with truth, on these opinions.

8 Τινὲς δὲ τῶν φυσικῶν σύνοδον τῶν ἐναντίων συνυφαίνουσιν, οἷον θερμοῦ καὶ <ψυχροῦ>, ξηροῦ καὶ ὑγροῦ. Καὶ γὰρ τὸ ζῆν ἀπὸ τοῦ ἀναζεῖν ὑπὸ τοῦ θερμοῦ καὶ τὴν ψυχὴν ἀπὸ τοῦ ἀναψύχεσθαι ὑπὸ τοῦ ψυχροῦ ὠνομάσθαι ἀποφαίνονται, καὶ ἅμα ἐπ' ἀμφοτέρων < . . . > ἢ τὸν ἀναπνεόμενον ἀέρα ψυχὴν νομίζουσιν· ὥσπερ Ἀριστοτέλης μὲν ἐν   5
τοῖς Ὀρφικοῖς ἔπεσί φησι λέγεσθαι τὴν ψυχὴν εἰσιέναι ἐκ τοῦ ὅλου ἀναπνεόντων ἡμῶν φερομένην ὑπὸ τῶν ἀνέμων· ἔοικέ γε μὴν αὐτὸς ὁ Ὀρφεὺς χωρὶς ὑπολαμβάνειν εἶναι καὶ μίαν τὴν ψυχήν, ἀφ' ἧς πολλὰς μὲν εἶναι διαιρέσεις, πολλὰς δὲ καὶ μέσας ἐπιπνοίας καθήκειν ἐπὶ τὰς μεριστὰς ψυχὰς ἀπὸ τῆς ὅλης ψυχῆς.   10

9 Τινὲς μὲν τῶν Ἀριστοτελικῶν αἰθέριον σῶμα τὴν ψυχὴν τίθενται· ἕτεροι δὲ τελειότητα αὐτὴν ἀφορίζονται κατ' οὐσίαν τοῦ θείου **367** σώματος, ἣν ἐνδελέχειαν καλεῖ Ἀριστοτέλης, ὥσπερ δὴ ἐν ἐνίοις Θεόφραστος, ἢ τὸ ἀπογεννώμενον ἀπὸ τῶν θειοτέρων γενῶν ὅλων, ὥσπερ ἄν τις νεωτερίσειεν ἐν ταῖς ἐπινοίαις· ἢ τὸ συγκεκραμένον τοῖς   15
σώμασιν, ὥσπερ οἱ Στωικοὶ λέγουσιν· ἢ τὸ τῇ φύσει συμμεμιγμένον ἢ τὸ τοῦ σώματος ὂν ὥσπερ τὸ ἐμψυχοῦσθαι, αὐτῇ δὲ μὴ παρὸν τῇ ψυχῇ ὥσπερ ὑπάρχον, οἷα δὴ λέγεται περὶ ψυχῆς παρὰ Δικαιάρχῳ τῷ Μεσσηνίῳ.

366: 1 συνόδων FP: corr. Canter. **2** καὶ (post θερμοῦ) om. F. ψυχροῦ add. Heeren. **4** ἢ FP: καὶ Canter; secl. Wachs.; lacunam statuit Festugière, sic supplevit <ἐτυμολογοῦσι πρὸς τὴν οἰκείαν δόξαν· ἢ γὰρ ψυχὴν τὸ πῦρ λέγουσιν>. **5** μὲν del. Meineke. **6** φυσικοῖς FP: Ὀρφικοῖς Gaisford ex Ar. l.s. ὡς εἰσὶν F, ὡς εἰσὴν P: εἰσιέναι Canter; πως εἰσιέναι Meineke. **9** μέσας FP: ἀμέσους conj. Usener. **367:** 13 ἐνδελέχειαν FP: ἐντελέχειαν corr. Heeren. **14** γενῶν om. P. **15** ἐν del. Usener. ταῖς ἐπινοίας susp. Heeren. **17** ὥσπερ τὸ ἐμψυχῶσθαι FP: ὥσπερεὶ ἐψυχῶσθαι vel ἐνεψυχῶσθαι Meineke, ὥσπερ τὸ ἐψυχῶσθαι Wachs., ἐμψυχοῦσθαι Festugière. δὲ FP: δὴ Wachs. **18** ὥσπερ corruptum; fort. ὁπωσοῦν Wachs. ὑπάρχον FP: ὑπάρχειν Wachs.

Some Miscellaneous Opinions (Mainly Materialist)

8. Certain of the physical philosophers make the soul a union woven together from opposites, such as hot and <cold,> dry and wet. For they derive the word "live" from "to boil up" due to heat, and the word "soul" from "to cool down" due to cold, and in both cases <they produce etymologies to accord with their beliefs; for either they say that fire is the substance of the soul,> or they consider that the air breathed into the body is soul, as, according to Aristotle, it is said in the Orphic poems that the soul enters into us from the Universe, borne by the winds, when we breathe; and it seems certainly that Orpheus himself considered that the soul was separate and one, and that out of it there spring many divisions, and that many intermediary "breaths" descended to the individual souls from the universal soul.

9. Certain of the Aristotelians make the soul a body composed of aether. Others define it as the essential perfection of the divine body, which Aristotle calls "perpetual motion," as indeed does Theophrastus in some places; or that which is produced from all the more divine classes of being, if one may suggest an innovation on this doctrine; or that which is intermixed with bodies, as the Stoics would have it; or that which is intermingled with the principle of growth or that which belongs to the body as a "being ensouled" — not present to the soul itself as belonging to it — which is said about the soul by Dicaearchus of Messene.

[Ἐν ταὐτῷ· περὶ δυνάμεων ψυχῆς]

10 Πλάτων μὲν οὖν οὐχ ὡς ἑτέρας τὰς δυνάμεις ἐν ἑτέρᾳ τῇ ψυχῇ ἐνεῖναι ἡγεῖται, συμφύτους δ᾽ αὐτὰς καὶ κατὰ μίαν ἰδέαν συνυφεστηκέναι λέγει διὰ τὴν ἀσύνθετον οὐσίαν τῆς ψυχῆς. Ἀριστοτέλης δὲ ὡσαύτως ἁπλῆν οὐσίαν, ἀσώματον, εἴδους τελεσιουργὸν τὴν τῆς ψυχῆς　5 ὑποθέμενος, οὐ ποιεῖ τὰς δυνάμεις ὡς ἐν συνθέτῳ τινὶ τῇ ψυχῇ παρούσας. Ἀλλὰ μὴν οἵγε ἀπὸ Χρυσίππου καὶ Ζήνωνος φιλόσοφοι καὶ πάντες ὅσοι σῶμα τὴν ψυχὴν νοοῦσι τὰς μὲν δυνάμεις ὡς ἐν τῷ ὑποκειμένῳ ποιότητας συμβιβάζουσι, τὴν δὲ ψυχὴν ὡς οὐσίαν προϋποκειμένην ταῖς δυνάμεσι προτιθέασιν, ἐκ δ᾽ ἀμφοτέρων τούτων　10 σύνθετον φύσιν ἐξ ἀνομοίων συνάγουσιν.

368 Ταύτῃ | τοίνυν αἱ δυνάμεις αὐτῆς τῆς ψυχῆς καθ᾽ αὑτὴν ἢ τοῦ ἔχοντος τοῦ κοινοῦ μετὰ τοῦ σώματος θεωρουμένου ζῴου, καθ᾽ οὓς μὲν ἡ ψυχὴ διττὴν ζωὴν ζῇ, καθ᾽ αὑτήν τε καὶ μετὰ τοῦ σώματος, ἄλλως μὲν πάρεισι τῇ ψυχῇ, ἄλλως δὲ τῷ κοινῷ ζῴῳ, <ὡς> κατὰ Πλάτωνα καὶ　15 Πυθαγόραν· καθ᾽ οὓς δὲ μία ζωὴ τῆς ψυχῆς ἐστιν ἡ τοῦ συνθέτου, συγκεκραμένης τῆς ψυχῆς τῷ σώματι, ὡς οἱ Στωικοὶ λέγουσιν, ἢ δούσης ὅλην τὴν ἑαυτῆς ζωὴν εἰς τὸ κοινὸν ζῷον, ὡς οἱ Περιπατητικοὶ διισχυρίζονται, κατὰ τούτους εἷς ἐστιν ὁ τρόπος τῆς παρουσίας αὐτῶν ὁ ἐν τῷ μετέχεσθαι ἢ ἐν τῷ κεκρᾶσθαι τῷ ὅλῳ ζῴῳ.　20

367: 1 δυνάμεως FP: corr. Meineke. Post ψυχῆς add. lemma πλάτωνος P. 3 συνεφεστηκέναι P. 4 σύνθετον FP: corr. Wyttenbach. 5 τελεσιουργὸν P², τελεσιουργοῦ FP¹. 6 ὑποτιθέμενος Heeren. 10 προτιθέασιν FP: τιθέασιν Wachs. 12 αὗται F (with space left before it), ταῦτα P: ταύτῃ Usener, αὗται Heeren.
368: 13 καθ᾽ ἃς F. μὲν <οὖν> Heeren. 15 ὡς add. Heeren. 17 ἢ δούσης P², ἡδούσης FP¹. 18 ὅλην P², ὅλης FP¹. αὐτῆς Heeren. 20 κερᾶσθαι P¹: συγκεκρᾶσθαι Meineke.

II. *The Powers of the Soul*

How the Powers Inhere in the Soul

10. Now Plato does not think that the powers exist in the soul as separate from it, but says that they are naturally conjoined with the soul and coexist with it in a single form because of the incomposite essence of the soul. And Aristotle similarly, since he posits that the essence of the soul is simple, incorporeal, and productive of form, does not regard the powers as present in any kind of composite soul. On the other hand the followers of Chrysippus and Zeno, and all those who consider the soul a body, join the powers together as though they were qualities in a substrate and consider the soul a substance that underlies the powers, and from both of these[1] they construct a composite nature made up of dissimilar elements.

In the following way, then, the powers belong to the soul in itself or to the common living being that possesses the soul and is conceived as existing along with the body. According to those who think that the soul lives a double life, one in itself and one in conjunction with the body, they are present in the soul in one way but in the common animal in another, as Plato and Pythagoras think. According to those, on the other hand, who think that there is a single life of the soul, that of the composite — because the soul is commingled with the body, as the Stoics say, or because the soul gives its whole life to the common living being, as the Peripatetics confidently assert — according to them there is a single way in which the powers are present: by being shared in or by being mingled with the whole living being.

---

[1]   That is, from the powers on the one hand and the soul itself on the other.

11 Πῶς οὖν διακρίνονται; Κατὰ μὲν τοὺς Στωικοὺς ἔνιαι μὲν διαφορότητι <τῶν> ὑποκειμένων σωμάτων· πνεύματα γὰρ ἀπὸ τοῦ ἡγεμονικοῦ φασιν οὗτοι διατείνειν ἄλλα καὶ ἄλλα, τὰ μὲν εἰς ὀφθαλμούς, τὰ δὲ εἰς ὦτα, τὰ δὲ εἰς ἄλλα αἰσθητήρια· ἔνιαι δὲ ἰδιότητι ποιότητος περὶ τὸ αὐτὸ ὑποκείμενον· ὥσπερ γὰρ τὸ μῆλον ἐν τῷ αὐτῷ   5
σώματι τὴν γλυκύτητα ἔχει καὶ τὴν εὐωδίαν, οὕτω καὶ τὸ ἡγεμονικὸν ἐν ταὐτῷ φαντασίαν, συγκατάθεσιν, ὁρμήν, λόγον συνείληφε. Κατὰ δὲ τοὺς Ἀριστοτελικοὺς καὶ πάντας ὅσοι ἀμέριστον τὴν ψυχὴν διανοοῦνται κατὰ μὲν τὴν οὐσίαν αἱ δυνάμεις <οὐ διακρίνονται>, κατὰ δὲ εἴδη ὧν δύνανται ποιεῖν. Κατὰ δὲ Πλάτωνα ἄλλως μὲν λέγεται ἡ   10
ψυχὴ τριμερής, ὡς ἐν ἑτέραις οὐσίαις ζωῆς τριπλῆ παραλλάττουσα,
369   ἄλλως δὲ πολυδύναμος, οὐκέτι κατ᾽ | οὐσίαν ζωῆς διαφέρουσα, ἐν ταὐτῷ δὲ πολλαῖς ἰδιότησι διακρινομένη. Καὶ ὅλως μέρος δυνάμεως ταύτῃ διενήνοχεν, ᾗ τὸ μὲν μέρος οὐσίας ἑτερότητα, ἡ δὲ δύναμις ἐν ταὐτῷ γεννητικὴν ἢ ποιητικὴν διάκρισιν παρίστησιν.   15
[Ἐν ταὐτῷ· περὶ πλήθους δυνάμεων.]
12 Οἱ ἀπὸ Ζήνωνος ὀκταμερῆ τὴν ψυχὴν διαδοξάζουσι, περὶ <ἣν> τὰς δυνάμεις εἶναι πλείονας, ὥσπερ ἐν τῷ ἡγεμονικῷ ἐνυπαρχουσῶν φαντασίας, συγκαταθέσεως, ὁρμῆς, λόγου. Οἱ δὲ περὶ Πλάτωνα καὶ Ἀρχύτας καὶ οἱ λοιποὶ Πυθαγόρειοι τὴν ψυχὴν τριμερῆ ἀποφαίνονται,   20
διαιροῦντες εἰς λογισμὸν καὶ θυμὸν καὶ ἐπιθυμίαν· ταῦτα γὰρ εἶναι χρήσιμα πρὸς τὴν τῶν ἀρετῶν σύστασιν. Δυνάμεις δὲ τῆς ψυχῆς ἀναλογίζονται φύσιν καὶ φαντασίαν καὶ αἴσθησιν καὶ δόξαν καὶ κινητικὴν σωμάτων διάνοιαν καὶ ὄρεξιν καλῶν κἀγαθῶν καὶ νοήσεις. Ἀριστοτέλης δὲ εἰς πέντε αὐτὰς διαιρεῖ, φύσιν, αἴσθησιν, κίνησιν κατὰ   25
τόπον, ὄρεξιν, διανόησιν.

368: 1 ἔνιοι P. **2** ante διαφορότητι add. τῇ Heeren. τῶν add. Heeren. **3** ἄλλα καὶ ἄλλα FP: ἄλλα κατ᾽ ἄλλα Meineke, ἄλλα εἰς ἄλλα Heeren. **5** γὰρ τῶ P. **6** ἐδωδίαν P[1]. **9** οὐ διακρίνονται sugg. Wach; alii alia. **11** ὡς ἂν FP: ὡς ἐν Usener. τριπλῆ ζωῆς FP: ζωῆς τριπλῆ sugg. Wachs.
369: 14 ἤ FP: ἦ Heeren. **17** δοξάζουσιν Heeren. περὶ τὰς FP: μερικὰς Usener, ἐν ἑνὶ δὲ τὰς Heeren, <ἐν ἑκάστῳ δὲ> μέρει τὰς Meineke, περὶ <ἣν> τὰς Wachs, περὶ <νοοῦντες> sugg. Festugière. **18** ἐν ὑπάρχουσι P. **19** λόγου in textu F; in marg. P. **24** καὶ ἀγαθῶν FP: κἀγαθῶν Meineke.

How the Powers are Distinguished

11. How, then, are the powers distinguished? According to the Stoics, some are distinguished by the difference of the body parts that underlie them. For they say that ever different effluences extend from the ruling element, some to the eyes, others to the ears, others to other sense organs. Other powers are distinguished by their individual qualitative nature in the same substrate; for even as the apple has in the same body sweetness and pleasant odor, so also the ruling faculty comprises in the same substrate imagination, assent, appetition, and reason. According to the Aristotelians and all who consider the soul to be without parts, the powers <are not distinguished> in substance, but rather according to the kinds of effects that they can produce. According to Plato, in one sense the soul is called tripartite since it varies in three ways in different life-substances, but in another sense it has many powers, the soul not now exhibiting differences in the life-substance but being distinguished in the same substrate by many individual properties. And in general, a part differs from a power in this, that the part exhibits a difference of substance, whereas the power exhibits a differentiation in production or creation in the same substrate.

Multiple Powers in the Soul

12. The followers of Zeno believe that the soul has eight parts and that connected with these parts there are a multiplicity of powers, as for instance imagination, assent, appetition, and reason exist in the ruling element. Plato and his school, Archytas, and the rest of the Pythagoreans assert that the soul is tripartite, dividing it into reason, spirit, and desire, for these are useful for establishing the system of virtues. As to the powers of the soul, these philosophers include the powers of growth, imagination, perception, opinion, thought that moves the body, desire for good and evil, and intellection. Aristotle divides the powers into five: the powers of growth, perception, locomotion, desire, and thought.

[Ἐν ταὐτῷ· περὶ τῶν κατ᾽ οὐσίαν τῆς ψυχῆς καὶ τῶν προστιθεμένων αὐτῇ δυνάμεων.]

13 Πλωτῖνος αὐτῆς ἀφαιρεῖ τὰς ἀλόγους δυνάμεις, τὰς αἰσθήσεις, τὰς φαντασίας, τὰς μνήμας, τοὺς λογισμούς· μόνον δὲ τὸν καθαρὸν λογισμὸν εἰς τὴν καθαρὰν οὐσίαν αὐτῆς ἀνατείνει, ὡς ἔχοντα συμφυῆ   5
δύναμιν πρὸς αὐτὴν τὴν τῆς οὐσίας ἰδέαν. |

370   Οἱ δὲ περὶ Δημόκριτον Πλατωνικοὶ πάντα ταῦτα τὰ εἴδη τῶν δυνάμεων εἰς τὴν οὐσίαν αὐτῆς συνάγουσιν.

Ὁ δὲ Πλάτων καὶ αὐτὰς ἑαυτῶν ποιεῖ καὶ τῶν ζῴων, καθ᾽ ἑτέραν ἑτέραν ζωὴν διοριζόμενος ἑκάτερον.   10

Οἱ δὲ περὶ Πορφύριον καὶ Πλωτῖνον ἑκάστῳ μέρει τοῦ παντὸς τὰς οἰκείας δυνάμεις προβάλλεσθαι ὑπὸ τῆς ψυχῆς ἀποφαίνονται, καὶ ἀφίεσθαι μὲν καὶ μηκέτι εἶναι τὰς ζωὰς τὰς ὁπωσοῦν προβληθείσας [οἱ περὶ Πορφύριον καὶ Πλωτῖνον Πλατωνικοὶ] ἀφορίζονται παραπλη-σίως τοῖς ἀπὸ τοῦ σπέρματος φυομένοις, ὁπόταν εἰς ἑαυτὸ ἀναδράμῃ τὸ   15
σπέρμα· εἶναι δὲ καὶ ταύτας ἐν τῷ παντὶ καὶ μὴ ἀπόλλυσθαι τάχα ἄν τις ἐπινοήσειε καινότερον, οὐκ ἀπιθάνως.

Hense III,
p. 608.
25ff.   [Ἰαμβλίχου ἐκ τοῦ Περὶ ψυχῆς.]

609   **14** Τούτων οὐσῶν τῶν κοινοτάτων δυνάμεων εἰσὶ καὶ | ἄλλαι τῆς ψυχῆς δυνάμεις, κατ᾽ αὐτὴν μέν, οὐ μὴν συμπληρωτικαὶ αὐτῆς, ὡς ἡ   20
Wachs-   μνήμη κατοχὴ οὖσα φαντάσματος.
muth I,
p.317.
20ff.   [Ἰαμβλίχου ἐκ τοῦ Περὶ ψυχῆς.] |

15 Πάλιν τοίνυν περὶ τοῦ νοῦ καὶ πασῶν τῶν κρειττόνων δυνάμεων τῆς ψυχῆς οἱ μὲν Στωικοὶ λέγουσι μὴ εὐθὺς ἐμφύεσθαι τὸν λόγον, ὕστερον δὲ συναθροίζεσθαι ἀπὸ τῶν αἰσθήσεων καὶ φαντασιῶν περὶ   25
δεκατέσσαρα ἔτη. |

369: 1 ἐν ταυτῷ post δυνάμεων (2) transponit F. 1 περὶ τῆς οὐσίας τῆς ψυχῆς Heeren. 5 ἀνατείνει FP: ἀνατείνειν sugg. Wachs. συμφυῆ F.
370: 7 δὲ om. P. πλατωνικοὶ FP: secl. Heeren, ἀτομικοὶ Meineke. 9 αὐτὰς καὶ ἑαυτῶν sugg. Wachs. 9 καθ᾽ ἑτέραν ἑτέραν FP: καθ᾽ ἑκατέραν sugg. Canter mrg. 12 προβαλέσθαι P. 13. ἀμφίεσθαι P. οἱ περὶ ... Πλατωνικοὶ FP: secl. Heeren. 15 ἑαυτο P², ἑαυτόν FP¹. ἀναδράμῃ P, ἀναδράμοι F. 16 ἀπόλυσθαι P.
609: 19 οὐσῶν τῶν S Mᵈ A: οὖν τῶν Trincavelliani, inde vulg.
317: 24 λέγουσιν P.

Which Powers Belong to the Soul

13. Plotinus removes from the soul the irrational powers: those of perception, imagination, memory, and discursive reasoning. He includes only pure reason in the pure essence of the soul, on the grounds that it has a power bound up with the very nature of the soul's essence. Democritus the Platonist and his followers, however, attribute all these kinds of faculty to the essence of the soul. Plato assumes that the powers belong both to souls themselves and to the living beings, distinguishing each in accordance with each life.

Porphyry and Plotinus and their followers maintain that the soul projects its own powers to each part of the universe and that the lives, howsoever they have been projected, are dissolved and cease to exist, similar to objects that grow from a seed, when the seed withdraws into itself. One might perhaps propose not unpersuasively the rather novel theory that these powers continue to exist in the universe and do not perish.

On Memory

14. These are the most common powers of the soul, but there are still others that are proper to it in itself but that do not constitute essential parts of it, such as memory, which is the retention of an image.

On the Intellect

15. Again, as regards the intellect and all the higher powers of the soul, the Stoics say that the reason is not implanted in the soul at the outset but is acquired later around the age of fourteen from sensations and images. The followers of Plato and Pythagoras say that reason is present in the newly-born but is obscured by external influences and does not exercise its proper activity but remains dormant.

318   Οἱ δ᾽ ἀπὸ Πλάτωνος καὶ Πυθαγόρου παρεῖναι μὲν καὶ ἐν τοῖς
ἀρτιγενέσι τὸν λόγον φασίν, ἐπισκοτεῖσθαί γε μὴν [ἐν] τοῖς ἔξωθεν καὶ
μὴ ἐνεργεῖν τὴν οἰκείαν ἐνέργειαν, ἀλλ᾽ ἡσυχάζειν.

Ἤδη τοίνυν περὶ τοῦ νοῦ πολλοὶ μὲν Περιπατητικοὶ τὸν ἐκ
σπέρματος καὶ [τὸν] ἀπὸ τῆς φύσεως ἄλλον νοῦν ὑποθέμενοι, ὡς αὐτί-   5
κα μάλα ἀποβλαστάνοντα ἀπὸ τῆς πρώτης γενέσεως, καὶ χωριστὸν καὶ
θύραθεν ἐπικαλούμενον ἕτερον παραγίγνεσθαι λέγουσιν ὀψιαίτατα,
ἐπειδὰν τελειωθῇ μὲν ὁ κατὰ δύναμιν νοῦς, ἐπιτηδείως δὲ μετέχῃ τῆς
κατ᾽ ἐνέργειαν νοήσεως.

Πολλοὶ δὲ αὐτῶν τῶν Πλατωνικῶν καὶ τὸν νοῦν τῇ ψυχῇ ἅμα τῇ   10
πρώτῃ εἰσόδῳ αὐτῆς εἰς τὸ σῶμα συνεισάγουσιν, οὐδὲ εἶναι ὅλως
ἑτέραν μὲν αὐτήν, ἕτερον δὲ αὐτῆς τὸν νοῦν.

Wachs-
muth I
p. 370.
14ff.   [Ἐν ταὐτῷ· περὶ τῶν ἐνεργειῶν τῆς ψυχῆς.]

16 Τίς οὖν ἀνήκοός ἐστι τῆς Περιπατητικῆς δόξης, ἢ τὴν ψυχὴν
ἀκίνητον μὲν εἶναί φησιν, αἰτίαν δὲ κινήσεων; Εἰ δὴ καὶ ἀνενέργητόν   15
ἐστι τὸ ἀκίνητον, ἔσται καὶ χορηγὸν τῶν ἐνεργειῶν τὸ τῆς ψυχῆς
ἀνενέργητον. Εἰ δ᾽ ὡς ἔνιοι λέγουσι, τέλος καὶ συνοχὴ καὶ ἕνωσις καὶ
μόνιμος αἰτία τῶν κινήσεών ἐστιν ἡ ἐνέργεια καὶ ταύτην ἐν ἑαυτῇ
συνείληφεν ἡ κατ᾽ Ἀριστοτέλην ἀκίνητος ἐντελέχεια τῆς ψυχῆς, ἔσται
ἀπὸ τῆς τελειοτάτης ἐνεργείας προϊοῦσα [ἀπὸ τῆς ψυχῆς] ἡ ἐν τοῖς καθ᾽   20
ἕκαστα τῶν ζῴων ἔργοις ἀπεργασία.

318: 2 ἐν FP: del. Usener. **4** περὶ τοῦ νοῦ secl. Wachs. male. τὸν (ante ἐκ) P², τῶν
FP¹. **5** σπέρματος P², σπερμάτων FP¹. τὸν del. Usener. **5/6** ante ὡς αὐτίκα et ante
καὶ χωριστὸν (6) Heeren perperam add. τὸν μὲν et τὸν δὲ. **7** ἐπικαλούμενον susp.
Wachs.; ἐπεισαγόμενον sugg. Usener. ὕστερον FP: ἕτερον Usener. **8** δὲ om. P.
9 μετέχειν FP: corr. Usener. **10** τῆς ψυχῇ FP: corr. Usener. **11** συνεισαγάγουσιν P.
370: 14 ἢ P², ἢ FP¹. **15** ἐνενεργητὸν P. post ἐστι add. καὶ F. **18** ἡ P², ἢ FP¹. **20** ἀπὸ
τῆς ψυχῆς secl. Heeren.

Now, concerning the intellect, many Peripatetics posit one intellect from seed and from the natural world, which arises immediately at the moment of birth. They add that a second intellect, which they call separate and external, comes into being along with it but arises very late, when the potential intellect is actualized and participates appropriately in actual intellection. On the other hand, many of the Platonists themselves introduce the intellect into the soul at the same time as the first entry of soul into body, and they absolutely do not differentiate the soul from its intellect.

III. *On the Activities of the Soul*

16. Who, then, is ignorant of the Peripatetic doctrine that the soul is unmoved but is the cause of motions? But if the unmoved is inactive, the inactive element of the soul will be the originator of activities. And if, as some say, (the soul's) activity is the end, the principle of coherence and unity, and the stable cause of motions and if the unmoved "entelechy," as Aristotle terms it, of the soul comprehends this activity within itself, then whatever is accomplished in the individual actions of animals will proceed from the most perfect type of activity.

Αὕτη τοίνυν κατά γε Πλάτωνα πολλοῦ δεῖ ἡ αὐτὴ εἶναι τῇ συμφύτῳ τῆς ψυχῆς οὐσίᾳ καὶ ζωῇ. Δῆλον γὰρ ὅτι δίδοται μὲν εἰς τὸ κοινόν, ἀλλ᾽ ἐπεὶ μεταβολὴ καὶ διαίρεσις καὶ παράτασις περὶ τὸ σῶμα

371 καὶ κατὰ χρόΙνον καὶ τόπον διάστασις ἐπισυμπίπτει, ὧν οὐδέν ἐστιν ἐν τῇ καθ᾽ αὑτὴν ἀσωμάτῳ ζωῇ, φανερὸν δὴ καὶ τοῦτο γέγονεν, ὡς οὐδὲν   5
ὑπάρχει κατὰ Πλάτωνα τῶν τοῦ συνθέτου ζῴου κινημάτων ἴδιον αὐτῆς τῆς ψυχῆς. Οὐκοῦν ὥσπερ ζωὴ κατ᾽ αὐτὸν ἦν διττή, ἢ μὲν χωριστὴ τοῦ σώματος, ἢ δὲ κοινὴ μετ᾽ αὐτοῦ, οὕτω καὶ ἐνεργήματα <τὰ> μὲν ἴδια ἔσται τῆς ψυχῆς, τὰ δὲ κοινὰ καὶ τοῦ ἔχοντος. Καὶ τούτων τὰ μὲν ἀπὸ τῆς ψυχῆς προκατάρχοντα, τὰ δὲ ἀπὸ τῶν τοῦ σώματος παθημάτων   10
ἐγειρόμενα, τὰ δὲ ἐξ ἀμφοῖν ἐπίσης ἀνακινούμενα· πάντα δὲ ὡς ἀπ᾽ αἰτίας τῆς ψυχῆς ὡρμημένα. Ὥσπερ δὴ καὶ τῆς κατὰ τὴν ναῦν φορᾶς κοινῆς οὔσης πρὸς τὸν κυβερνήτην καὶ τὸν ἄνεμον, τὰ μὲν ἄλλα τοιαῦτά ἐστιν, ὡς ἄνευ αὐτῶν μὴ γίγνεσθαι τὴν κίνησιν, ὁ δὲ κυβερνήτης καὶ ὁ ἄνεμος τὴν κυριωτάτην αἰτίαν περιέχουσιν ἐν ἑαυτοῖς τῆς φορᾶς, οὕτως   15
ἄρα καὶ ἡ ψυχὴ αὐτή τε ὅλῳ χρῆται τῷ σώματι καὶ τὰ ἔργα μεταχειρίζεται, ὡς ὄργανον ἢ ὄχημα τὸ σῶμα περιέχουσα· ἔχει δὲ καὶ καθ᾽ αὑτὴν οἰκείας κινήσεις, ὅσαι τοῦ συνθέτου ζῴου ἀπολυόμεναι αὐταὶ καθ᾽ αὑτὰς ἀπόλυτοι τὰς κατ᾽ οὐσίαν ζωὰς τῆς ψυχῆς ἐνεργοῦσιν, οἷαι δή εἰσιν αἱ τῶν ἐνθουσιασμῶν καὶ τῶν ἀύλων νοήσεων καὶ   20
συλλήβδην ἐκείνων, καθ᾽ ἃς τοῖς θεοῖς συναπτόμεθα.

Οὐ μὴν ἔτι γε τούτοις συγχωροῦσιν οἱ σῶμα τὴν ψυχὴν ὑπολαμβάνοντες, οἷον οἱ Στωικοὶ καὶ ἄλλοι πλείονες· οὐδ᾽ ὅσοι συγκεκρᾶσθαι αὐτὴν εἰς τὴν γένεσιν οἴονται, ὥσπερ οἱ πλεῖστοι τῶν

372 φυσικῶν· οὐδὲ ὅσοι βλάστημα αὐτὴν ἀπὸ Ι τῶν σωμάτων ποιοῦσιν ἐν   25
ἁρμονίας εἴδει οὖσαν. Πάντες γὰρ οὗτοι σωματοειδεῖς τὰς κινήσεις αὐτῇ ἀποδιδόασιν.

370: 1 κατὰ τε FP: κατά γε (vel κατὰ) Meineke. δεὶ FP², δὴ P¹. **3** περί F, om. sed add. m. 1 mrg. P: παρὰ Heeren.
371: 7 ἡ FP: ἦν Usener; secl. Meineke. **8** τὰ add. Usener. **12** ὁρμημένα P. δὴ ἐν τῆς P. **16** αὐτῇ P. ὅλη F, ὅλη P: corr. Canter. **18** τὸ σύνθετον ζῷον FP: corr. Heeren. ἀπολλυόμεναι FP: ἀπολελυμέναι Meineke, ἀπολυόμεναι Heeren. **19** αὐταὶ καθ᾽ αὑτὰς ἀπόλυτοι Heeren, ἀπόλυτοι secl. Wachs. **22** ἔτι τε FP: corr. Meineke. **24** αὐτὴν P², αὐτὸν FP¹.
372: 26 πάντα FP: corr. Heeren.

Now, according to Plato, the acts accomplished are far from being identical with the congenital essence and life of the soul. For it is clear that he assigns the acts to the common living being, but since change, divisibility, corporeal dimensionality, and extension in time and space coincide with these acts, none of which is present in the incorporeal life taken by itself, it plainly follows that according to Plato none of the motions of the composite living being is proper to the soul itself. And so, just as life for him was double — the one separated from body and the other in common with it — so also some operations will be proper to the soul and others will be common also to what possesses it.[2] And of these, some arise first from the soul, some are aroused from the passions of the body, and some are stirred up from both equally. But all arise from the soul as their cause. And indeed just as, when the motion of a ship is caused jointly by the helmsman and the wind, other elements are necessary for motion to occur, but the helmsman and the wind encompass in themselves the primary cause of the motion, so also the soul itself makes use of the whole body and administers its acts, encompassing the body as an instrument or vehicle; but it possesses also movements proper to itself, and souls free in themselves that are separated from the composite living being produce the essential lives of the soul, e.g., those of divine possession, of immaterial intellection and, in a word, of those by which we are joined to the gods.

Certainly those who think that the soul is a body, as do the Stoics and a good many others, do not agree with these statements; nor do those who think that the soul is combined with the body for the purpose of generation, as most of the natural philosophers do; nor do those who make the soul some sort of attunement sprouting from bodies. For all these assign corporeal motions to the soul.

---

[2] I.e., to the body.

17 [Ἐν ταὐτῷ· περὶ τῶν ἔργων τῆς ψυχῆς.]

Πότερον οὖν πασῶν τῶν ψυχῶν τὰ αὐτὰ ἔργα ἀποτελεῖται, ἢ τὰ μὲν τῶν ὅλων τελεώτερα, τὰ δὲ τῶν ἄλλων ὡς ἕκασται διειλήχασι τὴν προσήκουσαν ἑαυταῖς τάξιν; Ὡς μὲν οἱ Στωικοὶ λέγουσιν, εἷς τέ ἐστιν ὁ λόγος καὶ ἡ αὐτὴ πάντως διανόησις καὶ τὰ κατορθώματα ἴσα καὶ αἱ 5
αὐταὶ ἀρεταὶ τῶν τε μεριστῶν καὶ τῶν ὅλων· καί που Πλωτῖνος καὶ Ἀμέλιος ἐπὶ ταύτης εἰσὶ τῆς δόξης (ἐνίοτε γὰρ <οὐχ> ὡς ἄλλην τὴν μεριστὴν ψυχὴν παρὰ τὴν ὅλην, μίαν δὲ αὐτὴν πρὸς ἐκείνην εἶναι ἀφορίζονται)· ὡς δ᾽ ἂν εἴποι Πορφύριος, πάντῃ κεχώρισται τὰ τῆς ὅλης ψυχῆς παρὰ τὴν μεριστὴν ἐνεργήματα. 10

18 Γένοιτο δὲ κἂν ἄλλη δόξα οὐκ ἀπόβλητος, ἡ κατὰ γένη καὶ εἴδη τῶν ψυχῶν ἄλλα μὲν τὰ τῶν ὅλων παντελῆ, ἄλλα δὲ τὰ τῶν θείων ψυχῶν ἄχραντα καὶ ἄυλα, ἕτερα δὲ τὰ τῶν δαιμονίων δραστήρια, τὰ δὲ τῶν ἡρωικῶν μεγάλα, τὰ δὲ τῶν ἐν τοῖς ζῴοις καὶ τοῖς ἀνθρώποις θνητοειδῆ καὶ τὰ ἄλλα ὡσαύτως ἔργα διαιρουμένη. Τούτων δὴ διωρισμένων καὶ 15
τὰ ἐχόμενα τούτων τὴν ὁμοίαν λήψεται διάκρισιν.

19 Οἱ μὲν γὰρ μίαν καὶ τὴν αὐτὴν πανταχοῦ ψυχὴν διατείνοντες ἤτοι γένει ἢ εἴδει, ὡς δοκεῖ Πλωτίνῳ, ἢ καὶ ἀριθμῷ, ὡς νεανιεύεται οὐκ ὀλιγάκις Ἀμέλιος, εἶναι αὐτὴν ἐροῦσιν ἅπερ ἐνεργεῖν. Οἱ δ᾽ ἀσφαλέστερον τούτων διαταττόμενοι καὶ προόδους πρώτας καὶ | 20
373 δευτέρας καὶ τρίτας οὐσιῶν τῆς ψυχῆς διισχυριζόμενοι προχωρεῖν εἰς τὸ πρόσω, οἵους ἄν τις θείη τοὺς καινῶς μὲν ἀπταίστως δὲ ἀντιλαμβανομένους τῶν λόγων, τὰ μὲν τῶν ὅλων ψυχῶν καὶ θείων καὶ ἀύλων ἐνεργήματα ἐροῦσιν οὗτοι πάντως δήπου καὶ εἰς οὐσίαν ἀποτελευτᾶν· τὰ δὲ τῶν μεριστῶν κρατουμένων ἐν ἑνὶ εἴδει καὶ 25
διαιρουμένων περὶ τοῖς σώμασιν οὐδαμῶς συγχωρήσουσιν εὐθὺς εἶναι ταῦθ᾽ ἅπερ ἐνεργοῦσι.

372: 1 Περὶ τῶν ἔργων τῆς ψυχῆς. Ἐν ταυτῷ Gaisford. 2 τὰ μὲν P², τὸ μὲν FP¹. 3 ἕκαστοι FP: corr. Heeren. 4 post μὲν add. οὖν Heeren. 6 τε om. P. που om. P. 7 οὐχ ante ὡς add. Usener. 8 μίαν] ἐνίοτε Canter mrg. 9 post ἀφορίζονται clausula in FP: interpunctionem corr. Meineke. 11 καὶ FP: κἂν Meineke. 15 ἄλλα FP: ἄλλων Usener. 18 γένη ἢ εἴδη F. ἢ καὶ F, καὶ καὶ P. 19 ἐνεργεῖ sugg. Heeren.
373: 22 ante τοὺς add. κατὰ Heeren. κενῶς F. 23 τῶν λόγων om. P. 25 καὶ ante κρατουμένων add. Heeren. 26 περὶ: ἐπὶ sugg. Wachs. 26/27 οὐδαμῶς . . . ἐνεργοῦσι om. P.

IV. *On the Acts of the Soul*

17. Do all souls perform the same acts, or are those of universal souls more perfect, while those of the other souls correspond to the appropriate rank of which each partake? As far as the Stoics are concerned, reason is one, intellection absolutely identical, right actions equal and the virtues the same in the case of both the individual and the universal souls; Plotinus and Amelius are presumably of this opinion also (for on occasion they define the individual soul as being no different from the universal, but as being one with it); but according to Porphyry, on the other hand, the activities of the universal soul are totally distinct from the individual soul.

18. Another view, however, might be proposed which should not be rejected, which divides souls according to genera and species, making a difference between the perfect acts of universal souls, the pure and immaterial activities of divine souls and, different from these, the efficacious activities of daemonic souls and the great-hearted activities of heroic souls, and the acts of a mortal nature proper to animals and men, and so on for the rest. When these things have been defined, the features that are dependent on them admit of the same sort of distinction.

19. Those who maintain that the soul is one and the same on every level either generically or specifically, as is the opinion of Plotinus, or even numerically, as Amelius often rashly maintains, will say that the soul itself is identical with its acts. Others, making a more prudent distinction and insisting that it is by a downward sequence of primary, secondary and tertiary processions that the different essences of souls continually proceed, such as one would expect of those who enter upon the discussion (of these matters) with arguments which are novel but unshakeable, will say that the operations of universal and divine and immaterial souls in all cases come to accomplishment in their essences also, but they will by no means agree that individual souls, confined as they are in one single form and divided out among bodies, are to be immediately identified with their acts.

20 Κατὰ δὴ τὴν αὐτὴν μέθοδον προῖτω καὶ ἡ συγγενὴς πρὸς ταύτην
διαίρεσις. Λέγω δὴ προσπεφυκέναι μὲν ταῖς δυνάμεσι τὰ ἔργα ἐκείνων
τῶν ψυχῶν τῶν αὐτοτελῶν καὶ μονοειδῶν καὶ χωριστῶν ἀπὸ τῆς ὕλης,
ὡς ἂν φαίη ἡ νεωστὶ παρευρεθεῖσα ἥδε αἵρεσις, ἐοικέναι δὲ ταῖς τῶν
καρπῶν ἀπογεννήσεσιν ἐπὶ τῶν ἀτελεστέρων καὶ περὶ γῆν   5
ἀπομεριζομένων. Ἐπὶ δὴ τούτοις δεῖ νοεῖν ὡς οἱ μὲν Στωικοὶ πάσας τῆς
ὁποιασοῦν ψυχῆς τὰς ἐνεργείας συμμιγνύουσιν τοῖς διοικουμένοις καὶ
ἀψύχοις, οἱ δ' ἀπὸ Πλάτωνος οὐ πάσας. Εἶναι μὲν γάρ τινας δυνάμεις
τῆς ψυχῆς αἳ τοῦ σώματος ὡς ὕλης ἐφάπτονται, ὡς τὴν αἰσθητικὴν καὶ
ὁρμητικήν, καθαρωτέρας δὲ τούτων τὰς μηδὲν σώματι προσχρωμένας,   10
ὡς τὴν νοεράν.
21 Τὰ μὲν οὖν τῶν σωματοειδῶν δυνάμεων ἔργα κατ' οὐσίαν μὲν
Πλάτων οὐ συνάπτει τοῖς σώμασιν, κατ' ἐπιστροφὴν δὲ κοινωνεῖν φησί,
τὰ δὲ τῶν χωριστῶν ἀπολύει πάντη τοῦ κατατείνεσθαι εἰς τὰ σώματα.
Ἤδη τοίνυν καὶ τὰ μὲν τῶν ὅλων καὶ θειοτέρων ἔργα ἄμικτα εἶναι διὰ   15
τὴν καθαρότητα αὐτῶν τῆς οὐσίας, τὰ δὲ τῶν ἐνύλων καὶ μεριστῶν
μηκέθ' ὡσαύτως εἶναι ἄχραντα· καὶ τὰ μὲν τῶν ἀνιουσῶν καὶ
ἀπολυομένων τῆς γενέσεως ἀφίεσθαι τὸ λοιπὸν τῶν σωμάτων, τὰ δὲ τῶν
374 κατιουσῶν συμπλέκεσθαι | αὐτοῖς πολυειδῶς καὶ συνυφαίνεσθαι. Καὶ
τὰ μὲν τῶν ἐποχουμένων τοῖς αὐτοειδέσι πνεύμασι καὶ δι' αὐτῶν   20
τιθεμένων εὐκόλως, ἅπερ ἂν ἔλωσιν, ἄνωθεν ἀπραγμόνως ἐκφαίνειν τὰ
σφῶν ἔργα· τὰ δὲ τοῖς στερεωτέροις σώμασιν ἐνσπειρό-μενα καὶ
κατεχόμενα ἐν αὐτοῖς ἀναπίμπλασθαι ἀμωσγέπως τῆς τούτων φύσεως.
Καὶ τὰ μὲν τῶν ὅλων ἐπιστρέφειν εἰς ἑαυτὰ τὰ διοικούμενα, τὰ δὲ τῶν
διῃρημένων αὐτὰ ἐπιστρέφεσθαι πρὸς ταῦτα ὧν ἐπιμελοῦνται.   25

373: 1 αὐτῶν F. 4 παρευρεθεῖσα P, πορευθεῖσα F. 9 αἳ FP², αἱ P¹. 10 καὶ προτέραν
μὲν τούτων P, καὶ πρότερον μὲν τούτων F: καθαρωτέρας δὲ τούτων Canter mrg. 15
κατὰ FP: καὶ τὰ Heeren.
374: 20 αὐτῶν FP] αὑτῶν Wachs. male. 21 ἕλωσιν FP: θέλωσιν Usener. 24
ἐπιστρέφει P. εἰς αὐτὰ P¹. 25 post ἐπιμελοῦνται clausula in F.

20. Let us proceed by the same method of enquiry to a distinction akin to that which has just been discussed. I say, then, that the acts are an outgrowth of the powers in the case of those souls which are complete in themselves, simple in nature and separate from matter, as this view which we have just unveiled would put it, and that in the case of the less perfect souls, which have an existence divided about the earth, their acts are similar to the putting forth of fruit by plants. In this connection, one should note that, while the Stoics conjoin all the actions of the soul, of whatever type it may be, to the inanimate parts governed by it, the followers of Plato do not so conjoin all. For there are on the one hand, they say, certain powers which are linked to the body as a material base, such as perception and appetition, but there are certain powers purer than these which do not employ the body at all, such as intellection.

21. As for the acts of the bodily powers of the soul, Plato does not link them to the body in their essence, but says that they communicate with it by 'conversion,' and he frees the acts of the separated powers completely from any tendency towards bodies. So then the acts of universal and more divine souls are unmixed because of the purity of their essence, but those of individual souls immersed in matter are not unsullied to the same extent; and the acts of souls which are ascending and being freed from generation divest themselves of bodies for the future, while those of souls which are descending are entwined and interwoven with them in sundry ways. And those souls which are mounted upon pneumatic bodies of a uniform nature and which by means of them arrange calmly whatever they choose, from the start express their acts without any difficulty; but those who are sown in more solid bodies and imprisoned in them, are suffused, in one way or another, by the nature of these. Furthermore, the universal souls direct towards themselves the things which they administer, whereas the particular souls are themselves directed towards the objects of their care.

48 TEXT

22 Κατ᾽ ἄλλην τοίνυν ἀρχὴν τῆς τῶν αὐτῶν διακρίσεως ἡ μὲν Περιπατητικὴ δόξα τοῦ ζῴου μόνως καὶ τοῦ συνθέτου τίθεται τὰ ἔργα τῆς ψυχῆς. [Πλάτων δὲ τῆς ψυχῆς αὐτὰ πρώτως προτάττει, εἶθ᾽ οὕτως εἰς τὸ κοινὸν δίδωσιν.] Πλάτων δὲ καὶ Πυθαγόρας ὑπερφυῆ τὴν οὐσίαν αὐτῆς καὶ γεννητικὴν τῆς φύσεως προτάττοντες πρεσβύτερα αὐτῇ καὶ   5
τιμιώτερα πρὸ τῆς φύσεως τὰ ἔργα διδόασιν· ἄρχεσθαί τε αὐτὴν οὐ ποιοῦσιν ἀπὸ τῆς φύσεως, αὐτὴν δὲ ἀφ᾽ αὑτῆς καὶ περὶ αὑτὴν ἐξηγεῖσθαι τῶν οἰκείων ἐνεργειῶν ὑπολαμβάνουσιν, ὅσα τέ ἐστιν ἐν αὐτῇ καλὰ καὶ σπουδαῖα κινήματα τῆς φύσεως ὑπερέχοντα καθ᾽ αὑτὰ ἐξαιροῦσιν.   10
23 Ἤδη τοίνυν καὶ ἐν αὐτοῖς τοῖς Πλατωνικοῖς πολλοὶ διαστάζουσιν, οἳ μὲν εἰς μίαν σύνταξιν καὶ μίαν ἰδέαν τὰ εἴδη καὶ τὰ μόρια τῆς ζωῆς καὶ τὰ ἐνεργήματα συνάγοντες, ὥσπερ Πλωτῖνός τε καὶ Πορφύριος· οἳ δὲ εἰς μάχην ταῦτα κατατείνοντες, ὥσπερ Νουμήνιος· οἳ δὲ ἐκ
375   μαχομένων αὐτὰ συναρ|μόζοντες, ὥσπερ οἳ περὶ Ἀττικὸν καὶ   15
Πλούταρχον. Καὶ οὗτοι μὲν προϋποκειμένων τῶν ἀτάκτων καὶ πλημμελῶν κινημάτων ἐπεισιέναι φασὶν ὕστερα τὰ κατακοσμοῦντα αὐτὰ καὶ διατάττοντα καὶ τὴν συμφωνίαν ἀπ᾽ ἀμφοτέρων οὕτως συνυφαίνουσι·
κατὰ μὲν Πλωτῖνον τῆς πρώτης ἑτερότητος, κατ᾽ Ἐμπεδοκλέα δὲ   20
τῆς [πρώτης] ἀπὸ τοῦ θεοῦ φυγῆς, καθ᾽ Ἡράκλειτον δὲ τῆς ἐν τῷ μεταβάλλεσθαι ἀναπαύλης, κατὰ δὲ τοὺς Γνωστικοὺς παρανοίας ἢ παρεκβάσεως, κατ᾽ Ἀλβῖνον δὲ τῆς τοῦ αὐτεξουσίου διημαρτημένης κρίσεως αἰτίας γιγνομένης τῶν καταγωγῶν ἐνεργημάτων· τῶν δ᾽ αὖ διισταμένων πρὸς τούτους καὶ ἀπὸ τῶν ἔξωθεν προσφυομένων   25
προστιθέντων ὁπωσοῦν τῇ ψυχῇ τὸ κακόν, ἀπὸ μὲν τῆς ὕλης Νουμηνίου καὶ Κρονίου πολλάκις, ἀπὸ δὲ τῶν σωμάτων αὐτῶν τούτων ἔστιν ὅτε καὶ Ἁρποκρατίωνος, ἀπὸ δὲ τῆς φύσεως καὶ τῆς ἀλόγου ζωῆς Πλωτίνου καὶ Πορφυρίου ὡς τὰ πολλά.

374: 2 περιπατητικὴ F, περιπατητικοὶ P: περιπατητικῶν vulg. **3** post ψυχῆς clausula in F et P. Additur in P lemma πλάτωνος. Πλάτων δὲ . . . δίδωσιν del. Usener. **4** δίδωσιν F, δίδωσι P: τίθησιν Heeren ex cod. Aug. Esc. post δίδωσιν clausula in F et P. Πλάτων (ante δὲ καὶ) susp. Canter. **7** ἑαυτὴν F. **10** ἐξαίρουσιν FP: ἐξαιροῦσιν Wachs. **11** διαστάζουσιν P¹, διστάζουσιν P²: διαστασιάζουσιν Wachs. **14** κατατείναντες Heeren.
375: 18 οὕτω P. **19** συνυφαίνουσι P, συμφαίνουσι F. **20** πρώτης secl. Wachs. **24** καταγωγῶν susp. Heeren. ἐνεργημάτων. τῶν δ᾽ αὖ FP: ἐνεργημάτων ἐνίων αὖ Wachs. sugg. **27** ἔστι δ᾽ ὅτε Usener. **28** ἀποκρατίωνος P. **29** post τὰ πολλά clausula in FP.

22. Taking the distinction between acts from another point of departure, the Peripatetic doctrine is that the acts of the soul concern only the living being and the composite. [Plato situates them primarily in the soul, but then assigns them thus to the composite.] But Plato and Pythagoras, placing its essence in the highest rank, as being supernatural and a generator of natural life, grant its acts to be superior to and more worthy of honor than Nature; further, they do not make the soul derive its origin from the realm of Nature; but hold that the soul, derived from itself and attached to itself, animates its own activities, and such motions within it as are beautiful and good, which surpass the realm of Nature, they place on a higher level by themselves.

23. There has been much controversy within the Platonic School itself, one group bringing together into one system and form the various types and parts of life and its activities, as for example Plotinus and Porphyry; another, exemplified by Numenius, setting them up in conflict with each other; and another again reconciling them from a postulated original strife, as for instance Atticus and Plutarch. These last maintain that there supervene on pre-existing disorderly and irregular motions other later ones which organize and arrange them, and from both of them they thus weave together a web of harmony.

The activities which induce the soul to descend are caused, according to Plotinus by the "primal otherness," according to Empedocles by "the flight from God" (Fr. 115 D-K.), according to Heraclitus by "the rest which consists in change" (Fr. 84a D-K.), according to the Gnostics by "derangement and deviation," according to Albinus by "the erring judgement of a free will." While of those who are at variance with these thinkers and who would attach evil to the soul in some way from elements which have accrued to it from outside, Numenius and Cronius in many places derive it from matter, Harpocration also, on occasion, from the very nature of bodies, while Plotinus and Porphyry most of the time derive it from Nature and the irrational life.

50 TEXT

24 Κατὰ δὲ Ἀριστοτέλην εἴδεσι ζωῆς καὶ ἄλλοις ὅροις ταῦτα χωρὶς ἀπὸ τῶν ἀνθρωπίνων διακέκριται. Κατὰ δ' αὖ τοὺς Στωικοὺς ἀτελέστερα ἀεὶ ἀπομερίζεται τὰ τοιαῦτα τῆς ζωῆς ἐνεργήματα καὶ ὅσῳ ἂν ᾖ προϊόντα προσωτέρω τῆς ἀλογίας, τοσῷδε μᾶλλον ἐπὶ τὸ ἀτελέστερον ἀποφέρεται τὰ καταδεέστερα τῶν πρεσβυτέρων. Ὡς δ' 5 ἐγώ τινων ἀκήκοα Πλατωνικῶν, οἷον Πορφυρίου καὶ ἄλλων πολλῶν, ἀφομοιοῦται ἀλλήλοις τὰ μὲν ἀνθρώπεια τοῖς θηρείοις, τὰ δὲ τῶν ζῴων τοῖς ἀνθρωπείοις, ἐφ' ὅσον πέφυκε τὰ διακεκριμένα καθ' ἑτέρας οὐσίας ὁμοιοῦσθαι πρὸς ἄλληλα. |

376 **25** [Ἐν ταὐτῷ· περὶ μέτρου ψυχῆς.] 10

Οἱ μὲν δὴ μίαν οὐσίαν τῆς ψυχῆς ἀριθμῷ τιθέμενοι, πληθύοντες δὲ αὐτήν, ὡς Ἀμέλιος οἴεται, σχέσεσι καὶ κατατάξεσιν, ἤ, ὡς οἱ Ὀρφικοὶ λέγουσιν, ἐπιπνοίαις ἀπὸ τῆς ὅλης, ἔπειτα ἀνασχόντες ἀπὸ τοῦ πλήθους τῆς ὅλης ἐπὶ τὴν μίαν ψυχὴν ἀποθεμένην τὰς σχέσεις καὶ τὰς εἰς ἕτερον κατατάξεις καὶ ἀναλύοντες ἀπὸ τῆς εἰς τὰ μεταλαβόντα 15 διαιρέσεως, ἀπολυομένης τῆς τῶν μετασχόντων ἀποδιαλήψεως, τηροῦσιν αὐτὴν ὅλην πανταχοῦ τὴν αὐτήν, μίαν οὐσίαν τε αὐτῇ διδόασι καθ' ἓν πεπερασμένην.

Οἱ δ' ἐν ἀπείροις κόσμοις, ὥσπερ δὴ οἱ περὶ Δημόκριτον καὶ Ἐπίκουρον νομίζουσιν, ἀπὸ τῶν ἀπείρων ἀτόμων κατὰ συντυχίαν 20 συνερχομένων <συνισταμένοις> συνίστασθαι ἀπὸ τῶν τοιῶνδε στοιχείων τὰς ψυχὰς ἡγούμενοι ἀπείρους αὐτὰς εἶναι ἑπομένως ταῖς οἰκείαις ὑποθέσεσιν ἀποφαίνονται. Καὶ οἱ μὲν ἐκ σπερμάτων αὐτὰς γεννῶντες ἑκάστου δυναμένου πολλὰ σπείρειν καὶ τοῦδε προϊόντος ἀεὶ καὶ οὐδαμῇ ἱσταμένου κατὰ τὴν γέννησιν καὶ ἐν τῷ γίγνεσθαι ἀεὶ τὸ 25 ἄπειρον ἀπολείπουσιν. Οἱ δὲ κατὰ μεταβολὴν ἐξ ἑνὸς ζῴου φθειρομένου πολλὰ ζῷα καὶ πολλὰς ζωὰς παράγοντες ἐν τῷ μεταβάλλειν συνεχῶς καὶ μηδέποτε ἐπιλείπειν τὴν ἐκ τῆς μεταβολῆς

375: 2 ἀπὸ: ἐπὶ Usener. post διακέκριται clausula in F. 4 τόσῳ δὲ P. 7 ἀνθρώπια FP. θηρίοις FP: corr. Meineke. 8 ἀνθρωπίοις FP.
376: 10 Περὶ μέτρων ψυχῆς. Ἐν ταὐτῷ Gaisford. μέτρα FP: μέτρου Canter, μέτρων Gaisford. 11 πληθύοντες FP: πληθύουσαν Wachs., πληθύνοντες Festugière. 12 ἤ add. Heeren. ὅσοι F¹, ὡς οἱ F²P. 13 ἀνασχέοντες P¹, ἀναχέοντες FP²: ἀναστοιχειοῦντες Lobeck, ἄγχοντες Usener, ἀναστέλλοντες vel ἀναστρέφοντες Wachs., ἀνασχόντες Festugière (dubitanter). 14 ἀποθεμένας FP: corr. Usener, ἀποθεμένης Lobeck. 15 ἤ (post κατατάξεις) FP: καὶ Canter. 16 ἀποδιαλήψεως FP: διαλήψεως Heeren. 17 οὐσίαν om. P. 21 post συνερχομένων lacunam statuit Wachs.; <συνισταμένοις> ex. gr. Festugière. 21/22 ἀπὸ τῶν τοιῶνδε στοιχείων del. Heeren. 22 αὐτὸς P. 25 γέννησιν FP: γένεσιν Heeren. 26 ἄπορον FP: corr. Canter mrg. 27 ante πολλὰ add. καὶ Heeren.

24. According to Aristotle, on the other hand, it is by forms of life and other characteristics that these activities are distinguished from human ones. According to the Stoics, again, such inferior activities of life are continually detaching themselves in the sense of becoming less perfect, and the further they advance in the progress towards unreason, the more the inferior are separated from the superior in the direction of imperfection. Finally as I have heard from certain Platonists, such as Porphyry, and many others, human activities show similarity to those of wild beasts, and those of animals to those of men, in so far as activities distinguished by being based on different essences are to be assimilated to one another.

V. *The Number of the Souls*

25. Some posit that the essence of the soul is numerically one but then multiply it (as Amelius thinks by its relations and assignments or as the Orphics say by breaths from the Whole Soul), then rise from the multiplicity of the whole to the one soul that has laid aside these relations and locations relative to others, and free it[3] from its division into the things that partake of it. These thinkers, inasmuch as they reject its subdivision into its participating parts, preserve it completely whole and the same, and grant to it a single essence that is given limitation through individuation.

Others think, as Democritus, Epicurus, and their followers do, that in infinite worlds <composed of> infinite atoms assembled according to chance, souls are composed of these same elements; these thinkers conclude, conformably with their own hypotheses, that souls are infinite. Those who derive souls from seeds, since each person can produce many seeds and this process continues forever without ceasing, bequeath an infinity of souls because of this production and ceaseless begetting. Others, through the process of change, produce many animals and many forms of life from one animal that has perished,

---

[3] I.e., the Whole Soul as single (= "the one soul that has laid aside these relations and locations relative to others"). There is no pronoun in the Greek text.

διαδεχομένην ἀειγενεσίαν ταύτῃ τὸ ἀπέραντον πλῆθος τῶν ψυχῶν
ἐπινοοῦσιν ἐν τῷ ἀεὶ πλεῖον γίγνεσθαι. Οἱ δὲ τῆς φύσεως τὴν ψυχὴν |

377 μὴ διακρίνοντες πάλιν δὴ καὶ οὗτοι κατὰ διαίρεσιν τὸ ἄπειρον τῶν
ψυχῶν γίγνεσθαι προσομολογοῦσιν, ἐπειδὴ καὶ ἕκαστον τῶν φυομένων
δένδρων μεριζόμενον ταὐτόν ἐστι τῷ ὅλῳ καὶ τῶν ἴσων αὐτῷ φαίνεται 5
γεννητικὸν εἶναι.

Οἱ δ᾽ ἀπὸ Πλάτωνος ἀγενήτους καὶ ἀφθάρτους αὐτὰς προστη-
σάμενοι ἑστάναι ἀεὶ κατὰ τὴν αὐτὴν συμμετρίαν ἀφορίζονται, οὔτε γὰρ
προστίθεσθαί τι αὐταῖς ἀπὸ τῆς γενέσεως οὔτε ἀφαιρεῖσθαι ἀπ᾽ αὐτῶν
μεθιστάμενον εἰς τὰ ἀπολλύμενα. Τοῦτο δὴ τὸ μέτρον οἱ μὲν περὶ 10
Πλωτῖνον εἰς τὸν τέλεον ἀριθμὸν ὡς οἰκεῖον προσβιβάζουσι.

[< Ἐν ταὐτῷ· περὶ διαφορᾶς καθόδου τῶν ψυχῶν.>]

26 Πλωτῖνος μὲν καὶ Πορφύριος καὶ Ἀμέλιος ἀπὸ τῆς ὑπὲρ τὸν
οὐρανὸν ψυχῆς καὶ πάσας ἐπίσης εἰσοικίζουσιν εἰς τὰ σώματα.

Πολὺ δὲ διαφερόντως ἔοικεν ὁ Τίμαιος τὴν πρώτην ὑπόστασιν τῶν 15
ψυχῶν ποιεῖν, τὸν δημιουργὸν διασπείροντα περὶ πάντα μὲν τὰ
κρείττονα γένη, καθ᾽ ὅλον δὲ τὸν οὐρανόν, εἰς ὅλα δὲ τὰ στοιχεῖα τοῦ
παντός. Ἔσται δὴ οὖν καὶ ἡ σπορὰ ἡ δημιουργικὴ τῶν ψυχῶν
διαιρουμένη περὶ τὰς θείας δημιουργίας καὶ ἡ πρώτη τῶν ψυχῶν
πρόοδος συνυφισταμένη, μεθ᾽ ἑαυτῆς ἔχουσα τὰ δεχόμενα τὰς ψυχάς· ἡ 20
μὲν ὅλη τὸν ὅλον κόσμον, αἱ δὲ τῶν ἐμφανῶν θεῶν τὰς κατ᾽ οὐρανὸν
σφαίρας, αἱ δὲ τῶν στοιχείων αὐτὰ τὰ στοιχεῖα μεθ᾽ ὧν καὶ ψυχαὶ
συνεκληρώθησαν καθ᾽ ἑκάστην τοιαύτην λῆξιν, ἀφ᾽ ὧν δὴ αἱ κάθοδοι
γίγνονται τῶν ψυχῶν ἄλλαι ἀπ᾽ ἄλλων διακληρώσεων, ὡς βούλεται
ἐνδείκνυσθαι σαφῶς ἡ τοῦ Τιμαίου διάταξις. | 25

376: 1 ταύτην P. ἀπέρατον P. **2** ἐν τῷ ἀεὶ πλεῖον γίγνεσθαι del. Heeren.
377: 5 δένδρου FP: corr. Heeren. τὸ ὅλῳ P. αὐτῷ FP: αὐτῷ Heeren. **6** post εἶναι
clausula in FP. **9** προτίθεσθαι F. **10** μεθιστάμενα F. **11** προβιβάζουσι FP: corr.
Canter int. **12** lemma om. FP: transposuit Wachs., ex 379.11. **15** διαφερόντος P. **17**
ὅλα δὲ FP: ὅλα τε Heeren. **19** περὶ τὰς FP: παρὰ τὰς Usener. **21** θεῶν om. P. **22** post
καὶ add. αἱ Heeren. **25** post διάταξις clausula in FP.

and, because change is continuous and the perpetual generation that arises from change never fails, they regard the number of souls as unlimited because more are always coming into existence. Still others do not distinguish the soul from the principle of growth but acknowledge in their turn that an infinite number of souls comes into being through division, since each cutting taken from a live tree is the same as the whole tree and seems able to produce another equal to it.

The followers of Plato, on the other hand, since they say that souls are ungenerated and indestructible, determine that the souls stand always in the same proportion; for nothing is either added to them from being born or removed from them in death. This proportion Plotinus and his followers liken to the Perfect Number, as being appropriate to it.

VI. *The Descent of Souls*

A. Various kinds of descent of souls

26. Plotinus, Porphyry, and Amelius assign equal status to all souls and bring them forth from the supracelestial soul to reside in bodies.

The depiction of the soul's first coming into existence seems very different in the *Timaeus*. The Demiurge sows them among all the superior classes, throughout all the heaven, and into all the elements of the universe. Thus, the demiurgic sowing of souls will be divided around the divine creations, and the first procession of souls will come into existence along with it and will comprise the receptacles for the souls. The Whole Soul will take up its abode in the whole universe, the souls of the visible gods in the heavenly spheres, and the souls of the elements in the elements themselves to which souls were also assigned in each such allotment. From these places occur the souls' descents, some from some allotments, others from others, as it is clearly the purpose of the account in the *Timaeus* to show.

378 Ἄλλη τοίνυν αἵρεσις τῶν Πλατωνικῶν οὐ κατὰ τοὺς δημιουργικοὺς
κλήρους, οὐδὲ κατὰ τὰς διαιρέσεις τῶν κρειττόνων γενῶν οἷον θεῶν,
ἀγγέλων, δαιμόνων, ἡρώων, οὐδὲ κατὰ τὰς νομὰς τοῦ παντὸς διακρίνει
τὰς ἀπὸ τῶν διαφερόντων τόπων καταβάσεις τῶν ψυχῶν· τιθεμένη δὲ
τὴν ψυχὴν ἀεὶ εἶναι ἐν σώματι, ὥσπερ ἡ Ἐρατοσθένους καὶ Πτολε- 5
μαίου τοῦ Πλατωνικοῦ καὶ ἄλλων, ἀπὸ σωμάτων αὐτὴν λεπτοτέρων εἰς
τὰ ὀστρεώδη πάλιν εἰσοικίζει σώματα· διατρίβειν μὲν γὰρ αὐτὴν εἰς
μοῖράν τινα τοῦ αἰσθητοῦ, καθήκειν γε μὴν εἰς τὸ στερεὸν σῶμα ἄλλοτε
ἀπ᾿ ἄλλων τοῦ παντὸς τόπων. Καὶ τούτους Ἡρακλείδην μὲν τὸν
Ποντικὸν ἀφορίζειν περὶ τὸν γαλαξίαν, ἄλλους δὲ καθ᾿ ὅλας τοῦ 10
οὐρανοῦ τὰς σφαίρας, ἀφ᾿ ὧν δὴ δεῦρο κατιέναι τὰς ψυχάς· τοὺς δὲ
περὶ σελήνην ἢ ἐν τῷ ὑπὸ σελήνην ἀέρι λέγειν αὐτὰς κατοικεῖν καὶ ἀπ᾿
αὐτῶν κάτω χωρεῖν εἰς τὴν περίγειον γένεσιν, τοὺς δὲ ἀπὸ σωμάτων
ἀεὶ στερεῶν πίπτειν εἰς ἕτερα σώματα διισχυρίζεσθαι. Ἀπὸ μὲν δὴ
τοσούτων καὶ οὕτω διαφερόντων μερῶν γίγνεσθαι διαφερούσας τὰς 15
τῇδε καθόδους, αὐτοὺς δὲ τοὺς τρόπους διίστασθαι πολυειδῶς.

27 Ἡράκλειτος μὲν γὰρ ἀμοιβὰς ἀναγκαίας τίθεται ἐκ τῶν ἐναντίων,
ὁδόν τε ἄνω καὶ κάτω διαπορεύεσθαι τὰς ψυχὰς ὑπείληφε καὶ τὸ μὲν
τοῖς αὐτοῖς ἐπιμένειν κάματον εἶναι, τὸ δὲ μεταβάλλειν φέρειν
ἀνάπαυσιν. Οἱ δὲ περὶ Ταῦρον Πλατωνικοὶ πέμπεσθαι τὰς ψυχὰς ὑπὸ 20
θεῶν εἰς γῆν λέγουσιν, οἳ μὲν ἑπομένως τῷ Τιμαίῳ παραδιδόντες ὅτι
379 εἰς τελείωσιν τοῦ παντός, ὥστε εἶναι καὶ ἐν τῷ κόσμῳ τοσαῦτα ζῷα,
ὅσα εἰσὶν ἐν τῷ νοητῷ. Οἳ δὲ εἰς θείας ζωῆς ἐπίδειξιν τὸ τέλος
ἀναφέροντες τῆς καθόδου. Ταύτην γὰρ εἶναι τὴν βούλησιν τῶν θεῶν,
θεοὺς ἐκφαίνεσθαι διὰ τῶν ψυχῶν· προέρχονται γὰρ εἰς τοὐμφανὲς οἱ 25
θεοὶ καὶ ἐπιδείκνυνται διὰ τῶν ψυχῶν καθαρᾶς καὶ ἀχράντου ζωῆς.

Κατ᾿ ἄλλην τοίνυν διαίρεσιν οἱ μὲν ἑκούσιοι τρόποι νοοῦνται τῆς
καθόδου ἢ ἑλομένης αὐτῆς τῆς ψυχῆς τὴν διοίκησιν τῶν περὶ γῆν, ἢ
πειθαρχούσης τοῖς κρείττοσιν, οἱ δὲ ἀκούσιοι βιαζομένης ἐπὶ τὸ
χεῖρον ἕλκεσθαι. 30

378: 1 πλωτινικῶν P. 2 γενῶν om. P. 4 τιθεμένην FP: corr. Heeren. 6 λεπτοδέρμων
Gaisford, λεπτομερῶν Meineke. 7/8 εἰς μοῖράν τινα sugg. Usener. 11 post τὰς
ψυχάς clausula in FP: interpunctionem corr. Canter. 18 ὁδόν᾿ P, ὁδόντες F: ὁδόν τε
Heeren. 19 ante τοῖς add. ἐν Heeren. 20 post ἀνάπαυσιν clausula in FP. πέμπουσι
FP: corr. Canter. 22 καὶ om. Heeren.
379: 22 ἐν τῷ <αἰσθητῷ> κόσμῳ Meineke. 23 post νοητῷ clausula in FP. εὐθείας FP:
θείας Lobeck. 25 διὰ τῶν ψυχῶν . . . ἐπιδείκνυνται (26) om. Heeren in errore. εἰς
ἐμφανὲς FP: εἰς τὸ ἐμφανὲς Meineke, εἰς τοὐμφανὲς Wachs.

Another set of Platonists does not make this distinction that the descents of souls occur from different places according to the allotments of the Demiurge, according to the divisions of the superior classes (as for example, gods, angels, daemons, and heroes), and according to the distributions in the universe. Rather they posit that the soul is always in a body (as Eratosthenes, Ptolemy the Platonist, and others do) and make it pass from subtler bodies into dense bodies. For, they assert, the soul spends time in some portion of the sensible world, and descends into solid body at different times from different places in the universe. These places from which the souls descend here Heraclides of Pontus locates around the Milky Way; others throughout all the heavenly spheres. Some say that souls dwell around the moon or in the air under the moon and that they descend from there into earthly creation, while others firmly maintain that they always fall from solid bodies into other [solid] bodies. The various descents into this realm take place from so many and such different places, and the manner [of these descents] also differs in many ways.

27. Heraclitus holds that changes necessarily occur from opposites and supposes that souls travel both the road up and the road down and that for them to remain in place is toil but to change is rest. Taurus and his followers say that the souls are sent to the earth by the gods. Some of them, consistently with the *Timaeus*, teach that this occurs for the completion of the universe so that there will be just as many living things in the cosmos as there are in the intelligible realm. Others attribute the goal of the descent to the demonstration of divine life. For this is the will of the gods: to show themselves as gods through the souls. For the gods come forth into the open and show themselves through the pure and immaculate lives of souls.

According to another principle of division, some kinds of descent are thought to be voluntary (when the soul itself either chooses to administer the terrestrial realm or obeys its superiors) and others involuntary (when the soul is forcibly dragged to an inferior existence).

[Ἐν ταὐτῷ.]

28 Οὐχ ἡ αὐτή ἐστι πασῶν τῶν ψυχῶν κοινωνία πρὸς τὰ σώματα, ἀλλ᾽ ἣ μὲν ὅλη, ὥσπερ καὶ Πλωτίνῳ δοκεῖ, προσιὸν ἑαυτῇ τὸ σῶμα ἔχει ἐν ἑαυτῇ, ἀλλ᾽ οὐκ αὐτὴ πρόσεισι τῷ σώματι, οὐδὲ περιέχεται ὑπ᾽ αὐτοῦ· αἳ δὲ μερισταὶ προσέρχονται τοῖς σώμασι καὶ τῶν σωμάτων γίγνονται 5 καὶ ἤδη κρατουμένων τῶν σωμάτων ὑπὸ τῆς τοῦ παντὸς φύσεως εἰσοικίζονται εἰς αὐτά. Καὶ αἳ μὲν τῶν θεῶν θεῖα σώματα, νοῦν μιμούμενα, ἐπιστρέφουσι πρὸς τὴν ἑαυτῶν νοερὰν οὐσίαν· αἳ δὲ τῶν ἄλλων θείων γενῶν, ὡς ἕκασται ἐτάχθησαν, οὕτω κατευθύνουσιν ἑαυτῶν τὰ ὀχήματα. Ἔτι γε μὴν αἱ καθαραὶ ψυχαὶ καὶ τέλειαι καθα- 10 ρῶς εἰσοικίζονται εἰς τὰ σώματα ἄνευ παθημάτων καὶ τῆς στερήσεως τοῦ νοεῖν· αἱ δ᾽ ἐναντίαι ἐναντίως.

380 Ἀττικῷ < δὲ> καὶ < ἄλλοις τισὶ> Πλατωνικοῖς | οὐ συνδοκεῖ, καθ᾽ ἕνα δὲ τρόπον συντεύξεως τὰς ὅλας ψυχὰς τοῖς σώμασι συνάγουσιν, ὡσαύτως ἀεὶ μὲν καὶ ἐπὶ πάσης ἐνσωματώσεως τῶν ψυχῶν 15 προϋποτιθέντες τὴν ἄλογον καὶ πλημμελῆ καὶ ἔνυλον ψυχήν, ἐν αὐτῇ δὲ κατακοσμουμένῃ τὴν κοινωνίαν τῆς λογικῆς ἐπεισάγοντες.

29 Οἶμαι τοίνυν καὶ τὰ τέλη διάφορα ὄντα καὶ τοὺς τρόπους τῆς καθόδου τῶν ψυχῶν ποιεῖν διαφέροντας. Ἡ μὲν γὰρ ἐπὶ σωτηρίᾳ καὶ καθάρσει καὶ τελειότητι τῶν τῇδε κατιοῦσα ἄχραντον ποιεῖται καὶ τὴν 20 κάθοδον· ἡ δὲ διὰ γυμνασίαν καὶ ἐπανόρθωσιν τῶν οἰκείων ἠθῶν ἐπιστρεφομένη περὶ τὰ σώματα οὐκ ἀπαθής ἐστι παντελῶς, οὐδὲ ἀφεῖται ἀπόλυτος καθ᾽ ἑαυτήν· ἡ δὲ ἐπὶ δίκῃ καὶ κρίσει δεῦρο κατερχομένη συρομένη πως ἔοικε καὶ συνελαυνομένη.

<Τινὲς δὲ τῶν νεωτέρων οὐχ οὕτως> διακρίνουσιν, οὐκ ἔχοντες 25 δὲ σκοπὸν τῆς διαφορότητος εἰς ταὐτὸ συγχέουσι τὰς ἐνσωματώσεις τῶν ὅλων, κακάς τε εἶναι πάσας διισχυρίζονται καὶ διαφερόντως οἱ περὶ Κρόνιόν τε καὶ Νουμήνιον καὶ Ἀρποκρατίωνα.

379: 1 ἐν ταὐτῷ· περὶ διαφορᾶς (διαφορὰς P) καθόδου τῶν ψυχῶν FP: ἐν ταὐτῷ add Wachs.; Περὶ διαφορᾶς καθόδου τῶν ψυχῶν. Ἐν ταὐτῷ Gaisford. 3 αὐτῇ P: αὐτῇ Heeren. ἔχειν FP: corr. Canter. ἐν ἑαυτῇ P, ἐν αὐτῇ F. 4 πρόεισι FP: corr. Canter. 10 σχήματα FP: corr. Canter mrg. γε om. P. 11 οἰκίζονται P. 13 ἢ πλατωνικοῖς FP: <δε> καὶ <ἄλλοις τισι> Πλατωνικοῖς Heeren, καὶ Πλατωνικοῖς Meineke.
380: 13/14 καθ᾽ ἓν δὲ πρῶτον FP: καθ᾽ ἕνα δὲ τρόπον Canter, Heeren. 17 post ἐπεισάγοντες clausula in FP. 21 διὰ γυμνασίαν F², δι᾽ ἀμνασίαν F¹P. τῆς οἰκείων P. 24 post συνελαυνομένη clausula in FP; in F versus dimidia pars vacua relicta. 25 τινὲς δὲ τῶν νεωτέρων οὐχ οὕτως add. Heeren.

B. The Soul's Encounter with the Body

1. *Are the Embodiments of All Souls the Same or Do They Differ According to Each Soul's Rank?*

28. The association of all souls with bodies is not the same. The Whole Soul, as Plotinus also believes, holds in itself the body that is appended to it, but it is not itself appended to this body or enveloped by it. Individual souls, on the other hand, attach themselves to bodies, fall under the control of bodies, and come to dwell in bodies that are already overcome by the nature of the Universe. The souls of gods adapt their bodies, which imitate intellect, to their own intellectual essence; the souls of the other divine classes direct their vehicles according to their allotment in the cosmos. Furthermore, pure and perfect souls come to dwell in bodies in a pure manner, without passions and without being deprived of intellection, but opposite souls in an opposite manner.

Atticus and <certain other> Platonists, however, do not agree with this view; they unite all souls with bodies by a single method of incorporation. Always in the same way in every embodiment of souls, they first posit an irrational, disorderly, enmattered soul and then introduce an association of the rational soul with this soul as it is being brought into order.

2. *Do Embodiments vary by the Purpose of the Descent, or is Every Embodiment an Evil?*

29. Furthermore, I actually think that the purposes for which souls descend are different and that they thereby also cause differences in the manner of the descent. For the soul that descends for the salvation, purification, and perfection of this realm is immaculate in its descent. The soul, on the other hand, that directs itself about bodies for the exercise and correction of its own character is not entirely free of passions and was not sent away free in itself. The soul that comes down here for punishment and judgment seems somehow to be dragged and forced.

<Certain more recent philosophers> — especially Cronius, Numenius, Harpocration and their school — do not make these distinctions, but, lacking a criterion of differentiation, they conflate the embodiments of all souls into one single kind and maintain that all embodiments are evil.

30 Δεῖ δέ που καὶ τοὺς βίους τῶν ψυχῶν κατανοεῖν πρὶν ἐλθεῖν εἰς σῶμα, ὡς ἄρα καὶ οὗτοι πολλὴν ἔχουσιν ἐν ἑαυτοῖς διάστασιν· ἀπὸ δὲ διαφόρων τρόπων ζωῆς διάφορον ποιοῦνται ἑαυτῶν καὶ τὴν πρώτην σύνοδον. Οἵ τε γὰρ νεοτελεῖς καὶ πολυθεάμονες τῶν ὄντων, οἵ τε συνοπαδοὶ καὶ συγγενεῖς τῶν θεῶν, οἵ τε παντελεῖς καὶ ὁλόκληρα τὰ 5 εἴδη τῆς ψυχῆς περιέχοντες, πάντες ἀπαθεῖς καὶ ἀκήρατοι ἐμφύονται πρώτως εἰς τὰ σώματα· οἱ δὲ ἀπὸ τῶν ἐπιθυμιῶν ἄδην ἀναπεπλησμένοι καὶ ἄλλων παθῶν μεστοὶ μετὰ παθῶν συνέρχονται πρώτως τοῖς σώμασι.
|

381   [Ἐν ταὐτῷ.]   10

31 Κατὰ δ᾽ Ἱπποκράτην, τὸν τῶν Ἀσκληπιαδῶν, ὅταν πλασθῇ τὸ σπέρμα (τότε γὰρ ἐπιτηδείως ἔχειν αὐτὸ μεταλαμβάνειν ζωῆς), κατὰ δὲ Πορφύριον ἐν τῇ πρώτῃ ἀπογεννήσει τοῦ τικτομένου πρώτως ἡ κατ᾽ ἐνέργειαν ζωοποιία καὶ παρουσία τῆς ψυχῆς φύεται. Γένοιτο δ᾽ ἂν καὶ ἄλλη τις δόξα οὐδέπω καὶ νῦν ῥηθεῖσα, ἡ λέγουσα πλείονας μὲν εἶναι 15 τὰς δυνάμεις καὶ τὰς οὐσίας τῆς ψυχῆς, κατὰ καιροὺς δὲ ἄλλοτε ἄλλως, ᾗπερ ἂν ἐπιτηδείως ἔχῃ τὸ γιγνόμενον σῶμα, τὰ μὲν πρῶτα τῆς φύσεως μεταλαμβάνειν, ἔπειτα τῆς αἰσθήσεως, εἶτα τῆς ὁρμητικῆς ζωῆς καὶ τότε δὴ τῆς λογικῆς ψυχῆς, ἐπὶ δὲ τῷ τέλει τῆς νοερᾶς. Τοσαῦτα καὶ ἡ κατὰ τοὺς χρόνους συμφυομένη κοινωνία τῶν ψυχῶν πρὸς τὰ σώματα 20 δέχεται δοξάσματα.

380: 4/5 οὔτε συνοπαδοὶ P. 6 περιέχον P, περιέχον (supra ν, τ sprscr. F): corr.
Canter. 7 ὑπὸ Meineke. 8 ἄλλως sugg. Meineke.
381 10 titulum in textu habet P, mrg F. 11 κατὰ μὲν Heeren. τὸ FP: τὸν Canter. 15
καὶ νῦν] εἰς τὰ νῦν Heeren. 16 ἄλλως FP: ἄλλους sugg. Meineke. 17 ᾗπερ ἂν FP:
ᾗπερ ἂν Canter, εἴπερ ἂν Heeren, εἰσκρίνεσθαι, ἂν Meineke. ἔχει P. 19 καὶ ἡ FP:
γὰρ ἡ Meineke, γὰρ καὶ ἡ Heeren.

3. *Embodiments Differ according to the Different Lives that Souls Led Before their Descent*

30. One must also consider the lives of souls before they entered into body, since these lives have great individual variation. From different manners of life souls experience a different first encounter with the body. For, those who are "newly-initiated," who have seen much of reality and are companions and kinsmen of the gods, and who are fully perfected and encompass the parts of their soul complete are all first implanted free of passions and pure into body. As to those, on the other hand, who are sated with desires and full of passions, it is with passions that they first encounter bodies.

C. When and How Embodiment Occurs

1. *When Does Life Begin?*

31 <. . .> According to Hippocrates the Asclepiad, life is actually created and the soul becomes present when the sperm is formed into an embryo (for it is then suitably disposed to share in life); while according to Porphyry it is as soon as the child is born. Some other opinion might arise, not expressed as yet, that there are very many powers and essential properties of the soul and that at critical moments, in different ways at different times, when the body that is coming into being is suited to do so, it partakes first of the vegetative life, then of sensation, then of the appetitive life, then of the rational soul, and lastly of the intellectual soul. These are the many opinions concerning the times at which the soul becomes associated in a natural union with the body.

32 Ἀλλὰ μὴν ἕν γε τῷ τόπῳ τῆς εἰσόδου τῶν ψυχῶν, καθ᾽ ὃν
ἐπιζητοῦμεν πῶς εἰσκρίνεται, μία μέν ἐστι τριπλῆ δόξα ἡ ἕλκουσα ἀπὸ
τῶν ἐκτὸς τὴν ψυχὴν ἐν τῇ καλουμένῃ συλλήψει ἢ διὰ προθυμίαν τοῦ
γεννῶντος διὰ τῆς ἀναπνοῆς, ἢ διὰ προθυμίαν τῆς ὑποδεχομένης μήτρας,
ὅταν αὕτη ἐπιτηδείως ἔχῃ πρὸς τὴν κράτησιν, ἢ διὰ συμπάθειαν ἀμφοῖν,   5
ὅταν κοινῇ συμπνέοντα ἀμφότερα ἑλκτικὴν ἔχῃ τὴν ἰδιότητα
συγκινουμένης καὶ τῆς φύσεως· ἢ δὲ κατ᾽ ἀνάγκην εἰσδύνειν ποιεῖ
<αὐ>τὴν αὐτοκίνητον εἰς τὸ ὀργανικὸν σῶμα ἤτοι ἀπὸ τοῦ παντός, ἢ τῆς
(382. 11) ὅλης ψυχῆς, ἢ τῆς δημιουργίας πάσης. | Οἱ δὲ καθαρώτεροι τῶν
Πλατωνικῶν, ὥσπερ δὴ οἱ περὶ Πλωτῖνον, ἄρχεσθαι μὲν τῆς κινήσεως   10
τὸ ὀργανικὸν σῶμά φασιν ἀπὸ τούτων τῶν μερῶν, δουλεῦον εἰς τὴν
γέννησιν ταῖς χρωμέναις αὐτῷ δυνάμεσιν, αὐτὰς δὲ τὰς δυνάμεις
ἀπολύτους εἶναι τῶν μεριστῶν σωμάτων διισχυρίζονται.
382   **33** Ἤδη τοίνυν καὶ ἡ χρῆσις τοῦ σώματος πολλῆς δεῖται διακρίσεως.
Οἳ μὲν γὰρ προσεοικέναι αὐτὴν λέγουσι νεὼς κυβερνήσει, ἧς καὶ   15
ἀπολύεσθαι χωρὶς δύναται ὁ κυβερνήτης· οἳ δὲ ὀχήματος ἐπιβάσει
κοινὴν πορείαν καὶ διακομιδὴν ἡνιοχούσῃ προσοικειοῦσιν αὐτήν· οἳ
δὲ ὡς μᾶλλον ἁρμόζουσαν συνεργείᾳ ἀπ᾽ ἀμφοτέρων ἰσομοιρούσῃ, ἢ
συννεύσει καὶ ῥοπῇ πρὸς τὸ σῶμα, < ἢ> ἐπικράτεια τοῦ σώματος
ἀποδιδόασιν αὐτῆς τὴν ὁμοιότητα· οἳ δὲ οὐδὲν τούτων συγχωροῦσιν, ὡς   20
δὲ μέρος τὴν ψυχήν φασιν εἶναι ἐν ὅλῳ τῷ ζῴῳ, οἳ δὲ ὡς τέχνην
ἐμπεφυκέναι τοῖς ὀργάνοις, ὥσπερ εἰ ἦν ἔμψυχος < ὁ> οἴαξ.

381: 1 τρόπῳ sugg. Heeren. 2 <καὶ> πῶς Meineke. 4 <τὴν> προθυμίαν sugg.
Heeren. 4 διὰ τῆς ἀναπνοῆς FP: διὰ τὴν ἀναπνοὴν Heeren; transposuit Usener post
συλλήψει (3). μήτρας FP: secl. Meineke, μητρὸς Heeren. 5 αὐτὴ FP: corr. Meineke.
κράτησιν F, κατάστασιν P: ἐγκράτησιν Heeren. 7 συγκρινομένης sugg. Heeren. 8
τὴν FP: <αὐ>τὴν (sc. τὴν ψυχὴν) Usener. αὐτοκίνητον <δύναμιν> sugg. Meineke. 9
post πάσης clausula in FP.
382: 9 οἱ δὲ καθαρώτεροι ... διισχυρίζονται, (13) hic habent FP: post οἴαξ
transposuit Wachs. 12 γένεσιν FP: corr. Meineke. 13 τὰς om. P.
382: 14 καὶ om. Heeren. 15 λέγουσιν ὡς FP: λέγουσι νεὼς Meineke. 16 ἀπόλλυσθαι
F, ἀπόλυσθαι P: ἀπολελύσθαι Usener, ἀπολύεσθαι Léveque. δύναται χωρὶς F. 17
προσοιχοῦσιν FP: corr. Canter. 18 ὡς μᾶλλον ἁρμόζουσαν post αὐτὴν (17) habent
FP: transposuit Wachs. 19 <ἢ> ante ἐπικρατείᾳ Festugière; ἐπικρατεῖ sugg. Usener.
20 οἳ δὲ οὐδὲν ... οἴαξ infra post διατρίβουσιν (p.621.6) habent FP: transposuit
Wachs. 22 <ὁ> add. Wachs. (coll. Plot. Enn. 4.3.21.13).

2. *How the Soul Enters the Body*

32. Now, on the topic of the entry of souls, we are investigating how the soul enters into the body. One opinion, that the soul is drawn in from those in the surrounding atmosphere during what is called "conception," has three variants: the soul is drawn in either because of the desire of the begetter through breathing in, or because of the desire of the womb that receives the sperm when the womb is suitably disposed to retain it, or because of the united desire of both[4] when, by jointly breathing together, they possess the property of drawing the soul in since the nature of the sperm has also been excited. Another theory makes the soul self-moving and has it enter into the organic body by necessity, either from the universe, or from the Whole Soul, or from the whole created realm. The purer of the Platonists, however, as for instance Plotinus and his school, say that the organic body, which for the purpose of generation submits itself to the powers that make use of it, makes a beginning of the motion arising from these quarters, but they confidently assert that the powers themselves are independent of the individual bodies.

3. *How the Soul Employs the Body*

33. Further, we must carefully distinguish also the ways that the soul may be said to use the body. For some compare this use to steering a ship, from which the pilot can be separated. Others associate it with mounting a chariot and directing a common course and journey. Others propose for it, as more fitting, a similarity to an equally-balanced cooperation of soul and body, or to a convergence and declension of the soul towards the body, <or> to a mastery of the body by the soul. Others, however, grant none of these, but say that the soul is like a part in the whole living entity; others still that it is like a skill implanted in instruments, as if a rudder were ensouled.

---

[4] I.e., both the male partner and the womb, presumably.

[< Ἐν ταὐτῷ.>]

34 Περὶ τῆς κοινωνίας τῆς πρὸς τοὺς θεοὺς τῶν ψυχῶν γέγονέ τις διαμφισβήτησις τῶν μὲν λεγόντων ἀδύνατον μίγνυσθαι θεοὺς ταῖς κατεχομέναις ψυχαῖς ἐν τῷ σώματι, τῶν δὲ διατεινομένων μίαν εἶναι κοινὴν πολιτείαν τῶν καθαρῶν ψυχῶν πρὸς τοὺς θεοὺς καὶ εἰ ὅτι 5 μάλιστα ἐν τοῖς σώμασι διατρίβουσιν· οἳ δὲ μόνοις δαίμοσιν ἢ καὶ ἥρωσιν ὑποτιθέασιν αὐτὰς εἰς κοινὴν συνουσίαν.

35 < Πολυειδῶς διαφέρονται οἱ βίοι αἱρετοὶ κατὰ τοὺς φιλοσόφους>,
383 ἄλλοι μὲν, οἱ βελτίονες, κρινόμενοι κατὰ | Πλάτωνα καθάρσει καὶ ἀναγωγῇ καὶ τελειώσει τῆς ψυχῆς· ἄλλοι δὲ, οἱ χείρονες, τοῖς 10 ἐναντίοις τούτων ἀντιδιαστελλόμενοι· κατὰ δὲ τοὺς Στωικοὺς τῇ κοινωνίᾳ καὶ τῷ καλῷ τῷ τῆς φύσεως ἐξηρτημένῳ· κατὰ δὲ τοὺς Περιπατητικοὺς τῇ κατὰ φύσιν τε συμμετρίᾳ καὶ τῇ ὑπὲρ τὴν ἀνθρωπίνην φύσιν νοερᾷ ζωῇ προτιμώμενοι· κατὰ δὲ Ἥριλλον ἐπιστήμῃ· κατὰ δὲ Ἀρίστωνα ἀδιαφορίᾳ· κατὰ δὲ Δημόκριτον 15 εὐσχημοσύνῃ· κατὰ δὲ τοὺς ἄλλους μέρει τινὶ τοῦ καλοῦ· ἢ τῇ ἀοχλησίᾳ καθ᾽ Ἱερώνυμον ἢ ἄλλοις τισὶ τρόποις διαγωγῆς τὸ αἱρετὸν ἔχοντες, ἀφ᾽ ὧν οἱ κατὰ μέρος φύονται βίοι ἄπειροι περὶ τὴν γένεσιν διαιρούμενοι· περὶ ὧν οὐδὲν δεῖ πολυπραγμονεῖν, ἀλλὰ εἰς τὸ ἄπειρον αὐτοὺς μεθιέντας χαίρειν ἐᾶν. 20

382: 1 titulum om. FP: add. Wachs. **6** post διατρίβουσιν clausula in P. **7** αὐτὴν FP: corr. Wachs. **8** lacunam statuit Meineke, Wachs.; <πολυειδῶς διαφέρονται οἱ βίοι> add. Festugière exempli gratia; πολυειδῶς ... φιλοσόφους addivimus.
383: 10 post τῆς ψυχῆς clausula in F. **11** post ἀντιδιαστελλόμενοι clausula in F. ἐναντίως FP: corr. Wachs. **12** post ἐξηρτημένῳ clausula in F. **14** ἀνθρωπίνη P. post προτιμώμενοι clausula in F. post ἐπιστήμη clausula in F. **15/16** post ἀδιαφορίᾳ clausula in F. **16** εὐθημοσύνη sugg. Meineke. post εὐσχημοσύνη clausula in F. **17** ἀνοχλησίᾳ P. **18** ἔχοντες susp. Wachs.

4. *Do Pure Souls Associate with the Gods?*

34. Concerning the association of souls with the gods, a dispute has arisen between those who say that it is impossible for souls enclosed in bodies to mingle with the gods and those who contend that there is a single common polity of pure souls with the gods, even if the pure souls spend a great deal of time in bodies. Others, on the other hand, postulate that these souls share a common association only with daemons or even with heroes.

VII. *Life and Death*

A. The Choice of a Way of Life

35. <The preferred modes of life vary in many ways.> According to Plato, the better are marked out by purification, elevation and perfection of the soul, while the worse are distinguished by the opposite of these. According to the Stoics, lives are deemed more valuable on the basis of the community of humanity and the good that is dependent on nature; according to the Peripatetics, on the basis of due proportion in accordance with nature and by an intellectual life superior to human nature; according to Herillus, on the basis of knowledge; according to Ariston, on the basis of (achieving) indifference; according to Democritus, on the basis of good configuration. According to others, lives are worthy of choice on the basis of some part of the good: they base their choice either on freedom from disturbance (as is the opinion of Hieronymus) or on other ways of leading a life, from which arise the infinite number of individual lives divided about the realm of becoming. We need not trouble ourselves about them, but should dismiss them from our thoughts since they regress into infinity.

Ἐν ταὐτῷ· περὶ θανάτου.

36 Ἐπειδὰν μετὰ τὸν τῇδε βίον ἡ τελευτὴ συμπίπτῃ, τί ποτε συμβαῖνόν
ἐστι; Πότερον ὥσπερ ἐν τῇ γενέσει προϋπῆρχεν ἢ συνυφίστατο ἢ
ὑστέρα πως ἐπεγίγνετο τοῖς σώμασιν ἡ ψυχὴ κατὰ τὰς διαφόρους
αἱρέσεις, οὕτω καὶ ἐν τῷ ἀποθνήσκειν προφθείρεται τοῦ σώματος ἢ   5
συναπόλλυται αὐτῷ ἢ καὶ διαμένει καθ᾽ ἑαυτὴν μετὰ τὴν ἐνθένδε
ἔξοδον; Τὸ μὲν οὖν πᾶν κεφάλαιον τοιοῦτον· μέρη δὲ αὐτοῦ καὶ ἡ
κατὰ τὰ εἴδη διαίρεσις δέχεται πολλὰς τοιαύτας ἀμφισβητήσεις· ἆρά γε
πνιγμῷ τῶν ἀρτηρίων ἀποκλειομένων τοῦ δέχεσθαι τὸ ἐκτὸς πνεῦμα, ἢ
ἐκλυομένου τοῦ τόνου καὶ παριεμένου, ἢ τοῦ θερμοῦ   10
ἐναποσβεννυμένου πως εἰς τὰ εἴσω τὰ ζῶντα πρότερον εἰσαῦθις
384 ἀποθνήσκει· Ἀλλ᾽ εἰ οὕτως γίγνεται ὁ θάνατος, | προαναιρεῖται ἢ
συναναιρεῖται ἡ ψυχὴ τῷ σώματι, καθάπερ Κουρνοῦτος οἴεται.

Εἰ δὲ ὡς δύναμις ὑποκειμένου, ὥσπερ δὴ ἁρμονία λύρας ἢ
τελειότης, προαφίσταται τοῦ σώματος ἐν τῷ ἀποθνήσκειν ἡ ψυχή,   15
προφθείρεται μὲν οὐδαμῶς (οὐδὲ γὰρ διὰ κινήσεως πρόεισιν εἰς τὸ μὴ
εἶναι), ἀλλ᾽ ἐξαίφνης εἰς τὸ μὴ εἶναι μεθίσταται ἀχρόνως καὶ ἄνευ
φθορᾶς, ὥσπερ δὴ καὶ ἔστιν ὅτε ἔστιν ἀθρόως οἷον ἀστραπῆς
ἐκλαμπούσης. Ἔσται δὴ οὖν τὸ μὲν ζῆν τῷ ζῴῳ ἀπὸ τοῦ ἔχειν τὸ τῆς
ζωῆς εἶδος· τὸ δὲ καλούμενον ἀποθνήσκειν ἀπὸ τοῦ μὴ παρεῖναι αὐτὸ   20
ἢ μὴ ἔχεσθαι· ἧς πολλοὶ Περιπατητικοὶ δόξης προεστήκασιν.

Εἰ δὲ παρέσπαρται μὲν καὶ ἔνεστιν ἡ ψυχὴ τῷ σώματι καθάπερ ἐν
ἀσκῷ πνεῦμα, περιεχομένη ἢ συμμιγνυμένη πρὸς αὐτὸ καὶ ἐγκινουμένη
ὥσπερ τὰ ἐν τῷ ἀέρι ξύσματα διὰ τῶν θυρίδων φαινόμενα, δῆλόν που
τοῦτο ὅτι ἔξεισιν μὲν ἀπὸ τοῦ σώματος, ἐν δὲ τῷ ἐκβαίνειν διαφορεῖται   25
καὶ διασκεδάννυται, ὥσπερ Δημόκριτος καὶ Ἐπίκουρος ἀποφαίνονται.

383: 1 Περὶ θανάτου· Ἐν ταὐτῷ. Gaisford; ἐν ταὐτῷ F mrg. habet. 4 τῷ σώματι F. 6
ἐνθέδε P. 9 ὑποκλειομένων P. 10 περιεμένου P. τοῦ θερμοῦ ἢ FP: corr. Meineke.
11 ante πως add. τοῦ δὲ ψυχροῦ ἐγγιγνομένου Meineke.
384: 13 συναιρεῖται P. 16 οὐδὲν Meineke. 17 ἀχρόνως FP: ἀχράντως Usener. 19
ἐλλαμπούσης FP: corr. Meineke. τὰ ζῷα FP, τῷ ζῴῳ sugg. Heeren. 22 προέσπαρται
P. 22/23 καθάπερ ἐν ἀσκῷ FP: καθαπερεὶ ἀσκῷ Meineke. 23 περιεχόμενον P.
συμπιγομένη P. 24 ξύσματα etiam P. 26 post ἀποφαίνονται clausula in F.

B. On Death

36. When the end comes after life here, what follows? Is the case like that of birth, where according to different philosophical opinions the soul either pre-exists bodies or comes into existence along with them, or in some way is born after them, so that also in death it either perishes before the body, or dies along with it, or survives by itself after its departure from the body? Such is the essence of the topic in its entirety. But its parts and its division into individual topics admit of many disputed questions, as follows.

Do creatures that were once alive die immediately by suffocation when the arteries are prevented from taking in air from outside, or when the vital tension slackens and weakens, or when the internal heat in the internal organs is somehow quenched? But if death comes about in this way, the soul is destroyed either previously to or simultaneously with the body, as Cornutus thinks.

If, on the other hand, the soul is like a potentiality inhering in an object — as for instance the harmony of a lyre — or like the perfection of an object, and departs from the body in death, it by no means is corrupted before the body (for it does not proceed to non-being through motion), but immediately changes to non-being without time elapsing or the soul being corrupted, just as, when it exists, it exists instantaneously, like lightning flashing. Life, then, will exist in the living thing because it possesses the form of life, but that which is called death will exist because life is not present to it or is not possessed by it. Many of the Peripatetics champion this opinion.

On the other hand, if the soul is diffused throughout and exists within the body like air in a wineskin, is surrounded by or mingled with the body, and is moved within it like motes in the air that are visible through windows, it is clear that it departs from the body and that in the very departure it is dispersed and scattered, just as Democritus and Epicurus say.

37 ... τοὺς δὲ περὶ Πλωτῖνον τῆς στάσεως προϊσταμένους ἐκείνης τῆς χωριζούσης αὐτὰς ἀπὸ τοῦ λόγου, ἢ καὶ ἀφιείσης εἰς τὴν γένεσιν, ἢ καὶ ἀφαιρούσης ἀπὸ τῆς διανοίας, ἀφ᾽ ἧς πάλιν διττῆς δόξης γίγνεται διάκρισις. Ἤτοι γὰρ λύεται ἑκάστη δύναμις ἄλογος εἰς τὴν ὅλην ζωὴν τοῦ παντὸς ἀφ᾽ ἧς ἀπεμερίσθη, ᾗ καὶ ὅτι μάλιστα μένει ἀμετάβλητος,   5
ὥσπερ ἡγεῖται Πορφύριος· ἢ καὶ χωρισθεῖσα ἀπὸ τῆς διανοίας ἡ ὅλη ἄλογος ζωὴ μένει καὶ αὐτὴ διασῳζομένη ἐν τῷ κόσμῳ, ὥσπερ οἱ παλαιότατοι τῶν ἱερέων ἀποφαίνονται. |

385 **38** Κατὰ ταὐτὰ δὴ οὖν καὶ περὶ τῶν μέσων οὐσιῶν ψυχῆς τε καὶ σώματος πολὺ διαφερόντως διατάττονται. Οἳ μὲν γὰρ εὐθὺς αὐτὴν τὴν   10
ψυχὴν αὐτῷ τῷ σώματι τῷ ὀργανικῷ συνοικίζουσιν, ὥσπερ οἱ πλεῖστοι τῶν Πλατωνικῶν· οἳ δὲ μεταξὺ τῆς τε ἀσωμάτου ψυχῆς καὶ τοῦ ἀγγειώδους αἰθέρια καὶ οὐράνια καὶ πνευματικὰ περιβλήματα περιαμπέχοντα τὴν νοερὰν ζωὴν <τίθενται> προβεβλῆσθαι μὲν αὐτῆς φρουρᾶς ἕνεκεν, ὑπηρετεῖν δὲ αὐτῇ καθάπερ ὀχήματα, συμμέτρως δ᾽ αὖ   15
καὶ πρὸς τὸ στερεὸν σῶμα συμβιβάζειν μέσοις τισὶ κοινοῖς συνδέσμοις αὐτὴν συνάπτοντα. |

Wachs-
muth I,
p.454.10ff.

[Ἰαμβλίχου ἐκ τοῦ περὶ ψυχῆς]
39 Πλωτῖνος δὲ καὶ οἱ πλεῖστοι τῶν Πλατωνικῶν ἀπόθεσιν τῶν παθῶν καὶ τῶν μορφωτικῶν διαγνώσεων, δόξης τε πάσης ὑπεροψίαν [τε] καὶ   20
τῶν ἐνύλων διανοήσεων ἀπόστασιν, πλήρωσίν τε ἀπὸ νοῦ καὶ τοῦ ὄντος, ἀφομοίωσίν τε τοῦ κατανοουμένου πρὸς τὸ κατανοοῦν τὴν τελεωτάτην κάθαρσιν ὑπολαμβάνουσιν. Ἔνιοι δὲ καὶ τούτων πολλάκις ἀποφαίνονται περὶ τὴν ἄλογον ψυχὴν καὶ τὸν δοξαστικὸν λόγον ἐμφύεσθαι τὴν κάθαρσιν· τὸν δὲ λόγον αὐτὸν τὸν οὐσιώδη καὶ τὸν νοῦν   25
τῆς ψυχῆς ἀεὶ ὑπερέχειν τοῦ κόσμου καὶ συνῆφθαι τοῖς νοητοῖς αὐτὸν καὶ οὐδέποτε δεῖσθαι τελειώσεως καὶ ἀπολύσεως τῶν περιττῶν.

384: 1 lacunam ante τοὺς sign. Heeren. **2** ἀμφιείσης P. ἀφαιρούσας F, ἀφερούσας P: corr. Canter. **5** ἢ καὶ FP: ᾗ καὶ Heeren, εἰ καὶ Meineke. ὅτι del. Heeren. **7** διασώζεται sugg. Heeren. post κόσμῳ clausula in FP.
385: 9 τὰ αὐτά FP. **10** αὐτὴν om. Heeren. **12/13** τοῦ ἀγγελιώδους P, τῆς ἀγγελιώδους (sc. ψυχῆς) F, Wachs.: ἀγγειώδους Ferguson (*Hermetica* IV, p.574). **13** fort. ante αἰθέρια intercidit <τίθενται> Wachs. fort. post περιβλήματα <ἅ> sugg. Wachs. **14** περιαμπέχοντα P¹. **15** post ἔνεκεν add. λέγουσιν Heeren.
454: 18 Lemma om. FP (P habet πλωτίνου καὶ ἑτέρων): add. Wachs., post Canterum. **20** τε ante καὶ secl. Wachs. **21** ἀπόστασιν sugg. Heeren. **23** post ὑπολαμβάνουσιν clausula in F. **25** ἐμφύεσθαι P, ἐφίεσθαι F: στρέφεσθαι sugg. Usener. **27** ἔδεσθαι F, ἔσεσθαι P: δεῖσθαι Heeren.

C. The Soul After Death

37. < . . .> Plotinus and his school, on the other hand, champion the opinion that separates the irrational faculties from the reasoning element, either releasing them into the realm of generation or separating them from the discursive reasoning. From this opinion arises a choice between two doctrines. Either each irrational faculty is freed into the whole life of the universe from which it was detached, where each remains as far as possible unchanged, as Porphyry thinks. Or the whole irrational life continues to exist, separated from the discursive reasoning and preserved in the cosmos, as the most ancient of the priests declare.

38. In the same way there are very different views concerning the substances intermediate between body and soul. For some join the soul itself immediately to the organic body, as do the majority of Platonists. Others <say> that between the incorporeal soul and the earthly <body> ethereal, heavenly, and pneumatic wrappings surrounding the intellectual life-principle are brought forth for its protection, serve it as vehicles, and also bring it together in due proportion with the solid body, joining it thereto by means of certain intermediate common bonds.

VIII. *Eschatology*

A. Judgment, Punishment, and Purification

What Purification Entails

39. < . . . > Plotinus, on the other hand, and most Platonists, consider the most perfect purification to be a divestment of the passions and of the knowledge that makes use of images, a disdain for all opinion, a disassociation from thought involved with matter, a being filled with Intellect and Being, and an assimilation of the thinking subject with the object of its thought. Some of them also often say that purification concerns the irrational soul and the opinionative part of the reason, but that the essential reason itself and the intellect of the soul are always superior to the cosmos, are joined to the intelligible realm, and are never in need of perfection or of release from superfluous elements.

40 Ἀλλὰ δὴ τὸ μετὰ τοῦτο διελώμεθα, ὑπὸ τίνων ἕκαστα τούτων ἐπιτελεῖται, τὸ τῆς κρίσεως λέγω, τὸ τῆς δίκης ἔργον, τὸ τῆς καθάρσεως. Ὡς μὲν δὴ οἱ πλεῖστοι Πυθαγόρειοι καὶ Πλατωνικοὶ λέγουσιν, ὑπ᾽ αὐτῶν τῶν μεριστῶν ψυχῶν· ὡς δὲ οἱ ἀκριβέστεροι ἐν αὐτοῖς, ὑπὸ τῶν καθολικωτέρων καὶ τελειοτέρων ψυχῶν καὶ τῆς μιᾶς 5
καὶ ὅλης ψυχῆς καὶ τῆς τάξεως τοῦ παντὸς καὶ τοῦ νοῦ τοῦ
455 βασιλεύοντος καὶ τῆς ὅλης διακοσμήσεως· | ὡς δ᾽ οἱ ἀρχαιότεροι διατείνονται, <ὑπὸ> τῶν ἐμφανῶν θεῶν, καὶ μάλιστα δὴ πάντων ἡλίου, τῶν τε δημιουργικῶν αἰτιῶν τῶν ἀφανῶν, τῶν τε κρειττόνων γενῶν πάντων, ἡρώων φημὶ καὶ δαιμόνων καὶ ἀγγέλων καὶ θεῶν, ἐξηγουμένων 10
αὐτῶν τῆς ὅλης συστάσεως.

41 Τί ποτε οὖν αὐτῶν ἐστι τὸ τέλος, οὗ ἕνεκα πρώτως [αὐτῶν]
ὑφεστήκασι; Κρίσεως μὲν ἄμικτος καθαρότης τῶν ἀγαθῶν, χωριστή τε
αὐτῶν τῶν καλῶν τελεότης, ἀφεστηκυῖα τὸ παράπαν ἀπὸ τῶν ἀτελῶν,
ὑπερβολή τε ἐξῃρημένη τῶν κρειττόνων αὐτὴ ἑαυτῇ, πρὸς ἣν οὐδὲν 15
δύναται συντάττεσθαι τῶν χειρόνων οὐδέποτε. Καὶ ταῦτα τοῖς
παλαιοτέροις ἀρέσκει τὰ κεφάλαια αὐτῆς, ἄλλοις δ᾽ ἂν ἴσως εὐταξία
καὶ διάστασις τοῦ χείρονος ἀπὸ τοῦ βελτίονος καὶ τὰ τοιαῦτα μᾶλλον
ἂν δόξειεν εἶναι κυριώτερα τῆς ὠφελείας αὐτῆς αἴτια.

42 Δίκης δ᾽ ἂν εἴη τὸ τέλεον ἐν τῷ τὰ βελτίονα τῶν χειρόνων 20
ἐπικρατεῖν καὶ ἐν τῷ τὸ κακὸν κολούειν καὶ ἀνατρέπειν καὶ ἀφανίζειν
τὸ παράπαν καὶ ἐν τῷ τὴν ἀνάλογον καὶ κατ᾽ ἀξίαν ἰσότητα τοῖς πᾶσιν
ἀπεργάζεσθαι. Πρὸς δὴ ταῦτα δοκοῦντα τοῖς πρεσβυτέροις οἱ μὲν τὴν
κατ᾽ ἀριθμὸν ἰσότητα ἢ πολλαπλασίωσιν, οἳ δὲ τὸ ἀντιπάσχειν τὰ αὐτὰ
ἅπερ οἱ δράσαντες προηδίκησαν, οἳ δὲ τὴν ἀπαλλαγὴν τῆς κακίας, οἳ δὲ 25
ἄλλο τι τοιοῦτον ὑποτίθενται ἀπ᾽ αὐτῆς τὸ λυσιτελοῦν, καὶ περὶ ταύτας
τὰς αἱρέσεις ἑλίσσονται οἱ πολλοὶ Πλατωνικοὶ καὶ Πυθαγόρειοι.

455: 8 ὑπὸ add. Heeren. 12 αὐτῶν secl. Wachs. 14 τῶν om. P. 15 αὐτὴ ἡ αὐτὴ FP: αὐτὴ ἑαυτῇ Heeren. 16 χειρόνων. οὐδέποτε FP: corr. Usener. post οὐδέποτε add. δὲ Heeren. κατὰ FP: Καὶ Usener. 20 δ᾽ ἂν F, κἂν P. δέον FP: τέλεον Usener. 21 καλὸν FP: corr. Canter mrg. κολούειν F, κωλύειν P. 22 ἀνὰ λόγον sugg. Wachs. 23 post ταῦτα add. τὰ Heeren. post πρεσβυτέροις clausula in F. οἶμαι P, ἶμαι F: οἱ μὲν Canter mrg. 27 post Πυθαγόρειοι clausula in FP.

The Agent of Judgment, Punishment and Purification

40. Let us then next determine what agency accomplishes each of these processes of judgment, punishment and purification. Most Pythagoreans and Platonists say that it is the individual souls themselves; the more precise among them say the more universal and perfect souls, the one Whole Soul, the arrangement of the universe, and the Intellect which rules over the whole universe. The more ancient authorities maintain that it is the visible gods (especially the Sun), the invisible demiurgic causes, and all the superior classes, by which I mean heroes, daemons, angels and gods, since they themselves preside over the whole system.

The End for which they exist

41. What then is their end, for the sake of which they primarily exist? The end of judgment is an unmixed purity of what is good, a separated perfection of what is beautiful that is completely removed from what is imperfect, and the transcendent superiority of what is superior itself by itself, with which nothing inferior can ever combine. These principal ends of judgment were pleasing to the ancients, but for others perhaps orderly arrangement, separation of the worse from the better, and such things would rather seem to be more important reasons for its usefulness.

42. The end of punishment would consist in the better prevailing over the worse, in the curbing, routing, and complete elimination of evil, and in the accomplishment of proportional and merited equality for all. In the face of this doctrine of the ancients, some suppose that the advantage deriving from punishment is arithmetic equality or multiplication, others suffering the same punishments that one inflicted when one was first acting unjustly, others deliverance from vice, and others something else of this sort. Many Platonists and Pythagoreans hover around opinions such as these.

43 Καὶ μὴν τῆς γε καθάρσεως ἀφαίρεσις τῶν ἀλλοτρίων, ἀπόδοσις τῆς
456 οἰκείας οὐσίας, τελειότης, ἀποπλήρωσις, αὐτάρκεια, ἄνοιδος ἐπὶ τὴν
γεννησαμένην αἰτίαν, συναφὴ πρὸς τὰ ὅλα τῶν μερῶν, δόσις ἀπὸ τῶν
ὅλων εἰς τὰ μεριστὰ δυνάμεως καὶ ζωῆς καὶ ἐνεργείας καὶ τὰ τοιαῦτα
νοείσθω ὡς πάντων χρησιμώτατα. Οἳ δὲ οὐ πείθονται τοῖς ἀρχαιοτέροις   5
ταῦτα προστησαμένοις αὐτῆς τὰ ὄντως συμφέροντα, λύσιν δὲ ἀπὸ
σώματος καὶ ἀπαλλαγὴν τῶν καταδέσμων καὶ φθορᾶς ἐλευθέρωσιν καὶ
γενέσεως ἄφεσιν καὶ τὰ τοιαῦτα σμικρὰ τέλη προΐστανται αὐτῆς, ὡς τὰ
προέχοντα τῶν ὅλων, ἐν οἷς εἰσιν οἱ πολλοὶ Πλατωνικοὶ καὶ
Πυθαγόρειοι, ἄλλοι κατ᾽ ἄλλας αἱρέσεις διεστηκότες.   10
44 Ἔτι δὲ τὰ πέρατα τῶν τριῶν τούτων διελώμεθα, μέχρι πόσου δή
τινος ἀποτελευτᾷ αὐτῶν ἕκαστον. Κρίνονται μὲν δὴ μέχρι τοῦδε αἱ
ψυχαί, μέχρις ὅσου συντάττονται εἰς τὴν γένεσιν καὶ τοῦ παντὸς οὐκ
ἀφίστανται καὶ συμμίγνυνταί πως πρὸς τὰ διαφέροντα· αἱ δὲ ἀφειμέναι
ἀπόλυτοι καὶ ἀμιγεῖς καὶ ἀδέσποτοι παντελῶς καὶ αὐταὶ ἑαυτῶν οὖσαι   15
καὶ πεπληρωμέναι τῶν θεῶν ὁμοῦ καὶ τῆς κρίσεως παντάπασιν
ἀπελύθησαν. Οὐ μὴν ἔτι γε τοῖς ἀρχαιοτέροις περὶ τοῦδε συμφωνοῦσιν
οἱ Πλατωνικοὶ καὶ Πυθαγόρειοι, πάσας δὲ αὐτὰς ὑπάγουσιν ὑπὸ τὴν
κρίσιν.
45 Ὡσαύτως δὴ οὖν καὶ περὶ τῆς δίκης οἱ μὲν παλαιότεροι τὰς   20
ἀχράντους ψυχὰς καὶ τὰς ὁμονοητικῶς συναφθείσας τοῖς θεοῖς
ἐντεῦθεν ἤδη τοῖς θεοῖς ἐντιθέασι καὶ ἐκβαινούσας τῶν σωμάτων ἄνευ
τῆς δίκης ἀνάγουσιν εἰς τοὺς θεούς· οἱ δὲ Πλατωνικοὶ πάσας μετὰ τὴν
δίκην εἰς τὴν οὐσίαν ἀπὸ τῆς γενέσεως ἀπολύουσι.
457 **46** Γένοιτο δ᾽ ἂν καὶ περὶ τῆς καθάρσεως ἡ | αὐτὴ ἀμφισβήτησις, <εἰ>   25
οἱ αὐτοὶ μὲν ἄνδρες καὶ ταύτης ὑπερέχειν φασὶ τὰς ψυχὰς ὅσαι θεοῖς
συνέπονται, οἱ δ᾽ ἄλλοι πάλιν οἳ μὲν περιόδους τῆς ψυχῆς περικοσμίους
καθάρσεως εἶναι διατάττονται, ὥσπερ τινὲς Πλατωνικοί, οἳ δὲ καὶ
τούτων αὐτὴν ὑπερέχουσαν προτάττουσιν, ὥσπερ δὴ λέγει Πλωτῖνος.

455: 2 ἀναπλήρωσις sugg. Heeren.
456: 6 ὄντα (α corr. in ως) P. **9** οἱ om. Heeren. **10** post διεστηκότες clausula in FP.
11 δὲ om. P. **12/13** μεχρὶ τοῦδε αἱ ψυχαί om. Heeren. **13** ὅσου FP: ὅσον vulg.,
Heeren. τὴν om. F. **14** ἀφέμεναι FP: corr. Usener. **15** ἀπόλυτοι secl. sugg. Wachs.
καὶ αὐταὶ FP: corr. Heeren. **16** τῶν θείων sugg. Meineke. **17** post ἀπελύθησαν
clausula in FP. **19** post κρίσιν clausula in FP. **20** δὴ οὖν καὶ] μὲν οὖν sugg. Heeren.
22 ἐντεῦθεν FP: αὐτόθεν sugg. Usener. **23** post τοὺς θεοὺς clausula in FP. **24** post
ἀπολύουσι clausula in F. καὶ om. Heeren.
457: 2 5 εἰ add. Usener. **26** post οἱ add. γὰρ Heeren. **27** συνέπονται FP:
συνάπτονται sugg. Canter.

43. Let us consider the following as the most useful of all the ends of purification: removal of foreign elements, restoration of one's own essence, perfection, fulfillment, self-sufficiency, ascent to the engendering cause, conjoining of parts to wholes, and the gift of power, life, and activity from wholes to individuals. Others, however, are not persuaded by the ancients when they emphasize the real benefits of purification, but they give prior place to deliverance from the body, release from bonds, freedom from decay, escape from generation, and such minor ends of purification, as though these were superior to the universal ones. Among these thinkers are many Platonists and Pythagoreans, although they differ among themselves about the specifics of the doctrine.

The Limits of Judgment, Punishment, and Purification

44. Let us next determine the limits of these three processes and to what extent each of them is carried out. Souls are judged to the extent that they are combined with generation, are not separated from the universe, and are commingled in some way with things different. But those souls that have been let go free, are unmixed, are entirely unmastered, are themselves of themselves, and are filled with the gods, are thereby also entirely freed from judgment. The Platonists and Pythagoreans, however, do not agree with the ancients on this matter, but subject all souls to judgment.

45. In the same way also concerning punishment the ancients place among the gods henceforth and immediately the immaculate souls that are united with the gods by sharing in their intellect. They say that these souls, when they depart from their bodies, ascend to the gods without punishment. The Platonists, on the other hand, release all souls from generation into their true being after punishment.

46. The same dispute would also arise concerning purification. For the same men say that souls that follow the gods are superior to it too, while the others say the opposite. Some of the latter, such as certain Platonists, declare that there are places of purification for the soul within the cosmos. Others, such as Plotinus, prefer that the soul be above these places.

[Ἐν ταὐτῷ.]

47 Περὶ τῆς ἐπικαρπίας τῶν ψυχῶν, ἣν κομίζονται εἰσαῦθις, ἐπειδὰν ἐξέλθωσι τοῦ σώματος < . . . > εἰς ἀγγέλους δὲ καὶ ἀγγελικὰς ψυχάς, τὸ ὅλον δὴ τοῦτο οἱ πρεσβύτεροι. Καὶ τηροῦσι μὲν αὐτὴν ἐπὶ τῆς οἰκείας τάξεως Πλούταρχος καὶ Πορφύριος καὶ οἱ παλαιότεροι· Πλωτῖνος δὲ 5
πάντων τούτων αὐτὴν ἀφίστησιν.

48 Οἱ δ᾽ ἀρχαιότεροι παραπλησίαν τοῖς θεοῖς κατὰ νοῦν διάθεσιν ἀγαθοειδῆ καὶ προστασίαν τῶν τῇδε αὐτῇ ἀπονέμουσι καλῶς, Πορφύριος δὲ καὶ τοῦτο ἀπ᾽ αὐτῆς ἀφαιρεῖ. Τῶν δὲ πρεσβυτέρων τινὲς ὑπερέχειν μὲν αὐτὴν λογισμοῦ φασι, τὰ δὲ ἔργα αὐτῆς οὕτω 10
διηκριβωμένα ἀφορίζονται, ὡς οὐκ ἂν ἐξεύροι τῶν λογισμῶν ὁ καθαρὸς καὶ τελειότατος . . . Πορφύριος δὲ αὐτὰς ἀφαιρεῖ παντάπασιν ἀπὸ τῆς ἀδεσπότου ζωῆς, ὡς οὔσας συμφυεῖς τῇ γενέσει καὶ πρὸς ἐπικουρίαν δοθείσας τοῖς συνθέτοις ζῴοις.

49 Ὁ δὲ παρὰ Πλάτωνι Τίμαιος ᾗπερ ἐσπάρησαν διαφερόντως ὑπὸ τοῦ 15
δημιουργοῦ, ἄλλαι μὲν εἰς ἥλιον, ἄλλαι δὲ εἰς γῆν, ταύτῃ καὶ τὴν

458 ἄνοδον αὐτὰς ἀνάγει, μὴ ὑπερβαίνουσαν | τὸν ὅρον τῆς οἰκίας ἑκάστην πρὸς τῆς δημιουργικῆς καταβολῆς.

50 Ἕνωσιν μὲν οὖν καὶ ταυτότητα ἀδιάκριτον τῆς ψυχῆς πρὸς τὰς ἑαυτῆς ἀρχὰς πρεσβεύειν φαίνεται Νουμήνιος, σύμφυσιν δὲ καθ᾽ 20
ἑτέραν οὐσίαν οἱ πρεσβύτεροι διασῴζουσι. Καὶ ἀναλύσει μὲν ἐκεῖνοι, συντάξει δὲ οὗτοι προσεικάζουσι· καὶ οἳ μὲν ἀδιορίστῳ συναφῇ, οἳ δὲ διωρισμένῃ χρῶνται. Οὐ μέντοι κρατεῖται ὁ διορισμὸς αὐτῶν ὑπὸ τοῦ κόσμου ἢ κατέχεται ὑπὸ τῆς φύσεως, ὥσπερ τινὲς τῶν Πλατωνικῶν ὑπειλήφασιν· ἀνεῖται δὲ πάντῃ ἀφ᾽ ὅλων, ὥσπερ ἐπὶ τῶν χωριστῶν 25
οὐσιῶν τουτὶ νοοῦμεν.

457: 1 περὶ τῆς . . . τοῦ σώματος tituli instar post ἐν ταὐτῷ ponunt FP. 2/3 εἰς αὖτις F. 3 locus mutilatus; lacunam post σώματος statuit Wachs., Festugière sugg.: <οἱ μὲν πρεσβύτεροι λέγουσι πορεύεσθαι αὐτὰς εἰς θεοὺς μὲν καὶ θείας ψυχάς,> εἰς ἀγγέλους δὲ καὶ ἀγγελικὰς ψυχάς. δὲ FP: τε Heeren, del. Meineke vel post ψυχὰς add. ἔλθωσι. εἰς ἀγγέλους FP: ἰσαγγέλους sugg. Usener. post ψυχάς lacunam statuit Wachs. 4 δὴ τοῦτο] διάδουσιν Heeren, Canter int. post οἱ πρεσβύτεροι lacunam statuit Meineke. 5 οἱ παλαιότεροι] οἱ Πλατωνικοί sugg. Heeren; sed melius ἄλλοι Πλατωνικοί Wachs. post παλαιότεροι clausula in FP. 6 ἀφίστασιν P¹. 8 post καλῶς clausula in FP. 9 τούτους FP: τοῦτο Heeren. 11 ἐξεύρῃ F. post τελειότατος lacunam statuit Festugière. 14 post ζῴοις clausula in FP. 15-458, 18 Festugière transposuit post 16. 15 ᾗ παρεσπάρησαν sugg. Usener. ἤπερ FP: corr. Canter. 1 7 ὑπερβαίνουσας sugg. Usener.
458: 17 οἰκίας FP: τῆς οἰκείας vulg., Heeren post ἑκάστην transp.; οἰκίας sugg. Festugière. ἕκαστον FP, ἑκάστην sugg. Heeren. 18 πρὸς τῆς FP: πρόσθεν sugg. Wachs., <τάξεως> ante πρὸς τῆς sugg. Heeren. post καταβολῆς clausula in FP. 19 (ἕ)νωσιν F, ἕνωσιν P², ἐνῶσι P¹. 2 0 σύμφησιν P. 2 2 προσεοίκασι FP: προσεικάζουσι Festugière. 22 συναφεῖ FP: corr. Heeren. 23 διαχωρισμένη F. αὐτῶν om P. κόσμου in ras. F. 24 πλατωνικῶν in ras. F. 25 ἀχωρίστων FP 26 post νοοῦμεν clausula in FP.

B. The Reward of Souls

47. Concerning the souls' reward, which they attain subsequently, when they depart from the body <. . .> to angels and angelic souls; this in general is the opinion of the ancients. Plutarch, Porphyry, and the ancients preserve it in its proper rank. Plotinus separates it from all of them.

48. The ancients rightly attribute to the soul a disposition, good in form, similar to that of the gods in intellect and a superintendence over things in this realm; Porphyry, however, removes from it this latter characteristic. Some of the ancients furthermore claim that it is superior to the reasoning element, and define its acts so precisely that not even the pure and most perfect reasoning element could attain them. < . . . > Porphyry removes them completely from the independent life, on the grounds that they belong naturally to generation and were given as an aid to composite living beings.

49. < . . . > Plato's Timaeus, however, elevates them in their ascent even as they were sown variously by the Demiurge, some into the Sun, others into the Earth, none overstepping the boundary of the abode established in the demiurgic sowing.

50. < . . . > Numenius seems to prefer a unity and undifferentiated sameness of the soul with its principles, whereas the ancients preserve a coalescence with a different substance. The former compare it to a dissolving, the latter to a co-arrangement. The former treat it as a union without individuation, the latter one with individuation. Their individuated existence is not, however, governed by the cosmos or controlled by nature, as some of the Platonists have supposed, but is completely released from the universe, as we conceive to be the case with separated substances.

51 Οἱ δὲ περὶ Πορφύριον ἄχρι τῶν ἀνθρωπίνων βίων . . . τὸ δ᾽ ἀπὸ τούτου ψυχῶν ἄλλο εἶδος τὸ ἀλόγιστον ὑποτίθενται. Ἔτι τοίνυν Πορφύριος μὲν ἀφομοιοῖ τὴν ψυχὴν τοῖς πᾶσι, μένουσαν καθ᾽ ἑαυτὴν ἥτις ἐστίν . . .

52 Κατὰ δὲ τοὺς Πλατωνικοὺς ἐπιμελοῦνται τῶν ἀψύχων.　　　5

53 Ἀπολυθεῖσαι δὲ τῆς γενέσεως κατὰ μὲν τοὺς παλαιοὺς συνδιοικοῦσι τοῖς θεοῖς τὰ ὅλα, κατὰ δὲ τοὺς Πλατωνικοὺς θεωροῦσιν αὐτῶν τὴν τάξιν· καὶ ἀγγέλοις ὡσαύτως κατ᾽ ἐκείνους μὲν συνδημιουργοῦσι τὰ ὅλα, κατὰ δὲ τούτους συμπεριπολοῦσιν.

Wachs-
muth II,
p. 6.9ff.

[Ἰαμβλίχου ἐκ τοῦ Περὶ ψυχῆς.]　　　10

6.10 **54** Πόσῳ δὴ οὖν βέλτιον Ἡράκλειτος παίδων ἀθύρματα νενόμικεν εἶναι τὰ ἀνθρώπινα δοξάσματα.

Wachs-
muth II,
p.207.15ff.

[Ἰαμβλίχου ἐκ τοῦ Περὶ ψυχῆς.]

55 Ἡ γὰρ συνακολουθοῦσα παντὶ τῷ βουλήματι τοῦ διδάσκοντος τῶν μανθανόντων, αὕτη πασῶν ἐστι μουσικωτάτη τε καὶ ἀρίστη ἀκρόασις.　　　15

458: 1 post βίων lacunam statuit Heeren; suppl. Festugière ex. gr. <τὴν ἀθανασίαν διατείνεσθαι λέγουσι>. **3** μενούσης F. αὐτὴν F. **4** post ἐστίν lacunam statuit Festugière; suppl. ex gr. <οὐ μὴν τῶν τῇδε ἀξιοῖ τὰς ψυχὰς προΐστάναι>. **5** ἐπιμελοῦνται <καὶ> sugg. Wachs. **7** θεωροῦσιν FP: τηροῦσιν Heeren.
6: 10 lemma mrg P, in textu habent FL, sed in L solum ὁ ἀμβλίων (ὁ rubr.) ἐκ τοῦ Wachs. Cum P, ἐκ τῶν F. **11** νενόμικεν FPL, ἐνόμισεν vulgo. **12** δοξάσαντα L.
207: 15 αὕτη corr. Meineke pro αὐτὴ; καὶ ἡδίστη Meineke.

51. < . . . > Porphyry and his school, as far as human lives; and they posit another class of souls after this, the irrational. Further, Porphyry assimilates the soul to the universe, although it remains what it is in itself.

52. < . . . > According to the Platonists, they care for inanimate things.

53. After the souls have been freed from generation, according to the ancients they administer the universe together with the gods, while according to the Platonists they contemplate the gods' order. According to the former, in the same way they help the angels with the creation of the universe, while according to the latter they accompany them.

Fragmenta Incertae Sedis

54. How much better Heraclitus, who considered human opinions to be the playthings of children.

55. For a student's manner of listening is most cultured and best of all, when it adapts itself to every intention of the teacher.

COMMENTARY TO IAMBLICHUS' *DE ANIMA*

1

'Αριστοτέλης μὲν οὖν . . . This is a reasonably accurate summary of Aristotle's survey of previous opinions on the nature of the soul in *De Anima* 1.2. Aristotle begins (403b25ff.) by stating that "there are two (characteristics) in respect of which that which is ensouled is considered to differ from that which is soulless: movement (κίνησις) and the capacity for sensation (τῷ αἰσθάνεσθαι)." By 'movement', as he makes clear directly, he means both the capacity for self-movement, and the ability to move other things. Iamblichus' substitution of 'knowledge' (γνῶσις) for sensation, or sense-perception, is partially, at least, justified by 404b28, where Aristotle resumes his initial definition by saying, "Since, then, the soul appears to contain an element which produces movement and one which produces knowledge (γνωριστικόν) . . . ", and his repeated use of γιγνώσκειν thereafter (e.g. 405a18, a24, b13). "Subtlety of essence" (λεπτότης) and incorporeality are introduced at 405a6ff., where the Atomists and then Diogenes of Apollonia (405a21ff.) are asserted to postulate that soul is fire or air respectively because that element is "composed of the finest particles and most incorporeal of the elements" (λεπτομερέστατόν τε καὶ μάλιστα τῶν στοιχείων ἀσώματον). And in the summing-up, at 405b11-12, Aristotle declares that "all (thinkers), then, distinguish the soul by more or less these three (character-istics), movement, sensation, and incorporeality." He does not, however, employ the phrase ἀσώματος ὑπόστασις.[1]

The phrase "discovering a limit for the boundless" (πέρας τῶν ἀπείρων ἀνευρών) is a nice rhetorical flourish, possibly, in view of his immediately following remarks, not devoid of irony.

'Εγὼ δὲ ὁρῶ . . . Iamblichus begins his critique by condemning the vagueness and ambiguity of Aristotle's terminology, though with little justification. Aristotle is, of course, perfectly well aware of the different types of *kinêsis;* indeed, he could claim to have been the first

---

[1] This phrase first appears in Origen, *Comm. In Joh.* 1.5. It is in Proclus, *PT* 1, p. 57.15 S-W; *In Tim.* 1.33.20; *In Parm.* 1049.20; *In Eucl.* 49.10. See Simplicius *In Phys.* 620.3.

to distinguish them (e.g. *Phys.* 3.1, 201a8ff., *Met.* 11.9, 1065b14ff.). In the present context, however, he could argue, he did not have to distinguish them, since the definition comprises all kinds of *kinêsis* equally. Iamblichus' distinction between motions κατὰ μεταβολήν and motions κατὰ ζωήν corresponds more or less to that of Aristotle between motion in the category of substance (that is, coming to be and passing away) and motions in the other categories (such as local movement and alteration), and Aristotle would say that earlier thinkers (about whom he is talking), in claiming soul to be the source of motion, made no distinction between types of motion.

As for Iamblichus' further distinctions, that between types of cognition that are 'figurative' (μορφωτικαί) and those which do not involve figure, is presumably a distinction between cognition which involves *phantasia* and that which transcends it, and we have ventured to translate it on that assumption.[2] But as we know, Aristotle declares (*DA* 3. 7, 431a16-17; cf. 431b2) that οὐδέποτε νοεῖ ἄνευ φαντάσματος ἡ ψυχή, "the soul never intelligizes without an image," so that he would dispute the basis of Iamblichus' distinction; but even if he conceded its validity, he would dispute its relevance, since the thinkers he is surveying did not even distinguish clearly between sense-perception and thought, never mind representational and non-representational thought.

The objection, on the other hand, to the use of *asômatos* to designate both particularly fine material substances such as fire or air and what is incorporeal in the strict sense is a good one, inasmuch as it draws attention to an ambiguity that seems to continue in Greek philosophical discourse long after Aristotle.[3] Aristotle does indeed, as noted above, explain Democritus' choice of fire as the substance of the soul by saying καὶ γὰρ τοῦτο λεπτομερέστατόν τε καὶ μάλιστα τῶν στοιχείων ἀσώματον, but all he means by that, after all, is "least corporeal," so that once again Iamblichus is being excessively pedantic.

---

[2] We do not find the adjective μορφωτικός used otherwise in this sense (more or less as a synonym for φανταστικός) before Proclus. He, however, uses it fairly frequently, e.g. *In Remp.* 1. 74, 27; 111, 22; 121, 2-3 (τὸν δὲ νοῦν ἄληπτον εἶναι ταῖς φανταστικαῖς ἡμῶν καὶ μορφωτικαῖς κινήσεσιν); 235, 18-19 (καὶ ἡ μὲν φαντασία νόησις οὖσα μορφωτικὴ . . .). It is probably an Iamblichean term. See further, section 39, below.

[3] In particular in certain Stoic circles, at least (if we may bring Philo of Alexandria into evidence on this point), the heavenly fire, or *pyr technikon*, could be described as *asômaton* by comparison with the sublunary elements. See Dillon (1998).

However, it is not really Iamblichus' purpose here to give a fair exegesis of Aristotle. He is merely using him as a launching-pad for his own exposition. It is hardly to be expected, after all, that Aristotle, writing about his own predecessors in the last quarter of the fourth century BCE, should be able to provide a totally adequate conceptual overview of the range of opinions on the soul that had emerged during the following five centuries or so. Nevertheless, he constitutes a useful starting point.

πολὺ δὲ καὶ τὸ ἀτελὲς αὐτῶν καὶ ἐνδεὲς· This is reminiscent of a certain line of criticism of Aristotle's *Categories,* raised by Stoic critics such as Athenodorus and Cornutus, which is reflected in Simplicius' *Commentary* (18, 26ff. Kalbfleisch), and which would be well known to Iamblichus. The complaint was that Aristotle's enumeration of categories was incomplete because it did not take in certain classes of word.

2

Τινὲς εἰς τὰς τῶν τεσσάρων στοιχείων . . . Like Aristotle (403b31ff.), Iamblichus begins his critique of previous opinions with the Atomists, Leucippus and Democritus (mentioned by Aristotle, but not by Iamblichus). Iamblichus also omits the fact, specified by Aristotle, that spherical atoms form fire as well as soul, but that is not essential to his purpose.

The phrase "completely filled with pure primal essence" is peculiar, as being quite unsuited to anything the Atomists themselves might have approved of.

3

Ὡς δὲ τῶν Ἀριστοτελικῶν τινες . . . We have here a statement of Aristotelian doctrine couched in interesting terms, which may reflect the formulations of later Peripatetics, from Strato of Lampsacus onwards. We seem to have, in all, three formulations of the doctrine, and fourthly a suggested further interpretation, itself subdivided into two alternative forms.

(1) εἶδος τὸ περὶ τοῖς σώμασιν seems to be an interpretation of Aristotle's formulation of his doctrine in *De An.* 2.1, 412a19, οὐσία ὡς

εἶδος σώματος φυσικοῦ δυνάμει ζωὴν ἔχοντος. The phrase περὶ τοῖς σώμασιν seems somewhat vaguer than ἐν τοῖς σώμασι or indeed σώματος but it is not quite clear what the distinction could be.

(2) ποιότης ἁπλῆ ἀσώματος. This, and the next formulation, may in fact be simply interpretations of the first one. Alexander of Aphrodisias uses the phrase ποιότης ἀσώματος of the soul (*De An.* 115.5).

(3) In this case, the third formulation is just a further specification of the second, reflecting the next sentence in the *De Anima:* ἡ δὲ οὐσία ἐντελέχεια, which takes in the concepts οὐσιώδης and τελεία. An "essential" quality, as specified in the above-mentioned chapter of the *Metaphysics* 4.14 (1020a33ff.), is one which goes to make up the essence of a thing, as opposed to an accidental feature of the thing in question.

(4) However, soul, if it is a quality, is plainly not just an *essential* quality, but might be seen as the sum-total of all qualities — this being what it is to be an entelechy. It is interesting that Iamblichus presents this, not as an explicit doctrine of any Peripatetics, but as a doctrine which one might reasonably deduce from their utterances, and with a formulation of the same type as he habitually employs to express his own opinion. The further distinction that he makes within this formulation refers to the distinction, made widely in Neoplatonic circles, between a supervenient characteristic of a thing (also termed ὑστερογενής, 'later-born'), which would have no substantial existence, and a pre-existent *logos,* such as would be a possible Platonist definition of the embodied soul (this latter, however, is an unlikely candidate for a Peripatetic definition). Festugière (179 note 2) dismisses the possibility that this is a personal view of Iamblichus because it is not consistent with Iamblichus' own doctrine of the soul. All that is necessary, however, is that Iamblichus should be concerned to present the Aristotelian doctrine in its most acceptable form. And this he would do here, if the stress be laid on προυπάρχον.

4

Μετὰ δὴ ταῦτα . . . We now move a little higher up the scale of dignity, to those who declare the soul to be a mathematical entity of some sort. That these include a number of respected Platonists, such as the Old Academics Speusippus and Xenocrates, and the Middle

Platonist Severus, as well as the Pythagoreans Hippasus and Moderatus, should imply that such a doctrine embraces at least an aspect of the truth. Certainly being expressed in geometrical or mathematical terms does not exclude the possibility that the soul's essence is immaterial. Nevertheless, these thinkers are not particularly commended for their views, and we "ascend" from them in section 6 to the doctrine that the soul is an incorporeal essence.

διευκρινημένως is a very rare adverb, so its appearance in Simpl. *In Cat.* 301.20, in a possibly Iamblichean context, may be significant. Otherwise it occurs only in Vettius Valens *Anth.* p. 309.12.

῎Εστι δὴ γένος ἕν . . . Platonist discussions of the composition of the soul will generally have taken place in the context of the exegesis of *Timaeus* 35A, and the identifying of "the substance which is indivisible and remains always the same" and "that which comes to be divisible about bodies." Iamblichus chooses to start with Severus, since he seems to be the most overtly geometrical theorist (though in fact it would be historically correct to present him as developing the doctrines of such Old Academicians as Speusippus and Xenocrates). He is stated to postulate the elements of the soul as being "figure" (σχῆμα), as the limit of extension (διάστασις), and extension itself. It is possible, however, that we have here either a textual error (σχῆμα for, say, στιγμή) or a mistake on Iamblichus' part. The geometrical "limit" of extension, after all, is not "shape," but the *point*. In Proclus' *Timaeus Commentary* (2.153, 21ff. Diehl) the doctrine of Severus is given as being that it is made up of *point* (σημεῖον) and extension. Possibly Severus may have used the term σχῆμα in the sense of the unitary principle of geometrical reality, and Proclus is interpreting this as a reference to the point. At any rate, this doctrine of the soul as the product of the two basic principles of the geometrical level of reality sounds very like a development of what should have been the doctrine of Speusippus (see below), though that is presented by Iamblichus in somewhat different terms.

We turn next to the definition of Speusippus (Fr. 54 Tarán), "the form of the omni-dimensionally extended." This definition is also given by Iamblichus in *DCMS* 9, though without attribution to Speusippus. Tarán, in his commentary (365ff.), seeks to impugn the accuracy of this report by arguing that it is in conflict with the testimony of Aristotle (*Met.* 1028b15-27 = Fr. 29 Tarán) to the effect that Speusippus ranked the soul, as a separate *ousia,* below numbers and magnitudes (*megethê*), but Tarán approaches the evidence of Aristotle far too literally. Aristotle is above all concerned to emphasize what he regards as the absurdity of Speusippus' view of the world, and is not interested in a sympathetic interpretation of subtleties of doctrine. Certainly, for Speusippus, the soul appears at a lower level than numbers and geometrical magnitudes, but that does not mean to say that it is not in some sense a mathematical or geometrical entity. What it adds, no doubt, is motion, or motivity — very like Xenocrates' conception of soul as a "self-moving number." Every level of being in Speusippus' universe appropriates the characteristics of its prior level, and adds something, and what it is proper for soul to add is motion and, no doubt, cognition, which would be in accord with Plato's account of the nature of soul in the *Timaeus,* which both Speusippus and Xenocrates are interpreting. If Aristotle is tendentious, then, Iamblichus is over-simplifying, in presenting Speusippus' definition as purely mathematical. There will have been a good deal more to it than this one-line definition can convey.

ἐν αἰτίᾳ δὲ . . . This is a characteristic way for Iamblichus to present his own views (cf. section 7, 365.26 - 366.11.; section 13, 370.1-13; section 18, 372.15-20). Here Iamblichus appears to want to combine the virtues of these two definitions, and refine them further. But how, precisely, is he proposing to do that? Festugière (181 note 1), following Levêque, suggests that Iamblichus wishes to identify the soul as the unity prior to continuous magnitude, from which this latter then derives, and refers in this connection to a comment of Iamblichus, quoted by Simplicius in his *Commentary on the Categories* (135.8ff. Kalbfleisch), where Iamblichus explains the existence of the two chief varieties of quantity, the continuous and the discrete, as deriving from the two corresponding "powers" (*dynameis*) of the One (no doubt to be identified with limit and unlimitedness, which Iamblichus held to derive from the One even in the henadic realm, cf. *In Tim.* Fr. 7 Dillon). This does not at first sight seem very relevant, but what Festugière presumably wishes to suggest is that Iamblichus sees Soul as combining within itself, at a lower level, the powers governing both discrete and continuous magnitudes, that is to say, numbers and geometrical figures, and that in this way both Severus and Speusippus are expressing a measure of the truth; and that indeed seems very probable.

Πάλιν τοίνυν ὁ ἀριθμὸς . . . Iamblichus now turns to those thinkers, beginning with "some of the (ancient) Pythagoreans" and culminating (on the scale of sophistication) with Plato, who consider the soul to be, in some form, number. The list of intermediate figures comprises Xenocrates, third head of the Academy, the first century C.E. Neopythagorean Moderatus, and the fifth century B.C.E. Pythagorean "acusmatic" Hippasus.

If we may credit Aristotle (*Met.* 1.5, 985b26ff.), the Pythagoreans held that things in general, including what we would consider abstract concepts such as 'justice', or 'marriage', were numbers in a quite literal sense (which Iamblichus expresses with the phrase ἁπλῶς οὕτως), according to which the numbers are immanent in the objects. The number of soul may have been "one" (if one credits Alexander of Aphrodisias, *comm. ad loc.*), "two" (according to Hippolytus, *Ref.* I 15, 2 — adducing the Pythagorean Ecphantus), or even "four" (according to Ps. Plut. *Epit.* 877A and Sextus Empiricus IV 6). What exactly the Pythagoreans in question had in mind here is very difficult to unravel. In the case of physical objects, such as "horse" or "tree," it seems that at least simple-minded members of the sect just drew assemblages of dots (since they thought of numbers in terms of systems of points), in the shape of, say, a horse, and then counted them, to get the "number" of horse,[4] but this procedure will not work for "justice," or "marriage," or "soul." In these cases, a degree of symbolism is evident[5]. It is quite possible, however, that the true Pythagorean doctrine was a good deal more sophisticated than this, and envisaged systems of mathematical, or quasi-mathematical, formulae corresponding to all the features of the physical universe. The important thing, at any rate, is that these formulae, or whatever they were, were not transcendent, but immanent, and in this way, as Aristotle points out, they differed from the Platonic forms.

From these we move to Xenocrates, whose definition of soul is given in the sources[6] as 'number moving itself' (ἀριθμὸς αὐτὸν

---

[4] Cf. Theophrastus *Met.* 6a19ff., where Archytas is recorded as (possibly ironically) commending Eurytus for doing just this.

[5] In the case of Soul, the choice of the number Four seems to have been determined by the circumstance that it is the first number that contains all the harmonic ratios, the octave (2:1), the fifth (3:2), and the fourth (4:3). Cf. Sextus Empiricus IV 6. On Pythagorean number symbolism in general, see W. Burkert, *Lore and Science in Ancient Pythagoreanism*, 465-82.

[6] Apart from the doxographic report of Aetius, there are a number of references to his doctrine in Aristotle (*De An.* I 2, 404b29; I 4, 408b32 ff. = Fr. 165 I-P/60 H.), and a fuller, if still hostile, account in Plutarch, *Proc. An.* 1012DE, which

κινῶν). Interestingly, in the *Placita* of Aetius (IV 2, 1, p. 386b Diels = Fr. 169 Isnardi Parente/ 60 Heinze), this formula is attributed to Pythagoras also, which may be an indication that Xenocrates himself, in some work or other (he wrote both a treatise *On the Soul,* and a work on the Pythagoreans), made some attempt to father his own doctrine on Pythagoras. The definition makes reasonably good sense when viewed as an exegesis of Plato's account of the composition of the soul in *Timaeus* 35Aff., which Xenocrates, according to Plutarch (*loc. cit.*), interpreted as describing, first the generation of number from the union of the Monad and the Indefinite Dyad, and then the generation of soul proper by the addition to this of the elements of Identity and Difference, which produce the 'self-moving' quality of soul, whereby it both gives form to, and then cognises, physical individuals. It is by no means clear, however, that Iamblichus has any very clear idea of what Xenocrates had in mind in proposing this definition. He presents him as simply a stepping-stone towards the more comprehensive 'mathematical' definition attributed to Plato, without indicating how he relates to it. He seems to be dependent on the same sort of bald doxographic report as we have from Aetius, rather than any work of Xenocrates in which he explained his position.

As for Moderatus, he, as a good Pythagorean, is probably also purporting to present the doctrine of Pythagoras, but propounding a doctrine quite compatible with that of the Old Academy. There is a textual problem here, first of all, which can be solved in one of two ways. The MSS. read λόγους περιέχουσαν (FP²) or περιέχουσα (P¹), which introduces a grammatical difficulty. We strictly need either a *masculine* participle in the accusative, agreeing with ἀριθμὸν, or a feminine participle in the *dative,* agreeing with τῇ ψυχῇ. Heeren chose the former solution, Festugière the latter. We judge the latter to be preferable as being more easily explicable paleographically, an "intelligent" scribe not quite seeing the point of the dative, and substituting an accusative (P¹'s reading being then a further error, which is duly corrected.)

While recognizing the validity of Festugière's solution, we feel that the text could be kept, at the cost of a slight anacoluthon, since in any case the following clause featuring Hippasus cannot be accommodated to the original construction. Iamblichus will then have simply forgotten his own construction.

---

makes plain the connection with the exegesis of the *Timaeus.*

To turn to the doctrine expressed here, it can be seen as essentially a version of that of Speusippus, overlaid with Stoic terminology. For Moderatus, the soul is to be regarded as numerical in its essence inasmuch as it "embraces *logoi*" — which we have translated, with some hesitation, as 'reason-principles'. The theory behind this would seem to involve equating the mathematical and geometrical entities of Speusippus' system, which are activated at the level of soul so as to take on the creative and paradigmatic functions of Plato's forms, with Stoic *logoi spermatikoi* — an equation we can see already operative in the thought of Philo of Alexandria (and so a feature of post-Antiochian Platonism). These *logoi* are viewed as essentially mathematical formulae, so that Soul, as embracing the totality of them, becomes the principle of Number, and as such structures matter by means of these to produce the physical universe. Moderatus is referred to just below, as we shall see, as describing the soul as a 'mathematical harmony', which would seem to tend in the same direction as this.[7]

As for Hippasus, we are doubtless dealing here not with any doctrine of the historical Hippasus, but with a (late Hellenistic?) pseudepigraphon[8]. Iamblichus refers to this definition of number by Hippasus as well at *In Nic.*, p. 10, 20 Pistelli, where he describes him also as defining number as "the primary model used in the creation of the world" (παράδειγμα πρῶτον κοσμοποιίας), which sounds like a reference to the Paradigm of the *Timaeus* (which we know that Speusippus equated with the Decad, cf. Fr. 28 Tarán). This definition tends in the same direction, but, without bearing the other definition in mind, it would not be easy to see what this has to do with the soul being a numerical entity. If, however, we recognize that we are dealing with a mathematicizing interpretation of the Paradigm of the *Timaeus,* then all is explained.

κοσμουργός is a rare word, occurring first here (and in the *In Nic.* passage) in extant literature[9]. It need not be attributed to 'Hippasus' himself, though such an attribution cannot be excluded. What it means to be a κριτικὸν ὄργανον is not entirely clear, but probably refers to the soul's role in *individuating* particulars, and arranging them in species and genera.

---

[7] On Moderatus' doctrine in general, see Dillon (1977) 344-51.
[8] Cf. Thesleff, 91-93.
[9] Syrianus twice (*In Met.* 123.8 and 142.23) uses the same definition when quoting from Hippasus. The term is found later in Proclus (e.g., *In Tim.* 1.362.9, 2.160.17, 2.232.16, and 2.263.17) and in Damascius (e.g., *In Parm.* 2.137.18 Ruelle).

ὡς δὲ ᾿Αριστοτέλης ἱστορεῖ . . . We come now, finally, to the definition of Plato, not one taken from the dialogues (not even from the *Timaeus*), but from Aristotle's report at *De Anima* 1.2, 404b18-24, of Plato's 'unwritten doctrines'[10]. Aristotle's text runs as follows: "We get a similar account [sc. to that in the *Timaeus*, of which Aristotle has just given a rather peculiar interpretation] in the talks about philosophy,[11] where he maintains that the Essential Living Being[12] is compounded of the idea itself of the One together with the primary length, breadth and depth, everything else being similarly constituted. And again, in another context:[13] intuitive knowledge[14] is symbolized by one, scientific knowledge by two (for it proceeds by a single route to a single conclusion); the number of the plane [sc. "three"] is opinion,[15] and the number of the solid [sc. "four"] is sense-perception."

By suppressing Aristotle's phrase ἔτι δὲ καὶ ἄλλως, Iamblichus contrives to combine more explicitly the two bits of doctrine that Aristotle is relaying here, thus aligning more clearly the soul's ontological role (as the source of three-dimensionality) with its epistemological one (as the focus of all levels of cognition, each level corresponding to a dimension). He may well be justified in this, though we cannot be sure that this account of Plato's doctrine is not derived from a work by one of his followers (perhaps Xenocrates, as has been suggested above, note 11). At all events, it is plain that Iamblichus is here making fairly uncritical use of the evidence of Aristotle as to Plato's doctrine, for which he has no other independent source.

---

[10] Cf. also *Met.* 14.3, 1090b20ff.

[11] If this may be taken to be the meaning of the phrase ἐν τοῖς περὶ φιλοσοφίας λεγομένοις. It seems to us that it must at least refer to some report of Plato's views, perhaps by Xenocrates, not to Aristotle's own lost work *Peri Philosophias*. This report is certainly here accepted by Aristotle, who should have known, as a reasonably accurate representation of Plato's oral speculations.

[12] If we may take it that αὐτὸ τὸ ζῷον refers in fact to the *autozôion*, that is to say, the Paradigm of the *Timaeus*. This in turn would seem to equate the Paradigm with the World Soul, which implies that Aristotle is here recognizing a non-literal interpretation of the *Timaeus*.

[13] If this is the meaning of ἔτι δὲ καὶ ἄλλως. In any case, Iamblichus ignores this little complication.

[14] This has to be the sense of *nous* in this context. Iamblichus presumably understands this.

[15] Presumably because opinion (*doxa*) may be true or false.

5

Ἔτι τοίνυν τὴν ἁρμονίαν ἴδωμεν . . . We turn next to a doctrine which is still mathematical, but distinguishable from purely mathematics-based theories, the doctrine that the soul acts as an attuning force on the various elements from which the body is composed[16], without itself being just the attunement[17] of those forces (as proposed, notably, by the Pythagorean Simmias in *Phaedo* 85e ff.). Plotinus, we may note, devotes a chapter of *Enn.* 4.7 (8[4]) to the refutation of the doctrine that the soul is just the *harmonia* of the body, and Iamblichus is careful to dismiss that theory at the outset here. What we seem to have here in fact is not so much a definition of the nature of the soul, as of the nature of its relation to the body. Moderatus, interestingly, is brought in again here, although he has just previously been identified as one for whom the soul is a numerical entity, but, if we take this as referring really to the manner of the soul's activity in the body, it need not be seen, as we have suggested above, as involving any contradiction.

This is followed by a rather curious interpretation of the *Timaeus* — though the use of 'Timaeus' as the author of the doctrine might seem to imply that the reference is properly to the *Peri psychas kosmou* of "Timaeus Locrus". However, as Festugière points out, there is nothing in that work that precisely corresponds to Iamblichus' assertion that "Timaeus refers harmony to the soul as being a mean and a conjunction in beings and lives and the generation of all things", although this is, broadly speaking, an accurate representation of what Plato is saying in *Tim.* 31B-32C, and 35A-36D (and thus *Tim. Locr.* 95E-96C). The actual collocution μεσότητα καὶ σύνδεσιν seems to be borrowed from *Tim.* 43D: μεσότητας καὶ συνδέσεις, where the topic is rather the disruption of these harmonizing means and conjunctions by the trauma of birth.

As for the doctrine of "Plotinus, Porphyry and Amelius", it is interesting to note that on this point, at least, Iamblichus presents all his immediate predecessors as being at one, but it is surprisingly difficult to come up with clear supporting texts, not just for Amelius,

---

[16] Strictly speaking, what Iamblichus says here is merely "let us look at attunement", but in the context we may assume that he is referring to the doctrine that the soul is in some sense an attunement of the body.

[17] We have been taught, by musically-aware Classicists, not to translate *harmonia* as 'harmony', but as 'attunement', so we follow that policy here.

but even for Plotinus and Porphyry. We have already noted that Plotinus, in *Enn.* 4.7, 8[4], rejects the doctrine of soul as being *no more than* an attunement. Here, however, what is in question is the concept of soul as a pre-existent attunement, or as the transmitter of *logoi* bearing *harmonia* from the intelligible world both to the physical cosmos as a whole and to the individual body. Despite the fact that this is certainly in accord with Plotinian doctrine (Festugière quotes such passages as 1.3, 1, 28ff., where Plotinus speaks of attaining to the knowledge of *noêtê harmonia*), or 1.6, 3, 28ff., where there is also talk of "imperceptible *harmoniai* " which create perceptible ones), there is no passage in the *Enneads* to which one can point for an explicit statement of this doctrine[18]. For Porphyry, on the other hand, one can at least point to section 18 of the *Sententiae*, where he speaks of the soul as a *harmonia khôristê*, a "transcendent attunement," which moves the strings (of the bodily senses) all by itself, while they are attuned by an immanent attunement. Since Porphyry in this passage is actually deriving inspiration from a passage of the *Enneads, 3. 6, 4,* 41-52, where Plotinus is employing the image of the soul as a *harmonia* controlling the strings of a lyre, this may indeed be the passage which Iamblichus has in mind. However, as Festugière suggests, the truth may lie in another direction. There is an interesting passage in Proclus' *Timaeus Commentary* (2.213.8 -215.28 Diehl), in which Proclus actually refers to the doctrines of Plotinus, Porphyry and Amelius on the question of the interpretation of the harmonic ratios on the basis of which the soul is constructed in *Tim.* 35BC — or rather to a somewhat fanciful exegesis of these which Amelius wishes to attribute to Plotinus *in his unpublished discourses* (ἐν ἀγράφοις συνουσίαις), and which Porphyry then in effect endorses. Porphyry is here quoted as talking of the soul as "filling the cosmos with *harmonia* (πάντα τὸν κόσμον ἁρμονίας πληροῖ)" and "directing everything in the cosmos in accordance with harmonic reason-principles (πάντα τὰ ἐγκόσμια κατὰ λόγους ἁρμονικοὺς ποδηγεῖν)." Iamblichus himself is then reported by Proclus as contributing an elaborate exegesis of his own (= *In Tim.* Fr. 53 Dillon). The important aspect of this sequence of doxographies, however, in the present context is that, although Iamblichus and his predecessors have their own interpretations of detail in regard to the numbers of the soul, they are all in broad agreement on the point that the soul confers *harmonia* on the physical world "according to

---

[18] Not, for instance, in the latter part (chs. 9-13) of 4.7, where one might have expected it.

reason-principles pre-existing in its essence," which is the doctrine attributed to them in common here, and from which Iamblichus himself does not dissent. What we may assume, I think, is that Iamblichus himself, in his *Timaeus Commentary,* reviewed the doctrines of his predecessors in much the terms relayed to us by Proclus, accepting Amelius' report of the oral opinions of Plotinus, and that he is giving us a summation of that account here. This will not, as we shall see, be the only occasion on which Iamblichus appears to be reporting doctrines of Plotinus which do not appear as such in the *Enneads.* He probably had access, resident as he was in Apamea, to the collected works of Amelius, including his hundred or so volumes of notes on Plotinus' *synousiai* (cf. Porphyry, *Vit. Plot.* 3).

The identity of the last class of authority referred to, πολλοὶ δή τινες τῶν Πλατωνικῶν καὶ Πυθαγορείων, is somewhat problematical, but is probably to be sought for among Middle Platonists of Pythagorean tendency, such as Nicomachus of Gerasa or Numenius, but also such non-Pythagoreans as Atticus or Harpocration, and perhaps even among members of the Old Academy. Indeed, if we consult the text of Proclus just prior to that mentioned above (i.e. *In Tim.* 2.212.3 - 213.7), we find a critique of anonymous earlier commentators who simply interpreted the numbers of the soul as referring to the distances relative to each other of the seven planetary spheres, and we find Porphyry himself (*ap.* Macrobius, *In Somn. Scip.* 2.3.15) criticizing anonymous *Platonici* for the same error. Iamblichus may be taken here as referring to this doctrine. Proclus distinguishes a multiplicity of different "immanentist'" interpretations, some identifying the numbers with the distances of the planets from each other and from the earth, others referring them to the differences in their speeds or sizes, but all have in common that they take the *harmonia* to be "interwoven with the cosmos and inseparable from the heaven."

6

Ἴθι δὴ οὖν . . . We now turn to what one would assume to be the properly Platonist doctrine of the soul, that it is an incorporeal essence. Here we find Iamblichus' immediate predecessors figuring once again, along with Numenius, but of course their previously discussed doctrine that the soul is a *harmonia,* in the sense of conferring *harmonia,* is not in conflict with this.

What Iamblichus does here is, first, to put all his immediate predecessors, starting with Numenius, in one basket, and then contrast with their oversimplified position a doctrine which, by its manner of introduction, is plainly indicated to be his own. The position which he criticizes involves making no essential distinction between the soul and the levels of being superior to it[19] — in particular the various levels of the intellectual realm — nor yet between various types of soul. The only distinction recognized is that expressed by a formula produced first, it would seem, by Numenius, "all things in all, but in each in a manner proper to its essence."[20] This is actually adopted as a basic principle by later Platonists from Porphyry on (cf. *Sent.* 10; and e.g. Syrianus, *In Met.* 81, 38ff.; Proclus, *Elem. Theol.* 103), so that Iamblichus is here setting himself interestingly in opposition to the mainstream of Platonist opinion.

As for Numenius, he is operating with a somewhat simpler metaphysical scheme than Plotinus and his successors. Although he makes a distinction between his supreme god, the Good, and a demiurgic secondary god (cf. Frs. 11-16 Des Places), it is not clear that he envisaged distinct levels of being (such as between the One and Intellect) as proper to these two, or again between either of them and the soul. We have the testimony of Proclus (*In Tim.* 2.153.17-25 Diehl = Fr. 39 Des Places) that he (like many before him, not least Xenocrates) derived the soul from the monad and indefinite dyad, and Iamblichus himself tells us further on (s. 52, p. 458.3-4W.) that he "seems to maintain the notion of a union and identity without distinction between the soul and its causal principles", so we must assume that, despite the degree of hierarchy that Numenius had introduced into his universe, he did not declare distinctions of essence between his various entities.

Plotinus himself does not employ the Numenian formula, but he states the doctrine clearly in a notable passage of 3.4 (3, 22ff.), which Iamblichus may have in mind:

> For the soul is many things, and all things, both the things above and the things below, down to the limits of all life, *and we are each one of us an intelligible universe* (καὶ ἐσμὲν ἕκαστος κόσμος νοητός), making contact with this lower world by the powers of soul below, but with the intelligible world by its powers above and the powers of the universe;

---

[19] Here we find no necessity to alter the text with Usener from ἐν αὐτῇ to γένη αὐτῆς. Admittedly, the phrase is repetitive, but not impossibly so for Iamblichus.

[20] Des Places (1973) 90 gives this whole section as Fr. 41 in his collection.

and we remain with all the rest of our intelligible part above, but by its ultimate fringe we are tied to the world below, giving a kind of outflow from it to what is below, or rather an activity, by which that intelligible part is not itself lessened. (trans. Armstrong).

This passage actually embodies also the doctrine peculiar to Plotinus, and sharply criticized elsewhere by Iamblichus (*In Tim.* Fr. 87), that a part of the soul remains "above", in permanent contact with the intelligible realm, but it constitutes a good statement of the position being criticized here. The only problem is to decide what Iamblichus has in mind by saying that Plotinus is "not completely consistently" committed to this view. What he may be thinking of is Plotinus' rather subtle doctrine concerning the relation between the All-Soul, or hypostasis of Soul, and the individual souls, as explored e.g. in 4.9 [8], and later in 4.3 [27], 1-8, but these discussions are not really relevant to the question of the relation of Soul to the levels of being superior to it. Certainly Plotinus felt that there was an ontological distinction between the One, Intellect and Soul (the various levels of being are set out particularly clearly in such a treatise as 5.1), but he also plainly held that the soul contained the higher levels οἰκείως κατὰ τὴν αὐτῆς οὐσίαν -- and on that phrase there rests a lot of weight.

For Porphyry the same would seem to hold good. Sentence 10 of his *Sententiae* runs as follows:

All things are in all, but in a mode proper to the essence of each:[21] in the intellect, intellectively; in the soul, discursively[22]; in plants, seminally, in bodies, imagistically (εἰδωλικῶς); and in the Beyond, non-intellectually and supra-essentially.

This would certainly seem to put Porphyry firmly in the "uniformity of essence" camp, but in such a passage as Sentence 30, for example, he does make a sharp distinction between the mode of activity of higher realities, down to and including universal soul, which generate what is below them without turning their attention[23] towards their products, and particular souls, which are compelled to do this, and something like this may be what Iamblichus is thinking of — especially if one takes into account what he says later, in section

---

[21] It should be noted, however, that in the MSS. U and N we find quite a different opening: "We do not cognize alike in all cases (οὐχ ὁμοίως μὲν νοοῦμεν ἐν πᾶσιν)", which gives quite a different sense. It is hard to know what to make of that.

[22] Taking this to be, in the context, the meaing of λογικῶς.

[23] He uses the verb ἐπιστρέφεσθαι for this process.

17 (372.9ff.W), where he lists the same sequence of authorities à propos the acts of the soul. We must, however, reckon with the probability that Iamblichus is being more than a little polemical here.

As for Amelius, we are precluded by lack of evidence from knowing to what Iamblichus is referring by his ironic phrase ἀστάτως ἐν αὐτῇ φέρεται,[24] but by referring once again to the passage of Proclus' *Timaeus Commentary* adduced in connection with the previous section, we can see that Amelius did conceive of the soul as containing "all the beings in the cosmos, gods, daemons, men, irrational animals" (213.13-15), which is very much what is said here.

7

Ἀλλὰ μὴν ἤ γε πρὸς ταύτην ἀνθισταμένη δόξα . . . At any rate, after this somewhat tendentious and no doubt over-simplified account of his predecessors' position, Iamblichus now proposes to state his own doctrine — though being careful to do so anonymously.[25] On the face of it, there seems nothing very different or revolutionary about what he is maintaining. After all, Plotinus and Porphyry, at least, would certainly reckon Soul as secondary to, and ontologically distinct from, Intellect[26], but it becomes apparent, as we go on, and if one takes into evidence the important doctrinal passages from Priscianus collected at the end of this edition,[27] that what Iamblichus has in mind is a doctrine that is quite distinctive.

It is not easy, first of all, to judge how much weight to give to the phrase δευτέραν καθ᾽ ἑτέραν ὑπόστασιν. We have chosen what is, if anything, a slight over-translation, "following upon Intellect, representing a distinct level of being," to bring out the full force of what Iamblichus wishes to claim. As becomes apparent from the evidence of Pseudo-Simplicius,[28] he wants to assert that the very essence of the

---

[24] A rare phrase, but Iamblichus uses it again in *De Myst.* 2.5, p. 80.6-7.

[25] On Iamblichus' devices for presenting his own doctrine in this work, see our Introduction, section II.

[26] For Plotinus, cf. e.g 4.1, 1, 41ff: "But again, next to that altogether indivisible nature (sc. Intellect) there is another reality following upon it, having indivisibility from that other nature, which, pressing eagerly on in its progress from the one to the other nature, established itself in the middle between the two, the indivisible and primary and the 'divisible which is in the sphere of bodies', which is upon bodies." (trans. Armstrong). This is, of course, part of an exegesis of *Tim.* 35A.

[27] See appendix, below.

[28] Cf., in particular, *In De An.* 89, 33ff. (Passage C), and 240, 33ff. (Passage D).

soul is such as to be truly median between the realm of unchanging-
ness and indivisibility which is that of Intellect, and that of change
and fragmentation, which is the physical world, and that requires that
it partake of the nature of both. This was a position so radical as to
put the whole Platonist system under strain, although Iamblichus sees
it only as a legitimate exegesis of Plato's account of the composition
of the soul in *Timaeus* 35A. That is the point of his specification of it
as "the middle term of divisible and indivisible beings, and of
corporeal and incorporeal."[29]

The next characterization of the soul, as τὸ πλήρωμα τῶν καθόλου
λόγων, while perfectly respectable in Platonic terms, has possible
Pythagorean overtones also, although the passage from the *Protrepticus* which Festugière adduces (ch. 4, p. 22, 5 Pistelli) concerns only
the phrase οἱ καθόλου λόγοι, in the context of their being cognized,
according to Archytas, by *sophia*. On the other hand, Proclus, in *ET*
prop. 177, declares that every intellect is a πλήρωμα εἴδων, "a totality
of forms", which is consistent with Soul being a *plêrôma* of *logoi*. The
actual term *plêrôma,* incidentally, which is originally characteristic
rather of Christian and Gnostic texts, seems to have been introduced
into Platonism by Iamblichus (e.g. *De Myst.* I. 8: *28*), and is then
taken up by such authorities as Proclus and Damascius. The only
remarkable thing about this definition, apart from the actual
terminology, is that Iamblichus should feel that it embodies a
doctrine distinct from that of his predecessors.

The next definition, too, does not seem to demarcate Iamblichus
very clearly from his immediate predecessors: "that which, after the
Ideas, is at the service of the work of creation" is surely a pretty fair
description of how the soul was viewed by Plotinus or Porphyry. Only
the terminology itself is distinctive. Plotinus does not use ὑπηρεσία in
this (or indeed any) connection,[30] while Plato himself, though frequently employing both verbal and nominal forms of this root, does
not use it in connection with the role of Soul in the universe. It is
possible, however, that Iamblichus is concerned to emphasize the
secondary status of the soul, both by using this term, with its strong
connotation of subordination, and by emphasizing that it is *subsequent
to* (μετὰ) the Ideas, and thus to Intellect.

---

[29] Accepting a necessary supplement to the text by Usener (see Apparatus).
[30] Porphyry does employ it six times (e.g., *De Abst.* 1.47.8; 2.47.14; *Ad Aneb.* 2.3a)
but never in connection with the activity of the soul.

Again, "that life which has life of itself, which proceeds[31] from the noetic realm" may be a formula designed to emphasize the distinct and *lower* mode of life proper to Soul, in distinction from Intellect, but once again it is hard to see that Plotinus or Porphyry would have any quarrel with this.

Lastly, the formulation "the procession (πρόοδος) of the classes of real Being as a whole to an inferior substance (εἰς ὑποδεεστέραν οὐσίαν)" seems to do little more than repeat the previous one, and once again, does not conflict with the views of Plotinus. Indeed, Festugière is able to adduce an apt passage from *Enn.* 4.8 [6], 6, 1ff., which is a good expression of Plotinus' doctrine of the necessity of the development of lower levels of being from higher:

> If, then, there must not be just one thing alone — for then all things would have been hidden, shapeless within that one, and not a single real being would have existed if that one had stayed still in itself, nor would there have been the multiplicity of these real beings which are generated from the One, if the things after them had not indulged in procession (μὴ τῶν μετ᾽ αὐτὰ τὴν πρόοδον λαβόντων), and thus taken on the rank of souls — in the same way there must not be just souls alone either, without the manifestation of the things produced through them. (trans. Armstrong, slightly emended).

Iamblichus now summons up the authority of all the founders of true philosophy to buttress his position, and in the process lays down a marker for the lines on which he will proceed throughout the rest of the treatise. How he feels that he can enroll Aristotle on his side one might well wonder, but in fact the strong distinction that Aristotle makes between the active and passive intellects in *De An.* 3.5 will have helped him to that end. One can see here clearly the degree to which Iamblichus' *De Anima* is a polemical treatise. As we have pointed out in the preface, Iamblichus did not compose this document out of a dispassionate interest in the history of Greek theories of the soul, but rather as a vehicle for the definition of his own distinctive position over against those of his immediate predecessors.

8

Τινὲς δὲ τῶν φυσικῶν . . . We now turn back, in the next two sections, to more primitive views of the soul, in what seems a rather peculiar

---

[31] This, once again, embodies a persuasive emendation by Usener; the προσελθουσῶν of the MSS. is meaningless in the context.

mode of procedure. One is even tempted to postulate that Stobaeus has got his extracts out of order, and that these sections should properly come after Section 2; but, with that expression of doubt, we may perhaps leave them where we find them. It is possible, after all, that, since the doctrines with which Iamblichus in fact deals here are, first, that of the Orphics, and secondly that of the Peripatetic School after Aristotle, he is just tidying up loose ends, by enumerating some doctrines that did not quite fit into his scheme of ascending degrees of sophistication and accuracy, but which deserved mention nonetheless.

At any rate, Iamblichus turns for a text on which to base himself to the last part of chapter 2 of Aristotle's *De Anima* I (405b23ff.), where Aristotle is summing up the various distinguishing characteristics which previous thinkers have attached to the soul — movement, sensation and incorporeality:

> All those who assume pairs of contrary opposites among their first principles also construct the soul from contraries; while those who suppose the first principle to be a pair of contraries such as hot and cold or the like, similarly also suppose the soul to be one of these. In this connection they appeal to etymology also; those who identify the soul with heat derive *zên* ('to live') from *zein* ('to boil'), but those who identify it with cold maintain that *psychê* ('soul') is so called after the cooling process (*anapsyxis*) connected with respiration. (trans. Hicks, slightly emended.)

It is actually by no means clear whom Aristotle has in mind here. Various of the commentators have various suggestions. Themistius (p. 25, 23ff.) thinks of Empedocles as the figure behind "those who suppose the first principle to be a pair of contraries", while Philoponus (p. 92, 2ff.) identifies Heraclitus as the figure who chooses 'hot' as the contrary of which the soul is composed, and Hippon (whom Aristotle has mentioned earlier, rather dismissively, at 405b2 as declaring the soul to be water) as the champion of 'cold'. It is possible that latter-day followers of Heraclitus (whom Plato satirizes for fantastic etymologies in the *Cratylus,* in the person of Cratylus himself) are responsible for the *zên/zein* etymology, while Plato himself, also in the *Cratylus* (399E), is responsible for the (ironic) derivation of *psychê* from *anapsychein.*

However this may be, Iamblichus, by linking this passage with a later one from 1.5, 410b27ff. (= *Orph. Fr.* 27 Kern), where Aristotle is once again criticizing those who derive the soul from the elements, and this time adduces the Orphic theory that "the soul, borne by the winds, enters from the universe into animals when they breathe," is able to identify at least the champions of soul as the principle of cooling with the Orphics. However, he goes on to provide more information about Orphic doctrine, which is not derivable from the *De Anima* passage, and which he produces again later, in section 25, p. 376, 4ff., to the effect that Orpheus propounded the doctrine of a single, transcendent soul, (a) "from which there are many divisions" — a statement which is obscure, but which may mean that all individual souls are to be seen as 'parts' of this universal soul;[32] and (b) that πολλαὶ καὶ μέσαι ἐπίπνοιαι descend from it into individual souls. The term *epipnoia* is remarkable, as denoting normally 'divine inspiration', though here it must mean just "breath." In what sense these are *mesai* is not entirely clear[33], but it may simply mean that they mediate between the universal soul and the particular ones; it could also imply, however, that there are various degrees of closeness between different types of particular soul and the universal which is their origin.

9

Τινὲς μὲν τῶν Ἀριστοτελικῶν . . . It is strange, perhaps, that, after Aristotle himself has been (rather optimistically) linked with Plato and Pythagoras as propounding what Iamblichus regards as the true doctrine of the soul, "certain of the Aristotelians" should be brought in here as holding to a more materialistic view of it; but in fact it was widely held, at least from Antiochus of Ascalon on, that the Peripatetics after Aristotle — beginning in many respects even with Theophrastus — deviated from the doctrine of Aristotle in the direction of a greater degree of materialism, culminating in the positions taken up by Strato of Lampsacus. In the case of the soul, of course, there is the complication that Aristotle, in the most advanced phase of his thought, held the soul to be simply "the first *entelecheia* of a natural body which has organs" (*De An.* 2.1, 412b5), but there is reasonable evidence that at an earlier stage of his development (as in his

---

[32] Festugière quotes here a passage from the *Corpus Hermeticum* (10.7), which does indeed propound this doctrine, but has otherwise no obvious relevance to anything Orphic. It is far more likely to exhibit Stoic influence.

[33] Usener's emendation ἀμέσους for MSS. μέσας here seems to serve no purpose.

dialogue *Eudemus*) he held to a more Platonic concept of the soul, or at least to a concept of the soul as a distinct substance of some sort, and that is what is being referred to here.

As to the details of doctrine presented here, there are some difficulties. The first view, that the soul is a body composed of ether — that is, in Aristotelian terms, the 'fifth substance', of which the heavens and the heavenly bodies are composed — is not attributed explicitly to anyone earlier than the early second century BCE. Peripatetic Critolaus of Phaselis, head of the Academy before Carneades,[34] but it was pretty certainly also the view of Heraclides of Pontus back in the fourth century. Heraclides is attested as holding that the soul is "light-like" (φωτοειδής, Aetius, *Plac.* 4.3, 6, p. 388 Diels), with the implication that it is material, and that its true home, from which it descends into embodiment, is in the Milky Way. This latter opinion is actually reported by Iamblichus later in the present work (s. 26, 378, 11ff.), but the difficulty is that there he seems to take Heraclides as a Platonist (which he could equally well be seen as) rather than as an Aristotelian, so we cannot be quite certain that he has him in mind here.[35]

It is the second definition, however, that causes most difficulty. Here the presentation of the soul as "the essential[36] perfection of the divine body" is linked to a term for it attributed by Theophrastus "ἐν ἐνίοις" (no doubt in his *Physikai Doxai*)[37] to Aristotle, ἐνδελέχεια[38]. There are plainly layers of confusion here, but there are also some traces of valid doctrine. As mentioned above, Aristotle, at an earlier

---

[34] He is reported by Tertullian (*De An.* 5. 1) and Macrobius (*Somn. Scip.* 1, 14, 20) to have declared the soul to be composed of the *quinta essentia*. Cf. F. Wehrli, *Die Schule d. Ar.* Vol. 10.

[35] W. Theiler, 'Ein vergessenes Aristoteleszeugnis', *JHS* 77 (1957), p. 130, does make the identification, and it is not unreasonable.

[36] If that is what is meant by κατ' οὐσίαν. Without the article, it seems best to link it closely with τελειότητα rather than θείου σώματος.

[37] At any rate (as Festugière points out) this definition turns up in the doxographers, specifically Epiphanius (*Adv. Haer.* 3.31-2, p. 592 Diels), with Theophrastus' name linked to that of Aristotle. It is not quite clear, admittedly, either from the present text or from that of Epiphanius, that Theophrastus attributed this doctrine to Aristotle as well as adopting it himself "in some places," but it seems reasonable to assume this from the mode of their juxtaposition.

[38] It is quite misguided of Heeren to emend to ἐντελέχειαν here. Certainly there is confusion at the back of this between the two terms, but this term is sufficiently well attested elsewhere (see below) to be retained here. It is, for one thing, very probable that, at least in later antiquity, the cluster -*nt*- was hardly distinguishable from -*nd*- (as in Modern Greek), which would certainly encourage the confusion.

stage of his development, does seem to have accepted that the soul was a separable substance — probably initially an immaterial one (he is reported by the Pseudo-Simplicius[39] in his Commentary on the *De Anima* , p. 221, 29ff [= *Eudemus,* Fr. 8 Ross] to have "declared that the soul is a type of Form [εἶδός τι]"), but later, perhaps, as having thc same substance as the heavens. Here it seems to be asserted (on the authority of Theophrastus?) that the soul is taken to be somehow the essence and perfection of the heavenly realm, as if it were indeed its *prôtê entelecheia,* as well as being characterized by *endelecheia,* that is to say, perpetual self-motion. The linking of the terms *teleiotês* and *endelecheia* would lend substance to the hypothesis of a confusion between *endelecheia* and *entelecheia,* but it seems hardly possible that either Theophrastus or even Iamblichus himself (who knew the text of Aristotle's *De Anima* perfectly well) could have been guilty of such a confusion. There must be something more substantial behind this. We find, after all, in Cicero's *Tusculan Disputations* 1.10: *22,* a most interesting testimony as to Aristotle's doctrine (which may derive from Antiochus of Ascalon[40]). Aristotle is here presented as discussing *mens* or *animus,* 'mind', rather than *anima,* 'soul', but in the context that is not of much importance; Cicero is discussing the nature of soul. Aristotle is stated to "consider that there is a special fifth nature (*quintam quandam naturam*) from which comes intellect (*mens* . . . he employs a fifth class (of element) without a name, and accordingly applies to the actual soul (*animus*) a new term, *endelecheia,* descriptive of a kind of uninterrupted and perpetual movement." Philo of Alexandria, also, at *Somn.* 1.30, in the course of a doxography closely resembling that given by Cicero just above (*ibid.* section 19), lists *endelecheia* as a possible definition of the nature of the soul, though without attribution. The confusion (if confusion it is) between *entelecheia* and *endelecheia* is already well established, then, by the mid-first century BCE. What it seems to give evidence of, however, is a tradition, supported by Theophrastus, that Aristotle, at some stage of his development, held that the soul was of the same substance as the heavens, was characterized, like the heavenly bodies, by perpetual self-motion, and was in some sense the perfection of the

---

[39] On the unknown identity of the author, see our introduction, section III. This commentary is, by its author's admission, heavily dependent on the *De Anima* of Iamblichus.

[40] Although there are difficulties about this; cf. the discussion in Dillon, *Middle Platonists,* 96-102.

essence of that realm. Certainly he changed his view on this question at least in respect of the *soul* (what he thought of the nature of the Active Intellect is another matter) — in the process developing the neologism *entelecheia* on the model of the existing *endelecheia* — but not all of his successors followed him in this (though in fact a man like Critolaus may be thinking rather of the active intellect than of the human soul when propounding his doctrine). And so the 'confusion' is bequeathed to the doxographic tradition.

The next definition, "that which is produced from all the more divine classes of being", seems, strangely, to be an effort at interpretation by Iamblichus himself — at least, the terminology used, ὥσπερ ἄν τις νεωτερίσειεν ἐν ταῖς ἐπινοίαις, is characteristic of his introduction of his own views. But what is his view here? He is commenting on the Peripatetic doctrines that make the soul an ethereal substance (whether "ethereal body" or "the essential perfection of the divine body"). But Iamblichus would in no way agree that the soul, which for him is incorporeal, is ethereal. Thus, the innovation he suggests cannot be that the *soul* is ethereal.

Iamblichus says that the entity in question is "generated from all the more divine classes." It is possible that Iamblichus is thinking not of the soul but of the soul's vehicle (ὄχημα), which for him is ethereal. But the Greek clause presents certain difficulties for this interpretation. Iamblichus (*In Tim.* Frr. 81 and 84) believes that the vehicle is created whole by the Demiurge, not piecemeal in the soul's descent as the soul collects portions of ether from the ethereal bodies of the visible gods. (The latter theory is Porphyry's, against which Iamblichus argues.) Further the phrase "more divine classes" (θειότερα γένη) is an odd one to apply to the encosmic gods. The phrase appears nowhere else in Iamblichus' extant writings and appears to be unique among Neoplatonic authors. We interpret it as referring not solely to the visible gods but to all the classes superior to the human soul: visible gods, angels, daemons, and heroes. (In this sense, it would be equivalent to the more usual κρείττονα γένη). No philosopher, however, has argued that these lower divinities provided ethereal substance to the soul's vehicle or collection of ethereal envelopes.

We are led to two conclusions: Iamblichus is discussing some sort of ethereal body and this body is amassed from the classes of being superior to or more divine than the human soul itself. Iamblichus seems to have believed that although the soul's ethereal vehicle was created whole, there were still pneumatic additions made to the soul in its descent to earth.[41] These seem to be material accretions, but there is no reason to think that they did not include ethereal accretions as well. This would make these ethereal envelopes akin to the lower, pneumatic vehicle of Syrianus and Proclus, to which doctrine Iamblichus' ethereal and material envelopes may have formed part of the background. Be that as it may, Iamblichus would have denied that these ethereal envelopes are the vehicle. Rather they would be accretions added to the vehicle during the soul's descent, which make the soul more and more bodily.

If this is Iamblichus' theory of psychic accretions, then the "innovation" here in the *De Anima* is a direct criticism of the Peripatetics' view of the soul. It is not the soul that is ethereal. They have defined the wrong entity. The ethereal body they describe is actually something very much lower: the ethereal and pneumatic envelopes collected during the soul's descent to earth.

We find next a definition taken from the Stoics, who have not hitherto figured in his doxographic survey. The formulation τὸ συγκεκραμένον τοῖς σώμασιν seems to be a reference to the Stoic doctrine of 'total mixture' (κρᾶσις δι' ὅλων) as a description of the mode of contact between soul and body (*SVF* 1.145; 2.473; 48 Long-Sedley), but if so, it is not a definition of the *essence* of the soul, which is a fiery *pneuma*. It may be, however, that Iamblichus is equating this in his mind with the Aristotelian 'fifth substance' or ether (as was widely done in later antiquity), and is thus taking the Stoics to be merely adapting this variety of Peripatetic doctrine to their own purposes.

All the formulations up to this, then, are presented as taking to soul to be composed of ether. The final one[42], on the other hand, that of Dicaearchus, is quite uncompromisingly reductionist, being an even more extreme version of that propounded by Aristotle himself in the *De Anima*. Fortunately, we have a rather fuller account of Dicaearchus' doctrine presented by Cicero in *Tusc. Disp.* 1.10 (21), from a dialogue of his *On the Soul,* just prior to the testimony on Aristotle mentioned above:

---

[41] See Finamore (1985) 12-15.

[42] Or two — it is not clear how far the two last views are intended to be distinct, as opposed to two formulations of the same doctrine. If the former, and "that which is intermingled with the *physis* (growth-principle?)" is distinct, it is not easy to see to whom it can be attributed.

> On the other hand, Dicaearchus in that discussion, of which the scene is laid in Corinth, and of which he gives an account in three books, introduces a number of the learned men who took part in the discussion as speakers in the first book; in the other two he represents Pherecrates, an old native of Phthiotis, descendant (he says) of Deucalion, as arguing that the soul is wholly non-existent and an entirely empty name, and that the terms *animalia* and *animantes* have no reference (*frustra appellari*); neither in man nor in beast is there a mind or a soul (*animum vel animam*), and all the capacity we have of action or sensation is uniformly diffused in all living bodies and cannot be separated from the body, seeing that it has no separate existence and that there is nothing apart from one single body fashioned in such a way that its activity and power of sensation are due to the natural combination of the parts. (trans. J.E. King, somewhat emended)

Iamblichus' language is somewhat obscure due to its compression, but it is much clarified by the passage from Cicero just quoted. It becomes apparent that Dicaearchus is intent on trumping the position of his master in the *De Anima,* by producing, if possible, an even more extreme formulation — one not far removed, indeed, from that of Gilbert Ryle. One is not even to speak of such a thing as "soul;" just of "being ensouled"[43] as an aspect of bodily existence.

Iamblichus adds an editorial note of his own to Dicaearchus' doctrine. The phrase we have set off with dashes ("not present to the soul itself as belonging to it") seems to be Iamblichus explaining how far from the "truth" Dicaearchus has strayed. This condition of ensoulment is not even a property belonging to or caused by the soul.

We are a far cry, suddenly, from soul as an ethereal body. However, Iamblichus does manage in this paragraph to provide a brief survey of two quite different tendencies within the Peripatetic tradition on the subject of the soul, both stemming from Aristotle.

10

Having discussed the nature of the soul, Iamblichus turns in the next few sections to the soul's powers, activities, and acts. He begins with the various powers of the soul (sections 10-15).

---

[43] A small textual problem here: the MSS. have ἐμψυχῶσθαι, which is an impossible form. Meineke, followed by Wachsmuth, opted for the perfect of the simple verb, ἐψυχῶσθαι; Festugière (whom we follow) for the present of the compound verb, ἐμψυχοῦσθαι, which gives a rather better sense.

In section 10, Iamblichus contrasts the "correct" view of Plato and others (Aristotle, Pythagoras), that the soul is incomposite and that the powers belong to the soul in itself, with the "incorrect" view of Stoics and Later Peripatetics, who think that the soul is a body.

Πλάτων μὲν οὖν . . . Plato says that souls are incomposite (*Phd.* 78b), although elsewhere he stresses that souls have parts: *Rep.* 435a-442d, 580de, *Phdr.* 246ab, 253c-e, *Tim.* 89e. At *Tim.* 69b-71a, the three parts of the soul are allotted three different areas of the body.

The phrase "incomposite essence" (ἀσύνθετον οὐσίαν) comes from a suggestion by Wyttenbach. The MSS have σύνθετον, i.e. "composite," but this reading is inapposite here. Thus, we adopt Wyttenbach's correction.

Ἀριστοτέλης δὲ ὡσαύτως . . . This may come as a surprise. This doctrine, of course, is not what Aristotle thinks but what Iamblichus thinks that Aristotle thinks. For Aristotle's definition of soul as "the first entelechy of a natural body which potentially has life," see *De An.* 412a27. Iamblichus' conception of Aristotle's theory of soul, then, is that the soul is simple and incomposite, causes form (of life) in the body, and thus is associated with various somatic powers. When it comes to the soul's essence, Iamblichus would argue, Aristotle would agree with Plato that it is incomposite. (Another reason for accepting Wyttenbach's correction above.) The agreement of Plato and Aristotle is Iamblichean dogma. Thus the distinction between Plato and Aristotle, on the one hand, and the Stoics and materialists, on the other, is that for the former the soul is simple and forms a temporary conglomerate with corporeal powers, whereas for the latter the soul itself is a composite of soul and powers.

Ἀλλὰ μὴν οἵγε ἀπὸ Χρυσίππου καὶ Ζήνωνος . . . This sentence on the Stoics forms the first half of *SVF* II.826 (= 28F Long and Sedley).

προτιθέασιν ("consider") is the reading of the MSS. Wachsmuth suggested τιθέασιν, but this seems unnecessary, as Festugière says (192 note 1). Iamblichus uses the term six times in his extant works: *DCMS* 15.40 and 17.38; *De Myst.* 3.31 (p. 180.12); 4.5 (p.187.13), 8.3 (p. 264.14), 8.4 (p. 267.5).

Ταύτῃ τοίνυν . . . We read ταύτῃ with Usener, Wachsmuth, and Festugière. The MSS readings are problematic. F has αὗται; P ταῦτα, which could be rendered "and furthermore," but this seems unlikely with τοίνυν following. Heeren proposed αὗται, but "these powers" suggest a previously mentioned list, not in the text. The reading ταύτῃ has the added benefit of allowing the translator to divide the long Greek sentence into three parts: a description of how the powers will be allotted to the soul, the allotment of Plato and Pythagoras, and the allotment of the Stoics and Peripatetics. The first English sentence will introduce the next two (ταύτῃ will have its usual sense of "in the following way"); the second will expound what Plato thought (adding that Pythagoras does so as well); the third what the Peripatetics and Stoics thought. (The last two sentences are signaled by καθ' οὓς μέν and καθ' οὓς δέ.)

ἡ ψυχὴ διττὴν ζωὴν ζῇ . . . On the double life of the soul, see *De Myst.* 3.3 and below in *De An.* 370.3-4 W: "Plato assumes that they [i.e., the powers of the soul] belong to [the souls] themselves and to the [composite] living beings, distinguishing each in accordance with each life [i.e., the incarnate and discarnate lives]."

ὡς οἱ Περιπατητικοί . . . Festugière (192 note 4) compares Aristotle, *De An.* 414b29, but Aristotle is there discussing the impossibility of a general definition of soul and arguing that mortal beings with higher types of souls necessarily have the lower types as well but not *vice versa*. Iamblichus is not referring to Aristotle (who, he has already said, agrees with Plato that the soul is not a composite but is, in essence, simple — and therefore has a "double life") but to later Peripatetics, who in Iamblichus' opinion misinterpreted their master. (See notes to section 8, above.) Alexander of Aphrodisias, *De An.* 17.11-15, for example, argues that the soul is inseparable from body because the soul is the body's form. At 20.26-21.13 Alexander argues that the soul's relation to body is not like that of a pilot to a ship (and hence that the soul is not a separate and separable entity). He also questions, if the soul were separate from body, what agency would bring them together and how they would remain combined into a unity (21.13-21).

Iamblichus would argue that for both Plato and Aristotle, the essence of the soul is simple and not given over *entirely* to the body. The soul is separate and ultimately separable from its body.

11

Πῶς οὖν διακρίνονται; Iamblichus, having argued that Plato believes that the powers naturally coexist within an incomposite soul, moves on to consider how the various powers, different as they are, can be said to exist in a single soul. He contrasts the Stoics, Aristotelians, and Plato (κατὰ μὲν τοὺς Στωικοὺς . . . κατὰ δὲ τοὺς Ἀριστοτελικοὺς . . . κατὰ δὲ Πλάτωνα).

Κατὰ μὲν τοὺς Στωικοὺς . . . The Stoics distinguish the powers of the soul by two means, both corporeal. First, the powers are distinguished by the different bodily organs in which they exist. (*Pneumata* extend from the ruling element to these organs.) Second, the powers are distinguished by a common property of a single body-part itself. Just as an apple as a whole shares certain qualities (sweetness, scent, etc.), so the ruling element shares certain common powers.

πνεύματα γὰρ ἀπὸ τοῦ ἡγεμονικοῦ φασιν οὗτοι διατείνειν ἄλλα καὶ ἄλλα . . . We retain the reading of the manuscripts, ἄλλα καὶ ἄλλα. Wachsmuth, following Meineke, reads ἄλλα κατ' ἄλλα. Festugière translates "souffles, divers selon les diverses parties du corps." Heeren suggested ἄλλα εἰς ἄλλα, i.e., "some effluences to some, others to other [parts of the body]." Neither change is necessary. The clause, as it stands in the manuscripts, asserts that the ruling element emits various πνεύματα; the following clauses state where these πνεύματα go. The "ruling element" is the controlling element in the animal (in a human being, it is reason), and the powers extend from it as πνεύματα to the bodily organs.

Iamblichus explains that the πνεύματα extend from the ruling element to the five sense organs. Each *pneuma* travels to its own proper bodily seat. From other sources (*SVF* II.827, 828, 830, 832, 836, 879), we learn that there are two other such πνεύματα: seed that extends to the testicles and voice to the vocal chords. (See also section 12, below.) In these cases, the powers are differentiated by their physical location in the body: the eye has sight, the ear hearing, etc. Note that each bodily part has a single power.

Besides these powers that reside in a specific bodily part, Iamblichus continues, there are powers that are in the ruling power itself. These are different powers in a single bodily substrate, existing like taste and odor in a single apple. Iamblichus lists four of these powers: imagination, assent, appetition, and reason. This seems to be the only place where these four powers are so listed. Aetius (*SVF* II.836) substitutes sensations for reason: "The Stoics say that the ruling element is the highest part of the soul. It produces images, assents, sensations, and appetitions. They call this part 'reason' (λογισμός)." Diogenes Laertius (*SVF* II.837) says that in the ruling element "images and appetitions arise and from there reason (λόγος) comes." Iamblichus claims that reason is a power of the ruling element rather than being the ruling element itself. The point seems to be that these powers of the soul follow in a sequence. An image is presented. The mind assents to the image. Appetition follows. In a rational act, the assent and appetite are in accordance with reason, and the ruling element can be said to have made a rational choice. In animals and small children presumably there is only irrational assent to the image. See *SVF* II.52 and 74. On this topic, see A. A. Long and D. N. Sedley, *The Hellenistic Philosophers*, Vol. 1 (Cambridge 1987) 53-54; B. Inwood, *Ethics and Human Action in Early Stoicism* (Oxford 1985) 29-33; and A. A. Long, "Soul and Body in Stoicism," *Phronesis* 27 (1082) 49-51. For the Stoic συγκατάθεσις, the assent the mind gives to the images, see *SVF* III.177; for ὁρμή, see *SVF* III.169-177.

ὥσπερ γὰρ τὸ μῆλον . . . The example of the apple to describe how one substrate can have many different powers without having different parts seems to be a commonplace. It is in Porphyry, *Concerning the Powers of the Soul*, 253F.68-70 Smith: "For example now, all of the powers of an apple are in a single apple, but the parts [of the apple] are separated, some in one place and others in another" (αὐτίκα τοῦ μήλου αἱ μὲν δυνάμεις πᾶσαι ἐν ἑνί, τὰ δὲ μέρη ἄλλα ἀλλαχοῦ κεχώρισται). And it appears in Alexander of Aphrodisias' commentary on Aristotle's *De Anima* 31.4-6: To divide the soul is "as if someone were to divide an apple into odor, color, form, and sweetness. For such a division of an apple is not like one of a body, even if an apple is altogether corporeal" (ὡς ἂν εἰ τὸ μῆλόν τις διαιροίη εἴς τε εὐωδίαν καὶ εἰς εὔχροιαν καὶ εἰς σχῆμα καὶ εἰς χυμόν. ἡ γὰρ τοιαύτη τοῦ μήλου διαίρεσις οὔτε ὡς σώματος γίνεται, εἰ καὶ ὅτι μάλιστα σῶμα τὸ μῆλον). On the distinction between powers and parts, see below in this section.

Κατὰ δὲ τοὺς Ἀριστοτελικοὺς καὶ πάντας ὅσοι ἀμέριστον τὴν ψυχὴν διανοοῦνται . . . The defining characteristic of these "Aristotelians" is their belief that the soul does not have parts. Aristotle himself was opposed to the concept of the parts of the soul. He raises the issue four times in the *De Anima* (402b1-5, 411b5-30, 413b13-32, 432a22-b7).

In 411a26-b3, Aristotle raises the same question with which Plato began his discussion of the parts of the soul in *Rep.* 436ab. Do the soul's powers (which Aristotle lists as knowledge, perception, opinion, appetite, and wish) belong to the whole soul or to its parts (πότερον ὅλη τῇ ψυχῇ τούτων ἕκαστον ὑπάρχει . . . ἢ μορίοις ἑτέροις ἕτερα;)? If, as some say, the soul is divisible (μεριστή, b5), what unifies the disparate parts of the soul? It is not the body, he says (411b7), for it is rather the soul that unifies the body. But whatever else would make the soul one would then be soul (b8-9). But then the problem merely arises again: what unifies this soul? And the argument would continue to infinity (b9-14). Furthermore, if the whole soul held the whole body together, wouldn't each of the parts of the soul hold together some part of the body? But, if so, it is hard to see what part of the body the intellect holds together (b14-19). Thus it would seem that the soul does not have parts.

Furthermore, there is the problem of plants and some insects that have been cut in two. Each segment continues to live, if even for only a short time, and has all the powers of the original whole plant or animal (b19-24). In 413b16-24, Aristotle adds that, in the case of insects, several powers of the soul are found in each half: perception, locomotion, imagination, desire, and pleasure and pain. Thus, these "parts" of the soul are not divisible, but continue to cohere even in the separate segments of the insect. Afterwards (413b24-27) Aristotle states that the intellect may be separable. The other "parts," however, are not separable, but can be distinguished in definition (λόγῳ, b27-32).

In 432a22-b3, Aristotle criticizes the Platonic tripartite division of soul. In a certain sense, Aristotle says, there are not merely three parts (λογιστικὸν καὶ θυμικὸν καὶ ἐπιθυμητικόν) or even two (τὸ λόγον, τὸ ἄλογον) but an infinite number (ἄπειρα). Aristotle is using hyperbole, but his point is that there are many other so-called "parts" of the soul: nutritive, perceptive, imaginative, and desiderative — if one posits separate parts of the soul (εἴ τις θήσει κεχωρισμένα μόρια τῆς ψυχῆς). Furthermore, if one did accept a tripartite or bipartite division of soul, then the desiderative would in turn have to be split, since desires are involved in all the parts (b3-7). Thus, leaving the problematic intellect aside, the soul should not be divided into parts.

Alexander of Aphrodisias also believed that the soul was without parts, at least insofar as parts imply magnitude (30.29-31.1): "For the soul is not divisible into parts whether in the manner of number or even of magnitude" (ἡ δὲ ψυχὴ οὐ μόνον οὐχ ὡς μέγεθος, ἀλλ' οὐδὲ ὡς ἀριθμός ἐστι μεριστή). Iamblichus therefore is most probably alluding to later Peripatetics like Alexander. (We have already seen that Iamblichus believes that Aristotle agreed with Plato.) For Alexander, of course, the soul is the inseparable form of the body. The "productive intellect" (νοῦς ὁ ποιητικός), however, is different: it comes from outside (ἔξωθεν γινόμενος), is neither a part nor a power of our soul (οὐκ ὢν μόριον καὶ δύναμις τις τῆς ἡμετέρας ψυχῆς), and is alone immortal (108.22-109.1). The other powers of the soul (nutritive, perceptive, etc.) do not inhere in a "part" of the soul but belong to the composite of soul plus matter. Thus, Iamblichus concludes that for Aristotelians such as Alexander the soul's powers do not belong to the essence of the soul but are determined by the effects that the powers produce. Indeed Alexander makes a similar claim (31.1-4): "For we do not divide it [i.e., the soul] as we divide a composite from its separated constituents, but we make a division of the soul by an enumeration of the powers it possesses and by a discovery of their differences (οὐ γὰρ εἰς ἃ διαιροῦμεν αὐτήν, ὡς ἐκ τούτων κεχωρισμένων συγκειμένην διαιροῦμεν, ἀλλὰ τῇ τῶν δυνάμεων ὧν ἔχει καταριθμήσει καὶ τῇ τῶν διαφορῶν αὐτῶν εὑρέσει τὴν διαίρεσιν αὐτῆς ποιούμεθα). The comparison to the qualities in an apple (translated above) follows immediately. Thus, for Alexander, each power is known by its effect.

Κατὰ δὲ τοὺς Ἀριστοτελικοὺς . . . <οὐ διακρίνονται> αἱ δυνάμεις . . . Something has clearly dropped out of the MSS in this sentence. The adopted reading is Wachsmuth's, who is followed by Festugière. The sentence draws a distinction between distinguishing powers κατὰ τὴν οὐσίαν and κατὰ εἴδη. Wachsmuth's suggestion simply and elegantly draws the contrast between the two methods of distinguishing powers. Other suggestions are more radical. Heeren hypothesized: κατὰ μὲν τὴν οὐσίαν ἀμέριστοι αἱ δυνάμεις, κατὰ δὲ εἴδη μέρισται καθ' ἃ δύνανται ποιεῖν ("In essence the powers are without parts, but they are divided specifically in accordance with what they can produce.") Usener proposed: κατὰ μὲν τὴν οὐσίαν μία δύναμις, κατὰ δὲ εἴδη ὧν δύνανται πλείονες ("In essence there is one power, but in the kinds of effects that they can produce many"). All of these suggestions tend in the same general direction, but we prefer the simplicity of Wachsmuth's solution.

Κατὰ δὲ Πλάτωνα . . . Having given the two "false" views of the soul (the Stoic doctrine that the soul's powers inhere in a material substrate and the Peripatetic doctrine that the soul's powers inhere only in a composite structure of form and matter), Iamblichus passes to the "true" Platonic doctrine. Iamblichus is here concerned with the difference between parts and powers as well as with the Platonic conception of a tripartite soul.

Plato sometimes presents the soul as having three parts (e.g., *Rep* 440e-441a, *Phdr.* 246ab, *Tim.* 69d-70e). In accordance with the *Timaeus*, Iamblichus interprets Plato to mean that the soul exists or functions in three different ways in three different parts of the body (ἐν ἑτέραις οὐσίαις ζωῆς). Here οὐσίαις in the plural indicates the body parts of head, breast, and liver. This use of the plural is reminiscent of ὑποκειμένων σωμάτων ("the body parts that underlie [the powers]") used in the sentence about the Stoics, above: "life substances" = "substrates" = "body parts." At other times, Iamblichus continues, Plato represents the soul as having many different powers. These are differentiated not by the body part they exist in (κατ' οὐσίαν ζωῆς, note the singular οὐσίαν for a single substance, i.e., one body part: "life substance" = "substrate" = "body part") but by different characteristics in the same substrate (ἐν ταὐτῷ δὲ πολλαῖς ἰδιότησι). But what is this substrate? It cannot be any individual body part, for that would entail that all powers of the soul require some body part, something Platonists wish to deny. Intellectual thought requires no bodily organ. The substrate must therefore refer either to the soul/body complex or to the soul alone, depending on the circumstances. Thus, for Iamblichus, Plato disagrees with the Stoics in that he claims that (1) there are in one sense three parts of the soul (not one for each organ) and (2) the soul's powers belong not to any individual body part (e.g., the ruling part) but in one way to the soul/body complex and in another to the soul as a whole.

In section 10, we learned that whereas both the Stoics and Peripatetics believe that the soul's powers belong solely to the composite of body and soul, Plato teaches that the powers can subsist both in the composite and in the soul itself. Thus, the powers exist "in the same substrate," i.e., either in the complex or in the separated soul itself. The difference between Plato and the Peripatetics according to Iamblichus would then be that the Peripatetics, in denying that the soul lives a life separate from the body, do not see that all of the soul's powers belong in some sense to the separated soul. Iamblichus' doctrine here is then consistent with that attributed to him by the Pseudo-Simplicius and Priscianus (see appendix) that the soul has, as it were, two essences: both a pure, separated essence and an essence that is activated when it resides in a body. Both essences are what the soul is, and any attempt to separate the two from the life of the soul is futile.

Κατὰ δὲ Πλάτωνα ἄλλως μὲν λέγεται ἡ ψυχὴ τριμερής . . . ἄλλως δὲ πολυδύναμος . . . Iamblichus introduces here and in the final sentence a distinction between part and power. Any part requires a substrate which distinguishes it from another part, which has its own substrate. Separate powers do not require separate substrates. This distinction is neither in Plato nor in Aristotle, but is part of a later tradition. (The tradition continues after Iamblichus as well. See Themistius, *In De An.* 3.7-16.) In order to discover the roots of this tradition, it will be necessary to consider a passage from Porphyry.

Porphyry has a lengthy discussion of the difference between part and power in his *Concerning the Powers of the Soul* (253F.1-122 Smith = Stobaeus I.350.8-354.18). He, like Iamblichus, states that different parts have different substrates but that different powers can subsist in the same substrate (253F.33-36: τὸ γὰρ ἑτερομερὲς εὐθὺς ὑποκειμένου παραλλαγὴν εἰσάγειν, τὸ δὲ ἑτεροδύναμον καὶ περὶ ἓν ὑποκειμένου ἐνίστασθαι). Cf. 253F. 63-76. Porphyry (253F.37-42) cites Longinus (3rd Century C.E., a pupil of Ammonius) on the matter of the tripartite vs. partless soul. Longinus, Porphyry reports, denies that the embodied soul (τὸ ζῷον) is πολυμερές but rather is ἀμερές and πολυδύναμον:

> Longinus denies that the living creature (τὸ ζῷον) has many parts (πολυμερές) but rather asserts that it has no parts (ἀμερές) but has many powers (πολυδύναμον). He says, following Plato, that the soul comes to have many parts in the body but in itself is without parts. That it does not have many parts does not mean that it also has one power, for a single thing without parts may have many powers

This is clearly a difficult tightrope to walk. Longinus implies that the embodied soul is in one sense ἀμερές (because presumably the soul itself is partless) yet becomes πολυμερές in the body (because the body has parts in which the soul's many powers reside). Compare Iamblichus' use of ἄλλως μὲν λέγεται ἡ ψυχὴ τριμερής versus ἄλλως δὲ πολυδύναμος here. Note too that Longinus denies that the soul has only a single power (μονοδύναμος), a point to which we will return shortly.

It is worth considering the rare term πολυδύναμος, which appears in both Porphyry's and Iamblichus' texts. It is preserved for the first time Porphyry's text, although Longinus may have used the term earlier. (The term also occurs in Porphyry 253F.48, where it is again opposed to πολυμερής.) The term is common in Neoplatonism after Porphyry and Iamblichus but occurs in no earlier writer. Philoponus, however, uses the term in relation to Democritus at *In De An.* 35.12 (= DK A105):

> For Democritus says that it [i.e., the soul] is without parts (ἀμερῆ) and does not have many powers (πολυδύναμον), saying that thinking is the same as perceiving and that these proceed from the same power (ἀμερῆ γάρ φησιν αὐτὴν Δημόκριτος εἶναι καὶ οὐ πολυδύναμον, ταὐτὸν εἶναι λέγων τὸ νοεῖν τῷ αἰσθάνεσθαι καὶ ἀπὸ μιᾶς ταῦτα προέρχεσθαι δυνάμεως).

But Philoponus is clearly re-stating Democritus' position about soul atoms, not giving a verbatim quotation. Since the same kinds of atoms make up the soul wherever the soul may be in the body, no part differs from another and the soul's "powers" are the same in the sense that every soul act is caused by the collision of atoms against soul atoms. For more on this fragment, see W.K.C. Guthrie, *A History of Greek Philosophy*, Vol. 2 (Cambridge 1965) 433 note 3. Compare Alexander, *In De An.* 27.4-7, where he says that Democritus thought that the soul has only a single power that seems multiple because of its various activities. Cf. 118.6-9 (= *SVF* II.823), where Alexander does not name those who believe that the soul has a single power (μία ἡ τῆς ψυχῆς δύναμις). Long and Sedley (II.178) argue that the reference is to the Stoics. What the Stoics and Atomists share is a belief that a single substance (the ruling faculty or the atomic soul-compound) have a single power but give rise to different sorts of activities. Alexander does not use the term πολυδύναμος in relation to Democritus or the Stoics, and in fact the term does not appear in Alexander's extant works.

Themistius, *In De An.* 3.14-16 (= *SVF* 2.824), uses the term πολυδύναμος and attributes it to an unnamed group of philosophers:

Some think that soul has many powers (πολυδύναμον) because it exists in a single substrate (ἐφ' ἑνὸς οὖσαν ὑποκειμένου), while others think that it has many parts (πολυμερῆ) and divide the parts by place.

Among the latter group, Themistius includes the Stoics and "perhaps" (τυχόν)[44] Plato, a reference surely to the *Timaeus* (cf. 37.4-6 and 93.33-94.2). Who would have Themistius included in the mysterious first group? Quite probably Middle Platonists such as those whom Iamblichus has in mind. Note that in Longinus', Porphyry's, and Iamblichus' interpretation, Plato fits into both positions delineated by Themistius.

It is likely therefore that the discussion of the "tripartite" *versus* "multi-powered" soul that we find in Porphyry and Iamblichus is part of the doxographic tradition on Plato and Aristotle, probably beginning in the Middle Platonic era. The "part" *versus* "power" terminology would have allowed Middle Platonists to differentiate themselves clearly from Stoics. We should now look at Porphyry's long account.

Porphyry begins his discussion of "powers" and "parts" (253F.1-122) by contrasting the Stoics, who say the soul has eight parts (on which see section 12 below), with Plato and Aristotle, who say the soul has three parts. (For Aristotle, Smith cites *EN* 1102b28-1103a1.) The mistake many philosophers make, Porphyry says, is in not realizing that this tripartite division is made for the sake of delineating the virtues (on which, see section 12, below) and is not all-inclusive since it does not take into account the imaginative, perceptive, intellective, and nutritive (253F.11-18). Indeed, Porphyry later asserts that "Aristotle denies that the soul has parts but rather powers" (τὰ μὲν μέρη παρῃτεῖτο᾿Αριστοτέλης ἐπὶ τῆς ψυχῆς, τὰς δὲ δυνάμεις οὐκέτι, 32-33). (Cf. Alexander of Aphrodisias 30.26-31.6, who argues that the soul has parts without magnitude and has many but not infinite powers.) Thus, Porphyry thinks that those who say that the soul has parts because it is a quantity (τὸ ποσόν) are wrong (77-87), whereas those like Nicolaus of Damascus (1st Century B.C.E.), who say that the parts of the soul are more like qualities, are

---

[44] R. B. Todd, in his translation of Themistius, *On Aristotle's On the Soul* (Ithaca 1996) 156 note 26 says that τυχόν must mean "indeed" since "Themistius was not uncertain about the Platonic doctrine of the alignment of capacities of the soul with organs of the body." The issue here, however, is not what Plato wrote in the *Timaeus* but what he *meant* when he wrote it. Longinus interpreted Plato so that he may apparently be attributing parts to the soul yet not actually be doing so. Themistius may be of the same mind.

closer to the truth (88-109). For Nicolaus, the "parts" of the soul are its powers housed in the body: to live, to perceive, to move, to think, to desire (100-107). The soul is itself partless but the living creature receives the imprints from the soul's activities (107-109).

> Nicolaus therefore understands "parts" of the soul as "powers" of the body that holds it (τοῦ ἔχοντος). For the living creature and the ensouled body generally (τὸ γὰρ ζῷον καὶ ὅλως τὸ ἔμψυχον) by having a soul has many powers, such as to live, to perceive, to move, to think, to desire, the cause and source of all of which is the soul. And so he posits that these powers, from which the ensouled body is said to do and suffer these things, are parts of the soul, as we have said. And since the soul is without parts, nothing prevents the body from receiving partially (μεριστῶς) those activities that are imparted from the soul (τὰς ἀπ᾽ αὐτῆς τῶν ἐνεργειῶν ἐνδόσεις, 100-109).

We can see that this theory differs from that which the tradition gave as Democritus' and the Stoics'. The soul no longer has a single power that is differentiated in its activities, but has multiple powers that are exhibited in its different activities. This is Iamblichus' opinion as well, as preserved by the Pseudo-Simplicius and Priscianus (see appendix). The body receives these multiple powers as if in parts (reason in the head, spirit in the breast, passions in the liver) but the soul is without parts. Thus, as Iamblichus says, the soul is in a sense tripartite but in a sense not.

Porphyry concludes (110-122) that the soul itself is partless but when it comes into relation with the body, it has parts along with the body (ἐν τῇ κατὰ σχέσιν ζωῇ ὑφίσταται τὰ μέρη, 116-117). He compares a seed of grain that has parts in relation to its reproduction after sowing (since the seed has in it potentially all the differentiated parts of the plant). "So too parts arise along with the partless soul in reproduction" (οὕτω καὶ ψυχῇ ἀμερίστῳ οὔσῃ ἐν τῇ σπορᾷ παρυφίσταται τὰ μέρη, 120-122). Thus, Porphyry agrees with Longinus and Nicolaus that the soul has no parts but a multitude of powers and yet can, in a sense, be said to have parts as well.

We have then a tradition that differentiates Stoics (who think that the soul has a single power that arises in different ways in different parts of the body) and a Middle Platonic interpretation of Plato (that the soul has many powers but no parts except as parts are expressed in a bodily substrate). There is also a distinction made between parts and powers on the basis of the underlying substrate: parts are distinguished by substrates; powers are not. Finally, although it is not in Porphyry, there is a distinction to be drawn between Stoics and

Atomists (who think that there is a single power in the soul) and others (who think that there are multiple powers).

Iamblichus makes use of this tradition, but adds to it as well. He differentiates the Platonic position not only from the Stoic but also from the Peripatetic. He criticizes Stoics and Peripatetics for saying that the soul exists only in a bodily substrate. Iamblichus brings to bear the doctrine of the soul's double life on the Middle Platonic position and argues that the soul is tripartite when it lives its bodily life but has many powers even when it lives its separated life. Thus the soul is without parts in its essence. Like Longinus and Nicolaus, Iamblichus has found a way to assert that the soul is both tripartite and partless. Finally, Iamblichus argues that Plato and Aristotle share the same conception of the soul.

12

Iamblichus now discusses the multiplicity of the soul's powers, again contrasting the Stoics with Plato. The distinction just made at the end of section 11, between parts and powers, continues here.

Οἱ ἀπὸ Ζήνωνος . . . On the Stoic eight parts of the soul, see *SVF* I.143, II. 827, 828, 830, 832, 836, 879. These are the five senses, the generative element, voice, and the ruling element itself. Porphyry, in the long passage on the soul's "parts" and "powers" (253F Smith, cited above in section 11) lists the soul's eight powers (ὀκταμερῆ, 5-11 = SVF II. 830).

περὶ τὰς δυνάμεις εἶναι πλείονας . . . The text is corrupt here. Festugière suggests περι<νοοῦντες>: "cependant qu'ils présument avec subtilité que les puissances sont plus nombreuses encore" (194). Although ingenious, this reading requires a substantial change that is not easy to justify. Festugière is following Usener's suggestion that διαδοξάζουσι take a participle here. Iamblichus, however, uses the verb with an object (as he does here) both at *Myst.* 4.6: *190.3* and (in the middle voice) at 8.5: *268.14*.

It seems most likely, therefore, that some word or words have dropped out after περὶ and that the missing object of περὶ is μέρη or a word referring to μέρη. Possible readings (*exempli gratia*) for this sentence include (a) περὶ <δὲ τὰ μέρη>, "and connected with the parts are a multiplicity of powers" or, more simply, (b) περὶ <ἣν>, "and connected with which [eight-part soul] are a multiplicity of powers" (the emendation of Wachsmuth, which we accept). At any rate, the sense is that each of the eight parts of the soul has many powers.

In *SVF* 2.879, lines 28-37, Calcidius preserves the Stoic belief in the eight parts of the soul; these parts flow from the heart (the seat of the ruling element) to the various bodily parts and "fill [the body] with vital breath [= πνεῦμα] and rule and control it with various innumerable powers (*innumerabilibus diversisque virtutibus*)." Thus, in this passage from Calcidius, the parts have various powers. Iamblichus is preserving a similar doctrine: there are eight parts of the soul embracing several powers, as e.g., the ruling element (being one part) has four powers.

Οἱ δὲ περὶ Πλάτωνα καὶ ᾿Αρχύτας καὶ οἱ λοιποὶ Πυθαγόρειοι . . . This time Plato is joined by Archytas and the Pythagoreans generally. It is no surprise that Plato is in harmony with Pythagoreans. Iamblichus' respect for Archytas (surely a late Hellenistic forgery attributed to Archytas) is plain in his commentary on the *Categories*, where Archytas is posited as a source for Aristotle.

The doctrine of the tripartite division of the soul is Platonic. There is no extant evidence that Archytas (or even Pseudo-Archytas) proposed a tripartite soul. There is, however, an intriguing text of the Pythagorean Aesarus of Lucania, "On the Nature of Man" *apud* Stob. 1.355.1-357.22, which does present the doctrine. His name may be Aresas, if the Pythagorean from Lucania mentioned by Iamblichus in *The Pythagorean Way of Life* (section 266) is the same Pythagorean philosopher, as seems likely.[45]

Both Wachsmuth and Festugière compare Porphyry, "On the Powers of the Soul," Fr. 253F.11-18 Smith (= Stobaeus 350.19-25). Like Iamblichus here, Porphyry asserts that Plato's division of the soul into three parts is "for the sake of the virtues" (ἕνεκα τῶν ἀρετῶν, 14-15) and should not be taken as implying that the soul is truly tripartite, "for the imaginative, perceptive, intellectual, and nutritive [parts] are not included in this division" (τὸ γὰρ φανταστικὸν καὶ αἰσθητικὸν καὶ τὸ νοερὸν καὶ <τὸ> φυτικὸν οὐ δήπου ἐν τῇ διαιρέσει ταύτῃ περιληφθήσεται, 15-18). Porphyry, however,

---

[45] Thesleff (48-50) accepts the identification, following Heeren.

refers not to Plato and Archytas but to Plato and Aristotle in the *Nicomachean Ethics*. This is probably a reference to *EN* 1.13, as Smith suggests (page 272). Iamblichus, who puts Aristotle firmly into the camp of those who say that the soul is incomposite in its essence (section 10, above), would have agreed with Porphyry in this instance. In the final sentence of this section, Iamblichus will add the desiderative power to Porphyry's list.

Ἀριστοτέλης δὲ εἰς πέντε αὐτὰς διαιρεῖ . . . See *De Anima* 414a29-32. Aristotle is not consistent. At 413a23-25 he lists intellect, perception, locomotion and rest, growth and decay; at 413b11-13, nourishment, perception, thought, motion; 432a22-b7, nutrition, perception, imagination, desire, and reason; at 433b1-5, nutrition, perception, intellection, deliberation, and desire.

13

This section on the irrational powers of the soul is divided into two parts. In the first paragraph, Iamblichus discusses to what the powers belong: the soul itself or the composite of soul and body. In the second paragraph the subject is the continued existence of these irrational powers. If the powers belong to the composite, what becomes of them when the soul returns to its disembodied state?

Πλωτῖνος αὐτῆς ἀφαιρεῖ τὰς ἀλόγους δυνάμεις . . . As is often the case, Iamblichus oversimplifies Plotinus' position. His statements do accord well with *Enn.* 1.1, however. In 1.1.2, Plotinus states that the soul is "a kind of form" (εἶδός τι); it has συμφυὴς ἐνέργεια of its own (lines 6-9). "For it is what it is always. And it does not perceive nor is there any discursive reasoning or opinion attached to it (lines 25-26)." See also *Enn.* 4.3.18, where the soul on departing the body does not use practical reasoning but a kind of reasoning closely connected with intellect; 4.4.1-7, where the separated soul does not have memory of the lower realm (but see 4.3.26-32, where Plotinus suggests a higher and lower division of imagination to go with a similar division of memories in the soul); and 1.1.7, where sensation does not belong to soul *per se.*

Οἱ δὲ περὶ Δημόκριτον Πλατωνικοὶ . . . Democritus the Platonist is an obscure and interesting figure. Longinus (*apud* Porphyry, *Vit. Plot.*

20.31 and 60) mentions him as a philosopher who wrote doxographical treatises. We know some of his doctrines from Proclus, *In
Tim.* 2.33.13ff. and Damascius, *In Phaed.* 1.503.3. Olympiodorus tells
us (*In Alc.* 70) that he wrote a commentary on that dialogue, and
from the allusions in Damascius we know that he wrote one on the
Phaedo. See L. Brisson's entry "Démocritos" in *Dictionnaire des
Philosophes Antiques* 2.7167. Here Iamblichus attributes to him the
doctrine that all the irrational powers (and indeed all the psychic
powers, rational and irrational) belong to the soul itself — a doctrine
extreme from the Neoplatonic point of view but perhaps not so
strange from a Middle Platonic one.

Ὁ δὲ Πλάτων καὶ αὐτὰς ἑαυτῶν ποιεῖ καὶ τῶν ζῴων . . . Iamblichus
again gives the distinction between the soul in itself and the soul in
the body: τῶν ζῴων i.e., the composite living being made up of soul
and body. See above, section 10. For Plato, according to Iamblichus,
some irrational powers are appropriate to the soul itself and others to
the composite of soul and body; each group or cluster (ἑκάτερον,
neuter) of powers can be distinguished according to whether it
belongs to the essence of the soul or to the composite of soul and
body. This is clearly Iamblichus' position as well, as we shall see. We
preserve the MSS. reading of καθ' ἑτέραν ἑτέραν, with Festugière.

Οἱ δὲ περὶ Πορφύριον καὶ Πλωτῖνον . . . According to Iamblichus,
both Plotinus and Porphyry believed that the powers were dispersed
into the universe from which they came. Iamblichus seems to
compare this theory to plants, but the exact meaning of the clause is
difficult to determine. Festugière (195-196 note 7), following
Léveque, takes σπέρμα ("seed") as a "reason principle" deriving from
the World Soul. The problem with this view is not so much that it
limits the meaning of "soul," which in this paragraph refers to
individual human souls with their irrational elements, as that it is an
unusual meaning for σπέρμα. Iamblichus may be comparing human
souls to the World Soul, of course, but the more natural meaning of
σπέρμα is "seed." If this were the case Iamblichus would be
comparing the human soul to a plant seed. But what then is the
meaning of "when the seed withdraws into itself?" Plants grow out of
seeds, but we do not think of seeds as withdrawing. Iamblichus may
be thinking of σπέρμα as a kind of perennial bulb, like a tulip bulb.
(Porphyry, *Sent.* 37.16-19, seems to use σπέρμα in this sense as well.)

The bulb is like the soul-in-itself; the tulip plant and flower like the irrational powers. As a bulb sends out the plant, so the soul "projects" its powers. When the bulb "withdraws into itself," i.e., when the source of life leaves the plant but remains in the bulb (over the winter), the plant withers, dies, and disappears. Like the powers it is dissolved and ceases to exist, but the bulb continues to exist and will put out leaves again.

εἶναι δὲ καὶ ταύτας ἐν τῷ παντί . . . The second sentence of this paragraph presents Iamblichus' own view. (For the use of the optative in a similar way, see introduction and section 9.) The Greek demonstrative (ταύτας) without a noun refers to the "irrational powers," the subject of this section. (Festugière [196] translates as "ces vies," which is also possible.) Iamblichus believes that the irrational powers continue to exist, preserved in the universe. See below, section 37. A similar view is presented in *In Tim.* Fr. 81. (Proclus, *In Tim.* 3.234.18 and following, presents a similar view of Porphyry to that given here by Iamblichus.) For Iamblichus the irrational soul itself (conceived of as psychic "powers" or "faculties") together with the soul's ethereal vehicle continues to exist separately from the rational soul when the soul ascends to the intelligible. See further, Dillon (1973) 371-377 and Finamore (1985) 11-27 and 144-155.

The sections on the soul's powers in general end here. From sections 10 through 13, Iamblichus asserts that the soul is a single and incomposite essence that undergoes a change of life when it enters the body. Nevertheless, the powers, rational and irrational, are present, albeit in different ways, to both the disembodied and embodied soul. These powers, which include imagination, perception, opinion, discursive thought, desire, and intellection, survive death.

There is a further complication that is not discussed in the surviving fragments and that indicates that Stobaeus has edited Iamblichus' text sharply. Iamblichus, like Numenius (Fr. 44), believed not that the soul had two parts (rational and irrational) but that there were two souls. In *De Myst.* 8.6 (269.1-12), Iamblichus records the doctrine of the Egyptians that there are two souls in human beings: one from the Intelligible Realm (equivalent to that created by the Demiurge in Plato's *Timaeus*) and another received from the circuit of the heavens (equivalent to that created by the younger gods). From Iamblichus, *In Tim.* Fr. 81 and Damascius, *In Phaed.* 1.177, as well as from the *De*

Anima, we learn that Iamblichus thought that this irrational soul was immortal. Iamblichus must think, therefore, that the rational soul itself has irrational powers that it activates through the irrational soul when embodied. This would be in keeping with the testimony of the Pseudo-Simplicius (see passage D in the appendix): "It is reasonable then, or rather, necessary that not the soul's activity alone but also its essence and the highest part itself — of *our* soul, I mean — is somehow crippled and slackened and as it were sinks down in the inclination toward what is secondary." There is therefore an innate weakness even in the pure rational soul that gives rise to the irrational powers that we see actualized in human behavior. This, it would seem, is in keeping with the *Phaedrus* myth, where the disembodied soul slips and falls.

14

This section has been transposed from Stobaeus 3.608.25-609.3 to this place by Festugière (196-197 note 4). As he points out, this section and the next (on Intellect) would form part of Iamblichus' discussion of each faculty of the soul. Stobaeus has not included the examination of the other powers in his anthology. The definition of "memory" given here is based on Aristotle, *de Mem.* 451a14: "the possession of an image as of an icon of which it is an image;" and Iamblichus' definition is found in Porphyry as well (*On the Powers of the Soul* Fr. 255 Smith = Stobaeus 3.605.12). Memory is said to be proper to the soul but not an essential part of it. Iamblichus seems to be following Aristotle's thesis that memory is in part bodily because it requires an image, which is a secondary "motion" of perception, itself partly a bodily faculty.

15

This passage was transferred from 317.20-318.15 by Festugière. It continues Iamblichus' examination of various powers of the soul.

οἱ μὲν Στωικοὶ λέγουσι μὴ εὐθὺς ἐμφύεσθαι τὸν λόγον . . . For the Stoic doctrine, see *SVF* 2.841 and 471a. Galen (2. 841) quotes Chrysippus: "Reason is a collection (ἄθροισμα) of concepts and preconceptions (τῶν ἐννοιῶν καὶ προλήψεων)." Cp. 3.181. Iamblichus uses the verb συναθροίζειν, which is a Platonic compound; cf., e.g., *Tim.* 44d7. On reason occurring at age 14, see 1.149, 2.83 and 764, and 3.17.

Οἱ δ' ἀπὸ Πλάτωνος καὶ Πυθαγόρου . . . For the doctrine, see Plato *Tim.* 43d-44a and Proclus, *In Tim.* 3.348.6-21. Proclus (348.19) claims that reason remains dormant (ἡσυχάζειν) in foolish adults as well, repeating Iamblichus' use of the verb here. It is possible that Proclus is paraphrasing Iamblichus' commentary in this section of his *Timaeus* commentary. It is not clear what Iamblichus has in mind here in the *De Anima* when he refers to Pythagoras. "Timaeus Locrus" omits this from his summary of the *Timaeus*, cf. 4.99d-100a.

Ἤδη τοίνυν περὶ τοῦ νοῦ πολλοὶ μὲν Περιπατητικοὶ . . . Iamblichus here refers to the Aristotelian doctrine of *De An.* 3.5, on the active and passive intellect. Aristotle calls the former "separate" (χωριστός) at 439a17 and "external" (θύραθεν) at *de gen. et cor.* 736b28. Under the interpretation given here, the passive intellect is (one might say) inherited genetically whereas the active intellect derives from higher sources. It is unclear when the former comes into play in human life, but the active intellect is described as existing *in potentia* until such time (much later in life) when it can become actualized. In this, it seems similar to the Platonic view of reason, given above. Again, the use of the plural ("Peripatetics") suggests that this is not Iamblichus' interpretation of *De An.* 3.5 but that of Peripatetic writers after Aristotle. In fact, Iamblichus may well be familiar with Alexander of Aphrodisias' commentary on the *De Anima*, 80.16-81.22, where this subject is discussed. A distinction like Iamblichus' is made between the "practical" and "theoretical" *nous.* Cf. especially 81.13-15: "Humans come into being not preserving this latter capacity (sc. νοῦς θεωρητικός) from the outset, but with the potentiality and capacity for receiving it, only acquiring it itself later."

Πολλοὶ δὲ αὐτῶν τῶν Πλατωνικῶν . . . This sentence is odd in two ways. First, the first half clearly continues the topic of the previous sentence (when the intellect enters the body), whereas the second half is on a second topic (the differentiation of soul from intellect). Second, the latter half of the sentence has no main verb but is instead in indirect statement with the accusative + infinitive construction. Ostensibly, the construction is based upon the main verb of the first half, συνεισάγουσιν ("introduce"), but this is an unusual verb to take indirect statement in this meaning (unless we assume some sort of zeugma). It is possible then that something has dropped out here or that Stobaeus has purposely condensed the material at this point. Most probably, however, this is an example of Iamblichus' writing style. The question of the interrelationship of soul and intellect is of great importance to him in this work, and he slips in a reference to it here although it is not strictly relevant to the discussion at hand. Possibly, in the next sentence, Iamblichus would have given his own view of the intellect's incorporation and, along with it, a further explanation of the intellect's superiority to other parts of the soul.

Iamblichus first raised the question of the soul's relation to intellect above in sections 6 and 7 (365.5-366.11 W). See also Festugière 199 note 1, Finamore (1985) 21-22, and Steel 24-5. Among those Platonists who did not differentiate soul from intellect he included Numenius, and to some degree Plotinus, Amelius, and Porphyry. He will raise the issue again in sections 17-18 (372.4-22 W) and 39 (454.18-20 W).

16

Iamblichus now turns from the soul's powers (δυνάμεις) to its activities (ἐνέργειαι). The distinction is Aristotelian. Each soul has the potentiality to act, e.g., (in the case of animals) to perceive. This power is actualized when the perceptive organ is actually perceiving something. For the distinction, see Aristotle's *De Anima* 415a14-22. For the doctrine as it pertains to sensation, see *De An.* 2.5.

The issue for Iamblichus concerns the activities of the soul *qua* soul (e.g., intellection) and the activities that involve body as well as soul (e.g., sensation). Iamblichus considers three views: those of the Peripatetics, Plato, and materialists like the Stoics. As is to be expected, Iamblichus inclines toward the views of the divine Plato.

Τίς οὖν ἀνήκοός ἐστι τῆς Περιπατητικῆς δόξης . . . With this slightly rhetorical flourish, Iamblichus begins with an investigation of a Peripatetic interpretation of Aristotle with which he does not agree. Here again the doctrine should be understood not as Aristotle's but as that of later Peripatetics who "misunderstood" Aristotle's "true" doctrine, even though Aristotle (*De An* 405b30-b25) does argue against the position that the soul moves itself. See also Festugière

(200 note1) who cites Aristotle, *De An.* 406b24-25 and 433a9-10, for Aristotle's view that the soul does not move the body by a physical motion but by the faculty of (rational) desire and intellection (προαίρεσις or ὄρεξις and νοῦς). To these two passages should be added 3.10-11, esp. 434a16-21: "the epistemic faculty (τὸ δ' ἐπιστη-μονικὸν = νοῦς) is not moved but remains at rest." This introduces the so-called "practical syllogism." The major (universal) premise (recognized by intellect) combines with the minor premise (recognized by the desiderative element) to produce action. Thus, it may be inferred that the intellect is the unmoved mover and desire the moved mover.

Alexander of Aphrodisias, *In De An.* 21.22-24.17, argues that the soul, as the form of the body, would be immovable in itself (εἴη δ' ἂν καὶ ἀκίνητος καθ' αὑτήν, 21.4-5). He compares the soul to heaviness, which causes bodies to move downward but does not itself move (22.7-10 and 23.29-24.1). Further the soul would seem to operate best when at rest, for that state is more like intellectual thought (22.23-23.5). It is probably Peripatetics like him that Iamblichus has in mind here.

Εἰ δὴ καὶ ἀνενέργητόν ἐστι τὸ ἀκίνητον . . . This is the first of two criticisms of the Peripatetic doctrine (which is itself a misunderstanding of Aristotle's true doctrine, as Iamblichus sees it). Iamblichus first argues that, according to this theory, for anything to be unmoved it must be inactive, but nothing inactive can originate activity. This is not a problem for Aristotle, however, for whom the unmoved soul is in activity.

The term ἀνενέργητος is of late coinage. It is found in Plotinus and Proclus, as well as in Alexander of Aphrodisias (*In De An.* 39.8).

The phrase "the inactive element of the soul" translates τὸ τῆς ψυχῆς ἀνενέργητον. In this construction that utilizes the neuter article plus the neuter adjective, there is no expressed noun. The idea seems to be "whatever aspect of the soul (whether all of it or a part of it) that is inactive." This inactive soul or aspect of soul, Iamblichus argues, cannot be the cause of activity.

Εἰ δ' ὡς ἔνιοι λέγουσι . . . This is the second half of Iamblichus' disjunctive criticism: either the intellect is unmoved and thus inactive (in which case it governs none of our activities) or the intellect is unmoved but active (in which case it governs all of our activities).

The point of the first disjunct is that only something in activity can control human actions; the second shows that if it is intellect, intellect would control all actions, not only human but animal as well. For Iamblichus, the problem is that many human actions involve the body; the intellect should not be in control of such lowly activities.

Αὕτη τοίνυν κατά γε Πλάτωνα . . . Iamblichus now contrasts Plato's doctrine with that of the Peripatetics. There is no noun expressed with the feminine demonstrative (αὕτη), but its antecedent is the immediately preceding word, ἀπεργασία. Iamblichus' point is that whatever acts are accomplished by the composite of body and soul together are not identical to the intellect ("the congenital essence and life of the soul"). For Iamblichus' view that individual embodied human souls are not identical with their acts, see section 19, below.

Δῆλον γὰρ ὅτι δίδοται μὲν εἰς τὸ κοινόν . . . This κοινόν is "the common living being that possesses the soul and is conceived as existing along with the body" (section 10, 368.2-3 W). See the notes to section 10, above.

Καὶ τούτων τὰ μὲν ἀπὸ τῆς ψυχῆς προκατάρχοντα . . . The Greek participle, προκατάρχοντα, is a Stoic term. Causes are προκαταρκτικά in the sense that they are the immediate or primary source of the effect, as beauty of unbridled passion (*SVF* 2.119). Iamblichus uses the verb in *De Myst.* 1.7 (21.8). There he contrasts the visible gods with purified human souls. The gods "arise first as the cause of all things" (αἴτιον προκατάρχει πάντων), whereas the souls are dependent in turn upon the gods (21.7-10). Below (22.1-8), Iamblichus contrasts them by their relation to Intellect. The gods possess it purely, but souls participate in a partial intellect. The point is that the soul is cause secondarily after the gods and acts appropriately when it acts through them as its primary cause. Here in the *De Anima*, it is the discarnate soul that is the primary cause. It is the only cause of the motions of the disembodied soul and the primary (προκαταρκτικόν) cause of the other motions.

Ὥσπερ δὴ καὶ τῆς κατὰ τὴν ναῦν φορᾶς . . . There are three problematic text readings in this sentence. First, in the phrase "the soul itself makes use of the whole body," the word for "whole" is given in the dative feminine (ὅλῃ) by F and in the nominative feminine (ὅλη) by P. The reading adopted here (dative masculine, ὅλῳ) is Canter's suggestion, followed by Wachsmuth and Festugière. F's reading is untenable. If P's is accepted, the phrase becomes "the whole soul itself makes use of the body" or, possibly, "every soul makes use of the body." But there is a further difficulty that suggests that the passage is irredeemably corrupt. Although F gives the word "itself" (αὐτή), P gives αὐτῆ, which yields no good sense but suggests the dative (αὐτῇ), which in turn would match F's reading of the feminine dative. Finally, if the whole phrase ΑΥΤΗΤΕΟΛΗ is irremediable, it could be a copyist's error for another word, such as αὐτοτελής ("perfect"). There is no "true" solution, but in the end whichever reading is adopted the sense is unchanged. Iamblichus' point is that the soul uses the body as an instrument. Cf. Proclus, *ET.* 196: πᾶσα ψυχὴ μεθεκτὴ σώματι χρῆται πρώτῳ ἀιδίῳ, where the body is the immortal vehicle, instead of the corporeal body as here.

For the clause "souls separated from the composite living being," the MSS. have τὸ σύνθετον ζῷον ἀπολλυόμεναι ("being destroyed as to their composite life"), which makes little sense. We read, with Festugière (201 note 5), Heeren's suggestion: τοῦ συνθέτου ζῴου ἀπολυόμεναι. Wachsmuth gives τοῦ συνθέτου ζῴου ἀπολελυμέναι, which carries the same meaning. We take the feminine plural to refer collectively to "souls."

Heeren bracketed the words αὐταὶ καθ' αὐτὰς ἀπόλυτοι ("[souls] free in themselves"), while Wachsmuth, followed by Festugière, bracketed ἀπόλυτοι ("freed"). The word ἀπόλυτοι is redundant after ἀπολυόμεναι, but that is not enough to condemn it. Iamblichus is not above repetition for the sake of emphasis. Festugière suggests ἀκώλυτοι, "sans empechement, librement," but the substitution is unnecessary.

Iamblichus here concludes his argument against the Peripatetics, in which he integrates arguments from Plato. In the end, the motive principle of the soul is not simply intellect. Rather, when the soul moves the body, it is like a helmsman and the wind moving a ship. The soul uses the body as its instrument. There are other secondary (necessary) causes as well, but the soul is the primary mover. (Iamblichus does not here seem to distinguish the two types of cause represented by wind and helmsman, unless perhaps the wind represents an external intellect.) When the soul moves the body it is not acting *qua* soul alone but *qua* composite. When the body is not involved, soul qua soul is the motive principle.

Οὐ μὴν ἔτι γε τούτοις συγχωροῦσιν οἱ σῶμα τὴν ψυχὴν ὑπολαμβάνοντες
. . . The triple list is reprised from section 9 (367.4-9 W), which
concerned those who considered the soul to be corporeal. There the
Stoics thought the soul to be "that which is combined with bodies"
(τὸ συγκεκραμένον τοῖς σώμασιν, 367,4-5 W); an unnamed person or
persons (in the present passage, natural philosophers) thinks soul is
"that which is mixed together with the principle of growth" (τὸ τῇ
φύσει συμμεμιγμένον, 367.6 W); and Dicaearchus thinks it "a property
of the body of being ensouled, which is not present to the soul itself
as if it belonged to the soul" (τὸ τοῦ σώματος ὂν ὥσπερ τὸ
ἐμψυχοῦσθαι αὐτῇ δὲ μὴ παρὸν τῇ ψυχῇ ὥσπερ ὑπάρχον, 367.6-9 W).
See our notes to section 9, above.

ἐν ἁρμονίας εἴδει οὖσαν . . . This is a verbatim quotation from Plato's
Phaedo 91d1-2. Socrates is summarizing the previous argument of
Simmias: "For Simmias, I believe, distrusts and fears that the soul,
although it is more divine and more beautiful than the body, will
perish before it since the soul is some sort of attunement (ἐν
ἁρμονίας εἴδει οὖσα)." One suspects that Iamblichus is purposely
putting Dicaearchus into the position of the foolish Simmias, whose
opinion on the soul was easily dismissed by Socrates (91d-92e).

17

Πότερον οὖν πασῶν τῶν ψυχῶν τὰ αὐτὰ ἔργα. . . We turn now from the
activities (*energeiai*) of souls to the consideration of their acts (*erga*).
What distinction, one might well ask, is Iamblichus seeking to make
here? From the previous section, we can see that *erga*, or *energêmata*,
may be regarded as the practical manifestations of *energeiai*, but, as
Festugière points out *ad loc.*, Iamblichus is not in fact intending to
make any strong distinction between *energeiai* and *erga* (this has, if
anything, been foisted on him by Stobaeus). What he is concerned
with in this section, instead, is a series of three problems relative to
the acts or activities of souls: (1) whether the acts of all types of soul
are the same (372, 4-22); (2) whether the soul is to be distinguished
from its acts (372, 23-374, 20); (3) the relations between the
irrational and the rational powers of the soul — with a digression on
the origin of evil in the soul (374, 21-375, 28).

(1) The alternative to the position that all souls perform essentially the same *erga* is that those of universal souls are more 'perfect' (*teleôtera*), while the nature of those of 'the rest' — that is to say, souls attached to various levels of individual body, from the heavenly to the various types of earthly, perform acts corresponding to their station and dignity. But what is to be understood by 'universal souls'? By *hai holai psykhai* here Iamblichus presumably means souls still attached directly to the universal Soul (*hê holê psykhê*), since there can only, strictly speaking, be one of these. Such souls, however, are more properly described as *holikai* (as, e,g,, at Procl. *In Tim.* 1.380.26, opp. *merikai*). This has to be a different distinction from that presented by Proclus, e.g. at *ET* props. 184-5, between 'divine' (*theiai*) souls and the rest, since divine souls include even those of the planets and the fixed stars, and these are distinguished from *holai psykhai* just below.

Starting with the Stoics (who are presented here simply as foils), Iamblichus launches into another critique of his immediate predecessors. The Stoics, of course, regard all souls as essentially one, being all "sparks" of the one fiery Logos (e.g.*SVF* 2. 633), and therefore they would not postulate different types of act for different levels of soul — though Iamblichus, in fact, speaks here rather of an identity of *logos,* intellection (*dianoêsis*), right actions (*katorthômata*), and virtues (*aretai*). They serve, then, as one end of a spectrum of positions, of which Iamblichus himself is the other pole. At various points between them are ranged Plotinus, Amelius, and Porphyry.

Plotinus and Amelius are presented as being nearest in doctrine to the Stoics, "on occasion defining the individual soul as being no[46] different to the universal, but as being one with it." How far this is a distortion of Amelius' position we are hardly in a position to judge[47], but as regards Plotinus it seems a gross oversimplification. Nonetheless, as Festugière notes *ad loc.,* some justification for it might be found in Plotinus' remarks at *Enn.* 4. 3, 4, 14ff., in the course of the enquiry with which he begins his great essay *On Problems about the Soul,* where, for the first eight chapters, he entertains the hypothesis that all souls are, in some sense or other, one. In the passage referred to here by Festugière, he advances the following suggestion, in response to the difficulty raised as to how all soul can be one, when some soul transcends body, and other soul is divided among bodies:

---

[46]   Accepting the necessity of Usener's insertion of οὐχ before ὡς.

[47]   On the doctrine of Amelius on the soul, see, however, Luc Brisson, 'Amélius: sa vie, son oeuvre, sa doctrine, son style', in *ANRW* II: 36. 2, 836-47.

> . . . unless, of course, one made the one stand by itself without falling into body, and then said that all the souls, the soul of the All and the others, came from that one, living together with each other, so to speak, down to a certain level and being one soul by belonging to no particular thing; and that, being fastened (sc. to the one) by their edges on their upper side, they strike down this way and that, like the light which, just when it reaches the earth, divides itself among houses and is not divided, but is one none the less. (trans. Armstrong)

Plotinus then goes on in fact (ll. 26ff.) to introduce the striking image of the lower aspect of the soul of the All as the soul of a great plant, while the lower aspect of our souls may be compared to maggots in a rotten part of the plant, and the higher (self-conscious) part to a gardener concerned about the maggots in the plant. All this betokens a much more nuanced and sophisticated view of the relations between the All-Soul and the individual soul than Iamblichus is giving him credit for here. It is true, however, to say that, basically, Plotinus does wish to maintain the unity of all soul, at least against any theory that wishes to drive an ontological wedge between the All-Soul and individual souls, and to that extent Iamblichus is justified. This tendency manifests itself much more pronouncedly in such early treatises as 4.2 and 4.9. On this see H. J. Blumenthal, "Soul, world-soul, and individual soul in Plotinus," in *Le Néoplatonisme, Colloque internationaux du CNRS,* Paris, 1971, 55-63 (reprinted in his collected essays, *Soul and Intellect,* Variorum: Aldershot, 1993).

Porphyry, on the other hand, Iamblichus wishes to distinguish quite sharply from his master and senior colleague, as declaring that the activities (*energêmata*) of the All-Soul are "totally distinct" (*pantê kekhôristai*) from those of individual souls. Once again, Iamblichus seems to us to be exaggerating and over-simplifying, but we have to recognise the limitations of our evidence. The two works of Porphyry on the soul of which we have fragments, the treatise *On the Soul: Against Boethus,* and that *On the Faculties of the Soul,* contain nothing in their surviving portions relevant to the topic, the former being concerned rather with arguments for the immaterality and immortality of the soul, and the latter with the faculties (*dynameis*) of the soul in the body. Our most relevant surviving passage is actually section 37 of the *Sententiae,* the beginning of which runs as follows:

> One should not think that it is by reason of the multiplicity of bodies that the multiplicity of souls comes about, but rather that it is prior to

bodies that they are both many and one, with the single universal soul not preventing the existence of many souls within it, and the many not effecting a partition of the single soul between them. For they distinguish themselves without cutting themselves off, nor fragmenting the universal soul into themselves, and they are present to each other without confusion, nor by making the universal a mere conglomeration; for they are not divided from one another by boundaries, nor, again, are they blended with one another, even as the many items of knowledge are not blended together in a single soul, and, again, are not merely juxtaposed in the soul like bodies, maintaining a distinction of substance, but they are qualitatively distinct activities (*poiai energeiai*) of the soul."

This, it must be said, is itself largely a paraphrase of Plotinus, *Enn.* 6.4.4.37ff., which chapter is a good statement of Plotinus' own position, but Porphyry does go on to expand on it, and is certainly adopting this position as his own. Porphyry does here, and further on in the *Sentences,* assert the distinctness of Soul as a whole from the many individual souls, in the sense that it is not just the sum-total of them, nor is it dispersed into them, but the overall thrust of the passage does seem to be the assertion of the unity of all soul, even as is that of *Enn.* 6.4.4. On the whole, it seems best to admit that we do not have the evidence, if any, on which Iamblichus is basing his claim.

18

Γένοιτο δὲ κἂν ἄλλη δόξα οὐκ ἀπόβλητος . . . At any rate, he now turns to the presentation of his own position (introduced in the usual modest and devious way), which is certainly a much more highly articulated one than that which he attributes to his predecessors. He proposes, as in the *De Mysteriis,* to make a distinction between pure or transcendent souls (here again termed *holai psykhai*), on the one hand, and then in turn the souls of the heavenly gods (*theiai*), daemons, heroes, and finally mortals, both men and irrational animals. We may compare his position here with, on the one hand, that expressed in the *De Mysteriis,* 1.5-7, where the distinctions between gods, daemons, heroes and souls proper are set out, and that expressed by Proclus in his *Commentary on the Timaeus* (3.245.19-246.4 Diehl), a passage very plausibly identified by Festugière (n. *ad loc.*) as being of Iamblichean inspiration (it leads up to *in Tim.* Fr. 82 Dillon):

We will not, then, accept the view of those more recent authorities who declare our soul to be 'of equal worth' (*isaxios*) with the divine, or 'of one substance' (*homoousios*) with it, or however they care to express it;[48] for let them hearken to Plato, when he talks of "seconds and thirds" (*Tim.* 41D), and when he separates off the particular (*merikai*) souls from the mixing-bowl, and represents them as being produced by the Demiurge on foot of a secondary level of intellection[49] — which is the same as to say a more particular level of intellection; for someone who says this is postulating essential differences between types of soul, not just differences of activity, as is the view of the divine Plotinus. For let it be accepted that the one class look to universal intellects, while the others do so to particular ones, and the former employ unadulterated (*akhrantoi*) intellections, while the latter turn away periodically from true being; and the former are always engaged in the construction and ordering of the universe, while the latter (only) sometimes journey about with the gods[50]; and the former are always moving and directing fate, while the latter sometimes come under the power of fate and 'the laws of fate' (41E); and the former lead towards the intelligible, while the latter are allotted the rank of followers; and the former are divine only, while the latter are transferred from time to time into different orders of being, daemonic, heroic, or mortal . . .

This is Proclus talking, but he is pretty certainly here relaying the views of Iamblichus. Some pages further on, at 247.16-25, the views of Iamblichus himself are quoted (= Fr. 82 Dillon), making it clear that he wished to postulate clear distinctions between the different levels of soul:

According to the divine Iamblichus, the mixing-bowl is single,[51] a certain life-giving cause that comprehends all life and gathers it together, sustaining itself by means of demiurgic reason-principles, which penetrate through all life and through all soul-orders, and which allot to each soul within its proper sphere appropriate measures of coherence, to the souls of the original mixture (sc. divine souls) primal measures because of their being the first to be mixed, and to those mixed in the second session secondary measures; for according as is their rank relative to each other, such is the procession from the mixing-bowl which they are allotted, receiving thence the defining bounds of their life.

---

[48] We may note that Iamblichus in fact employs both these adjectives in criticising Porphyry's position in *De Myst.* 3.21.

[49] We take this to be the meaning of κατὰ δευτέραν νόησιν, this being an interpretation of what the Demiurge is described as doing in 41d.

[50] A reference to the myth of the *Phaedrus* 248a.

[51] The Middle Platonist Atticus had, oddly, decided that there were actually two mixing-bowls (247, 12-14).

Iamblichus thus finds in Plato's rather cryptic reference to "seconds and thirds" at 41d support for his doctrine of *essential* differences between various levels of soul, and *a fortiori* differences in their acts.

19

Οἱ μὲν γάρ ... The differentiation from his predecessors is continued in the next section. Plotinus' views we have considered, but on Amelius more might be said. Iamblichus here characterizes him as going beyond Plotinus in a rash assertion[52] of the actual numerical identity of all souls. Some further light may be thrown on this allegation by another passage from the same part of Proclus' *Timaeus* commentary (3.246.23-28), which overtly concerns, not Amelius, but Theodorus of Asine. Theodorus, however, in many respects seems to have taken over the doctrinal positions of Amelius,[53] and this would seem to be one of those cases. At any rate, Proclus makes the same accusation against Theodorus as Iamblichus makes against Amelius:[54]

> This, then (sc. the continuation of the passage quoted above), is directed against those who consider our soul to be of one substance (*homoousios*) with that of the universe and with all others, and that we are all things without qualification (*askhetôs*), planets and fixed stars and everything else, even as those too are, as is the view of Theodorus of Asine; for such presumptuous talk (*megalorrhêmosynê*) is far removed from the doctrine of Plato.

Here we may suspect that Proclus is simply substituting Theodorus for Amelius, since he is the most recent (post-Iamblichean) exponent of such a doctrine, and this helps to disguise the fact that Proclus is taking over this whole passage from Iamblichus' commentary. At all

---

[52] The verb νεανιεύεται here has a sarcastic ring. It is probably borrowed from Plato's *Gorgias* 482c4.

[53] Cf. Werner Deuse, *Theodoros von Asine: Sammlung der Testimonien und Kommentar*, Wiesbaden, 1973, 12-13.

[54] For other passages where Proclus seems to be taking over a criticism of Amelius by Iamblichus, and transferring it, on his own initiative, to Theodorus, cf. 2.277.26ff., where Proclus speaks of Iamblichus "excoriating all such speculation (sc. as that of Theodorus) in his chapter entitled 'Refutations of Amelius and his school, and of Numenius' " (= *In Tim.* Fr. 57 Dillon), and 3.333.28ff., where "Plotinus and Theodorus" are credited with a position which Iamblichus is attacking (Fr. 87), whereas the original culprits must have been Plotinus and Amelius. There is an outside possibility that Iamblichus might have attacked Theodorus, since he was a pupil of his, and so a younger contemporary, but it is on the whole less likely than that Proclus is indulging in editorializing.

events, it seems plain that Amelius went even beyond Plotinus (who, as we can observe, holds a fairly subtle and complex position on this question) in asserting the essential unity of all soul, which would entail it being true of all souls that their essences are involved in every act that they perform.

To this position Iamblichus once again opposes his own view (modestly disguised as "those who make a more prudent distinction"), going back to his interpretation of the "seconds and thirds" of *Tim.* 41d as referring to a hierarchy of levels of soul. In the present context, the distinction is between divine and pure souls, whose acts (*energêmata*) eventuate, or come to fulfillment in, their essence (εἰς οὐσίαν ἀποτελευτᾶν), and individual, embodied souls, which are not necessarily essentially identified with all of their acts.

Now what, we may ask, does such a distinction signify? One might suggest that, in the case of pure souls, every act (and these acts would inevitably be of a continuous or repetitive nature) is an expression of their essence, so as to be virtually indistinguishable from it, and every act necessarily comes to fulfillment; in the case of the souls of the heavenly bodies also, their activities, being circular and perfectly regular, are entirely in harmony with their essence, and always come to completion. In the case of human souls, on the other hand, many activities are initiated which (a) are not intimately involved with their essences, and (b) never come to completion, for one reason or another, and this is a function of being separated out among individual bodies, with the limited consciousness that goes with that.

Remarkably enough, some light seems to be thrown on the distinction that Iamblichus is making here by a passage from Plotinus, *Enn.* 5.1.12, 1-10:

> Why, then, when we have such great possessions,[55] do we not consciously grasp them, but are mostly inactive in these ways, and some of us are never active at all? They are always occupied in their own activities (*energeiai*), while Intellect, and what is prior to Intellect, is always engaged with itself, and Soul — the "ever-moving" — likewise. For not everything which is in the soul is immediately perceptible by us, but it reaches us when it enters into perception; but when a particular active power (*energoun*) does not give a share in its activity to the perceiving power, that activity has not yet pervaded the whole soul. (trans. Armstrong, slightly emended)

---

[55] Sc. as union with Soul, Intellect, and even the One, such as he has been describing in ch. 10 above.

What Plotinus is saying here has an application, at least, to the distinction that Iamblichus is making. Normal human consciousness is simply not in touch with the whole of itself, and so its acts cannot be identical with its essence.

20

Κατὰ δὲ τὴν αὐτὴν μέθοδον . . . Iamblichus here continues the exposition of his own doctrine. In the case of the class of pure souls, which he characterizes here as "complete in themselves" (*autoteleis*), "uniform" (*monoeides*), and "separate from matter" (*khôristai apo tês hylês*), acts arise naturally (*prospephykenai*) from their powers (*dynameis*), whereas embodied, individual souls produce acts distinct from their faculties, rather in the manner of plants producing fruit. The point of this comparison, presumably, is that the fruit is an external, separable, manifestation of the potency of the plant, even as an action or product of an embodied soul is distinct from its producer, but the image remains a rather odd one.

Iamblichus now seems to change the subject rather abruptly, in making a distinction between the Stoics who, consistent with their materialist doctrine of the soul, postulate that all the activities (*energeiai*) of the soul are linked to, and indeed arise from, the body (a position he has already criticized earlier, in section 10 above), and the Platonists, who distinguish between activities that are involved with the body, such as acts of sense-perception, and other that are not, namely acts of pure intellection.

21

Τὰ μὲν οὖν τῶν σωματοειδῶν δυνάμεων ἔργα . . . This continues the distinction between Stoics and Platonists made just above, and makes the point that even activities involved with the body are only linked with it "by conversion" (κατ᾽ ἐπιστροφήν) — in other words, that the soul, even when exercising these activities, remains to some degree 'above' the body, preserving an essence which transcends it. The doctrine here is in accord with that of Plotinus and Porphyry, including the rather unusual use of *epistrophê*, which normally refers to the "reversion" of a lower level of being upon a higher, the more normal term for the downward attention of a superior entity being *neusis* (e.g. Plot. *Enn.* 1.6.5.49; 3.6.5.25; 4.4.8.54). However, Plotinus, at *Enn.* 4.3.4.22ff. (the continuation of a passage referred to in section 17, above, and which Iamblichus seems to have in mind), says:

> The Soul of the All would always remain transcendent because it would have nothing to do with coming down, even with its lower part, nor with a turning (*epistrophê*) to the things here below, but our souls would come down because they would have their part marked off for them in this sphere, and by the turning (*epistrophê*) to them of that which needs their care. (trans. Armstrong)

— where we find *epistrophê* used in both senses. For the actual doctrine expressed here we may turn rather to *Enn.* 3.6.5.23ff., where in fact *neusis* is used (as noted above) for downward attention. There the purification of the passionate part of the soul is described as consisting in restraining it from extensive inclination to what is below it (τῇ μὴ πολλῇ νεύσει καὶ τῇ περὶ τὰ κάτω μὴ φαντασίᾳ), implying that what are vulgarly regarded as acts arising from its union with body only arise from its excessive inclination towards it. (Plotinus is concerned in the first five chapters of this tractate to assert the essential impassibility of the soul.)

In Porphyry, we find the same doctrine expressed in *Sent.* 7: "A soul binds itself to body through directing its attention (*epistrophê*) towards the passions which derive from it, and is freed from it, in turn, through the attainment of impassibility (*apatheia*)."[56]

On this question, then, Iamblichus has no quarrel with his immediate predecessors. He presents us, however, with a scenario of souls rising and descending from and towards union with body which emphasizes the variety of situations in which souls may find themselves, resulting in corresponding differences in their *erga*. The implication is, presumably, that his predecessors have not given due regard to this variety of situations.

Καὶ τὰ μὲν τῶν ἐποχουμένων ... Here a distinction is made between souls "mounted upon *pneumata* of a uniform[57] nature (ἐποχουμένων

---

[56] Ψυχὴ καταδεῖται πρὸς τὸ σῶμα τῇ ἐπιστροφῇ τῇ πρὸς τὰ πάθη τὰ ἀπ᾽ αὐτοῦ καὶ λύεται δὲ πάλιν διὰ τῆς ἀπ᾽ αὐτοῦ ἀπαθείας.

[57] The adjective αὐτοειδής, although an extremely rare word, is not unattested. Simplicius uses it of the vehicle in *In De Cael.* 469.7 (τὸ αὐτοειδὲς ... ὄχημα). Marcus Aurelius uses it of the soul at 11.12 (σφαῖρα ψυχῆς αὐτοειδής). Thus, although one may be tempted to correct the word to αὐγοειδής, which is regularly

τοῖς αὐτοειδέσι πνεύμασι)" and those "sown in more solid bodies".
The former cannot refer to the heavenly gods (who are, rather,
theiai), but to souls which have not, or not yet, descended into bodies,
and are therefore "pure." A passage of Proclus (*In Tim.* 2.81, 21ff.)
illustrates this distinction rather well (he is discussing the reason why
the world as a whole does not require sense-organs, in connection
with *Tim.* 33C):

> In this passage he [i.e., Plato] is obviously doing nothing else than
> freeing the universe from the mode of life proper to individuals[58] and
> the organs appropriate to this, which are attached to us when we
> descend into generation; for when we remain above we have no need
> of such multifarious life-modes and the particular organs that go with
> them, but there suffices for us the luminous vehicle (ὄχημα
> αὐγοειδές), which contains in a unified mode all the senses. So seeing
> that we ourselves, when we have dispensed with generation, are free
> from all life of this sort, what are we to assume in the case of the
> universe?

So then, for Proclus as for Iamblichus the vehicle under discussion is
proper to pure souls, and they, by virtue of it, perform their *erga*
without any trouble (*eukolôs*), in contrast to ourselves, who are
burdened with solid bodies.

Καὶ τὰ μὲν τῶν ὅλων ... On the other hand, what is the contrast
intended here between the acts of αἱ ὅλαι ψυχαί and those of αἱ
διῃρημέναι? Universal souls (as suggested above, in commentary to
section 17), should properly be those that are attached to no body,
but are still united to the Universal Soul (ἡ ὅλη ψυχή), since they are
opposed to souls that are μερισταί, or in this case 'divided' among
individual bodies. However, these souls do have areas of concern of
some sort to administer, which they cause to turn towards (ἐπιστρέφειν) themselves, in contrast to the experience of individualized
souls, which must themselves turn their attention towards what they
administer (primarily their bodies).

22

Κατ᾽ ἄλλην τοίνυν ἀρχὴν ... Iamblichus now once again (cf. section
15 above) contrasts the Peripatetic position (which only recognizes
psychic activities as being those of an ensouled body, since the soul

---

used of the vehicle in Neoplatonism, there seems to be no necessity of doing so.

[58] This seems the best translation of μεριστὴ ζωή in this context.

has no independent status) with that of Pythagoras and Plato,[59] who declare the soul's essence, and therefore its acts, to be such as to transcend 'nature' (*physis*) — "nature" signifying the realm of animate body. This very basic and uncontroversial distinction is merely a prelude to further controversy with his immediate predecessors.

[Πλάτων δὲ τῆς ψυχῆς . . . δίδωσιν.] This sentence is plausibly excised by Usener as a gloss on what follows. Both MSS show their discomfort with it by leaving a space, and in the case of P, inserting Πλάτωνος before it. It certainly adds nothing and interferes with the flow of the thought.

ὑπερέχοντα καθ᾽ αὐτὰ ἐξαιροῦσιν. We adopt here the emendation of Wachsmuth, ἐξαιροῦσιν for ἐξαίρουσιν of MSS., ἐξαιρέω and its derivatives being the more usual term in Neoplatonic circles for "removing" in the sense of "causing to transcend."

23

Ἤδη τοίνυν καὶ ἐν αὐτοῖς τοῖς Πλατωνικοῖς . . . Iamblichus now launches into a rather comprehensive survey of his Platonist predecessors, beginning from Plotinus and Porphyry, but continuing back to Numenius and other Middle Platonists, on two topics which might seem quite distinct to us, but which apparently were closely allied in his mind. The first is the question of the essential unity or otherwise of the soul; the second that of the causes of the soul's descent, a topic which anticipates somewhat one that is taken up more fully a little later (sections 26-31, p. 377.11ff. W), but which gains its relevance here from the fact that Iamblichus is focussing on the *energêmata* that bring about descent into the body.

He structures his first doxography in reverse chronological order, though managing to arrange his three sets of authorities into a sort of Hegelian synthesis. Plotinus and Porphyry he characterizes as viewing the various activities and "parts" of the soul as essentially concordant — *syntaxis* here having the sense of "framework" or "structure." This cannot be intended to deny that Plotinus and Porphyry, like all Platonists, maintained the existence of a tension

---

[59] Note the characteristic pairing of Pythagoras and Plato, as at 365.4; 366.6; 368.5; 369.9.

between the rational and the irrational parts of the soul. Festugière (208 note 1) assumes that Iamblichus is here exhibiting a confusion between Plotinus' (and Porphyry's, cf. *Sent.* 37) doctrine of the (articulated) unity of all souls with the All-Soul (as set out e.g. in *Enn.* 4.3.1-8), and what is at issue here, which is the (articulated) unity of each soul with itself. There is, however, no need to suppose Iamblichus confused on this point. As opposed to Numenius — with whom the contrast is being set up — Plotinus and Porphyry (and all subsequent Platonists) did maintain the basic unity of the human soul, despite the tension within it of irrational and rational elements. Indeed, in his more extreme moods (e.g., *Enn.* 3.6.1-5), Plotinus excludes the irrational impulses, and even sensation, from the soul proper, relegating them to a projection, or "trace" (ἴχνος) of soul, which arises only in connection with embodiment.

Numenius, on the other hand, is attested, on the evidence of Porphyry (*On the Faculties of the Soul,* Fr. 253 Smith = Num., Fr. 44 Des Places), as maintaining that we possess "not three parts of soul, nor even two, the rational and the irrational, but *two souls,*" and that they are at war with each other, reflecting the two opposed souls which he saw at work in the universe (cf. Fr. 52, ll. 64ff, Des Places, from Calcidius), and which he discerned in Plato, *Laws,* Book 10. This is an interestingly radical theory, in face of which Plotinus and Porphyry are plainly supporters of a unitary soul.

Plutarch and Atticus, on the other hand, can be seen as combining a belief in an original irrational soul, independent of divinity, with a conviction that such a soul is taken in hand by god and made rational and harmonious, this being the process described in the *Timaeus*, of which they adopted a literal interpretation (cf. particularly, for Plutarch, *Proc. An.* 1014BC, and for Atticus, Procl. *In Tim.* 1. 381.26 - 382.12 Diehl = Fr. 23 Des Places — though there, as elsewhere, he is linked inextricably to Plutarch). For Plutarch and Atticus, in contrast to Numenius, the original irrational soul does not survive as such after its ordering by the Demiurge, except as a residual element of recalcitrance; Numenius seems to hold to a more uncompromisingly dualist view. The language used here by Iamblichus, κατακοσμοῦντα . . . διατάττοντα . . . συμφωνίαν . . . συνυφαίνουσι, is all thoroughly Platonic, without being particularly distinctive.

κατὰ μὲν Πλωτῖνον τῆς πρώτης ἑτερότητος . . . Iamblichus moves here with some abruptness, by means of a genitive absolute clause, from the question of the composition of the human soul to that of the reasons for its descent into the body. One might reasonably suspect a lacuna, or some abridgement of his original on the part of Stobaeus, but it is possible to provide a coherent translation, so we may leave the text as it is, noting only that the topic has changed somewhat.

Iamblichus takes his start from Plotinus' assertion at the beginning of *Enn.* 5.1, in answer to his question "what made the souls forget their father, God?": "The beginning of evil for them was audacity and coming to birth and *the primal otherness* and the wishing to belong to themselves (5.1.1, 2-6)." For Plotinus, this *prôtê heterotês* is best seen as an aspect of the indefinite dyad, which manifests itself initially in the development of Intellect from the One, but also in that of Soul from Intellect, and of the individual souls from the All-Soul.[60] However, the adducing of Empedocles and Heraclitus immediately after this seems to point to Iamblichus also having in mind such a passage as *Enn.* 4.8.1, where Plotinus quotes, first Heraclitus (l. 11) and then Empedocles (l. 18),[61] on the question of the reasons for the descent of the soul. The relevant passage (1.11-23) reads as follows:

> Heraclitus, who urges us to investigate this (sc. why the soul comes to be in the body), positing "necessary changes" from opposite to opposite, and saying "the way up and the way down" and *"changing it is at rest"* (μεταβάλλον ἀναπαύεται) and "it is weariness to toil at and be subjected to the same things," has left us guessing, since he has neglected to make clear to us what he is saying, perhaps because we ought to seek by ourselves, as he himself sought and found. And Empedocles, when he said that it is a law that sinful souls should fall into this world, and that he himself has come here as *"an exile from the gods"* (φυγὰς θεόθεν), who "put his trust in raging strife," revealed just as much as the riddling statements of Pythagoras and his followers about this and many other matters (and besides, he is unclear because he writes poetry).

If indeed Iamblichus has this passage in mind — and we cannot be quite certain of this — it is interesting to see what use he makes of it. Plotinus is stressing the obscurity of the utterances of both Presocratic sages; Iamblichus simply abstracts one characteristic utterance of each and presents it as a dogma. In fact, the positions of

---

[60] Cf. J.M. Rist, 'The Problem of 'Otherness' in the *Enneads'*, in *le Néoplatonisme: Colloques internationaux de la C.N.R.S.*, Paris, 1971, 77-87, repr. in *Platonism and its Christian Heritage*, Aldershot, 1985

[61] We may note that, though Plotinus here quotes them in the order Heraclitus-Empedocles, when he refers to them again in 4.8, 5.5-8, he gives the order Empedocles-Heraclitus, which is the one that Iamblichus adopts.

both Empedocles (an original fall from grace through willfulness)[62] and Heraclitus (an inherent restlessness, which makes change seem like a relief) can be related to the first reason for the "forgetfulness of the Father" in 5.1.1, 2, *tolma,* or "audacity" — which is, of course, in turn related by Plotinus in that passage to the "primal otherness."

Iamblichus now continues his doxography with the opinions of "the Gnostics" and of Albinus. It is by no means so clear whence he derives these. Plotinus does, of course, attack the Gnostics in *Enn.* 2.9, and their doctrine of the fall of the soul in chs. 10-12, but he does not use the terms *paranoia* or *parekbasis* in that connection, concentrating his fire instead on the concept of the Gnostic Sophia, and her fall through inquisitiveness and restlessness. What Plotinus seems to be criticizing in particular is the Valentinian myth of the fall of Sophia, but he does not concern himself with the motivation of Sophia in doing what she does. Her initial failing, however, could well be described as *paranoia,* in the sense of "perverted or deviant intellection," and *parekbasis,* in the sense of "deviation from normality, or from correct conduct." Iamblichus might, then, have had access to some Gnostic texts himself, but there would be nothing very strange in that, after all.

As for Albinus, the problem of trying to relate this report of his doctrine to what we find in ch. 25 of the *Didaskalikos* does not arise if that document ceases to be attributed to Albinus, but is returned to the shadowy Alcinous, as is now more or less the consensus of scholars. On the other hand, even if one were to persist in claiming it for Albinus, bearing in mind the type of document which the *Didaskalikos* is, the disagreement between it and what Albinus might have said elsewhere, when propounding his own view, need not be regarded as absolute. In *Did.* ch. 25, p.178.34ff., we find three possible reasons proposed for the fall of the soul: (1) the will of the gods; (2) intemperance (*akolasia*); and (3) love of the body (*philosômatia*) — this last being interpreted as a natural affinity for embodiment.[63] Among these possibilities, the second obviously relates most closely to what we have here, without being identical with it: "the erring judgement of a free will" could reasonably be seen as being the natural result of *akolasia.* Certainly, Albinus, in whatever work he

---

[62] Wachsmuth wished to excise πρώτης from the Empedocles reference, presumably expecting that it has strayed in from the Plotinus reference just before, but it seems possible that Iamblichus included it.

[63] The analogy that Alcinous produces is that of fire for asphalt, 178.39.

propounded this view, would have had to provide some explanation of what the cause and/or effect of such an erring judgment was.

τῶν δ᾽ αὖ διισταμένων πρὸς τούτους . . . To whom, we may ask, does *toutous* refer here? It might at first sight appear to refer back to *houtoi* in l. 20 — skipping over the intervening digression — that is to say, Plutarch and Atticus, but in fact one can recognize a plausible contrast with the immediately preceding authorities since they postulate, in each case, an internal cause of declination for the soul, while the following authorities take this as coming from the outside. Three sets of authorities, first Numenius and his colleague Cronius (= Fr. 43 Des Places), then Harpocration (who is presented elsewhere as being a follower of both Atticus and of Numenius),[64] and then Plotinus and Porphyry, are being presented as regarding evil as something introduced into the soul "from the outside." The contrast made here may be seen to refer to Plutarch and Atticus as well, which may seem surprising since they are often presented as dualists; but in respect of the particular issue being discussed here, it can be seen to make sense.

As pointed out above, Plutarch and Atticus are portrayed as presenting the demiurgic "ordering" of the soul as supervening on the original disordered state of the soul, in such a way that there no longer survives an independent source of evil, at least as far as the soul is concerned.[65] Numenius, Cronius and Harpocration, on the other hand, in Iamblichus' view, and even Plotinus and Porphyry, see evil as persisting independently of the soul.[66] Numenius sees it as coming to the soul from matter (cf. esp. Fr. 52 Des Places, from Calcidius), which he identifies with the Indefinite Dyad, and whose independence from, and co-eternity with, God, the Monad, he asserts strongly, in opposition to certain fellow-Pythagoreans (Fr. 52.15ff.). Harpocration's position seems to be presented here as, if anything,

---

[64] Cf. J.M. Dillon, "Harpocration's Commentary on Plato . . . ", *CSCA* 4 (1971), 125-7 (repr. in *The Golden Chain,* Aldershot, 1990, Essay XIV), and *The Middle Platonists,* pp.258-62.

[65] Plutarch does, certainly, seem to wish to maintain an independent source of evil in the universe as a whole, identified by him in the *Is. et Os.* with Ahriman (369E) and Seth-Typhon (371B), as well as with the Pythagorean-Platonist Indefinite Dyad (370EF, cf. also *Def. Or.* 428E).

[66] What the force of the qualifications πολλάκις, ἔστιν ὅτε, and ὡς τὰ πολλά might be, in connexion with these three doctrinal positions, is not clear. Iamblichus is hardly alleging vacillation; he may just mean that these authorities do not make their views clear on every occasion.

even more world-negating than that of Numenius. For him, it is the
body itself, not matter, that is the cause of evil for the soul. The body
is, therefore, not just a morally neutral entity, but intrinsically evil.
Now no doubt Harpocration did adopt a thoroughly negative attitude
to incarnation (we find him being presented later [380.14-19] as
linked with Numenius and Cronius as holding that *all* entries of souls
into body are evil), but there may be a more philosophically interesting reason for his difference with Numenius on this point. We seem
to have, in Plotinus' *Ennead* 1.8 [51], *On What are and Whence come
Evils,* ch. 8, the refutation of an argument which denies that matter is
the origin of evil in the soul, claiming that this must be due to the
body, as being something which has form, and so can act on something else (matter being too formless to constitute a positive source
of evil), and this is most naturally attributed, on the basis of the
information available to us, to Harpocration:

> But if someone says that we do not become evil because of matter —
> giving as a reason that ignorance is not caused by matter, nor are bad
> desires; for even if it is the case that their coming into existence is
> caused by the badness of body, it is not the matter but *the form* that
> causes them, heat, cold, bitter, salt, and all the forms of flavor, and
> also fillings and emptyings, and not just fillings, but fillings with
> bodies of a particular quality;[67] and in general it is the qualified thing
> which produces the distinction of desires, and, if you like, of falsified
> opinions, so that form rather than matter is evil — he too will be
> compelled all the same to admit that matter is evil. (trans. Armstrong,
> slightly adapted).

Plotinus goes on to argue that form or quality (*poiotês*) does not by
itself cause evil (even as the form Fire itself does not burn), but only
when it has become mingled with matter in the body, so that it is
matter that remains the ultimate cause of evil. He does not, however,
seem entirely to dispose of Harpocration's point (if it is he), which is
that those things generally accounted evils in the soul are perverted
qualities, and thus their origin must be traced to something already
imbued with form, which would be the body itself. One seems to see
here traces of an interesting intra-school dispute, out of which
Harpocration comes not badly.

   As for Plotinus and Porphyry, this linking of them with Middle
Platonic dualists seems rather incongruous, in view of the way in

---

[67] All this seems to be based on Plato's connecting of evils in the soul with
imbalances in the bodily constitution at *Tim.* 86bff. — an interesting use of that
interesting passage.

which they have been distinguished from them earlier, but once
again, Iamblichus could adduce texts to support his allegation. In
Enn. 1.8, from which we have just quoted, Plotinus would seem
unequivocally to identify matter as the ultimate source of evil in the
soul, as in everything else, but some remarks in *Enn.* 4.4.44.31ff., for
instance, where he is talking about the snares of *praxis* as opposed to
theoria, might lend themselves to such a position as Iamblichus is
attributing to him here:

> This is what the magic of nature (φύσις) does; for to pursue what is
> not good as if it were good, drawn to the appearance of good by
> irrational impulses (ἀλόγοις ὁρμαῖς), belongs to one who is being
> unwittingly led where he does not want to go. And what would
> anyone call this other than magical enchantment (γοητεία)?

The villain here is certainly *physis* and not matter; and *physis* operates
on the soul by means of *alogoi hormai*. So one could argue that the
immediate, if not the ultimate, cause of evil in the soul was sometimes seen by Plotinus to be 'nature', in the sense of the operations
of the irrational life-force immanent in the physical world.

Similarly, one can come upon passages of Porphyry on which the
same interpretation could be put. Festugière draws attention (211
note 1) to *De Abst.* 3.27 (p. 225.2-4 Nauck), where we find the remark:
"For in many people the motions and the needs of irrational nature
are the first stimulus to injustice";[68] and 4.20 (p. 262.24-5), in the
course of a discussion of pollution, where he says: "And the passions
also pollute the soul (reading τὴν ψυχὴν for τῆς ψυχῆς, with Nauck)
by involving it with the irrational, thus feminizing the masculine
element within."[69] Doubtless he made similar remarks elsewhere,
though neither in his case nor in that of Plotinus does it mean that
matter does not remain the ultimate cause of evil in the soul.
Nevertheless, Iamblichus' distinction here seems not to be devoid of
all justification.

24

Κατὰ δὲ Ἀριστοτέλην . . . This reference to Aristotle is decidedly
cryptic and might give evidence of an omission by Stobaeus. In

---

[68] ἐν πολλοῖς γὰρ τὰ τῆς ἀλόγου κινήματα φύσεως καὶ αἱ χρεῖαι ἀδικίας κατάρχει.

[69] μιαίνει δὲ καὶ τὰ πάθη τὴν ψυχὴν τῇ συμπλοκῇ τοῦ ἀλόγου, θηλυνομένου τοῦ
ἐντὸς ἄρρενος. The 'masculine element' refers presumably to the intellect.

particular, one would expect a κατὰ μέν clause before this one. First of all, we must identify the reference of ταῦτα. Festugière suggests that it refers back to the "disorderly and irregular motions" mentioned in ll. 2-3 above (disregarding the intervening passage about the causes of descent and of evil in the soul), and that what Aristotle is presented as maintaining is that such motions (or activities) are to be distinguished from (truly) human ones by "εἴδη ζωῆς and other defining characteristics (ὅροι)".[70] But the mention of ἐνεργήματα in the next sentence would seem to settle the matter in favor of "activities."

What, then, are these "forms, or types, of life?" In Aristotelian terms, presumably the various levels of soul set out in the *De Anima* and elsewhere, the nutritive soul (common to all living things), the sense-perceptive (present in all animals which have motion), the imaginative (shared by man with some of the higher animals), and the rational (peculiar to man). But what is missing in this sentence is an explicit reference to animal activities, such as is presented in the third sentence of this section (the one concerning Porphyry). We therefore tentatively suggest a lacuna here with a sentence beginning κατὰ μέν which would contain a reference to the activities of lower souls. Quite possibly the philosophers involved would have been Plato and the Pythagoreans, or alternatively certain Presocratics. If this is true, then there is no reason to alter the text with Usener, who proposed emendation of ἐπί for ἀπό. Rather, what Iamblichus says is that Aristotle separated the activities of lower kinds of soul from those of human soul by the kinds of life that each class of soul actualizes, a doctrine which is indeed Aristotelian.

Κατὰ δ' αὖ τοὺς Στωικούς . . .   In the case of the Stoics, it is easier, perhaps, to see what Iamblichus may have in mind. Festugière suggests that the reference is to the Stoic doctrine of the different levels of soul being distinguished by different degrees of 'tension' (*tonos*) in the *pneuma*, or vital spirit (cf. SVF 2.714ff. — and indeed this passage is included by von Arnim in that context, as Fr. 720). If

---

[70] This also assumes that we are to keep the ἀπό of the MSS. before τῶν ἀνθρωπίνων, against Usener's emendation to ἐπί, which would mean "in the case of human activities," and give the sense, presumably, that these activities, in human souls, were distinguished (from those in irrational souls?) "by forms of life and other modes of definition." This could be made sense of, certainly, if it were the reading of the MSS., but since the MSS. reading gives an acceptable sense, there seems no occasion to alter it.

so, however, Iamblichus is introducing into the Stoic theory a concept not present in the other testimonia, that the activities of lower levels of soul are "more imperfect" (ἀτελέστερα) than those of the higher, whereas in general the various degrees of *tonos* seem to be regarded as equally perfect in their way.

Ὡς δ᾽ ἐγώ τινων ἀκήκοα Πλατωνικῶν . . . Here Iamblichus does seem to be making reference to oral communications from Porphyry — and others. There is no difficulty, of course, about assuming this, since Porphyry is attested by Eunapius as his master; but it must be noted that ἀκούω does come to be used in peculiar ways in later Greek: e.g. Julian, *Or.* 5, 162C, speaks of "hearing" Xenarchus, a philosopher of the time of Augustus; and Proclus, *In Tim.* 3.25.2 Diehl, tells us "I heard such opinions expressed in argument by Theodorus" (τοιαῦτα γὰρ ἤκουσα τοῦ Θεοδώρου φιλοσοφοῦντος), which he could not have possibly have done in the normal sense. So it cannot be absolutely taken for granted that Iamblichus is referring to oral communication from Porphyry, much less "many others."

On the other hand, this may not much matter. The doctrine is one on which Iamblichus can be seen as opposing Porphyry, that is, on the question whether there is a generic difference, and not just one of degree, between the souls of animals and of men. There is an interesting passage of Nemesius of Emesa, *De Natura Hominis* (51, p. 117 Matthaei), in which he contrasts Iamblichus with his predecessors on the question of transmigration of human souls into animal bodies:

> Cronius, in his work *On Reincarnation* (for that is the term he uses for transmigration), wants all souls to be rational;[71] and a similar view is advanced by Theodorus the Platonist[72] in his essay entitled "That the Soul is all the Forms,"[73] and Porphyry likewise. Iamblichus, however,

---

[71] That is to say, at least *potentially* rational.

[72] Sc. Theodorus of Asine. Since Iamblichus is presented as opposing all these views, and since Theodorus (though a pupil of his) may probably be assumed to have written after him, Theodorus may here perhaps be seen, as in a number of other contexts, as a surrogate for his spiritual master Amelius, whom Iamblichus will really be criticizing (cf. comment on section 19 above). The position here advanced by Theodorus is certainly consistent with Amelius' known views. This raises, however, the awkward problem of Nemesius' sources. It may be that Nemesius is dependent for his knowledge of Platonist doctrinal positions on some later Platonist source, such as Plutarch of Athens, though the chronology is uncertain.

[73] Sc. of life: εἴδη here could better, perhaps, be rendered "classes" or "species," except that they would sound strange by themselves in a title, unless one gives the

taking the opposite tack to these, declares that the species of soul corresponds to the species of animal concerned, that is to say, the species of soul are different. At any rate, he composed a monograph entitled[74] "That transmigrations do not take place from men into irrational animals, nor from irrational animals into men, but from animals into animals, and from men into men."[75]

This is an important testimony, as it demonstrates the link between the doctrine of metempsychosis into animals and that of the basic homogeneity of all souls, both of which positions held by his immediate predecessors Iamblichus opposes. In the present passage, however, the final clause constitutes a problem. What does Iamblichus mean by introducing the qualification "in so far as things distinguished by being based on different essences are to be assimilated (ὁμοιοῦσθαι) to one another?" Surely for Porphyry (and Amelius) the situation is that all souls can be assimilated to one another, and that is the error which Iamblichus is combating?[76]

25

Iamblichus turns to a discussion of the number of souls in the universe.[77] This long section is divided by forms of οἱ μέν and οἱ δέ. The first group (οἱ μέν) is represented by Amelius and the Orphics, who think that souls are numerous but finite; the second (οἱ δέ) by materialists like the atomists, who think that souls are infinite in

---

title as something like "That Soul is (the same in) all Species."

[74] This seems an almost unbelievably unwieldy title, even for Iamblichus, but at least it makes clear the subject-matter of the treatise. It seems necessary, by the way, to read ἐπιγραφόμενον for the MSS. ἐπίγραφον (or to excise it, as Matthaei would prefer).

[75] Κρόνιος μὲν γὰρ ἐν τῷ περὶ παλιγγενεσίας (οὕτω δὲ καλεῖ τὴν μετενσωμάτωσιν) λογικὰς πάσας εἶναι βούλεται· ὁμοίως δὲ καὶ Θεόδωρος ὁ Πλατωνικὸς ἐν τῷ "Ὅτι ἡ ψυχὴ πάντα τὰ εἴδη ἐστί, καὶ Πορφύριος ὁμοίως· Ἰάμβλιχος δὲ τὴν ἐναντίαν τούτοις δραμών, κατ᾽ εἶδος ζῴων ψυχῆς εἶδος εἶναι λέγει, ἤγουν, εἴδη διάφορα. γέγραπται γοῦν αὐτῷ μονόβιβλον ἐπιγραφόμενον, "Ὅτι οὐκ ἀπ᾽ ἀνθρώπων εἰς ζῷα ἄλογα, οὐδὲ ἀπὸ ζῴων ἀλόγων εἰς ἀνθρώπους αἱ μετενσωματώσεις γίνονται, ἀλλὰ ἀπὸ ζῴων εἰς ζῷα, καὶ ἀπὸ ἀνθρώπων εἰς ἀνθρώπους.

[76] In *De Abstinentia* 3.2-6, Porphyry has an interesting discussion of the degree to which animals can participate in language, as a sign of their participation in rationality (λόγος), which includes an account of a pet partridge which he raised in Carthage (chapter 3.7).

[77] This, on the basis of the preserved text, is necessarily the meaning of the chapter heading in Stobaeus (περὶ μέτρου ψυχῆς). We accordingly adopt Canter's emendation (μέτρου) of the MSS μέτρα, since a genitive is required. Gaisford's μέτρων may equally well be correct.

number — this group is further subdivided into three (οἱ μέν . . . οἱ δέ . . . οἱ δέ); the third (οἱ δέ) is represented by Platonists who think that the soul is finite but unvaried in number — this group includes Plotinus' followers (οἱ μέν). (One expects another οἱ δέ. It seems likely that Stobaeus has abruptly ended a longer passage in Iamblichus' work.)

Οἱ μὲν δὴ μίαν οὐσίαν τῆς ψυχῆς ἀριθμῷ τιθέμενοι . . . Iamblichus first considers those who hold that the essence of the soul is numerically one. Into this camp he places Amelius and the Orphics.

πληθύνοντες δὲ αὐτὴν . . . There is no reason to alter the reading of the MSS, πληθύνοντες. It is true that this verb is usually intransitive while πληθύνειν is transitive, but even Festugière (212 note 3), who would change to the transitive verb, admits (with LSJ) that this need not be so since both Proclus and Damascius use πληθύειν in the passive. Indeed, Iamblichus himself at De Myst. 1.6, p. 19.13 uses it passively: τὸ μὲν δαιμόνιον φῦλον ἐν τῷ ἑνὶ πληθυόμενον ("the tribe of daemons is multiplied in unity").

ὡς ᾿Αμέλιος οἴεται, σχέσεσι καὶ κατατάξεσιν . . . On Amelius, see sections 6 (365.16-17 W), 17 (372.9-12 W), and especially 19 (372.23-26 W). Amelius' position in the final passage is here modified by the qualification that he postulated as the differentiating factor in souls σχέσεις καὶ κατατάξεις. Some light may be thrown on the meaning of κατάταξις by adducing a passage of the De Myst. 1.8: 23, where Iamblichus is criticizing a position taken up by Porphyry:

> We do not, however, accept the way in which your hypothesis distinguishes them [sc. the various properties of the divine classes of being], which declares that "the cause of the distinction now being investigated is the assignment (κατάταξις) of these entities to different sorts of body, specifically that of the gods to ethereal bodies, that of daemons to aery ones, and that of souls to bodies of earth." For this concept of "assignment," as for instance the assignment of Socrates to his tribe when this is exercising its prytany, is improperly predicated of the divine classes, seeing as they are all absolute and autonomous in themselves.

The point here is that the concept of κατάταξις (which seems to have been employed here by Porphyry, in the relevant section of his Letter to Anebo) presupposes a degree of subordination to external — and inferior — forces not suitable to divine beings, especially gods, but even to souls, and Porphyry is being criticized for postulating that, even as Amelius is here.

The terms κατάταξις and σχέσις are used together by Proclus, *In Tim.* 1.49, 29ff., in the course of an exegesis of the community of wives in the *Republic*, recalled at *Tim.* 18cd, which he sees as relating much more properly to the gods than to human society. The divine relationships, he says, seem paradoxical to us only because of our κατάταξις to a particular body, and the limitation on our consciousness resulting from that. He ends by characterizing our life in the body as an ἄσχετος σχέσις καὶ κατάταξις ἀκατάτακτος καὶ ἀδιαίρετος διαίρεσις, a sequence of paradoxical epithets with a strangely Iamblichean ring. What must be meant is a relationship and assignment to the body that holds within it the capacity for transcending itself (as well as a "division" that preserves the soul's indivisibility from its source). Cf. *In Tim.* 2.20, 4-9 and 285, 12-15, where these two terms are found again in conjunction.

Proclus *In Tim.* 2.213.9ff. (a commentary on *Timaeus* 35bc on the division of the World Soul into numerical proportions) discusses Amelius' doctrine of the soul. There Proclus tells us that Amelius thought that the World Soul contained or embraced the souls of gods, daemons, and human beings. These proceed from the World Soul and arrange themselves according to rank in the universe. Daemons have "a double relation (διττὴ σχέσις) because they are between gods and us." Thus their *assignment* to the universe and their *relation* to other souls in the universe defines them as daemonic. For Amelius, soul is numerically one (i.e., there is one World Soul from which all others come) but becomes many after procession. Iamblichus here characterizes him as saying that the only factor that causes souls to be many is the variety of their relationships to their receptacles; basically, it is all one soul.

ὡς οἱ Ὀρφικοὶ λέγουσιν, ἐπιπνοίαις ἀπὸ τῆς ὅλης . . . On the Orphic doctrine, see above, section 8 ("Aristotle [*De An.* 410b27-30] states that in the Orphic poems it is said that the soul enters from the universe, carried on the winds, when we breathe in (ἀναπνεόντων ἡμῶν)" (366.17-20 W). Orpheus thought that from the single soul "came many mediating breaths (μέσαι ἐπίπνοιαι) to individual souls from the Whole Soul" (366.22-24 W). In the present passage, the Orphic doctrine is that the Whole Soul is numerically one but is "multiplied" into individual souls by these "breaths" from the World

Soul, which (it would seem) individual souls "breathe in." This doctrine does not seem concordant with the otherwise-attested Orphic belief in the survival of the individual soul and in metempsychosis, as notable in the golden plates from Thurii (Fr. 32 Kern) and in some lines of "Orpheus" preserved by Vettius Valens (Fr. 228c, d Kern). In 228a,b, however, we find lines supporting Aristotle's position: ψυχὴ δ' ἀνθρώποισιν ἀπ' αἰθέρος ἐρρίζωται ("the soul in human beings derives its roots from the ether") and ἀέρα δ' ἕλκοντες ψυχὴν θείαν δρεπόμεσθα ("it is by drawing in the air that we acquire a divine soul"). The idea may be that immortal souls are floating around in the ether, waiting to be breathed in. On the Orphic belief, see W. K. C. Guthrie, *Orpheus and Greek Religion* 2nd ed. (Princeton 1993), 94-5 and 144-5 note 17.

ἔπειτα ἀνασχόντες ἀπὸ τοῦ πλήθους · · · The text is problematic, and there is no sure solution. (See the apparatus criticus for various suggestions.) Festugière (213 note 1) read ἀνασχόντες ("rise"), which is possible and remains close to the reading of the MSS. Some verb of motion seems necessary, since these philosophers are moving from the many individual souls caused by the Whole Soul back to the Whole Soul again, this time in its aspect of single soul separate from all others. As another possibility, though less plausible paleographically, one might suggest ἀναχωροῦντες ("withdraw").

τηροῦσιν αὐτὴν ὅλην πανταχοῦ τὴν αὐτὴν . . . The first way to "count" souls is to consider the change from a single "Whole Soul" to the individuated souls that proceed from it. This is basic Neoplatonic doctrine, based upon Plato's *Timaeus*. Iamblichus posits the Whole Soul as the unparticipated moment of the Psychic realm and divides the Soul of the Universe and individual souls from it (*In Tim.* Frr. 50, 54-56). (By "Whole Soul" here, however, Iamblichus may mean the Soul of the Universe; see below, section 26. If so, Iamblichus still differentiates it from individual souls by its rank and, hence, in its essence. See *In Tim.* Fr. 56 and Dillon [1973] 336-7.) The problem with the view of Amelius and the Orphics is, as we have seen before, that in the procession from Whole to partial souls, they think that the souls' essence does not change. Thus the multiplication whether by "relations and assignments relative to other" souls or by "breaths" does not cause the differentiation in kinds of souls that Iamblichus favors. The difference between the Whole Soul and its parts (they think) is simply that the Whole Soul is an undivided soul sharing the same essence with them. For Iamblichus, this will not do.

Iamblichus may be suggesting a second problem for these thinkers as well. How can the Whole Soul be one and separate from the souls that proceed from it yet be their cause? It is clear from the first clause that this is just what these thinkers believe: the Whole Soul is one but multiplied. The phrase "the multiplicity of the whole" must refer to the multiplicity of souls that arise or proceed from the Whole Soul, i.e., a multiplicity contained in the Whole Soul. Amelius and the Orphics are said to "rise" from a multiplicity-from-unity back to a unity-before-multiplicity, whereby the World Soul is again single but now unrelated to the individual souls that have come from it. The Whole Soul is said to have "laid aside these relations and assignments [i.e., those we find in the lower individual souls] relative to other [souls]." They "free it from its division into the things [i.e., souls] that partake of it." It is insofar as they deny the Whole Soul's subdivision *after* it has been subdivided that they can claim that the Whole Soul is one but many.

Οἱ δ' ἐν ἀπείροις κόσμοις . . . Iamblichus now begins a discussion of those who believe that the number of souls is infinite. He first places the atomists in this group. Iamblichus briefly discussed their doctrines in section 2, above. Here only a little more is added. Soul-atoms, and thus souls, are plainly infinite in number, just like other classes of atoms. Souls are material, and disperse on the death of the individual.

κατὰ συντυχίαν συνερχομένων <συνισταμένοις> συνίστασθαι . . . With Festugière (213 note 4) we insert συνισταμένοις as required syntactically. Even for Iamblichus, this string of compounds beginning with the Greek prefix συν- is noteworthy.

Οἱ μὲν ἐκ σπερμάτων αὐτὰς γεννῶντες . . . Festugière wishes to connect the school of thought alluded to here with those mentioned in section 16, above, and to propose that they are medical theorists. That may well be so, but in the earlier passage Iamblichus merely attributes the doctrine that "the soul enters into combination with the body for the purpose of generation" to οἱ πλεῖστοι τῶν φυσικῶν, which Festugière renders, strangely, "la plupart des médecins." Surely Iamblichus means only "physical philosophers," primarily the early

Ionians, presumably. It is not clear who these theorists are, but the point of their inclusion is that they postulate one soul per seed (or rather, per successfully fertilized egg), which would imply an ever-increasing number of souls.

The word ἀπολείπουσιν ("leave behind") has a technical meaning of "bequeath" in wills. See *LSJ* I.1. Iamblichus is probably punning on the notion of materialists bequeathing an infinite number of souls to posterity via infinite procreation. The idea of desertion (of wife or child) is inherent in the term as well.

Οἱ δὲ κατὰ μεταβολήν . . . The identity of this group is also obscure. Perhaps it is a reference to the production of maggots from the dead carcasses of cows (as Festugière suggests, 214 note 1), but probably the doctrine is wider and includes any growth from dead matter, e.g., flowers from manure. Like the previous group, they postulate the possibility of an infinite number of souls. The concept of change here is consistent with that of the natural philosophers for whom change is a natural and eternal part of the world.

Οἱ δὲ τῆς φύσεως τὴν ψυχὴν μὴ διακρίνοντες . . . The natural philosophers in this sub-group are concerned with proving the infinity of souls from the ability of plants and trees to reproduce themselves from cuttings. As Festugière points out, it is hardly appropriate to see the Stoics as those being referred to here, as Lévêque had suggested,[78] since they precisely *did* distinguish the level of *physis* from that of *psychê* proper. On the phenomenon, see Aristotle, *De Anima* 413b16-19: ἐπὶ τῶν φυτῶν ἔνια διαιρούμενα φαίνεται ζῶντα καὶ χωριζόμενα ἀπ' ἀλλήλων, ὡς οὔσης τῆς ἐν τούτοις ψυχῆς ἐντελεχείᾳ μὲν μιᾶς ἐν ἑκάστῳ φυτῷ, δυνάμει δὲ πλειόνων ("In the case of plants, some parts after they have been divided and separated from other parts seem alive since the soul in them is actually one in each plant but potentially many"). See also 409a9-10 and 411b19-30.

It is common to these last three sub-groups that they postulate the possibility of a progressive infinity of souls. It may seem curious that Iamblichus should pick them out as suitable foils for Amelius and the Orphics, but in fact the theory of an *ever-increasing* multiplicity of souls, rather than that of a static infinity of souls, can be seen as the opposite pole to the doctrine of the essential unity of all soul.

---

[78] *Apud* Bouillet, *Les Ennéades de Plotin*, 2 p. 647 note 5.

Οἱ δ' ἀπὸ Πλάτωνος . . . And so we reach finally, as the synthesis of this opposition, the Platonists. Iamblichus presents the (mainstream) Platonist tradition (having already presented Amelius' doctrine as deviant) as positing a fixed and limited number of souls, pre-established in accordance with divine providence, and recycling themselves endlessly. On the Platonic doctrine, see *Republic* 10.611a4-9 and *Timaeus* 41d8-e1.

οἱ μὲν περὶ Πλωτῖνον . . . The "followers of Plotinus" would no doubt include Amelius,[79] who was much given to arithmetical speculations, and probably Porphyry as well, although we have no indication of this. At any rate, these "followers of Plotinus" connect this pre-ordained number of souls with the Platonic "Perfect Number." Plato twice mentions the term "Perfect Number." In *Rep.* 546b3-4 it refers to a period of time during which the gods beget offspring (θείῳ γεννητῷ), which may be related by Plotinus' followers to the divine begetting of souls. In *Tim.* 39d2-7, it refers to the "perfect year," i.e., the amount of time it takes for all the planets to complete their heavenly journey. Since Plato says (*Tim.* 41d8-e1) that souls are equal in number to the stars (which the Neoplatonists took to include planets but did not interpret to mean one soul to one heavenly body, since there must be more human souls than divine ones), one can easily imagine a Neoplatonist trying to work out a mathematical "perfect number" corresponding the Demiurge's creation of soul. Plotinus certainly does not speculate on this issue in his published works, although Amelius may have referred to such a doctrine of his master.[80] In any case, this divine number must remain mysterious, although there is some possibility that, as Adam suggests in his commentary on the *Republic*, *ad loc.*, it was seen as being the square of 3600, which would be the number of days in a cycle of 36,000 years of 360 days each, the so-called "Great Year" of 12,960,000 days. Dodds (1963[2]) 301-303, while discussing the concept of ἀποκατάστασις in Proclus, *El. Th.* 199-200, cites Proclus, *In Tim.*3.93.22ff where he connects the Perfect Number with ἀποκατάστασις.

---

[79] The fact that Amelius is accused of declaring that all souls are one does not preclude the possibility that he also speculated on the total number of pre-ordained instantiations of it.

[80] This would not, after all, be the only instance in which Amelius referred to "unwritten doctrines" of his master. Cf. Proclus, *In Tim.* 2.213.9ff., on the significance of the numbers of the soul.

Here this section on the number of souls existing in the universe abruptly ends. Iamblichus would certainly have agreed with Plato's doctrine that the number of souls remains constant. Whether he had his own theory about that number's association with the Perfect Number, we do not know.

26

Iamblichus now turns to the topic of the soul's descent. It is impossible to determine how much material Stobaeus has cut between the end of the last section and the beginning of this.

'Εν ταὐτῷ· περὶ διαφορᾶς καθόδου τῶν ψυχῶν . . . Wachsmuth transposed this lemma from 379.11 W. Festugière follows him in this, agreeing that it was "badly placed." Nevertheless, he finds the title unsatisfactory even in this place and re-titles the section, "Points de départ et buts de la descente" (page 216 note 1). In truth the topics of this section are many. Iamblichus begins by contrasting three groups on the soul's descent and embodiment: (1) Plotinus, Porphyry, and Amelius, (2) Plato in the *Timaeus*, and (3) other Platonists (377.13-378.21 W). The topic here is the places in the universe from which the soul can be said to descend. The first group thinks it is simply from the Hypercosmic Soul; the second gives a hierarchy of places (hypercosmic, encosmic, sub-lunar); and the third posits some particular place above the earth. Next Iamblichus turns to the question of whether the soul's descent is voluntary or not (378.21-379.10 W). We assign a different section number to each of the two major divisions and allow the MSS. title to stand while admitting that each section could be titled separately.

Πλωτῖνος μὲν καὶ Πορφύριος καὶ 'Αμέλιος . . . See section 17, above (372.9-14 W), where (we are told) Plotinus and Amelius make the universal soul and individual souls the same, but Porphyry distinguishes them. Also, in section 6 (365.14-21 W), Plotinus and Amelius hold somewhat (but not consistently) to the view that all souls are equal, whereas Porphyry appears to be of two minds on the subject. Iamblichus believes that different classes of soul (e.g., divine and human) should be placed in distinct categories. See the notes to section 15, above. Iamblichus would agree that the individual human soul comes from the Supracelestial Soul (*In Tim.* Fr. 54.8-11), but he would add further steps to the process. See below and Finamore (1985) 59-60.

Πολὺ δὲ διαφερόντως ἔοικεν ὁ Τίμαιος . . . Iamblichus now embarks on an interpretation of *Timaeus* 41d-42a, where the Demiurge blends human souls from the remnants of the ingredients from which he had created the divine souls, distributes them among the stars, and prepares for their eventual birth as human beings. This interpretation differs from the doctrine of Plotinus, Porphyry, and Amelius in two ways. First, not all souls are equal (and in fact the human soul is much inferior to those above it). Second, the descent is considered in various stages and does not occur immediately from the Supracelestial Soul.

In this paragraph, Iamblichus mentions several Neoplatonic doctrines concerning the soul's descent: the first existence of souls, their "sowing" among the planets and stars, and their descent into the material realm. For a full discussion, see Finamore (1985) 60-91. The "first coming into existence" (πρώτη ὑπόστασις) is the soul's earliest and highest existence at the supracelestial level; the "sowing" (σπορά) brings the soul into the cosmos and associates it and its ethereal vehicle with a soul and vehicle of a leader-god; the descent (κάθοδος) brings the soul into the world of generation and into its corporeal body.

εἰς ὅλα δὲ τὰ στοιχεῖα τοῦ παντός . . . Festugière (216-217 note 5) interprets τὰ στοιχεῖα as "planètes," but this is incorrect. See Finamore (1985) 73. The sowing of the human soul and vehicle takes place into all the superior classes of soul (visible gods, angels, heroes, daemons, etc.) who exist above and below the Moon. The "elements" refer to the bands of fire, air, and water between the Moon and earth.

ἡ σπορὰ ἡ δημιουργικὴ τῶν ψυχῶν διαιρουμένη περὶ τὰς θείας δημιουργίας . . . We read περί with FP. The Demiurge sows the souls with their vehicles around the vehicles of the gods and other superior classes.

ἡ πρώτη τῶν ψυχῶν πρόοδος . . . The "first procession" (πρώτη πρόοδος) is that from the Mixing Bowl (*Tim.* 41d4-7). See Iamblichus, *In Tim.* Fr. 82 and Finamore (1985) 89-90.

ἡ μὲν ὅλη τὸν ὅλον κόσμον . . . The Whole Soul (ἡ ὅλη ψυχή) is presumably the Soul of the Universe (ἡ τοῦ παντὸς ψυχή).

"Αλλη τοίνυν αἵρεσις τῶν Πλατωνικῶν . . . Iamblichus now turns to the third major grouping, another set of Platonists (who differ from Plotinus, Amelius, and Porphyry, whose views he has given above). Iamblichus discusses the views of various Platonists who do not follow the *Timaeus* but believe that the human soul *always* exists in some body, heavenly or earthly. He differentiates four different "bodies" or starting points whence the soul descends: (1) the Milky Way, (2) the stars and planets, (3) the Moon or the air just under it, and (4) other solid bodies. (Note that Iamblichus lists the abodes in descending order from the top of the cosmos down.) F. Cumont, *After Life in Roman Paganism* (New Haven 1922) 91-109, esp. 93-94, has discussed these psychic abodes. Of these four, the last is different in that it does not allot the soul a heavenly abode at all, but rather holds that the human soul passes from one corporeal body to another. The problem with all four views, as far as Iamblichus is concerned, is that they do not make use of the different abodes established in his interpretation of the *Timaeus* and they do not allow the soul a separated, non-bodily (earthly or otherwise) existence.

Plotinus, *Enn.* 4.3.9.1-8 discusses the soul's entry into body (πῶς ἐγγίγνεται σώματι ψυχή), distinguishing two ways that a soul may enter a body. Either it is already occupying a body (whether of earth or air or fire) or it occupies no body before entering into some body (εἰς ὁτιοῦν σῶμα, i.e., a body of earth, air, fire, etc.). Plotinus' first means of entry is similar to the thinkers Iamblichus discusses here. Indeed, Plotinus divides this first class into two subdivisions. The first is when the soul enters from one body to another (γίνεται ψυχῇ ἐν σώματι οὔσῃ τῇ τε μετενσωματουμένῃ); the second when the soul enters from aery or fiery body into an earthly one. The latter is like the opinions of the first three groups discussed by Iamblichus, where the soul goes from ethereal ("fiery," for Plotinus) or aery bodies to earthly ones; the former like the fourth, where the soul goes from earthly body to earthly body. The souls that may enter into bodies for the first time, which Plotinus discusses at greater length, is similar to the conception of the *Timaeus*, where the soul's πρώτη ὑπόστασις is without body. Iamblichus' discussion differs from Plotinus' in two ways: it is more detailed and more doxographical. It is possible therefore that Iamblichus has taken Plotinus' treatise and supplemented it with material of his own. Alternatively, Plotinus' discussion may already be part of a larger set of discussions about the soul's embodiment, in which case Plotinus may have condensed his material while Iamblichus took it over and added to it.

οὐ κατὰ τοὺς . . . Iamblichus by helpfully telling us what these "other Platonists" did not do (οὐ κατὰ τοὺς . . . οὐδὲ κατὰ τὰς . . . οὐδὲ κατὰ τὰς) tells us more about his own interpretation of the *Timaeus*. The human soul is "distributed" into its god's soul, is "sown" into the superior classes, and descends into the places allotted to it by the Demiurge (i.e., into its appropriate allotment in this life). The νομαί ("distributions") are the sending of souls around the souls of the gods. See Finamore (74-78 and 115 note 5). As the sowing establishes the human souls' vehicles in the vehicles of the gods and superior classes, so the distribution establishes the human souls in their souls. In these lines, Iamblichus is working in reverse order, from lowest allotment upwards.

If we take these lines together with the previous paragraph on the *Timaeus*, Iamblichus may be seen as presenting a carefully articulated interpretation of Plato's *Timaeus* that includes the soul's first incarnation by the Demiurge, its distribution (as incorporeal soul) into the souls of the planetary gods, the creation of its ethereal vehicle and placement into it, the sowing of the soul and vehicle into those of the soul's leader-god and the subsequent placement into the superior classes allotted to that god, and its final allotment in this realm and its placement under the laws of fate.

Ἐρατοσθένους καὶ Πτολεμαίου τοῦ Πλατωνικοῦ . . . Festugière (218 note 1), following Wachsmuth, believes that this Eratosthenes is not the mathematician from Cyrene, but another "Platonist" Eratosthenes. Dodds (1963²) 317-318 was at first hesitant, but in a note added to the second edition (348) he accepts that this is probably the Cyrenean. The reason for Dodds' change of heart is an article by F. Solmsen, "Eratosthenes as Platonist and Poet," *TAPA* 73 (1942) 192-213. Solmsen (198, cf. 201-202) argues that there is no other reference to a "Platonist" Eratosthenes in antiquity and that a passage in Proclus, *In Tim.* 2.152.26ff., which Festugière considers to refer to the "Platonist," is also to the Cyrenean and shows that Eratosthenes was interested in matters concerning Plato's *Timaeus.* Solmsen's arguments are cogent. We see little reason to unnecessarily multiply the number of philosophers named "Eratosthenes." If this attestation is correct, then the belief in "subtle bodies" (i.e., vehicles or envelopes of the soul) can be traced back to Hellenistic times.

On Ptolemy, see A. Dihle, "Der Platoniker Ptolemaios," *Hermes* 85 (1957) 315-325.

εἰς τὰ ὀστρεώδη . . . Literally "into oyster-like bodies." For the metaphor, see Plato, *Phaedrus* 250c5-6: we are surrounded by a body, "bound as an oyster."

Ἡρακλείδην μὲν τὸν Ποντικὸν . . . For Heraclides, see Gottschalk, *Heraclides of Pontus*, (Oxford 1980) 100-105. We have evidence here of a tradition within Platonism, represented initially by Heraclides (but also later by such figures as Antiochus of Ascalon) which actually regarded the soul as composed of aether or some fiery substance of great purity. This tradition is reflected in Philo of Alexandria as well; see Dillon (1998) 99-110.

27

Having explained different views of the soul's descent into body, Iamblichus now considers two ways of viewing the descent. The section is divided into two parts, each of which is further subdivided into two (by μέν . . . δέ). The first part (given in the first paragraph in this section) concerns the soul's descent as a necessary following of the laws of the cosmos; the second (given in the second paragraph) the distinction between a voluntary and involuntary descent. As we shall see, these two ways of looking at the descent are not contradictory but are two ways of viewing the same phenomenon. There is nothing in this section with which Iamblichus would disagree. He believes that the soul descends of necessity (in accordance with the *Timaeus*) and that different souls will either accept the need to descend or not. Below, in section 29, Iamblichus will distinguish three classes of souls, two of which will descend willingly in the necessary descent and one which will descend unwillingly "for punishment and judgment." On section 27, see Finamore (1985) 96-101.

Ἡράκλειτος μὲν . . . Heraclitus, frr. 60, 84a, and 84b. (Fr. 60 is from Hippolytus, *Refutation of All Heresies*; 84 a and b derive from Plotinus.) These fragments also appear grouped together in Plotinus, *Enn.* 4.8.1 (cf. 4.8.5), where they also concern the soul's descent. See Festugière (71-72).

Plotinus (*Enn.* 4.8.1.12-17) has the following to say about Heraclitus' "doctrine" on the descent:

> Heraclitus urges us to seek this [i.e., how the soul comes to be in body], positing that "changes necessarily arise from opposites" (ἀμοιβάς τε ἀναγκαίας τιθέμενος ἐκ τῶν ἐναντίων), and having said that "the road up is the road down" (ὁδόν τε ἄνω κάτω εἰπὼν) and "by changing it rests" (μεταβάλλον ἀναπαύεται) and "it is weariness to the same [souls?] to toil and to be ruled" (κάματός ἐστι τοῖς αὐτοῖς μοχθεῖν καὶ ἄρχεσθαι), he seems to hint, not caring to make the meaning clear to us, on the grounds perhaps that it is necessary to seek after it, just as he himself has discovered [the truth] after seeking it.

Two things, at least, are clear from this passage. First, these sayings of Heraclitus were already imagined by Plotinus' time to be related to the topic of the soul's descent into a body. Second, Plotinus himself found them hard to interpret. Since Plotinus refers the fragments to the soul, it is clear enough that the kind of descent hinted at is a *necessary* descent (ἀμοιβάς τε ἀναγκαίας); the change in the soul's state is part of the necessary *logos* controlling the cosmos.

Iamblichus is taking a similar tack. The change in the soul's status occurs by necessity (ἀμοιβὰς ἀναγκαίας τίθεται ἐκ τῶν ἐναντίων). This necessity is connected not only to the soul's descent but also to its reascent (ὁδόν τε ἄνω καὶ κάτω διαπορεύεσθαι τὰς ψυχάς). Both the descent and ascent are linked to some innate power in the soul by which it is more difficult for the soul to remain inactive than it is for it to yield to the descending and ascending (τὸ μὲν τοῖς αὐτοῖς ἐπιμένειν κάματον εἶναι, τὸ δὲ μεταβάλλειν φέρειν ἀνάπαυσιν). Indeed, no matter the truth of Iamblichus' interpretation of the sayings of Heraclitus, it seems that he is at greater pains than Plotinus to give them a consistent and comprehensible interpretation. The soul has an innate drive, as it were, that keeps it in motion. Its descent and reascent are necessary, and the soul cannot easily resist this inner drive. Thus, according to Iamblichus, the doctrines of Heraclitus are in agreement with that of the *Timaeus*, where the soul descends and is embodied according to necessity. As in section 26, above, it is possible that Iamblichus has Plotinus' passage in mind here, or that both are following a common text that deals with Heraclitus.

Οἱ δὲ περὶ Ταῦρον Πλατωνικοὶ . . . The doctrine attributed to Heraclitus (that the soul's descent is governed by necessity) is also attributed to "Taurus and his followers." Taurus (*floruit* 145 C.E.) was the teacher of Aulus Gellius (who preserves several anecdotes about him) and an Academic who wrote a commentary on Plato's *Timaeus*. (Excerpts are preserved in Philoponus, *De Aeternitate Mundi*.)

The periphrasis that Iamblichus uses here, "Taurus and his followers," is intriguing. Were there various students of Taurus who adopted two different ways of explaining the soul's "necessary" descent, or were these two ways in fact both taught by Taurus himself? Dillon (1977) 245-246 was the first to suggest that the two views were Taurus' and that Iamblichus is using the periphrasis "Taurus and his followers" to mean simply "Taurus." He argues correctly that the two opinions are compatible. In fact, the two opinions are clearly accepted by Iamblichus himself and folded into a single view. Although an authoritative answer cannot be given, it is not impossible that the opinions were both Taurus' originally.

οἳ μὲν ἑπομένως τῷ Τιμαίῳ . . . The first group of Taurians (or Taurus himself) claims that the gods send souls to earth for the completion of the universe (τελείωσις τοῦ παντός). The doctrine is from Plato's *Timaeus*. The Demiurge will create the four kinds of living creatures in order that there will be as many types of creature below as intellect discerns in τὸ ζῷον (*Tim.* 39e3-40a2). The Demiurge tells the creator gods that they must create the last three types of creature because the world must contain all the kinds of living creatures in order to be complete (τέλεος) (41b7-c2). Finally, at the end of the *Timaeus*, Plato writes that the universe he has described contains all the living creatures and is greatest, best, most beautiful, and most complete (μέγιστος καὶ ἄριστος κάλλιστός τε καὶ τελεώτατος) (92c5-9). See also Plotinus, *Enn.* 4.8.1.40-50, where he summarizes Plato's view in the *Timaeus*, esp. 47-49: individual souls were sent by the god for the perfection of the world (πρὸς τὸ τέλεον αὐτὸ εἶναι). Cf. Festugière 73-74, Dillon (1977) 245, and Finamore (1985) 121 note 63.

Οἳ δὲ εἰς θείας ζωῆς ἐπίδειξιν . . . The second group (or Taurus in an alternate explanation) gives a religious explanation. Certain souls descend into bodies purely, and these divine human beings display the life and thought of the gods through their own human lives. Iamblichus too posits a special superior class of human souls. These purified souls descend willingly in a necessary descent for the good of humanity and would include such "divine" philosophers as Plato and Pythagoras. See the notes to sections 29 and 30 (380.6-29 W) below.

It should be noted that Iamblichus breaks out of indirect discourse in the final sentence. In the previous two sentences, he gives the Taurian view using the infinitive in indirect discourse: "Others attribute the goal of the descent to the demonstration of divine life. For this [they say] is (εἶναι) the will of the gods: to show themselves as gods through the souls." But then Iamblichus uses the indicative mood, clearly approving the Taurian view: "For the gods come forth (προέρχονται) into the open and show (ἐπιδείκνυνται) themselves through the pure and immaculate lives of souls."

Κατ᾽ ἄλλην τοίνυν διαίρεσιν . . . Having approved the views of both Heraclitus and Taurus on the soul's necessary descent into body, Iamblichus now turns to a different way of looking at the descents. Given that the soul must descend, to what extent is the descent voluntary? Like Plotinus before him (*Enn.* 4.8.5), Iamblichus finds no contradiction between the descent that is necessary for the completion of the universe and soul's willingness or unwillingness in its individual descent. Iamblichus has already hinted at his solution when he discussed pure souls that descend to demonstrate divine will, for these souls are clearly willing participants in a necessary descent. These souls know and accept the will of the gods. Lesser souls descend unwillingly, being forced to descend and enter again into bodies for punishment for their past sins. See sections 29 and 30, below.

28

Sections 28-30 concern the human soul's encounter with the body. It was from here that the title to section 26-27 was transferred. We have supplied the titles given here for sections 28-30. Festugière (220) entitles the first section "Diverse selon la diversité des âmes," but this leaves out of account the second paragraph on Atticus and other Platonists who think that all embodiments are the same. Similarly, he (222) entitles section 29, "Diverse selon la diversité des buts," which again ignores the second paragraph in the section. Section 30 lacks a second paragraph that would offer a contrast to the doctrine given. This suggests that Stobaeus has again curtailed our text. Festugière (223) gives the title "Diverse selon les genres de vie différents des âmes avant la descente."

Οὐχ ἡ αὐτή ἐστι πασῶν τῶν ψυχῶν κοινωνία . . . This paragraph presents one view of the act of embodiment: different classes of souls join with bodies differently. The next paragraph presents an alternative view: all souls join bodies in the same way. This first paragraph, which certainly preserves Iamblichus' own doctrine (see *De Myst.* 1.8), uses the Iamblichean psychic differentiae to explain how embodiment is less a detriment to souls at the top of the hierarchy and more of one to souls at the bottom. Iamblichus takes us from the highest soul to the lowest.

The Greek word is κοινωνία, "partnership," "communion," "community." It is used of the "community of wives and children" in *Rep.* 464a9. Iamblichus uses the term indifferently of the soul's association with the body (here and 381.13-14 W) and with the gods (382.18 W). He uses it also of the association of the rational soul with the compound of irrational soul and body (380.5 W). Plotinus uses the term in *Enn.* 4.3.9.9-10: ψυχῇ κοινωνία σώματι. See also Galen, *de Placitis Hippocratis et Platonis* 643 Muller: τὴν πρὸς τἄλλα σώματα κοινωνίαν. The term has Stoic overtones (383.3 W) but has been fully adopted into the Neoplatonic vocabulary.

ἡ μὲν ὅλη, ὥσπερ καὶ Πλωτίνῳ δοκεῖ . . . The World Soul has the best relationship to body: it holds the cosmic body but is not held by it. As Iamblichus says, Plotinus (*Enn.* 4.3.9) holds a similar theory. In fact Plotinus uses similar terminology. The cosmos "is overcome and does not overcome; it is held but does not hold" (κρατούμενος οὐ κρατῶν, καὶ ἐχόμενος ἀλλ' οὐκ ἔχων, lines 37-8). See also Festugière 220 notes 3 and 4. Individual souls, however, consort with bodies more intimately.

Καὶ αἳ μὲν τῶν θεῶν θεῖα σώματα . . . The heavenly gods have absolute control over their (ethereal) bodies. As one continues down the scale through the superior classes (angels, heroes, and daemons), these souls become less and less able to control their vehicles (i.e., their own ethereal bodies). Human souls, who unite with corporeal bodies, have the hardest time, although it is easier for pure souls than for impure ones.

There is no reason to translate καί (line 18 W) as καίτοι ("cependent"), as Festugière wishes. Rather the conjunction is copulative. Iamblichus has just contrasted the whole soul with partial ones. Now he describes the various partial souls and their relationship with their bodies.

The ethereal bodies of the gods are said to "imitate intellect" in that they move in a circular motion. Note that the gods have an "intellectual essence" (νοερὰν οὐσίαν, line 20) whereas human souls have "a disposition, good in form, similar to that of the gods in intellect" (παραπλησίαν τοῖς θεοῖς κατὰ νοῦν διάθεσιν ἀγαθοειδῆ, *De An.* 457.13-14 W). Iamblichus is careful to keep classes of soul distinct.

῎Ετι γε μὴν αἱ καθαραὶ ψυχαὶ . . . These are the pure souls of section 27. See our notes to sections 29-30, below.

᾽Αττικῷ < δὲ> καὶ < ἄλλοις τισὶ> Πλατωνικοῖς . . . The Greek text is corrupt. The MSS. have ᾽Αττικῷ ἢ Πλατωνικοῖς ("Atticus or Platonists"), which makes little sense, because Atticus is after all a Platonist. The reading given here was suggested by Heeren and followed by Wachsmuth and Festugière. The "other Platonists" may be taken to include Numenius, who also subscribed to this psychic dualism, and Atticus' follower Harpocration of Argos. Cf. Dillon (1977), 374-378 and 260-261. Another possibility is that Πλατωνικοῖς is a scribal misreading for Πλουτάρχῳ which would unite Atticus with his normal comrade in arms (from the Neoplatonic perspective). This still leaves the Greek somewhat rough, but possible. Plutarch shared with Atticus a belief in a disorderly soul (cf. *De Proc. An.*, *passim* and section 23, above).

For Atticus, see section 23 (374.26-375.5 W). Festugière (221 note 4) cites and translates Proclus, *In Tim.* 2.153.25ff. and 3.234.8ff. On the latter passage, see Dillon (1975) 371-372. Atticus seems to have held that the soul is composed of a pre-existing mortal irrational component that is put in order by a higher, immortal rational component. The concept of a "disorderly" (πλημμελής) soul derives from Plato, *Tim.* 30a4. See Proclus *In Tim.* 1.381.26ff (translated by Festugière 208 note 3), who cites Atticus in this context. On the level of the cosmos, Atticus postulated both the World Soul and an evil

World Soul (responsible for the disorderly motion of matter before the Demiurge brought it into an orderly motion). At the level of human soul, he postulated an immortal and controlling rational soul along with a disorderly irrational one. On Atticus, see also Dillon (1977) 256-7.

Here Iamblichus contrasts Atticus' view of the soul's embodiment with his own. Clearly Atticus does not differentiate different classes of soul. Indeed for Iamblichus, Atticus believes that the embodiment of human souls parallels that of the cosmic soul. This would mean that every embodiment involves the rational soul taking over a body with its inherent disorderly motions, which are in turn presided over by an irrational soul. The rational soul is to impose order (hence the present participle, κατακοσμουμένη, "is being brought into order").

29

Οἶμαι τοίνυν καὶ τὰ τέλη διάφορα ὄντα . . . As in the previous section, Iamblichus begins by giving his own doctrine, then follows up with the views of "other Platonists." On this section, see Finamore (1985) 101-107.

Iamblichus here emphasizes the distinction of purposes of the soul's descent and posits a threefold distinction of embodiments based upon that. Elsewhere in the *De Anima* (and indeed just below), Iamblichus makes only a twofold division between pure and impure souls (sections 28 and 30, 379.22-25 and 380.23-9. W), but in *De Myst.* 5.18 he makes a similar threefold division of souls. On these divisions, see the notes to the next section. Iamblichus, in the present passage, has subdivided the category of impure souls into two: the mass of sinful humanity who descend into bodies for punishment of their past sins and those of greater purity who descend to better themselves. The highest category contains those completely pure.

Iamblichus believes, following the *Timaeus*, that all souls descend of necessity. The highest two classes of human souls recognize that their descent is for the best and make the necessary descent willingly. The lowest class of human souls does not see that the descent for punishment is a good thing and thus descends unwillingly.

<Τινὲς δὲ τῶν νεωτέρων οὐχ οὕτως> διακρίνουσιν . . . Both F and P leave a gap after what precedes with a strong stop. Heeren suggested

this addition, and he is followed by Wachsmuth and Festugière. The text is certainly corrupt. The verb διακρίνουσιν comes too abruptly at the beginning of its sentence; both a subject and some resumptive conjunction such as δέ are required. Heeren has supplied both, and we adopt his suggestion here.

οἱ περὶ Κρόνιόν τε καὶ Νουμήνιον καὶ ᾿Αρποκρατίωνα . . . Iamblichus has mentioned the views of Numenius, Cronius, and Harpocration on evil and the soul before in section 23 (375.12-16 W). There Numenius and Cronius think that evil becomes attached to the soul through matter, while Harpocration believes it arises from the material bodies themselves. See our notes to section 23, above. On the soul's embodiment as a misfortune, see Dillon (1977) 377 (Numenius), 380 (Cronius), and 260-261 (Harpocration).

30

In this section Iamblichus turns to the life of souls before they are ever implanted in bodies. On this section, see Finamore (1985) 107-110 and Finamore (1997) 168-171 and 173-176.

Οἵ τε γὰρ νεοτελεῖς . . . Iamblichus' vocabulary is intentionally reminiscent of the *Phaedrus*. For νεοτελεῖς καὶ πολυθεάμονες, see *Phdr.* 251a2, 250e1, and 248b4; for οἵ τε συνοπαδοὶ καὶ συγγενεῖς τῶν θεῶν, 248c3; for ὁλόκληρα, see 250c1-3. This embodies an important feature of Iamblichus' exegesis of the *Phaedrus*, reflected (through Syrianus) in Hermias' commentary. Iamblichus sees three categories of human souls presented clearly at 248aff. Cf. Hermias 157.5-159.3, although Hermias makes no mention there of the highest class of souls descending.

As the vocabulary suggests, Iamblichus is interpreting Plato's *Phaedrus* myth. Both here and in section 28 (379.22-25 W) he divides human souls into two classes. The embodiment of the higher class is without passions and pure; that of the latter affected by passions. Plato makes a twofold division of human souls also. After describing the journey of the gods (*Phdr.* 247c-e), Plato differentiates between those human souls who successfully follow the gods in this journey and manage with difficulty to see the Forms (248a) and those who do not see the Forms because their horses stumble and are dragged down along with others (248ab). Later (248cd), Plato says that the first group will remain always unharmed (ἀπήμονα, c4; ἀβλαβῆ, c5). Iamblichus seems to interpret this to mean that such a soul will descend and enter into a body purely and without being affected by passions.

We saw above (section 29, 380.6-14 W) that Iamblichus also promulgated a threefold division of souls, in which the lowest class here in section 30 was subdivided into souls either somewhat or very much impure. The reason behind the triple division can be found in the *Phaedrus* myth as well. Of the highest of his two classes of soul, Plato says (248c) that if such a soul can attain a vision of the Forms, it will be free for one revolution (= 10,000 years); and if it can do so always, it will always be free. The other souls shed their wings and fall to earth; in their first birth they become philosophers but in subsequent births the soul may not fare as well (248c-e). Now a soul that chooses the philosophical life for three successive 1,000-year periods escapes the cycle of births for the rest of the 10,000-year cycle (248e-249c). Iamblichus seems to be subdividing Plato's second class of souls into those that have had a better view of the Forms than others and who have the ability to choose the philosophical life thrice. They descend "not completely unaffected" (380.11 W) and through living in the body regain their connection to the Intelligible. (Hence, they descend διὰ γυμνασίαν καὶ ἐπανόρθωσιν τῶν οἰκείων ἠθῶν, 380.10 W.) The other souls are not so fortunate and continue to lead non-philosophical lives for the entire 10,000-year cycle.

Iamblichus makes a similar threefold distinction in *De Myst.* 5.18. There the highest human souls "using some supernatural power of intellect, stand aside from nature, are led around to the separated and unmixed Intellect, and at the same time surpass the powers of nature" (223.16-224.2). These are the pure souls once they have made their pure descent to this realm. Since they are unaffected by passions, they can easily re-establish direct contact with the higher world. The lowest class of human souls live in and are controlled by nature, are subject to fate, and use practical reasoning instead of intellect (223.10-16). The intermediate class carry on their lives between nature and Intellect; "some use both, others pursue a life mixed from both, and others are freed from the inferior and change to the better" (224.3-6). They are thus in a position to better themselves while living in the body. The distinction between the two lowest classes shows Iamblichus' pessimistic and optimistic sides. The lowest, the mass of humanity, is weighed down by the material world and find it difficult to ascend from it. The median class, however, through its involvement in appropriate theurgic acts, can rise from nature and make contact with the gods. Such a soul seems able to make up for its mediocre showing in the Intelligible world before its embodiment.[81]

There is one final difficulty that Iamblichus faces because of his belief in a class of pure souls. Plato intimates that his highest class of souls does not descend; it is simply "unharmed" (*Phdr.* 248c). It is the other souls that fall (248c). Iamblichus himself realized the difficulty. In *In Phd.* Fr. 5, we find that he claimed that these pure souls did not descend, but he further explains what he means by this. They can be said not to descend "by reason of the form of their life which creates a descent that does not involve generation and which never breaks its connection with the higher realm." (Cp. *In Phdr.* Fr. 7 and *De An.* 379.22-24.) What Iamblichus seems to imply is that pure souls do descend (and descend willingly) and become embodied, but they maintain such close contact with the Intelligible that the term "descent" is not strictly applicable. This is not to say that they always intellectualize (for they are souls not gods) but that they are free from the influences of matter and can much more easily ascend than other mortals, although they too require appropriate theurgical ritual (*De Myst.* 5.18, 225.1-5).

These pure souls are born in the bodies of the especially spiritual and philosophical. Iamblichus must have envisioned thinkers such as Pythagoras and Plato. Through the lives they led and the philosophy they left behind they have assisted in the "preservation, purification, and perfection" of those of us in this realm. Clearly they did descend into this realm and become embodied, but Iamblichus must think that the kind of example and instruction that they left to us signifies no ordinary kind of higher thought. In Iamblichus' terminology, they are turned away from the sensible realm (ἀπόστροφοι ἦσαν τῆς γενέσεως, *In Phdr.* Fr. 7), their connection to the Intelligible is unbroken (ἀδιάκοπον, *In Phd.* Fr. 5), and they become embodied without passions and without being deprived of intellection (ἄνευ παθημάτων καὶ τῆς στερήσεως τοῦ νοεῖν, *De An.* 379.23-4 W). All of this suggests that although these pure souls like all human souls

---

[81] For previous intimations of such a threefold distinction in Philo, Plotinus, and the Gnostic tradition, see Dillon (1989) 69-76.

require the gods' assistance in re-ascent to the Intelligible from the sensible realm, once they attain that realm they are more closely attuned to it than other lower souls because of their privileged position in the time before they were embodied.

31

We have supplied titles in sections 31-34. P has "In the same," i.e., in the *De Anima*, as does F in its margin. Section 31 concerns the time at which the soul becomes associated with body.

Κατὰ δ᾽ Ἱπποκράτην . . . The beginning of section 31 has been lost, for the sentence begins κατὰ δὲ Ἱπποκράτην, without a previous μέν clause, and ends by referring to the many (τοσαῦτα) opinions listed in it, but as it is there are only three listed.

It may be possible to determine how much of Iamblichus' text Stobaeus has omitted. Festugière (224 notes 1-3) cites Porphyry, *Ad Gaurum* as a possible source for Iamblichus. Porphyry includes the opinions of Hippocrates, as does Iamblichus, and of an unnamed philosopher, which Iamblichus uses below in the next section (381.16 W). Porphyry also provides another opinion, that of Numenius (fr. 36 des Places) that life begins when the sperm enters the mother's womb, and Festugière argues that this opinion would have occupied the missing μέν clause here in the *De Anima*. If so (as seems likely), Iamblichus would have given the three opinions chronologically according to release of sperm, conception, and birth. It is not clear why Stobaeus has chosen to omit the opinion of Numenius here. On Hippocrates, see *Nat. Puer.* 18.

Γένοιτο δ᾽ ἂν καὶ ἄλλη τις δόξα . . . This is Iamblichus' own opinion, as the use of the potential optative shows. Iamblichus appears to claim originality for this view, but it is hardly distinguishable from Stoic doctrine (e.g., *SVF* 2.83). In its claim that rationality comes late in human life, the doctrine is also in accord with Plato, *Tim.* 43a-44d. See section 15 (318.1-4 W).

Iamblichus does not, however, say when life begins. His point is that there are a number of powers and properties in the soul (as he has already shown in the *De Anima*) and that these become manifest in the human organism at different times. When precisely the soul housing these faculties and properties enters the body he does not say, but we may make an informed conjecture.

Proclus (*In Tim.* 3.322.18-31) believes that, according to Plato, the body is ensouled at the moment of birth. He argues specifically against the view that the gods place the soul in the sperm. Psellus (*De Omniafaria Doctrina* 115 = Porphyry, Fr. 267 Smith) records that while Hippocrates and Galen thought that the embryo was ensouled, Porphyry denied this, claiming that the embryo was not nourished by soul but by nature, as trees and plants are. Thus it was nourished through the mother, not through itself. Porphyry here is following the Stoic doctrine (*SVF* 2.806). It seems likely that Iamblichus would have followed this Neoplatonic tradition. (Proclus certainly gives no hint to the contrary, although he cites and contradicts Iamblichus on another matter a few lines later at 323.7-14.) It is interesting to note that Alcinous (178.34-39) believed that the embryo was ensouled. See Dillon (1993) 156. The view of Numenius (that the sperm entering the womb is ensouled) has already been noted. Clearly, as Iamblichus says, there are many opinions about the time of ensoulment.

Iamblichus' view, then, will be that neither the sperm when it enters the womb nor the embryo is ensouled. Rather, the embryo is nourished by the soul and body of the mother. It is ensouled at the moment of birth, but not all at once. It develops first a vegetative soul, then a perceptive one, then a rational one (when it starts using discursive reasoning), and finally an intellectual one (which of course not all human beings actualize). The time interval between vegetative and perceptive soul cannot be very great, perhaps only a few seconds. It is intriguing that Iamblichus posits an interval at all. Perhaps he has in mind the time of the actual birthing process followed by the newborn's subsequent cries. It is a fascinating question. If one assumes that life begins at birth, at what point does the child begin to feel and perceive as opposed to grow and feel hunger?

κατὰ καιροὺς δὲ ἄλλοτε ἄλλως . . . We preserve the reading ἄλλοτε ἄλλως with FP. Meineke altered the text to ἄλλοτε ἄλλους, and both Wachsmuth and Festugière follow him: "sometimes at some critical times, sometimes at others." There is, however, no need to alter the MSS. reading. It makes better sense to differentiate between when and how the body takes on the psychic δυνάμεις καὶ οὐσίαι.

32

Iamblichus explores three possible explanations for the way the soul enters the body. The first two are anonymous, and the third Iamblichus ascribes to the Plotinians.

Ἀλλὰ μὴν ἔν γε τῷ τόπῳ τῆς εἰσόδου τῶν ψυχῶν, καθ᾽ ὃν ἐπιζητοῦμεν πῶς εἰσκρίνεται . . . The Greek verb εἰσκρίνεσθαι seems to have taken on a technical meaning as the term for the entry of soul into body. See Alcinous *Did.* 178.35; Festugière 267 note 1; Iamblichus, *De Myst.* 1.8, p. 25.9, with des Places 51-52 note 2; Plotinus, *Enn.* 4.3.9.8 (ἡ εἴσκρισις).

This tripartite opinion corresponds to that set out in Porphyry *ad Gaurum* 35.9ff. (although it is not there subdivided into three). According to it, the heat of the sexual act draws in a soul "from the outside" while those engaged in sex are breathing in. This has affinities to the doctrine of the Orphics. See sections 8 (366.17-24 W) and 25 (376.4-5 W) and the notes there. The Whole Soul emits partial souls that are breathed in during the sexual act.

ἀπὸ τῶν ἐκτὸς τὴν ψυχὴν ἐν τῇ καλουμένῃ συλλήψει . . . The term "conception" (σύλληψις) is explained as a pun in Porphyry (35.16): "because what happens is similar to the capture of a bird" (διὰ τὸ ἁρπαγῇ πτηνοῦ ἐοικέναι τὰ γιγνόμενα).

The phrase "from those in surrounding atmosphere" translates the Greek ἀπὸ τῶν ἐκτός, "from those outside." Cf. Porphyry, *ad Gaurum* 35.11: ἐκ τοῦ περιέχοντος ἀέρος ("from the surrounding air").

ἢ διὰ προθυμίαν τῆς ὑποδεχομένης μήτρας . . . Meineke bracketed μήτρας; Heeren suggested μητρός. There is, however, no need to tamper with the reading of the manuscripts. It may sound odd to speak of the desire of the womb, but it is Platonic. In *Tim.* 91b7-c7, Plato says that the womb is an animal desirous of childbearing (ζῷον ἐπιθυμητικὸν τῆς παιδοποιίας, c2); if frustrated in this desire, the womb will wander and cause disease. The womb therefore has desires of its own. Porphyry too speaks of the womb in this way in the corresponding passage of the *Ad Gaurum* (35.9ff.).

συγκινουμένης καὶ τῆς φύσεως . . . This is another difficult phrase. we translate "since the nature of the sperm has also been excited" (literally: "nature also having been excited along with [them, i.e., the male and the womb]"). Festugière translates: "se trouve émue la force naturelle pourvoyeuse du sperme," following Porphyry, *ad Gaurum*. Heeren suggested reading συγκρινομένης καὶ τῆς φύσεως ("nature also having been brought into combination"), where "nature" refers to the combined nature of the male and female partners. This is unnecessary. Iamblichus' point seems to be that in order for the psychic exhalation from the Whole Soul to be drawn into a fetus and for conception to occur, both the male and the womb must be warmed by desire and be breathing in while the sperm must be "excited" or "in activity" so that the soul can attach itself to it.

ἢ δὲ κατ' ἀνάγκην εἰσδύνειν ποιεῖ . . . This second theory, unlike the first, makes use of the Platonic notion of a self-moved soul (αὐτοκίνητος). Instead of the soul being drawn into the body through inhalation, the soul itself "by necessity" enters bodies. Neoplatonists found the Platonic doctrine of the self-moved soul in *Phdr.* 245c5 and *Laws* 894b-895b, although modern editors read ἀεικίνητον in the *Phaedrus* text. See T. M. Robinson, *Plato's Psychology* 2nd ed. (Toronto 1995) 111-115. For Neoplatonic texts, see Hermias, *In Phdr.* 104.7, 9, and 15. It seems that Iamblichus himself read αὐτοκίνητον in Plato's *Phdr.* 245c, for in *In Phdr.* Fr. 2 we find him denying that the irrational soul is self-moved, an epithet reserved for rational soul alone. (See Dillon's commentary on this fragment, 249-250.) Neoplatonists differentiated between Intellect as Aristotle's unmoved mover, the soul as self-moved mover, and the body as that which is moved by something else. (See Proclus, *ET* 20 and Dodds' notes, pp. 206-208 and 201-202, where he cites *Th. Pl.* 1.14, where Proclus includes the category κινούμενα καὶ κινοῦντα, which matches Iamblichus' role for the irrational soul in *In Phdr.* Fr. 2.) This "self-moved" soul, then, descends into the body "by necessity" from somewhere in the universe. The "necessity" is probably that of the *Timaeus*, according to Iamblichus' interpretation of which every soul must descend into a body. See section 26, above (377.16-29 W). There Iamblichus held that the soul's descent began from the Intelligible, through the World Soul, into the souls of the gods and superior classes, and ultimately to this lowest realm. Here Iamblichus is less definite, saying it descends into body from either the Universe as a whole or from the World Soul itself or from the "created realm," i.e., the sublunary realm ruled by the visible gods.

Although Iamblichus would agree that the soul is self-moved and descends by necessity, this sentence does not represent Iamblichus' view. As we have seen, the soul's descent for Iamblichus follows a path determined by his interpretation of the *Timaeus*. The three disjuncts at the end of the sentence are not Iamblichean. Most probably, then, this is the opinion of some Middle Platonists. For the self-moving soul in Middle Platonism, see Alcinous 178.16-23; for the necessary descent, see Iamblichus on Calvenus Taurus in section 27, above (378.25-379.6). Alcinous himself gives four possible reasons for the soul's descent (178.37-39), all of which can be classified as "necessary," if not "voluntary." See Dillon (1977) 293-294 and (1993) 156-158.

<αὐ>τὴν αὐτοκίνητον . . . This is Usener's suggestion. Festugière would keep the reading of the manuscripts, τὴν αὐτοκίνητον. Although this is possible, it is doubtful that Iamblichus would have omitted the noun ψυχὴν with the adjective. The MSS. reading would yield an awkward translation: "Another theory makes the self-moving enter into the organic body . . ." We therefore adopt Usener's suggested change.

Οἱ δὲ καθαρώτεροι τῶν Πλατωνικῶν . . . Both manuscripts have this sentence here. Wachsmuth transposed it from this location to the end of the next paragraph. Festugière (226 notes 1 and 2) rightly argues that it belongs here. It represents a third theory of how the soul enters the body. As Festugière explains, the phrase "from these quarters" (ἀπὸ τούτων τῶν μερῶν) refers to "either from the universe, or from the Whole Soul, or from the whole created realm" in the previous theory and to "from those in the surrounding atmosphere" in the first; in the words "the organic body . . . makes first use of the motion," the motion is that of the self-moved soul of the previous theory. Festugière is wrong, however, that "independent" (ἀπολύ-τους) opposes "by necessity" in the previous theory. The independence meant here is that the rational soul with its rational faculties is separated from the life-in-body. This leaves open the possibility of whether or not the "descent" is free or necessary.

On Plotinus, see (with Wachsmuth and Festugière) *Enn.* 4.3.3 and 4.3.23. Plotinus does not wish to partition the soul so that one part is present in one sense organ and another in another. Rather the same part of soul is present to each organ, and it is the organ itself that causes the difference in function. The soul seems to use the whole body as an organ, at least insofar as perception is concerned (4.3.3.8-9 cf. 4.3.22.12-18). For the soul's independence, see (with Festugière) 4.3.23.33: the rational soul is not located in the head as if in a place, but the brain makes use of the rational soul.

Aristotle, in his definition of the soul, says that it is the first entelechy of an *organic* body (*De An.* 412a27-29). At *De An.* 412b16-17, after his famous description of the essence of an ax, Aristotle says of the human soul that it is the essence of a body "that holds the beginning of motion and rest in itself" (ἔχοντος ἀρχὴν κινήσεως καὶ στάσεως ἐν ἑαυτῷ). This seems to be the point of Iamblichus' description of the organic body starting motion even though the body is directed by the soul.

It is how Iamblichus interprets Plotinus here that is of importance. The use of the term "purer" (καθαρώτεροι) is a trifle sarcastic. Thus, according to Iamblichus, Plotinus and other Platonists of his school think that the soul does not strictly enter the body at all, but the powers of the soul use the organic body while remaining aloof from it. The problem for Iamblichus is the soul's independence, as we have seen before. If the rational soul (here called "the [rational] powers") is independent of the body, then it has not truly descended. For Iamblichus' view that the whole human soul descends, see *In Tim.* Fr. 87.

33

Iamblichus sets out seven ways in which the soul may be said to use a body. As in the previous section, he commits himself to none of them. The seven possibilities he lists come from the philosophical tradition.

Οἳ μὲν γὰρ προσεοικέναι αὐτὴν λέγουσι νεὼς κυβερνήσει . . . (1) First, Iamblichus says, the soul may make use of the body as a pilot does the ship. The image of the pilot appears as early as Plato's *Republic* 488a-489a, where the good pilot is compared to the philosopher (cf. *Politicus* 297a). In the context of the philosopher-ruler, a Platonist could easily make the leap from a pilot who guides his ship well, to a philosopher who rules his state well, to the rational part of the soul that guides the irrational and spirited parts well. In spite of this passage from the *Republic* and Iamblichus' claim in *In Phdr.* Fr. 6 that the pilot in *Phdr.* 247c7 is the One of the soul, Plato does not seem to be the source of the doctrine given here in the *De Anima*. Rather, Aristotle provides the necessary text in his own *De Anima*. After arguing that the soul is inseparable from the body because it is the entelechy of some body, Aristotle adds: "It is not evident whether the soul is an entelechy of the body as a sailor is to his ship" (ἔτι δὲ ἄδηλον εἰ οὕτως ἐντελέχεια τοῦ σώματος ἡ ψυχὴ ὥσπερ πλωτὴρ πλοίου, 413a8-9). These words of Aristotle caused no small problem for later interpreters.

Alexander of Aphrodisias (*De An.* 1.29) argues that even for Aristotle the pilot is not analogous to the soul, unless κυβερνήτης is taken to mean the pilot's τέχνη. For if the soul were like the pilot, the soul would be corporeal, would be limited to one part of the body, and would not be the soul of the whole body. He concludes that Aristotle did not think the soul was like the pilot of a ship.

Plotinus (*Enn.* 4.3.21) examines how the soul is present to the body. The first possibility he lists is "as a pilot in a ship" (lines 5-8). Plotinus approves this image in one way (because it shows that the soul is separable from the body) but objects to it because (1) the pilot is accidentally on the ship qua sailor (πλωτήρ) but it is unclear how he is there qua pilot (lines 9-11) and (2) the soul is in the whole body but the pilot is not in the whole ship (lines 11-12). On the other hand, at *Enn.* 1.1.3.20-24, Plotinus distinguishes between soul as unseparated form (i.e., as an entelechy of the body in Aristotle's sense) and "a form in contact with body, like a pilot." The upper part of the soul uses (χρώμενον) the body but is separate, while the lower part is mixed with body while using it at its level. Clearly, Plotinus, unlike Alexander, is straining to show how Aristotle could have said that a soul is both an unseparated entelechy and separated.

This desire to have Aristotle accept a Platonic higher soul continued in later Neoplatonism, and probably represents Iamblichus' view. Pseudo-Simplicius (*De An*, 96.1-10) thinks that Aristotle is distinguishing between the soul's life in the body and the soul's separated life. When the soul uses the body, it is unseparated; but in another sense the soul transcends the body, and the part that does not use the body is separable from the body as a pilot from his ship. Philoponus (*De An.* 224.10-225.31) also tries to make this statement jibe with the rest of Aristotle's psychology. He argues that the rational soul is in a way inseparable from the body, and in another separable

(224.28-37). Philoponus claims that this is true of the pilot as well, since there are some things he can do only by being on the ship but others that he does separated from the ship. In this he is like the rational soul, for it has certain activities that it can perform only when embodied and others it can perform only when separated.

This first use of body by soul, then, is an attempt to give Platonic meaning to an Aristotelian conundrum, but it applies only to the rational soul, not to the irrational. As such, Iamblichus would think it only a partly correct description. It is also likely that he, like the Pseudo-Simplicius and Philoponus, thought that it applies to the rational soul only when it is operating according to its (separated) essence.

ἧς καὶ ἀπολύεσθαι χωρὶς δύναται ὁ κυβερνήτης . . . Reading ἀπολύεσθαι with Léveque and Festugière (227 note 1). Cp. above, section 16 (371.19 W).

οἳ δὲ ὀχήματος ἐπιβάσει . . . (2) The soul may make use of the body as a charioteer guides the chariot. This image is Platonic, arising from the *Phaedrus* myth and from the *Timaeus* (41e and 69c). The emphasis Iamblichus places on the common (κοινήν) journey shows that it bears a special sense here, one complementary to the first. For while the first image emphasized the possibility of the rational soul's separation from body, this image concerns the rational soul's use of the body. (In *Tim.* 69c, the rational soul is housed in the head and uses the rest of the body as its "vehicle," i.e. to carry it about. Thus, soul and bodily vehicle may be said to follow a common course.) Here the soul follows the motion of the body, just as the charioteer follows that of the chariot. The connection between soul and body is, therefore, more intimate than in the preceding image. A greater degree of symbiosis results. (There is no need to see a reference to Iamblichus' doctrine of the ethereal vehicle of the soul here.)

οἳ δὲ ὡς μᾶλλον . . . (3-5) These three ways of describing the association of soul and body are connected. Either the association is evenly balanced, or the soul yields to body, or the body gives itself totally to soul. Festugière (227 note 3) ascribes the first to Aristotle's psychology. This is true, of course, but not for the Neoplatonic interpretation of Aristotle's psychology. Iamblichus may be thinking of Stoics or Epicureans here, but he need not have in mind any specific group.

The terms "convergence" and "declension" (σύννευσις, ῥοπή) have a Gnostic ring. For νεῦσις, see Plotinus *Enn.* 2.9.4.6-8 and 2.9.10.19, but Plotinus uses it himself, as Festugière 227 note 4 says. (Iamblichus uses it in *Myst.* 2.7, p. 84.16.) Iamblichus uses the verb συννεύειν in *In Tim.* Fr. 49.51 of the power of a sphere to converge upon itself (although this may be Proclus using the term and foisting it back upon Iamblichus). Proclus certainly uses the term (both as verb and noun) in *ET* 146 for the reversion of an hypostasis back to its first principle (like a circle converging on itself). Iamblichus' use of the term here for the soul's convergence to body seems unusual. (See also Festugière 227 note 4 for its use by Plotinus and Porphyry.) The verb ῥέπειν is used of declining toward bodies and is found in Iamblichus' own writings (*In Tim.* Frr. 16.9 and 22; *Myst.* 1.20, p. 64.8) and by Porphyry, *Sent.* 3-4, 28. On the two terms νεύειν and ῥέπειν, see also des Places 76 note 1. There seems to be, then, no definite school to which Iamblichus would be referring here.

The same is true of the mastery of the body by the soul, which is acceptable to Platonists, Aristotelians, and Stoics.

< ἢ> ἐπικράτεια τοῦ σώματος . . . Both manuscripts have the dative (ἐπικράτεια) without the conjunction. Usener suggested changing the dative to the verb ἐπικρατεῖ, and Wachsmuth prints his suggestion. We cannot make sense of this proposed reading in this sentence. We adopt Festugière's reading (227 note 5). He proposes that a conjunction (ἢ) has dropped out of the text.

οἳ δὲ οὐδὲν τούτων . . . (6-7) The soul is a part of the whole living thing. This same view is opposed by Plotinus in *Enn.* 4.3.20.30-34: "It is not as a part in a whole, for the soul is not part of the body . . . as a part in a whole living entity" (οὐ μὴν οὐδ' ὡς μέρος ἐν ὅλῳ, οὐ γὰρ μέρος ἡ ψυχὴ τοῦ σώματος . . . ὡς ἐν ὅλῳ μέρος τῷ ζῴῳ.). The final image is similar to that given by Alexander of Aphrodisias (above) and also appears in *Enn.* 4.3.21.11-21. Taken together, these last two methods are opposed. The first shows how the soul may be materially part of a body; the second how it may be formally part of it.

34

Iamblichus turns from the soul's association with body to its association with the gods. Strictly speaking, this section does not fit well with those on embodiment that come before it. Wachsmuth suggested making it a separate chapter. Festugière 228 note 1 remarks that it does not correspond to parallel passages in Tertullian and Aetius, but he nonetheless attaches it to the preceding sections. We do the same, but suspect that it is a paragraph from elsewhere in the *De Anima* that Stobaeus has placed here.

For Iamblichus, who pioneered the idea of the soul as mean between gods and the material realm and who increased the significance of theurgy in Neoplatonism, the issue of how the human soul and gods form a union is an important one. It is surprising that he does not clearly indicate his own view here. Two passages from the end of the *De Anima* show that Iamblichus would adopt the second opinion given here, that pure human souls can mix with the gods, but with certain restrictions. In section 53 (458.17-21 W), it is the view of the "ancients" (i.e., of Iamblichus) that "after they have been freed from generation, souls administer the universe with the gods." Iamblichus believes that pure human souls form a community with the gods after death and during ritual ascent. On this passage, see Finamore (1985) 153-155. Iamblichus also believes, however, that the human soul existed on a different level of reality from the gods and could not become completely unified with them. In section 50 (458.3-6 W), Iamblichus contrasts the opinion of Numenius of a "union and undifferentiated sameness" of soul and higher principles with that of the ancients of "a natural conjoining to a different substance." For Iamblichus, the pure human soul mixes with the gods but remains separate according to its own essence. Compare *Myst.* 2.2, where Iamblichus discusses the differences between heroes, daemons, and souls. The human soul, he says (69.9-14) "because of the good will of the gods and because of the illumination of light given from them, often mounts even higher, ascending to a greater and angelic order." Iamblichus at first says that the human soul ceases to exist in human boundaries but becomes angelic (69.14-16), but then softens this statement and says that it "always is defined according to a single category and by sharing (κοινοῦσα) it co-arranges (συντάττεται) itself with different higher causes at different times" (69.17-19).

The reference to daemons and heroes in the final sentence of this section is to the lowest two orders of the so-called superior classes (angels, daemons, heroes). According to this third opinion, pure human souls ascend only to the τάξις of these lower beings, not even to the angels. This would be opposed to *Chald. Or.* Fr. 138, according to which the souls of theurgists exist ἀγγελικῷ ἐνὶ χώρῳ.

For the Stoic view that the cosmos is a "city of gods and human beings," see *SVF* 2.528 (Arius Didymus, quoted in Eusebius, *Praep. Evang.* 15.15). Gods are the rulers; human beings the ruled. There is a κοινωνία πρὸς ἀλλήλους because they share in λόγος together.

35

The titles for sections 35-38 are not in the manuscripts. Festugière (229) has entitled the whole "Vie de l'âme dans le corps." We have divided it into four sections. The first concerns the soul's choice of the best life (which is probably made before it enters a body; see below.) The second concerns death. The third and fourth concern the fate of the irrational soul and vehicle after death.

The beginning words of section 35 are missing from both manuscripts. Wachsmuth marked the opening with an ellipsis. Festugière (229 note 1) argues that a main clause is required with a verb upon which the following Greek participles depend. He suggests πολυειδῶς διαφέρονται οἱ βίοι: "Les genres de vie se distinguent." We suggest: πολυειδῶς διακρίνονται οἱ βίοι αἱρετοὶ κατὰ τοὺς φιλοσόφους. Our inserted clause is similar to Festugière's but is meant to stress (1) the notion of a way of life that is (2) chosen by each person, as well as (3) the fact that different philosophical schools have defined the best way of life differently. These are the three issues that Iamblichus stresses throughout this paragraph. Like Festugière's, our insertion is meant *exempli gratia* and should not be taken as representing Iamblichus' precise words.

For a comparison of the doxography of this section with Cicero's *Lucullus* (= *Academica* book 2) 129-131 and *De Finibus* 2.34-35 and 5.16-23, see Festugière 261-262.

οἱ βελτίονες, κρινόμενοι κατὰ Πλάτωνα . . . Plato's supposed doctrine of the purification, elevation and perfection of the good soul and punishment of the bad leads Iamblichus' list. It has no correspondence to any of the three Cicero passages listed by Festugière. Iamblichus discusses the soul's purification after death in section 43 below (455.25-456.4). He says there that it includes the re-establishment of the soul's own essence, its perfection (τελειότης), and its elevation to the engendering causal principle (ἄνοδος ἐπὶ τὴν γεννησαμένην αἰτίαν). Thus all three "Platonic" attributes obtain: purification, elevation, and perfection. Plato, of course, does not mention all three, but he discusses purification in *Phaedo* 80c-81e, where he distinguishes between pure (philosophic) souls that go straight to their reward after death and the impure souls that require purification. Compare the Myth of Er, where some souls have a blissful vision of heaven for 1,000 years and other souls spend the 1,000 years in punishment for sins committed on earth (*Rep.* 615a-616b). (See also the final myth of *Gorg.* 523a-526d, where again the soul is judged after death and the souls of the wicked are punished, while the souls of the good receive their reward straightway.)

κατὰ δὲ τούς Στωικούς . . . For the Stoic doctrines of the association or community (κοινωνία) of human beings and life in accordance with nature, see *SVF* 1.179 and 2.528.

κατὰ δὲ τοὺς Περιπατητικοὺς . . . For Aristotle's theory of virtue as a mean and of the value of the contemplative life, see *Eth. Nic.* 2 and 10.7. For the view that the life of contemplation is "superior to human nature," see esp. *Eth. Nic.* 1177b26ff.: ὁ δὲ τοιοῦτος ἂν εἴη βίος κρείττων ἢ κατ' ἄνθρωπον. Both the Stoics and Aristotelians are mentioned in Cicero's texts.

κατὰ δὲ ῞Ηριλλον ἐπιστήμη· κατὰ δὲ ᾿Αρίστωνα ἀδιαφορία· κατὰ δὲ Δημόκριτον εὐσχημοσύνη . . . Herillus of Carthage, a pupil of Zeno of Citium, founded a distinctive Stoic sect of his own. His choice of knowledge as the supreme end of life represents an extreme of intellectualism. Cicero mentions him as one who considers *cognitio et scientia* to be the highest good (*Luc.* 129).

Ariston of Chios, another pupil of Zeno, took an extreme position as regards things "preferable" and "non-preferable" (προηγμένα and ἀποπροηγμένα), maintaining that all external things were totally "indifferent" (ἀδιάφορα) and that virtue was the only good. Cicero says that Ariston (*Luc.* 130) is one who thinks that the highest good is achievement of indifference (ἀδιαφορία).

Cicero does not mention Democritus. We cannot find the term εὐσχημοσύνη used in this sense of Democritus elsewhere in Greek literature. The reference is lacking in Diels-Kranz.

Hieronymus of Rhodes (290-230 BCE) was a philosopher and historian of literature who trained as a Peripatetic under Lycon but left to set up a school of his own. At *Luc.* 131 and *De Fin.* 5.20, we are told that he thinks that the highest good is the absence of pain. The term ἀοχλησία is also attributed to Speusippus (Clement, *Strom.* 2.133.4) and later to Epicurus (*Ep. Ad Men.* 62,12 Usener).

The role and place of this section in the *De Anima* is unclear. Stobaeus has placed it between sections dealing with the soul's descent and association with the body (and with the gods, if section 34 is rightly placed) and with death (the separation of soul from body). It may, therefore, be all that remains of Iamblichus' discussion of the life of the soul in the body.

There are two other possibilities, however, both suggested by Iamblichus' inclusion of the Platonic doctrine at the head of the paragraph. Festugière's study of Cicero's *Lucullus* and *De Finibus* clearly indicates that Iamblichus has added the Platonic material to a previously existing doxography. (Festugière 262 is hesitant about a single Hellenistic source for both Cicero and Iamblichus and thinks that if there were one, Iamblichus re-worked it with regard to the Platonic, Aristotelian, and Stoic schools.) Since the new material is directly attributed to Plato (κατὰ Πλάτωνα), it represents Iamblichus' own beliefs about the life to be chosen. It thus puts all the other theories in perspective. Where they miss the mark is in not understanding the importance of the disembodied life to the choice of earthly life.

This leads to the two possibilities to which we just referred. Is the choice of life the one that we make while embodied or that we make in the disembodied state? Clearly, for all the other opinions, the choice is made here and now. If Iamblichus interprets the Platonic choice of life in the same way, then this section is about the embodied life and the choices we make in it. Plato, however, when he discusses the soul's choice of life in the Myth of Er (*Rep.* 617d-620d), has the soul decide before it becomes embodied. If Iamblichus follows Plato in this, as seems likely since this is *the* most important description of the choice of life in Plato's writings, then Iamblichus' point becomes more interesting. For it is not a choice made on the basis of a single embodied life, but a study based on the whole life cycle (the 10,000-year cycle of the *Phaedrus*). As Plato says (*Rep.* 618b6-c6), the critical point is to learn how to choose the best possible life by gaining the knowledge to distinguish the good and bad lives (ἐπιστήμονα, βίον καὶ χρηστὸν καὶ πονηρὸν διαγιγνώσκοντα).

This is gained, according to the *Republic*, by learning it in this life but in the *Phaedrus* by learning it before embodiment. The two dialogues need not be, and for Iamblichus would not be, in conflict. Thus the ability to choose a good way of life is learned continuously both in the embodied and disembodied lives of the soul. This paragraph, then, is about training the embodied soul (via theurgy) to choose in its disembodied state the correct way of life for it to live in any of its embodied existences.

Further, this is probably the position the paragraph occupied in the *De Anima*. It falls between embodiment of soul and death (= separation or disembodiment of soul) and concerns a decision made before an embodied existence while the soul is disembodied. It seems naturally placed. Iamblichus may, of course, have had more to say than what is contained in this single paragraph.

There is one other possible allusion to Plato's Myth of Er. At the end of the paragraph, Iamblichus dismisses all the non-Platonic opinions about the choice of the best way of life. He says that there is an infinite variety of them but that this need not concern us. (This speaks volumes for their unimportance. These will not make a person ἐπιστήμονα, βίον καὶ χρηστὸν καὶ πονηρὸν διαγιγνώσκοντα. The lives are "infinite" because they include all the wrong choices, and evil is unbounded.) We can "dismiss them from our thoughts" (αὐτοὺς . . . χαιρεῖν ἐᾶν). Plato uses the same expression in the *Republic* while discussing the importance of the soul's preparation to gain that knowledge that will allow it to choose correctly. "It will dismiss all other matters from its thoughts" (τὰ δὲ ἄλλα πάντα χαιρεῖν ἐάσει, 618e2-3). It is true that the expression χαιρεῖν ἐᾶν is a common one, but the similar context for Plato's and Iamblichus' use of the term does suggest that Iamblichus has the passage from the *Republic* in mind. Both the unimportant studies (other than philosophy) for Plato and the other ways of life for Iamblichus will be a waste of time and should be dismissed from our thoughts. The important point is to train the soul in philosophy.

Iamblichus' paragraph is a rhetorical tour de force. He takes a pre-existing Hellenistic doxography on the τέλος of life and uses it as a foil to the ideal "Platonic" βίος. The non-Platonic views simply cannot stack up, except perhaps quantitatively, since they amount to an infinite number of wrongheaded βίοι. Iamblichus ends with a flourish: about these βίοι "we need not trouble ourselves" (πολυπραγ-μονεῖν, the identifying feature of the democratic βίος which Socrates and Plato condemned), but we "should dismiss them from our thoughts."

Plotinus, we may note, discusses the soul's choice of life in *Enn.* 3.4.5, in his study of the guardian daemon that Plato says is allotted to human souls in *Phd.* 107d and *Rep.* 620de.

36

Ἐν ταὐτῷ· περὶ θανάτου. . . . The MS. P gives the whole title, but F has simply ἐν ταὐτῷ in the margin. Festugière has "Sur la Mort" and adds subsidiary headings below that are not in the MSS.

Ἐπειδὰν μετὰ τὸν τῇδε βίον . . . This section on death is nicely structured. Iamblichus first sets out the topic's sum and substance (κεφάλαιον) here in the first paragraph. He states that just as there are three possibilities for the soul at birth (the soul may exist before, come into existence with, or come into existence after the body), so too there are three possibilities for the soul at death (the soul may perish before the body , or at same time with it, or may survive the body's death). Iamblichus then begins to examine the first two of these three "parts" (μέρη) of the topic in the following three paragraphs.

Stobaeus again has edited Iamblichus' text roughly. The section ends with a μέν solitarium and, more importantly, includes only views in which the soul is afforded no life after its separation from the body. Iamblichus would certainly have gone on to discuss other views of death in which the soul survived. The doxography may have been similar to the beginning sections of the *De Anima* (1-9) that culminate in the differences between Plotinus, Porphyry, Amelius, etc., and Iamblichus. But see our notes to the next section, below.

Ἆρα γε πνιγμῷ τῶν ἀρτηρίων . . . This paragraph presents the soul's departure as previous to or simultaneous with the body's death. The soul deteriorates with the body over time.

For the translation of ἀρτηρίων as "arteries," see Festugière 232 note 1, where he cites evidence from the "pneumatic" school of medicine and from the *Corpus Hermeticum*. Soul is present as pneuma in the body and travels through the arteries and veins. If these are cut, the pneuma is blocked; sickness or death ensues.

A second meaning of ἀρτηρία is possible, "windpipe." The term has this meaning in Plato's *Tim.* 70d1 and Aristotle's *De An.* 420b29. In both instances, however, it is used in the singular, whereas Iamblichus uses the plural. Plato has the plural in *Tim.* 78c6, where the god makes a device similar to a fish trap (κύρτος) so that the human body can breathe. Part of this device goes "through the windpipes" to the lungs. (The term ἀρτηρία signifies any tube, including the windpipe, artery, bronchial tubes, or aorta.) If we allow Iamblichus a similar use of plural for singular here, then we may translate: "when the windpipe is prevented from taking in air from outside." Iamblichus would then be referring to normal suffocation caused by loss of air to the lungs.

Diogenes of Apollonia was probably the originator of this doctrine that air or pneuma is the source if life, sensation, and thought. "Human beings and the other animals live by breathing in air, which is for them soul and intelligence . . . If it is removed, they die and intelligence ceases" (64B4 D-K = Fr. 8 Laks). This air, Diogenes says, is warmer than the air around us but cooler than that near the sun; further, its temperature differs in different creatures, and this fact explains why human beings have intelligence while other animals do not (64B5 = Fr. 9 Laks, cf. 64A19 D-K). In a passage preserved by Aetius (= 64A29 D-K), Diogenes explains that sleep is caused by the blood pushing the air from the veins to the heart and stomach; "if all the aery substance leaves the veins, death occurs." These theories passed into some of the Hippocratic texts and became part of Greek medical lore.

ἢ τοῦ θερμοῦ ἐναποσβεννυμένου . . . For the doctrine that the internal heat is quenched, see Empedocles in Aetius 5.24.2, who attributes to Empedocles the doctrine that sleep is caused by a moderate cooling of the blood while death is caused by its complete cooling (31A85 D-K).

καθάπερ Κορνοῦτος οἴεται . . . L. Annaeus Cornutus (c. 20-66 C.E.) was a Stoic philosopher, probably a freedman of Seneca, who taught both Persius and Lucan. Persius writes about him in his *Satires*. Cornutus' work "On the Nature of the Gods" survives, and contains much Stoic allegorizing and playful etymology. It is not at all clear why Iamblichus chooses him as the representative of a school of thought that has the soul perish with the body. Perhaps he composed a work on the subject of death.

Εἰ δὲ ὡς δύναμις ὑποκειμένου . . . This paragraph presents the soul as a potential state or the perfection or the form of the body. Here there is no deterioration with body, but the soul simply ceases immediately to exist (like attunement in an instrument) without any corruption or "motion" from being to non-being.

On the soul as the form of the body, see Aristotle, *De An.* 412a6-22, where Aristotle defines the body as potentiality and the form as actuality, then says: "Necessarily, soul is a substance in the sense of being the form of a natural body that potentially has life" (ἀναγκαῖον ἄρα τὴν ψυχὴν οὐσίαν εἶναι ὡς εἶδος σώματος φυσικοῦ δυνάμει ζωὴν ἔχοντος, 19-21). See also 414a12-14: "The soul is that by which especially we live, perceive, and think, so that it would be some sort of essence or form, but not matter or substrate" (ἡ ψυχὴ δὲ τοῦτο ᾧ ζῶμεν καὶ αἰσθανόμεθα καὶ διανοούμεθα πρώτως· ὥστε λόγος τις ἂν εἴη καὶ εἶδος, ἀλλ' οὐχ ὕλη καὶ τὸ ὑποκείμενον). We note again that Iamblichus attributes this view (that the soul is the form of the body) only to "many Peripatetics" and not to Aristotle himself, whose own *De Anima* Iamblichus would have interpreted differently and more in accordance with Plato. See section 2, above.

ἀλλ' ἐξαίφνης εἰς τὸ μὴ εἶναι μεθίσταται ἀχρόνως . . . We read ἀχρόνως with the manuscripts and Festugière. Wachsmuth follows Meineke in printing ἀχράντως, "without defilement," which misses the point that the change is immediate and all at once.

Ἔσται δὴ οὖν τὸ μὲν ζῆν τῷ ζώῳ ἀπὸ τοῦ ἔχειν τὸ τῆς ζωῆς εἶδος· . . . Heeren would read τῷ ζώῳ for τὰ ζῷα, not without justification. The accusative is very awkward; it would have to be an odd use of the accusative of respect. The dative singular is a relatively easy emendation.

Εἰ δὲ παρέσπαρται μὲν καὶ ἔνεστιν . . . This paragraph describes the atomic view of the soul as a configuration of atoms held together by the body and intermingled with it. For the atomists, the soul is dispersed at the time of death. The atoms continue to exist but not as the same compound in the same body and, hence, not as a soul. Again there is no deterioration of soul at death, but its withdrawal from the body does take place over time. In this theory, as in the previous two, the soul does not survive death intact.

ἔνεστιν ἡ ψυχὴ τῷ σώματι καθάπερ ἐν ἀσκῷ . . . We keep the reading of the manuscripts. There seems little reason to alter the text to καθαπερεῖ ἀσκῷ with Meineke and Wachsmuth. Iamblichus uses καθάπερ above, at the end of the second paragraph of section 36 (384.1-2 W) as a subordinating conjunction, καθάπερ Κορνοῦτος οἴεται; and below in the next section (385.8 W) as a subordinating conjunction with an ellipsis of the verb, καθάπερ ὀχήματα. The repetition ἔνεστιν . . . ἐν is not unusual in Greek. Iamblichus himself uses the construction in section 10 (367.11-12 W): ἐν ἑτέρᾳ τῇ ψυχῇ ἐνεῖναι. He uses the construction with the verb ἐνιδρύειν in section 5 (364.19-20): τὴν ἐν σώμασιν ἐνιδρυμένην and in section 6 (365.10-12 W): ἐν τῇ μεριστῇ ψυχῇ . . . ἐνιδρύουσι. Iamblichus also uses the construction with ἐνυπάρχειν in section 12 (369.7-8 W): ἐν τῷ ἡγεμονικῷ ἐνυπαρχούσων. It is odd that Iamblichus uses σώματι without the preposition just before ἐν ἀσκῷ, but not impossible. He may even be thinking of the phrase καθάπερ ἐν ἀσκῷ πνεῦμα as a separate construction from ἔνεστιν ἡ ψυχὴ τῷ σώματι. Or perhaps he considers it more immediately under the influence of the prefixed ἐν in ἔνεστιν.

ὥσπερ Δημόκριτος καὶ Ἐπίκουρος ἀποφαίνονται . . . Iamblichus' vocabulary is reminiscent of the atomists, but gathered from divergent sources. For παρέσπαρται, see *Letter to Herodotus* 63: "The soul is a body made of fine particles diffused (παρεσπαρμένον) through the whole organism." The reference to air in the wineskin is not attested for the Atomists, but is in Epicharmus 23B10 D-K: ἅ γα φύσις τί ὤν; ἀσκοὶ πεφυσιαμένοι (from Clement, *Str.* 4.45). On the notion that atoms are like motes (ὥσπερ τὰ ἐν τῷ ἀέρι ξύσματα διὰ τῶν θυρίδων φαινόμενα), see Aristotle, *De An.* 404a3-4: Democritus calls spherical atoms fire and soul "similar to so-called motes in the air, which are visible in sunrays through windows" (οἷον ἐν τῷ ἀέρι τὰ καλούμενα ξύσματα, ἃ φαίνεται ἐν ταῖς διὰ τῶν θυρίδων ἀκτῖσιν). See also Lucretius 2.114-115. Iamblichus uses the Greek verb for "scatter" (διασκεδάννυται) used by Plato in *Phd.* 77e1 (διασκεδάννυσιν, cf. 77b5), when Socrates is mocking Simmias and Cebes for fearing (like children) that a high wind will scatter the soul after death.

37

τοὺς δὲ περὶ Πλωτῖνον . . . Heeren, followed by Wachsmuth and Festugière, marks a lacuna before this section. This is verified, as

Festugière also points out, by the opening δέ and the change of subject from what happens to the soul at death (the subject of section 36) to what happens to the "irrational faculties" (the subject of section 37). The MSS record a strong break here, starting the present section on a new line, but with no new heading.

It is impossible to be completely certain how much material intervened between these two sections. We have suggested above that Iamblichus may have listed opinions of many philosophers on the fate of the soul after death. If, however, instead of heavy-handed editing by Stobaeus we have a copying error caused by a scribe's eye moving from a τοὺς δὲ that began the next (missing) sentence in the section 36 to the τοὺς δὲ here in section 37, much less may have been lost. It is this second possibility that we think more likely.

Festugière (235) thinks that, besides the ending of the previous section and the beginning of this, a section that he calls "Fate of the Intellect" is missing. He then titles this section "Fate of the Irrational Powers" and the next "Fate of Intermediary Substances." (The entire part composed of the three sections is entitled "Fate of the Elements of the Composite Human Being.") This is intriguing, but by no means necessary.

Returning to the end of the last section, we can see that the missing δὲ clause would probably have been in opposition to the view that the soul "is diffused throughout and exists in the body." This opposing view could well have been the Platonist view and the third of the three possibilities Iamblichus himself listed in the first paragraph of section 36, viz., that the soul survives the death of the body. If this is the case (and it seems likely), then the possibility of a scribal error being the cause of the lacuna at the opening of section 37 is much more likely, for the Platonists to whom Iamblichus was referring could well have been "those around Plotinus." Hence the error would have been caused by skipping from one τοὺς δὲ περὶ Πλωτῖνον to another.

Moreover, the move from Atomists to Platonists is helpful in explaining the position of sections 37 and 38. In the lacuna, Iamblichus would have discussed the view that the soul survives death. This would have raised the issue of which soul or parts of the soul survive. Damascius, *In Phd.* 1.177 preserves an example of this topic.

> Some philosophers, such as Numenius, think the soul is immortal from the rational soul to the ensouled condition (ἄχρι τῆς ἐμψύχου ἕξεως); others to nature, as Plotinus says somewhere [*Enn.* 4.7.14];

> others to the irrational soul, as of the ancients Xenocrates and Speusippus and of the more recent ones Iamblichus and Plutarch; others up to the rational soul alone, as Proclus and Porphyry; others to intellect alone, for they allow the faculty of opinion to perish, as many of the Peripatetics; others to the Whole Soul, for they allow individual souls to perish in the Whole.

On this passage, see Westerink's commentary (106-109). Iamblichus may have entertained a similar doxology, although he clearly could not have discussed philosophers who came after him. The discussion could well have culminated in discussion of the Plotinian school and in their opinion of the fate of the irrational part of the soul and the soul's vehicle, the topics of sections 37 and 38.

Further evidence can be gathered from Proclus, *In Tim.* 3.234.9-237.1. In a discussion of Plato's *Tim.* 41d1-2, where the Demiurge tells the "younger gods" to "weave mortal to immortal" and create living beings, Proclus himself presents a doxography concerning what part of the soul is mortal and what part immortal. The earlier part of the doxography, which includes Atticus and Albinus (234.9-18) and Porphyry (234.18-32), is almost certainly drawn from Iamblichus' own commentary. See Dillon (1973) 373. Atticus and Albinus believe that only the rational soul is immortal and that the irrational soul and vehicle are not. Porphyry would preserve the irrational soul and vehicle in the universe, but not intact. Rather, just as the faculties involved were gathered from the heavenly bodies in the soul's descent, so too they are given back to their sources in the soul's ascent. Proclus gives Iamblichus' own view (= *In Tim.* Fr. 81): both the irrational soul and vehicle are immortal.

The doctrine attributed to Plotinus' school here in the *De Anima* is similar to that attributed to Porphyry in Proclus' *Timaeus* commentary. The irrational faculties are detached from the reasoning element and returned to the ethereal and other bodies from which they originated. The doctrine of the priests also agrees with Iamblichus' doctrine in *In Tim.* Fr. 81: the irrational soul is preserved in the cosmos. On this, see further Finamore (1985) 11-27.

This is the first occasion upon which Iamblichus calls up the authority of "the priests" to re-enforce his own opinion. (He uses it more frequently below.) As to the identity of these priests, one can only speculate. One might naturally think of the wisdom of the Egyptian priests, as relayed through the Hermetic writings, or of the priests of Chaldaea, whose wisdom would be represented in the Chaldaean Oracles. This mode of expressing his opinion is an aspect of his concern to relate Platonism to the timeless wisdom of the ancients.

χωριζούσης αὐτὰς ἀπὸ τοῦ λόγου . . . The Greek pronoun αὐτὰς cannot refer to "souls," from the previous section, since it makes little sense to speak of separating souls from reason. The referent, which would have been in the missing section, is supplied from ἑκάστη δύναμις ἄλογος in the next sentence.

ἢ καὶ ὅτι μάλιστα μένει ἀμετάβλητος . . . We read ἢ καὶ, which Heeren suggested and Wachsmuth accepted. Festugière (236 note 1) reads ἢ καὶ with FP. This would set up not a double set of opinions, which the text clearly calls for, but a triple one: (1) either (ἤτοι) each irrational faculty is freed into the whole life of the universe from which it was separated off, (2) or (ἢ καὶ) each remains as far as possible unchanged, (3) or (ἢ καὶ) the whole irrational life continues to exist, separated from the discursive reasoning and preserved in the cosmos. Festugière argues that the second ἢ καὶ (the one introducing the third opinion) marks off Iamblichus' own theory which is opposed to the earlier disjunction. This earlier disjunction concerns the existence of the irrational powers *in parts*, where "certaines puissances se dissolvent (λύεται) dans la Vie universelle, certaines autres continuent d'exister le mieux possible." Thus this disjunction is the first half of the double opinion. Leaving aside the complexity of such a division, we note that the most natural way to take the second set of conjunctions (ἢ καὶ . . . ἢ καὶ) is as a disjunctive pair: "either this or this." This is exactly how Iamblichus uses them in the first sentence in this section. (Festugière sees this and tries unsuccessfully to explain the difference away, 235 note 3.) Heeren's suggestion solves the problem simply. On this reading, see also Dillon (1973) 375-376, Finamore (1985) 16-17, and A. Smith (1974) 65 note 19.

38

This section concerns the soul's vehicle, a purer body intermediate between the incorporeal soul and the corporeal body. On Iamblichus' doctrine of the vehicle as an ethereal body created whole from the gods themselves (and not merely gathered bit by bit from planetary ether and perhaps lower sources as well), see Iamblichus, *In Tim.* Frr. 81 and 84, Dillon (1973) 374-377 and 380, Dodds (1963) 319-321, and Finamore (1985) 11-27 and 167-168.

Iamblichus here provides two possible ways that the soul is connected to the body. It is either connected immediately to the body, or there are other intermediary bodies between them.

Οἳ μὲν γὰρ εὐθὺς . . . The first method is actually a denial of the existence of any type of vehicle or intermediate body. The soul is joined immediately to the corporeal body. Festugière (237 note 2) cites Alcinous, *Did.* 23, as an example. Alcinous, following Plato's *Timaeus* 44de and 69c-71a, believes that when the secondary gods received the immortal rational soul from the Demiurge, they placed it in the human head and "placed the rest of the body under it joining it to serve it as a vehicle."

οἳ δὲ μεταξὺ . . . The second method by which soul is connected to body involves a series of "ethereal, heavenly, and pneumatic wrappings." Festugière (237 note 4) cites the *Corpus Hermeticum* for this belief (see below). The idea of the soul putting on garments more and more material in its descent is also part of the Greek and Platonic traditions. See above, section 26 (378.6-9 W): "[Some Platonists] posit that the soul is always in a body (as Eratosthenes, Ptolemy the Platonist, and others do) and make it pass from subtler bodies into dense bodies." Plotinus says that souls (*Enn.* 4.3.15.1-5) first take on a heavenly body and then in the course of their descent add "more earthly bodies" (γεωδέστερα σώματα) (see Armstrong's note *ad loc.*). Porphyry (*ap.* Proclus, *In Tim.* 3.234.18-26) believes that the vehicle is gathered from the heavenly bodies in the soul's descent.

μεταξὺ τῆς τε ἀσωμάτου ψυχῆς καὶ τοῦ ἀγγελιώδους αἰθέρια καὶ οὐράνια καὶ πνευματικὰ περιβλήματα περιαμπέχοντα . . . The text is corrupt and no sure solution has been suggested. The sentence lacks a main verb in the Greek. Heeren suggested λέγουσιν ("say") after ἕνεκεν; Wachsmuth τίθενται ("posit") after αἰθέρια. (Wachsmuth would also add the relative pronoun ἅ after περιβλήματα, which is otiose.) We accept Wachsmuth's τίθενται but feel it would come more naturally after ζωήν.

The two manuscripts have ἀγγελιώδους ("like an angel"), a word not attested in *LSJ*, but P has it as neuter, F feminine. Wachsmuth follows F. As a feminine adjective, ἀγγελιώδους would modify an understood "soul." But this does not provide the contrast called for by the preposition μεταξύ ("between"). The phrase "between the incorporeal and the angelic soul" is incorrect because the περιβλήματα ("wrappings" or "garments") must exist between soul and body, not between two souls. (Another possibility is to say that the noun for "body" has fallen out of the text, and Iamblichus wrote "between the incorporeal, angelic soul <and body.>" One would then have to explain why Iamblichus would call the soul "angelic" here.) Festugière (237 note 3) adopts a suggestion by Ferguson, ἀγγειώδους ("like a vessel"). The image of the vessel for the body is common enough in antiquity, but the use of the adjective without a noun might seem abrupt.[82] Marcus Aurelius (10.38), however, does use it substantively (τὸ περικείμενον ἀγγειῶδες). This usage would justify Iamblichus' usage here.

αἰθέρια καὶ οὐράνια καὶ πνευματικὰ περιβλήματα περιαμπέχοντα τὴν νοερὰν ζωὴν <τίθενται> προβεβλῆσθαι . . . The verb προβάλλειν is a technical term among the Neoplatonists. For examples of its use in Iamblichus, see Finamore (1985) 28 note 9. Usually, the soul is said to "bring forth" or "project" lives or reason-principles from itself. These can be either from the soul in its highest aspect or from the soul in conjunction with the body (as composite) when it "puts forth" irrational lives. This is best understood in an Aristotelian context. The soul has certain powers (to think, to perceive, to grow), and the actualization of these powers is the soul "bringing them forth." See Simplicius, *in Cat.* 374-375 and Finamore (1985) 13.

For the term περιβλήματα, compare the use of περιβόλαιον in *CH* 10.17, 121.12-19:

> For it is impossible for the intellect to be established naked by itself in an earthly body (ἐν γηΐνῳ σώματι). Nor is it possible for the earthly body to bear such a great immortality or for so great a virtue to be in contact with a passive body. So it [i.e., the intellect] has taken the soul as a wrapping (περιβόλαιον), and the soul, which is itself something divine, uses the pneuma as a servant.

---

[82] Bazán (1997) 143 note 49 thinks that the adjective ἀγγειώδης is equivalent to the noun ἀγγεῖον. He cites *Ch. Or.* 157, where the noun is used for the compound of soul in body: σὸν <δὲ γὰρ> ἀγγεῖον θῆρες χθονὸς οἰκήσουσιν ("beasts of the earth will dwell in your vessel"). Psellus (who preserves this fragment) says that the vessel is τὸ συνθετὸν ἡμῶν κρᾶμα τῆς ζωῆς ("the composite blend of our life").

The extract from the *De Anima* ends here. It seems likely that Iamblichus would have gone on to give his own doctrine. According to him, the vehicle is not made up of mixtures from heavenly bodies but is created "from ether as a whole . . . neither subtracting from the divine bodies nor coming into existence through accumulation" (*In Tim.* Fr. 84.4-7: ἀπὸ παντὸς τοῦ αἰθέρος . . . οὔτε ἐλαττουμένων τῶν θείων σωμάτων οὔτε συμπεφορημένως τούτων ὑφισταμένων). The vehicle is an ethereal body created by the gods themselves to house the human soul (*In Tim.* Fr. 81.6-10: οὐχ ἁπλῶς ἀπὸ τῶν σωμάτων τῶν θείων . . . ἀλλ' ἀπὸ τῶν θεῶν αὐτῶν). See Finamore (1985) 11. The vehicle, then, is a single, non-compounded ethereal body that exists eternally. The rational soul is housed in it in its descent and can detach itself from it after its reascent to the vehicle of the soul's own leader-god. The ethereal vehicle remains with the god's ethereal vehicle; the rational soul can ascend even higher into the Intelligible realm and beyond. See Finamore (1985) 148-151. The concept of the heavenly garments gathered in descent Iamblichus seems to have transferred from coverings for the soul to coverings for the vehicle in its descent. See Finamore (1985) 15.

The next excerpt (454.10-458.21 W), which follows immediately in this edition, is separated by some sixty-nine pages in Wachsmuth's edition. It concerns the soul's fate in the afterlife, however, and as such may have followed soon after the end of this section.

39

['Ιαμβλίχου ἐκ τοῦ περὶ ψυχῆς] . . . The titles are not in the MSS. P has "Of Plotinus and Others," probably based on the first words of the section. Wachsmuth, following Canter's suggestion, prints "Iamblichus' On the Soul." Festugière assigns the section number (IV) and title "Eschatologie." He also adds titles for the individual paragraphs below. The title "Judgment, Punishment, and Purification" is his, based on section 40 (454.24-25 W). We have added the other titles below.

Πλωτῖνος δὲ καὶ οἱ πλεῖστοι τῶν Πλατωνικῶν . . . This paragraph concerns the role of purification according to the school of Plotinus and "most Platonists." The beginning of the section is missing, as evidenced by the particle δέ in the opening sentence. As will be seen, Iamblichus in this part of the *De Anima* tends to distinguish between the opinions of "the ancients" (i.e., Iamblichus' own opinion) and those of various unnamed Platonists and Pythagoreans. It is not likely, however, that the missing beginning dealt with Iamblichus' view of purification. The views of the "ancients" regularly follow, not precede, those of the "Platonists." What then was in the missing μέν clause? We suggest that it is the opinion of Plato himself. Stobaeus has omitted Iamblichus' words and substituted quotations from Plato's *Timaeus* (42a-d), *Gorgias* (523a-524a), and *Republic* (614b-616c) (Stobaeus 448.17-454.9).

The paragraph as we have it distinguishes two positions of the "Platonists." According to the first, the soul's purification involves the separation of all the lower aspects of soul from the higher. According to the second, purification concerns only the lower soul, while the higher soul is never in need of being purified.

Festugière (239 note 2) questions whether the purification that Iamblichus discusses is envisioned as occurring before or after death. In fact, as he says, either is possible. For Platonists, purification was a prelude to re-ascent, whether during life or after it. The use of purification is the same in each case. Certainly, however, the judgment and punishment discussed in the following paragraphs take place after death, and this suggests that this is Iamblichus' intention in the immediate context as well.

Plotinus discusses purification in his treatise on virtues (*Enn.* 1.2). He identifies the four Platonic virtues of the *Republic* (wisdom, temperance, courage, and justice) with civic virtues, differentiating them from the "purificatory" virtues, which he discovers in the *Phaedo*. These latter, he says, properly belong to the soul in itself (1.2.3.11-19). Possessing virtue is having a "likeness to god" (ὁμοίωσις πρὸς θεόν, lines 19-21; cf. 1.2.1.1-6 and Plato, *Tht.* 176ab). Plotinus is at pains to show that the soul alone has virtues, whereas Intellect and the One do not, since they do not have a disposition (διάθεσις, 1.2.3.20) toward and away from virtue as souls do. They are permanently in the state toward which souls strive and which they achieve only occasionally. Thus the soul, when it has the virtues and is therefore purified, becomes like god. Purification is a "removal of everything alien" to the soul in itself (ἀφαίρεσις ἀλλοτρίου παντός, 1.2.4.5-7). In *Enn.* 4.7.10, Plotinus says that the virtues exist in the soul, after it has been purified, and that such a purified soul is similar to the gods (lines 11-20); purification provides the soul with knowledge of the Intelligible (lines 41-47).

Iamblichus, then, has captured this conception of purification in this first sentence. Purification is a removal of the lower powers of soul from the soul itself. Iamblichus sets this out in five stages.

First, purification removes the passions and use of images. On the Greek τῶν μορφωτικῶν διαγνώσεων, see above, section 1 (363.5-6 W), αἱ μορφωτικαὶ ... γνώσεις. Festugière (178 note 1) compares Proclus' use of the term μορφωτικός in his *Republic* commentary. See especially 1.39.28-40.4: "Every god is without form (ἀμόρφωτος) even if he is envisioned in images (μορφωτικῶς). For there is no form in him, but rather from him, since he who envisions is not able to see the formless (ἀμόρφωτον) without an image (ἀμορφώτως) but sees according to its own nature with images (μορφωτικῶς)" and 111.19-23, where the faculty of imagination apprehends god "with images" (μορφωτικῶς). Festugière also cites 74.24-30, 120.25-121.3, and 235.18-21, where the term is associated with φαντασία. The term μορφωτικός then concerns a lower form of thought that makes use of images.[83] The term διάγνωσις underscores this meaning by use of the prefix δια- that carries the connotation of discursivity.[84]

---

[83] The term μορφωτικός is common in this sense in Proclus' works: *In Remp.* 2.107.21-22; *In Alc.* 1.245.15-246.3; 264.15-18; *In Parm.* 679.24-30; 804.1-11; 1025.9-11; *In Crat.* 129.7-10; and *In Tim.* 1.352.16-19. At *In Parm.* 946.37-947.2, Proclus presents a hierarchy of knowledge (γνῶσις) from perceptible to imaginative to opinionative to intellective. The imaginative is termed: αἱ δὲ τῶν τῆς φαντασίας προσδεόμεναι μορφωτικῶν γνώσεων. Cf. 994.32-42, where the same hierarchy occurs and where "imagination receives μορφωτικάς images of [the Forms]." See also, *In Tim.* 1.352.16-19: τὸ γὰρ αὐτὸ γινώσκει θεὸς μὲν ἡνωμένως, νοῦς δὲ ὁλικῶς, λόγος δὲ καθολικῶς, φαντασία δὲ μορφωτικῶς, αἴσθησις δὲ παθητικῶς. καὶ οὐχ ὅτι τὸ γνωστὸν ἕν, μία καὶ ἡ γνῶσις. Proclus makes a similar distinction in his commentary to Euclid 46.1-9; 51.17-52.3; 55.20-23; 94.19-21. The pseudo-Simplicius picks up the term in his *De Anima* commentary: 17.2-5; 214.16-21 (where he mentions Iamblichus); and 215.15-25.

[84] See also *De Myst.* 4.5, where Iamblichus is discussing why good people suffer. The problem is, Iamblichus says (187.7-10) that mere human beings cannot reason out (ἀναλογίζεσθαι) the complete life of the soul, including sins committed in previous embodiments. He goes on to say (187.10-12) that even in this current life many human injustices are concealed from human knowledge (λανθάνει τὰς διαγνώσεις ἀνθρωπίνας) whereas they are known to the gods (τοῖς δὲ θεοῖς ἐστι γνώριμα). The distinction between lesser human knowledge (with the δια- prefix) and the surer divine variety (without the prefix) echoes the use of the prefix here in the *De Anima*, where it refers to human ratiocination. See also *De Myst.* 10.3, where Iamblichus discusses an inferior kind of divination, based on watching for earthly signs of cosmic sympathy, in which the diviner reasons in a human way (ἀνθρωπίνως ... συλλογίζεται, 288.12-13) and "creates a kind of knowledge not distant from corporeal nature" (οὐ πόρρω τῆς σωματοειδοῦς τάξεως ποιεῖται τὴν διάγνωσιν, 288.14-15).

Second, there is the move away from "opinion." The term "opinion" (δόξα) is to be contrasted with "knowledge" (ἐπιστήμη), in the Platonic sense. Festugière (239 note 1) compares Plato, *Phd.* 84a and *Phdr.* 248b. See also Hermias, *In Phdr.* 160.18-20, where he comments on *Phdr.* 248b5 ("They [i.e., the imperfect souls who have just fallen from above] make use of the nourishment of opinion."): "That is to say they put forth (προβάλλουσι) the reason-principles of the sensible realm and live in accordance with them, no longer viewing the Intelligible but rather the sensible." The Platonic text represents what occurs in the soul's descent; Iamblichus' in the soul's ascent. Just as the descending soul loses its access to the Intelligible and takes on δόξα in its stead, so too during the ascent and "purification" the soul must leave δόξα behind.

Third, there is a move away from matter. The phrase ἡ ἔνυλος διανόησις again emphasizes the lower kind of thinking associated with embodied human souls. For the term ἔνυλος, see Festugière (239 note 2), who cites Aristotle's use of the term in *De An.* 403a25. The term is Neoplatonic and Iamblichean. See especially *De Myst.* 6.3, where Iamblichus is explaining that the gods are not directly involved in divination through animals, "for neither partially nor immediately nor materially (ἐνύλως) nor with any relation" are they involved with material particulars (243.5-8); *In Tim.* Fr. 10, where Iamblichus says that Solon (as transcendent Demiurge) has his creative activity hindered in the material realm "since material (ἔνυλα) motions and a material (ἔνυλος) disturbance become an impediment to the creative principles of the encosmic realm" (lines 20-22); Dillon (1973) lists other instances in his index (427). Cf. Proclus, *ET* 209.1-4, where the soul's vehicle becomes more material (ἐνυλοτέρων) in its descent and strips off material things (ἐνύλου) in its ascent.

Fourth and fifth, there is the positive doctrine of what the soul obtains: Intellect and intelligible reality. The assimilation of thought to thinker is an Aristotelian doctrine. See *De An.* 430a3-5: "For it [i.e., the intellect] is an object of thought like others. For with regard to things without matter, the thinker and the thought are the same (τὸ αὐτό ἐστι τὸ νοοῦν καὶ τὸ νοούμενον). For theoretical knowledge and the object of that knowledge are the same."

Strictly speaking this first view of purification is basically Platonic and one with which Iamblichus agrees. See *Protr.* 70.9 ff., cited by Festugière 239 note 4. He would, however, certainly have stressed the need for the gods and superior classes in the ascent.

Ἔνιοι δὲ καὶ τούτων πολλάκις ἀποφαίνονται περὶ τὴν ἄλογον ψυχὴν . . . In the second sentence, Iamblichus adds that "some" of these Platonists think that the soul's intellect is above purification. He again has Plotinus in mind. In *Enneads* 1.2.4 Plotinus likens purification to a conversion (ἐπιστραφεῖσα, line 16; ἐπιστρέφεται, line 17, and ἐπέστραπται, line 18). Virtue arises in the soul from this conversion toward the higher realms. The soul gains "a vision and an impression of the seen object, placed inside and working in the soul, like sight around what is seen" (θέα καὶ τύπος τοῦ ὀφθέντος ἐντεθεὶς καὶ ἐνεργῶν, ὡς ἡ ὄψις περὶ τὸ ὁρώμενον, lines 19-20). Thus, purification is the turning of the soul to the higher realities. Plotinus, however, then worries about this conversion. Did the soul not already possess this vision? Yes, he replies, but not actively (ἐνεργοῦντα) but as it were unilluminated (ἀφώτιστα, lines 20-23). In *Enn.* 3.6.5.14-30, Plotinus again refers to purification in this way, saying that the soul turns away from things below toward those above. Plotinus compares this conversion to the lower soul awaking from wrong-headed dreams (ἡ ἔγερσις ἐκ τῶν ἀτόπων εἰδώλων, line 24) and achieving an unclouded vision. Thus, as with the souls' "descent," its purification and resulting clear vision of the higher realms is always present to the soul. It must awake itself to it.

On Iamblichus' distinction between δοξαστικὸς λόγος and οὐσιώδης λόγος as a distinction between opinion in the embodied soul and thought in the disembodied soul, see Festugière (239 note 4). It may be based in part on Aristotle's distinction between the part of the soul that opines (δοξαστικόν, *EN* 1140b26) and the part that knows in *EN* 6.5. For οὐσιώδης used to describe what belongs to the soul in its disembodied essence, see, with Festugière (239 note 5) and Dodds (1963²) 300, Proclus *ET* 195, where the Intellect provides the soul with its "essential reason-principles" (οὐσιώδεις λόγους), and *In Tim.* 2.299.18 (ἐνέργεια . . . τοῦ οὐσιώδους τῆς ψυχῆς).

40

Ἀλλὰ δὴ τὸ μετὰ τοῦτο διελώμεθα, ὑπὸ τίνων ἕκαστα τούτων ἐπιτελεῖται . . . In this paragraph, Iamblichus considers who is responsible for the soul's judgment, punishment, and purification.[85]

---

[85] For a more detailed account of this section of the *De Anima*, see J. F. Fina-more, "What the Hades? Iamblichus and Proclus on Judges and Judgment in the

These three concepts arise from myths in several Platonic works: *Gorgias* 523a-526d, *Phaedo* 113d-114c, *Republic* 614b-621b (the Myth of Er), *Phaedrus* 248c-249d, and *Laws* 904c-905c. According to the Platonic myths the soul, after it lives its life on earth, leaves the body at death, and is removed to another place where it is judged. If the soul has led a good (especially philosophical) life, it gains its reward. If not, it undergoes some sort of punishment and is thereby purified.

Plato does not seem to hold souls accountable for judging, punishing, and purifying themselves. In *Gorg.* 524a, Rhadamanthus, Aeacus, and Minos judge the souls, but the soul goes elsewhere for punishment (525a). No specific individuals are said to be the agents in the *Phaedo*, although bad souls are said to be released from their punishments by the souls of their victims (114ab) and exceptionally good souls are said to have (previously) purified themselves by philosophy (οἱ φιλοσοφίᾳ ἱκανῶς καθηράμενοι, 114c2). Unnamed judges appear in the *Republic* (614cd); the souls are again taken elsewhere for punishment and purification. A voice prevents those who have not had sufficient punishment from leaving the place of punishment (615e-616a). The *Phaedrus* does not name the agents who judge or punish the souls in between their earthly lives. After being judged, some souls go to "places of punishment under the earth" (εἰς τὰ ὑπὸ γῆς δικαιωτήρια, 249a6-7) while others are taken to a heavenly place by Justice (a7-8). The agents are divine but unnamed in the *Laws*.

Plato's lack of specificity has led to disagreement among his followers. Proclus, *In Rep.* 2.128.3-140.25, argues that the place of punishment is the ether beneath the Moon and that the agents of the judgment include gods, daemons, heroes, and pure souls.[86]

Damascius (*In Phd.* 2.99; cf. 1.481) disputes Proclus' claim that the place of judgment (δικαστήριον) is the ether; rather (Damascius says) it is the whole cosmos. At 1.482, Damascius explains that Justice (who is, of course, in charge of punishment) heads a σειρά from heaven through earth: διὰ πάσης πρόεισι τῆς οἰκείας προόδου μεχρὶ καὶ τῶν ἀψύχων, οἷον ὑδάτων κριτικῶν καὶ πνευμάτων.

Iamblichus is concerned with earlier Platonists' views of what lay behind the soul's judgment, purification, and punishment after death. He isolates three groups but gives us no names.

Afterlife," *Mediterranean Perspectives* 1 (1998), 45-59.
[86] Finamore (1998) 50-52.

Ὡς μὲν δὴ οἱ πλεῖστοι Πυθαγόρειοι καὶ Πλατωνικοὶ λέγουσιν . . . According to Iamblichus, "most Pythagoreans and Platonists" claim that the agency of judgment, purification, and punishment is the soul itself. We can find no clear statement of this position in ancient texts. Iamblichus may be thinking of those who believe that souls are reincarnated immediately from one body into the next. See above, section 26 (378.16-18 W): Some Platonists "firmly maintain that [souls] always fall from solid bodies into other [solid] bodies." See notes there. Thus the soul's punishments take place in this world and are "self-inflicted" in the sense that they are caused by the soul's own actions either in this or a previous life.

ὡς δὲ οἱ ἀκριβέστεροι ἐν αὑτοῖς . . . Iamblichus' second group assigns agency to powers above the soul. The string of possibilities connected by the Greek conjunction καί is typical of Iamblichus' style. Here he seems to be arranging the conjuncts in ascending order. (They are not equivalent, as Festugière 240 note 3 claims.) The "more universal and perfect souls" are those souls above human souls, i.e., superior classes and visible gods; the Whole Soul is the Soul of the Universe; the "arrangement" (τάξις) of the universe must then be everything that is arranged therein, from the Soul of the Universe to the superior classes. The Intellect is of course hypercosmic but rules over the whole of generation; the term "universe" (διακόσμησις) was used by Aristotle to describe the whole universe (*Met.* 986a6). For διακόσμησις referring to the whole universe under the Intellect, see Iamblichus, *In Phdr.* Fr. 5, where he identifies the "heavenly vault" of *Phdr.* 247b1 with "the διακόσμησις situated immediately below" the Demiurge (lines 4-5).

Again it is impossible to say which "Pythagoreans and Platonists" Iamblichus has in mind here. Iamblichus' use of the phrase "the more precise among them" (οἱ ἀκριβέστεροι ἐν αὑτοῖς) indicates that he considers this group to hold a view more consistent with the truth. Iamblichus may be thinking that the first group has, as it were, put too much emphasis on Plato's teachings in the *Republic* that the soul, not the gods, is responsible for the soul's fate (αἰτία ἑλομένου· θεὸς ἀναίτιος, *Rep.* 617e4-5). For Iamblichus, the gods still have a role to play, as we shall see.

ὡς δ᾽ οἱ ἀρχαιότεροι διατείνονται . . . The "more ancient authorities" in the third group again represent Iamblichus' opinion. Whereas for the second group Iamblichus gave the agents in ascending order, for the third he gives them in descending order. First come the visible gods, especially the Sun. For the role of the Sun, Festugière (263-264) cites Proclus *In Tim.* 3.68.14ff.; on purificatory gods, 198.16ff. Julian, in his *Hymn to King Helios*, following Iamblichus, delineates a system of three "suns:" the Intelligible Sun (= the One), the Intellectual Sun (= the Intellect), which he identifies with Mithras, and the visible Sun. Each rules over the other gods at its level. Thus the visible Sun is the ruling god of the visible gods and therefore has greater powers. See Finamore (1985) 133-140.

The "invisible demiurgic causes" (τῶν τε δημιουργικῶν αἰτιῶν τῶν ἀφανῶν) do not refer to the hypercosmic gods, as Festugière says, but to the lower invisible gods. Iamblichus' distinction is based on an interpretation of Plato's at *Tim.* 41a3-5 between the gods "that revolve visibly" (ὅσοι τε περιπολοῦσιν φανερῶς) and those that "appear as they will" (ὅσοι φαίνονται καθ' ὅσον ἂν ἐθέλωσιν). Proclus, *In Tim.* 2.195.1ff., tells us that the former are the heavenly gods, the latter the sublunary gods. It is most probably an Iamblichean distinction; see Dillon (1973) 368. Thus the "invisible demiurgic causes" here are the sublunary gods in their demiurgic capacity. The subject of Plato's *Sophist* is, according to Iamblichus, the Sublunar Demiurge (*In Soph.* Fr. 1.1-2). Iamblichus may conceive of this entity as the "king" of other demiurgic sublunar deities, as the sun is king of the visible gods. Be that as it may, it is to these sublunar demiurges that Iamblichus alludes here.

Finally, beneath both the cosmic and sublunar gods are the usual array of superior classes ("heroes, daemons, angels, and [visible] gods"). Iamblichus' discusses these beings and their various *differentiae* in *De Mysteriis*, esp. in Book 2. These beings differ in essence from each other (2.1) and therefore have various different characteristics. In general, those of the higher classes (gods and angels) are purer and more elevated than those of the lower (daemons and heroes). In 2.5, Iamblichus distinguishes their "power to purify souls" (τὸ ἀποκαθαρτικὸν τῶν ψυχῶν, 79.7). Iamblichus here further divides angels into two classes: archangels and angels.

> In gods the power to purify souls is perfect; in archangels anagogic. Angels merely free souls from the chains of matter, while daemons drag them back into nature. Heroes lead them down into concern for perceptible works. (79.7-11)

Thus the *De Mysteriis* echoes the role of these superior classes in the soul's purification.

In the *De Anima* Iamblichus has set up a chain of divinities from the stars and planets above to the superior classes below to be responsible for the soul's judgment, punishment, and purification. It will be recalled that Proclus believed that the place of judgment (mentioned by Plato in *Phaedo* 107de) was "between earth and heaven" (μεταξὺ γῆς τε καὶ οὐρανοῦ, *ap.* Dam. *In Phd.* 1.481.1, cf. *In Remp.* 2.132.5-133.20), which Proclus interprets to be the ether (cf. 2.100). Damascius disagreed, preferring a series of places of judgment suitable to different classes of soul (1.481.4-7; 2.99). This is a later Neoplatonic "improvement," one to which Iamblichus would not have attained. If Iamblichus was the source of Proclus' belief, then Iamblichus' reasoning here becomes clear. The places of punishment for the soul are ethereal and therefore require agents who have ethereal bodies. The visible gods, the sublunary gods, and the superior classes all have ethereal vehicles and can act without intermediaries in the ethereal realm. (The superior classes can act directly on the soul even on the earth.) Thus the agents cannot be any higher than the visible gods, for the hypercosmic gods are not in the cosmos and do not have vehicles. Iamblichus would no doubt have agreed with Proclus' point that justice descends from the highest realms down to the ethereal beings and below them to the material realm (1.482), but he would have insisted that the actual agents were the ethereal gods and superior classes.

It should be remembered that the soul has an ethereal vehicle also. See Damascius, *In Phd.* 2.542, who like Proclus distinguishes a higher and lower vehicle. Iamblichus believed in a single ethereal vehicle, and it must be this one in which the soul is punished. Thus, ethereal divinities judge, punish, and purify souls in their ethereal vehicles in the ethereal cosmos.

41

Τί ποτε οὖν αὐτῶν ἐστι τὸ τέλος . . . This paragraph and the two that follow concern the τέλος of judgment, punishment, and purification, i.e., what condition of the soul is gained through these three processes. Again Plato's dialogues provide little evidence here. Iamblichus throughout divides the prevailing opinions into two, those of the "Platonists and Pythagoreans" (called simply "others" in section 41) and those of the ancients, who again represent Iamblichus' own thoughts.

Κρίσεως μὲν ἄμικτος καθαρότης τῶν ἀγαθῶν . . . As Festugière says (240-241 note 5), the ancients are concerned more with the highest aspects of judgment: the soul becomes purely good without a trace of anything inferior. How is this possible for the human soul, which is a mean between divine beings and material entities? Probably Iamblichus has in mind a temporary purity attained and sustained with the help of the ethereal divinities. In this way it would be similar to the purification of the vehicle in its ascent out of the body during theurgy. See Finamore (1985) 127-131. The "others" opt for "an orderly arrangement" (εὐταξία), which is probably a reference to the orderly arrangement of the three parts of the soul in the *Republic*. (See also, Pseudo-Plato, *Def.* 411d: "Justice is unanimity of the soul with itself and the orderly arrangement of the parts of the soul to and around one another," Δικαιοσύνη ὁμόνοια τῆς ψυχῆς πρὸς αὑτήν, καὶ εὐταξία τῶν τῆς ψυχῆς μερῶν πρὸς ἄλληλα τε καὶ περὶ ἄλληλα.)[87] This condition is possible even in an embodied state without theurgy, and hence is beneath the immediate concern of the ancients. The phrase "separation of the worse from the better" (διάστασις τοῦ χείρονος ἀπὸ τοῦ βελτίονος) is ambiguous. The adjectives are singular and probably neuter, but the exact reference is unclear. They may refer to parts of the soul, however, or to the separation of all kinds of vice from human character. Again, this sort of "judgment" involves the lower, embodied aspects of the soul.

ὑπερβολή τε ἐξῃρημένη τῶν κρειττόνων αὐτὴ ἑαυτῇ . . . The manuscripts have αὐτὴ ἡ αὐτή ("itself the same"), which may be correct but has a very odd ring to it. In this case, the transcendent superiority that the soul attains after its punishment remains the same and does not fluctuate, as the superiority possessed by an impure embodied soul would. Heeren suggested αὐτη ἑαυτῇ, which we read with Wachsmuth and Festugière. This reading seems more natural. The soul's superiority is pure (itself by itself) and thus uncombined with anything inferior.

πρὸς ἣν οὐδὲν δύναται συντάττεσθαι τῶν χειρόνων οὐδέποτε . . . The two manuscripts divide this sentence and the previous one as follows: They place a break between χειρόνων and οὐδέποτε, which would cause the previous sentence to end "with which nothing inferior can

---

[87] For εὐταξία used of the parts of the soul, see Proclus, *In Alc.* 325.8-12. At *In Tim.* 3.289.8-9, he says that the soul destroys its εὐταξία when it turns to passion.

combine" and this sentence to begin "These principal ends of judgment were never pleasing to the ancients." It is the beginning of this sentence that is impossible, for the ancients could not possibly disagree with the foregoing goals of judgment. We adopt the reading of Usener, which is followed by Wachsmuth and Festugière.

42

Δίκης δ᾽ ἂν εἴη τὸ τέλεον . . . Iamblichus now turns to the end of judgment. He again begins with the ancients and their more sublime explanation, before turning to "many Platonists and Pythagoreans."

ἐν τῷ τὴν ἀνάλογον καὶ κατ᾽ ἀξίαν ἰσότητα τοῖς πᾶσιν ἀπεργάζεσθαι . . . In distinguishing the doctrines of the ancients from those of the "Platonists and Pythagoreans" concerning the end of punishment, Iamblichus makes use of Aristotle's distinction between proportional and arithmetic justice. See, with Festugière 241 notes 1 and 2, *Nic. Eth.* 5.3.1131a24-33 and 5.4.1132a6-11. Cf. *Pol.* 1301b26-1302a1. For Iamblichus, punishment is proportional, that is it takes into account the offense and the type of soul that committed it. For the punishment and reward being according to merit, see *Phd.* 113d8-e1 and *Rep.* 615b7-c1.

Lesser Platonists and Pythagoreans allot the same punishment for the same offense. "Multiplication" in this context signifies that the punishment will be worse than the offense. See (with Festugière 241 note 2) *Rep.* 615ab, where Plato says that the punishment or reward will be ten times that of the original acts. The words "suffering the same punishments that one inflicted when one was first acting unjustly" refer to a basic law of retaliation. As Festugière says (241 note 3), Aristotle calls this a Pythagorean doctrine (*Nic. Eth.* 5.5.1132b21-1133a5). For the phrase "deliverance from vice," see Festugière 241-242 note 4, who compares the Platonic conception of punishment as a cure in *Gorg.* 525ab and *Laws* 854d.

καὶ περὶ ταύτας τὰς αἱρέσεις ἑλίσσονται οἱ πολλοὶ Πλατωνικοὶ καὶ Πυθαγόρειοι . . . The verb ἑλίσσονται seems to have a sarcastic ring to it. Indeed Iamblichus adopts a superior tone throughout sections 41-43, where he compares the opinions of the ancients to Platonists and Pythagoreans. In section 41, he writes Καὶ ταῦτα τοῖς παλαιοτέροις ἀρέσκει τὰ κεφάλαια αὐτῆς, ἄλλοις δ' ἂν ἴσως . . . ("These principal ends of judgment were pleasing to the ancients, but for others perhaps . . ."); in section 43 Οἳ δὲ οὐ πείθονται τοῖς ἀρχαιοτέροις ταῦτα προστησαμένοις αὐτῆς τὰ ὄντως συμφέροντα ("Others, however, are not persuaded by the ancients when they emphasize the real benefits of purification") and καὶ τὰ τοιαῦτα σμικρὰ τέλη προΐστανται αὐτῆς, ὡς τὰ προέχοντα τῶν ὅλων ("but they give prior place to such minor ends of purification, as though these were superior to the universal ones"). It is as if, in Iamblichus' eyes, the unnamed "Platonists and Pythagoreans" are blind to the obvious, and Iamblichus can only pity them.

The word ἑλίσσονται is, as far as we have been able to determine, used in this sarcastic way only here. It has a pedigree, however, associating it with the lower-order thinking and with the material realm. Plato (*Tht* 194a8-b6) uses the verb in a passage about when one is likely to make false judgments.

> Concerning those things which we know and perceive, in these matters opinion turns and twists and becomes true and false. (περὶ δὲ ὧν ἴσμεν τε καὶ αἰσθανόμεθα, ἐν αὐτοῖς τούτοις στρέφεται καὶ ἐλίττεται ἡ δόξα ψευδὴς καὶ ἀληθὴς γιγνομένη, 194b2-4)

The verb turns up in the *Chaldaean Oracles* (Fr. 163) in a negative description of matter, which "always twists around the maimed abyss" (πηρὸν βάθος αἰὲν ἑλίσσων, line 5).[88] Iamblichus cites a Pythagorean *symbolon* that uses the verb in *Protrepticus* 108.3-4: Στρωμάτων ἀναστὰς συνέλισσε αὐτὰ καὶ τὸν τύπον συνστόρνυε ("When you arise from bed, twist the coverlets and remove the imprint [of your body]"). He explains the *symbolon* at 122.22-123.2 as "twisting" the coverlets of ignorance to gain true knowledge of higher things. Thus in both the *Chaldaean Oracles* and the *Protrepticus*, the distortion inherent in the verb ἑλίσσειν is connected with the distortion of the material realm. Here, in the *De Anima*, Iamblichus connects that distortion with the thinking of the wrong-headed "Platonists and Pythagoreans."

43

Καὶ μὴν τῆς γε καθάρσεως ἀφαίρεσις τῶν ἀλλοτρίων . . . In this section, Iamblichus turns to the end of purification. He again draws a

---

[88] On this Oracle, see H. Lewy, *The Chaldaean Oracles and Theurgy* (Paris 1978) 295 note 137; 296 notes 139 and 143; and 297 note 147.

distinction between the "higher" form of purification stressed by the ancients (i.e., by Iamblichus himself) and the lower form championed by "many Platonists and Pythagoreans." As Festugière points out (242 note 3), Iamblichus supports these "lower" forms in his *Protrepticus* (70.9ff.), but adds to them the higher: "philosophy seems to us a release from human bonds, deliverance from generation, a return to being, knowledge of absolute truth, and purification for the soul" (φαίνεται ἡμῖν φιλοσοφία ἀπαλλαγὴν τῶν ἀνθρωπίνων δεσμῶν παρέχειν καὶ λύσιν τῆς γενέσεως καὶ περιαγωγὴν ἐπὶ τὸ ὂν καὶ γνῶσιν τῆς ὄντως ἀληθείας καὶ κάθαρσιν ταῖς ψυχαῖς). See also *De Myst.* 1.12, where Iamblichus discusses theurgical ascent of the soul: "The ascent through invocations provides to the priests a purification from passions, a release from generation, and union with the divine principle" (κάθαρσιν παθῶν καὶ ἀπαλλαγὴν γενέσεως ἕνωσίν τε πρὸς τὴν θείαν ἀρχήν, 41.18-42.1). Plotinus too recognizes two levels of purification (for higher and lower soul). See *Enn.* 1.2.5; for ἀφαίρεσις ἀλλοτρίου παντός, see *Enn.* 1.2.4.5-7. Thus Iamblichus does not reject purification for the embodied soul but prefers to emphasize that of the disembodied soul here, where the topic is the soul's lot after death. Hence he lays stress on the soul's return to its own essence and to the gods (called here "engendering cause" and "wholes"). Iamblichus thereby stresses the soul's dependence on gods for its purification. Cf. *De Myst.* 10.6 and 3.31 (pp. 178.3-179.12). (On the distinction between material and immaterial rituals based upon the soul's disembodied and embodied states, see *De Myst.* 5.15: "There are two kinds of ritual. One will be simple, incorporeal, and purified of all generation, which is appropriate for pure souls. The other is accomplished with bodies and every enhylic operation, which is not appropriate for pure souls or for those freed from all generation," 219.7-12. Cf. chapters 16-17. Iamblichus makes a threefold division in 5.18-19.)

44-46

Ἔτι δὲ τὰ πέρατα τῶν τριῶν τούτων διελώμεθα . . . As the sequel will show, by "limits" Iamblichus means which sort of souls undergo each of the three processes. Iamblichus holds that pure souls are not judged, punished, or purified after death, but that impure souls are. On the categories of pure and impure souls, see sections 28 (379.22-

25 W) and 30 (380.19-29 W) with the notes there. Iamblichus further subdivides the category of impure souls into two (souls that descend for "exercise and correction of its own character" and for "punishment and judgment"); see section 29 (380.6-14 W) with notes.

The vocabulary in section 44 is reminiscent of that in section 41 (455.6-15 W), which concerns the end (τέλος) of judgment. There, the purpose of judgment was to have the soul attain its pure, separated state. Thus, the more that souls are impure and polluted by the material realm, the more they are in need of judgment. The idea that souls are judged insofar as "they are combined with generation" (συντάττονται εἰς τὴν γένεσιν), recalls the goal (of judgment) that they have "a transcendent superiority . . . with which nothing inferior can ever combine" (ὑπερβολή τε ἐξῃρημένη . . . πρὸς ἣν οὐδὲν δύναται συντάττεσθαι τῶν χειρόνων οὐδέποτε, 455.9-11 W). The words "are not separated from the universe" (τοῦ παντὸς οὐκ ἀφίστανται) recall the goal that souls be "completely removed from what is imperfect" (ἀφεστηκυῖα τὸ παράπαν ἀπὸ τῶν ἀτελῶν, 455.9 W). To souls that are "commingled in some way with things different [i.e., from their true higher nature]" (συμμίγνυνταί πως πρὸς τὰ διαφέροντα) and "unmixed" (ἀμιγεῖς) we may compare the goal of "unmixed purity" (ἄμικτος καθαρότης, 455.7-8); while for "those souls that have been let go free" (αἱ δὲ ἀφειμέναι ἀπόλυτοι), we may compare section 29 (380.12 W), concerning the intermediate class of soul that is not completely pure: οὐδὲ ἀφεῖται ἀπόλυτος καθ' ἑαυτήν, "not let go [i.e., from the Intelligible] pure in itself." For souls that are "themselves of themselves" (αὐταὶ ἑαυτῶν), see section 12, concerning which faculties belong essentially to the soul. There Iamblichus says that Plato distinguishes between faculties that belong to the soul itself (αὐτὰς ἑαυτῶν, 370.3 W) and those that belong to the composite of soul and body. Cp. (in section 41 again), the goal of having a "transcendent superiority . . . itself by itself" (ὑπερβολή τε ἐξῃρημένη . . . αὐτὴ ἑαυτῇ, 455.9-10). It should be noted that Iamblichus is following the Platonic doctrine that judgment and punishment are for the souls' benefit (e.g., *Gorg.* 525b).

Iamblichus' point, then, is that pure souls are already purified and therefore in need of neither purification nor the preliminary stages of judgment and punishment that lead to purification. At the time of death, the pure souls are "themselves of themselves," i.e., what souls are essentially, pure and ready for contact with the gods. Impure souls, however, need further cleansing. Festugière (243-244 note 2) says that in the myths of the *Gorgias, Phaedo,* and *Republic,* all souls are judged. This is of course true, but Iamblichus would have found support for his thesis in his interpretation of the *Phaedrus.* If (as suggested above, in the notes to section 30) Iamblichus interpreted *Phdr.* 248a-d in such a way as to allow for the existence of pure human souls (i.e., the soul "that becomes a follower of the god and sees something of true reality" and is "always unharmed," *Phdr.* 248c3-5), such souls are not among the "others" in 249a5 who having been judged are then either punished under the earth (6-7) or carried to heaven for their reward (7-9). Thus Iamblichus reinterprets the judgments of *all* souls in *Gorg.* 524a-525d, *Phd.* 113de, and *Rep.* 614cd as referring to all impure souls only, just as he does *Phdr.* 249a.

Hermias, unfortunately, preserves none of Iamblichus' thoughts on this topic. In *In Phdr.* 162.29-163.19, he discusses the appropriate passage (*Phdr.* 248c3-8). He interprets Plato's statement that a soul that follows the god "is unharmed for another period" (μέχρι τε τῆς ἑτέρας περιόδου εἶναι ἀπήμονα, 248c4) as meaning that the soul "remains unharmed (ἀβλαβής, from c5) for that whole period; that is, it will not fall into generation" (163.1-2). The period is the one which Plato says lasts 1,000 years, but which later Neoplatonists took as variable. (See Damascius, *In Phd.* 2.147, discussing *Phd.* 113e6, that some souls never go out of Tartarus, a situation the exact opposite to the one in which the soul never descends. The answers to both puzzles are parallel, however, since the same reason that souls must exit Hades will be given for why they must not remain in heaven. Damascius says that Plato may be referring to a stay of a single period, which is Syrianus' solution; or a complete turning of the outer heaven, which is Proclus' solution; an orbit of any one of the planets or of the soul's ἀγελάρχης, which are unattributed solutions; or the period appropriate to the soul itself, which is Damascius' solution. Cf. Westerink Vol. 2, 364-366; Damascius, *In Phd.* 1.547 and Westerink Vol. 2, 278-281.) Hermias seems to follow Syrianus, although the term "period" is ambiguous. He adds that the soul can remain above only with assistance from the gods, daemons, and heroes. Hermias' position (and that of the other Neoplatonists mentioned by Damascius) may be a reaction to Iamblichus' controversial doctrine that pure souls did not (in some sense) descend (*In Phd.* Fr. 5).

After the judgment of these souls, the souls that have led a bad life are sent for punishment: to a "prison" for curable souls and to Hades and Tartarus for the incurable in *Gorg.* 525a7 (φρουρά), c8 (δεσμωτήριον), and 526b7 (Τάρταρος); to Acheron for curable souls and to Tartarus for incurable in *Phd.* 113de; "under the earth" for curable souls and to Tartarus for incurable in *Rep.* 615a2 and 616a4; "to places of punishment under the earth" in *Phdr.* 249a5-6. Those that have led a philosophical life are sent to a heavenly reward: to the "Isles of the Blessed" in *Gorg.* 526c5; to the surface of the Earth and to "places more beautiful" in *Phd.* 114bc; up to heaven in *Rep.* 614e5-6; "to some place in heaven" in *Phdr.* 249a6-7. In the *Laws* (904c-e), Plato makes a similar distinction: curable bad souls go to Hades, good souls go to a special holy place, and the incurably bad to the opposite place.

τὰς ἀχράντους ψυχὰς καὶ τὰς ὁμονοητικῶς συναφθείσας τοῖς θεοῖς . . . The phrase "by sharing in their intellect" translates the Greek adverb ὁμονοητικῶς. The adjectival form, when found in Plato, is used in the sense of ""harmonious" or "of one mind." See Plato, *Rep.* 554e4 and *Phdr.* 256b1. Here, however, it refers to the Iamblichean doctrine that the human soul is in a separate level of existence from the unmixed Intellect above and that the human soul participates in that Intellect through ascent to the gods. See above, section 6 (365.22-366.5 W) and Finamore (1997). Iamblichus may have coined this term in this sense. For a similar use of the adverb, see Iamblichus, *In Phil.* Fr. 6.

οἱ δὲ Πλατωνικοὶ πάσας μετὰ τὴν δίκην εἰς τὴν οὐσίαν ἀπὸ τῆς γενέσεως ἀπολύουσι . . . As in the previous section on the topic of judgment, so here on punishment the distinction between the ancients (i.e., Iamblichus) and the Platonists is that the former say that pure souls do not undergo these processes whereas the latter say they do. For the Platonists, the soul after it is punished returns to its οὐσία i.e., to its pre-embodied state before its earthly sins (but it is not yet, it seems, purified).

Γένοιτο δ᾽ ἂν καὶ περὶ τῆς καθάρσεως ἡ αὐτὴ ἀμφισβήτησις . . . In section 46, Iamblichus first differentiates the ancients (whom he calls "the same men") from the Platonists. The ancients again mark off pure souls as privileged, not being in need of purification. The Platonists say that all souls are purified. On the phrase "that follow the gods" (θεοῖς συνέπονται), see above, section 30 (380.24 W) and notes there. These are the pure human souls.

Iamblichus then divides the Platonists into two camps. As Festugière says (244 note 3), both groups are concerned with the place in which souls are purified. The word translated "place" is περίοδος in the Greek. The word may mean either "period of time" or "orbit" (as of a planetary god). Here it seems to have a spatial rather than temporal meaning. Festugière chooses the temporal sense, and he may be correct. The problem, however, is that the last clause would then bear a strange sense: "Others, such as Plotinus, prefer that the soul be above these (temporal) periods." In what sense can a soul be said to "be above" or "transcend" (ὑπερέχειν) a period of time? If this means that the souls are hypercosmic and in the realm of eternity, rather than that of time, then they are also "above the place of purification," which is encosmic. Thus, the meaning of both translations comes to the same thing. Otherwise, it is difficult to see in what sense Iamblichus could mean "(temporal) period" here.

The "orbit" or "area of circular ambit" for the soul while it undergoes purification may be either somewhere within the cosmos (περικοσμίους, i.e., somewhere between earth and the fixed stars) or somewhere above the sphere of the fixed stars.

This latter Platonic view is ascribed to Plotinus. Festugière (244 note 4) finds no passages in Plotinus corroborating Iamblichus' claim. Purification for Plotinus, however, is living in accordance with the higher part of the soul (*Enn.* 1.2.4). In *Enn.* 1.2.5, he says that the soul "perhaps gathers itself away from the body and to places of some sort" (ἀπὸ μὲν δὴ σώματος ἴσως μὲν καὶ τοῖς οἷον τόποις συνάγουσαν ἑαυτήν, lines 6-7). The soul is then unaffected by the body (lines 7-8). Once the soul is in this condition, it purifies its irrational part (lines 22-32). Thus, purification involves the soul withdrawing to its higher aspect (see *Enn.* 1.1.3.21-26) and the Intelligible Realm. Iamblichus probably saw this as saying both that all souls must undergo purification (for all souls must withdraw to their higher aspect) and that the place of purification is in the Intelligible Realm.

On Iamblichus' view of where (impure) souls are purified, Festugière cites John Lydus, *de Mensibus* 167.21ff.: "Iamblichus in the first book of his treatise 'On the Descent of the Soul,' mentions their restoration (ἀποκατάστασις), giving to Hades the area (χώρα) above the Moon up to the Sun, where he says the purified souls are located." As with the place of judgment, the place of purification would be ethereal. See Damascius, *In Phd.* 1.481 and the notes to section 40, above.

47-53

On the first three difficult and mutilated paragraphs, see Festugière 245 note 1, who indicates two lacunae in the text (at 457.9 and 457.19 W) and transposes the final sentence (on the *Timaeus* of Plato) so that it immediately follows the first sentence in section 47. We have preferred to preserve the paragraph as it appears in both manuscripts. Specific information is given below. In truth, the paragraph seems sketchy and disjointed. We suspect both that Stobaeus has excerpted material from a longer section in Iamblichus' original work and that Stobaeus' text is mutilated at points.

The title is from the first words of the section. The manuscripts have simply "In the Same," although the first incomplete set of clauses in the subsequent paragraph ("Concerning the souls' reward, which they attain subsequently, when they depart from the body . . .") are conjoined thereto, in P as a kind of heading. Festugière (245) gives as title "Récompense des Ames." See below.

Iamblichus turns to the soul's reward after death. If this part of the *De Anima* follows directly on Iamblichus' discussion of judgment, punishment, and purification, then the reward is not simply for the highest class of pure souls but also for impure souls that have led a good (philosophical) life and have undergone punishment, judgment, and purification. These would be the souls of the intermediate category in section 29 (380.6-14 W). See notes there along with section 30 and its notes.

Just as Iamblichus and other Neoplatonists struggled to interpret what Plato meant by "Hades" and other terms for the place of punishment, judgment, and purification, so too there was need of interpretation for the soul's ultimate reward. Plato, again, is far from clear. In *Gorg.* 526cd, the judges Rhadamanthus, Aeacus, and Minos send the philosophical soul to "the Isles of the Blessed." In *Phd.* 114bc, Plato divides these souls into two classes. Those who have lived well come to live on the surface of the "true" earth; those who have been purified by philosophy live without bodies in more beautiful places (*Phd.* 114c2-4). In *Rep.* 614c-e, souls of the just, after being judged, ascend through the opening into heaven (c3-6) and after 1,000 years descend from there pure and "tell of the beauty of an extraordinary vision" (d7-e4). In *Phdr.* 249ab, good souls after being judged "are carried by Justice to some place in heaven and live as worthily as their life in human form allowed" (a7-b1). In *Laws* 904de, an especially good soul is taken to a holy place.

Damascius, *in Phd.* 1.551, preserves a late Neoplatonic attempt to explain what Plato meant. He reinterprets Plato's double division of good souls (*Phd.* 114bc) into three. "Those without philosophy dwell on the heights of the earth with very subtle pneumatic bodies, those who practiced philosophy at the level of the polis live in heaven with luminous bodies, and those who are completely purified are restored to the hypercosmic place without bodies." As Westerink (Vol. 2, 282) says, the three groups correspond to those who lived according to ethical, social, and purificatory virtue.

Iamblichus could not have been Damascius' source for the triple division, for the concept of a double vehicle (one pneumatic, one luminous) begins with Syrianus. See Proclus, *in Tim.* 3.236.31-238.26; Finamore (1985) 168-169; Dillon (1973) 374; Dodds (1963^2) 319-321. He did, however, distinguish life in the (single ethereal) vehicle from a life separated from it. See Finamore (1985) 144-151. The human soul descends as a whole into generation. It re-ascends as a whole, in theurgy or after death, to the visible gods. Its ethereal vehicle attaches itself to the vehicle of its leader-god. In some rare cases (*De Myst.*5.20; 5.22; 10.7), the highest part of the rational soul (the "one of the soul," *In Phdr.* Fr. 6) can detach itself from the vehicle and ascend higher to the One itself. See Finamore *ad loc.* for further sources. If (as seems likely) Iamblichus accepted Plato's twofold division of good souls in *Phd.* 114bc, then it is also likely that those who "dwell on the earth's surface" remain in their vehicles and those who "reach habitations even more beautiful" are separated from their vehicles and mount higher.

In sections 47-53, Iamblichus discusses the soul's reward after death. This necessarily involves the soul in a purified ethereal vehicle, for the soul is punished and purified in that vehicle, as we have seen. (See Damascius, *In Phd.* 1.543 and 2.146, where it is the lower, pneumatic vehicle in which souls are punished after death.) Thus the soul is either already purified (and thus not in need of further purification after death) or it undergoes punishment and purification in its vehicle after death. The intermediate class of souls would undergo both purification in ritual ascent and purification after death. The reward is granted to pure souls and to the recently purified intermediate souls.

47

Περὶ τῆς ἐπικαρπίας τῶν ψυχῶν . . . The Greek word for "reward" is ἐπικαρπία, "produce" or "crop." It comes to mean any recompense or profit gained from any activity. Here it is the recompense for living a good life while on earth, that is, the soul's heavenly reward. This seems to have become the usual term in Neoplatonism for the soul's reward after death. Proclus uses it four times in regard to the soul's reward as described in the Myth of Er: *In Remp.* 2.97.22, 152.1-2, 172.7, and 175.17-18. Cf. *In Alc.* 121.2.

We translate the first sentence as it is given by both manuscripts. As mentioned above, FP attach the first set of clauses (before the ellipsis) directly to the title ("In the same"). It is indeed a possible solution to the problem of the mutilated text here. These clauses may not be Iamblichus' words but those of an editor (working after Stobaeus and before the composition of the archetype of FP) describing the topic of this section of Stobaeus' work.

If the words are Iamblichus' and belong to the text, then there is certainly a lacuna after them, for the next clause in FP begins with no verb and with an introductory δὲ: εἰς ἀγγέλους δὲ. There would have been a previous μέν clause in the original.

Festugière (245 note 1) suggests completing the text (exempli gratia) as follows: <οἱ μὲν πρεσβύτεροι λέγουσι πορεύεσθαι αὐτὰς εἰς θεοὺς μὲν καὶ θείας ψυχάς,> εἰς ἀγγέλους δὲ καὶ ἀγγελικὰς ψυχὰς ("<the ancients say that they go, some to the gods and divine souls>, some to angels and angelic souls>"). There are several points in favor of his suggestion. It provides the needed μέν clause, adds a main verb, and preserves the manuscripts' reading of εἰς ἀγγέλους. (Usener had suggested ἰσαγγέλους, which Wachsmuth adopted.)

There are problems with Festugière's supplement, however. First, the clause that follows ("this then in general is the opinion of the ancients") is unnecessary after the addition of "the ancients say." Iamblichus could, of course be summarizing the ancients' doctrine, but a summary would suggest that the doctrine was lengthier than the one presented here. Another problem is the inclusion of the words "some to the gods and divine souls." Festugière does not explain why he includes the mention of gods here. Perhaps he does so because below in section 53 (458.17-19 W), Iamblichus says: "After the souls have been freed from generation, according to the ancients they administer the universe together with the gods." Also, of course, there is need of a μέν to precede the δὲ, which occurs in the clause about the angels. (We will discuss the further problem of his inclusion of οἱ μὲν πρεσβύτεροι, which also requires an answering δὲ, below.)

There is, however, no need to add mention of gods or anything else here. Iamblichus may well be considering a passage from the *Chaldaean Oracles* (Fr. 138). Olympiodorus, *In Phd.* 10.14.8-10, is our source for this fragment. He is discussing *Phd.* 72b1-3, in the argument from opposites (*Phd.* 69e6-72e2). Life continually arises from death and returns to it. Olympiodorus first argues that Plato could not have believed in eternal punishment, explaining away passages in the *Gorgias* where Plato says the opposite (*in Phd.* 10.14.1-8), then uses evidence from the *Oracles* to prove that Plato likewise did not believe that souls could live eternally in the upper realms: "But he [i.e., Plato] does not wish that the souls of theurgists remain always in the Intelligible Realm, but that they also descend into generation, concerning whom the Oracle says 'in the angelic space'" (ἀγγελικῷ ἐνὶ χώρῳ). He is concerned with the souls of theurgists, souls which Iamblichus would consider pure. R. Majercik (193) explains the fragment as follows: "the point is that the post-mortem soul of the theurgist chooses to descend from the intelligible to the material sphere (via the angelic order), presumably to aid the ascent of souls." These are Iamblichus' highest class of souls, those which descend "for the salvation, purification, and perfection of this realm" (section 29, 380.8-9 W). As we have seen, Iamblichus hesitated over whether and how they could be said to descend. See notes to section 30, above.

Iamblichus also seems concerned with these souls and this Chaldaean fragment in *De Myst.* 2.2, which we also discussed in the notes to section 34. Iamblichus differentiates the activities of daemons, heroes, and souls. Souls are described as the lowest of the three and therefore more involved with the lower realm but also capable of ascending higher and uniting with the gods (θεοῖς τε συνάπτουσα, 67.7) although in a manner inferior to that of daemons and heroes (68.8-69.7). Although the soul has the eternity and sameness of daemons and heroes in a lesser degree, it can with the gods' assistance "ascend to a greater, angelic order" (ἐπὶ μείζονά τε τάξιν τὴν ἀγγελικὴν ἀναγομένη, 69.11-12). At this point, Iamblichus says, the human soul becomes an angelic one (69.12-14), but he then softens this by saying: "If it is necessary to speak the truth, it is always defined according to a single category and by sharing it co-arranges itself with different higher causes at different times" (69.16-19). This is certainly more in keeping with Iamblichus' stress on the differences between kinds of souls. Thus, if this is Iamblichus' attempt to interpret the Oracle, it seems that he does so by taking the words "angelic space" in the Oracle as equivalent to "angelic order" and then arguing that the human soul ascends to, exists at, and descends from this order because of the soul's purity without itself actually becoming an angel. On this interpretation, see Finamore (1985) 154-155.

To return to the passage in the *De Anima*, this partial sentence probably alludes to this Iamblichean doctrine. Pure souls, according to the ancients, ascend "to angels and angelic souls" (εἰς ἀγγέλους δὲ καὶ ἀγγελικὰς ψυχάς). Compare *De Myst.* 2.2: when the soul ascends, "it is wholly perfected into an angelic soul (εἰς ἀγγελικὴν ψυχήν) and a pure life" (69.12-14). Thus, the sentence in the *De Anima* alludes to pure souls only and discusses their τάξις after death.

Could the lacuna be filled simply with an infinitive such as ἐξελθεῖν ("go out")? This would have the benefit of connecting the two halves of the sentence: "Concerning the souls' reward, which they attain subsequently, when they depart from the body, <that they depart> to angels and angelic souls, this in general is the opinion of the ancients." There are two problems: the placement of δέ and the brevity of the doctrine of the ancients. Rather, it seems that much more is missing in the lacuna, including an earlier μέν clause, perhaps discussing the views of some Platonists on the rank to which souls attain after purification, and/or more information about the doctrine of the ancients, perhaps along the lines of *De Myst* 2.2, where Iamblichus explains that souls do not become literally angelic.

Καὶ τηροῦσι μὲν αὐτὴν ἐπὶ τῆς οἰκείας τάξεως Πλούταρχος καὶ Πορφύριος καὶ οἱ παλαιότεροι· Πλωτῖνος δὲ πάντων τούτων αὐτὴν ἀφίστησιν . . . Wachsmuth indicates a lacuna before this sentence, stating that αὐτὴν ("it") has no referent. The pronoun, however, certainly refers to "soul," which may have been written in the singular in the foregoing lacuna. Alternatively, the pronoun could have been substituted for the plural, if the plural noun "souls" were used previously. Iamblichus writes the plural ψυχάς, "souls," in the previous sentence, but these are angelic not human souls. Iamblichus does use the plural τῶν ψυχῶν of human souls in the beginning words of this section, if it is the beginning of the same sentence and if it is by Iamblichus and not merely a section title. (See above.) For such a switch from plural to singular, see section 26 (378.5-6 W): καταβάσεις τῶν ψυχῶν· τιθεμένη δὲ τὴν ψυχὴν ἀεὶ εἶναι ἐν σώματι ("descents of souls; positing that the soul is always in a body"). Festugière (245 note 1) cites the passage in a different context to prove the same point. Although the switch from plural to singular would not be a sufficient reason in itself to say that there is a lacuna here, there is still good reason for positing a lacuna.

Festugière (245 note 1), transposes the sentence concerning souls' proper heavenly abodes in the *Timaeus* from below (457.22-458.2 W) to here before this sentence. He argues rightly that in the *Timaeus* sentence the plural pronoun αὐτὰς must refer to "souls," whereas in the sentence just before it (457.19-22 W) the same pronoun refers to the soul's irrational powers or activities. Since Festugière thinks that the topic of the *Timaeus* sentence is the same as the topic of the first sentence in this section, viz., the τάξις to which souls attain after death, he argues that the *Timaeus* sentence should come immediately after that sentence. He further argues that the transposition creates the necessary antithesis between the doctrine of the ancients (in the first sentence) and the doctrine of Plato (in the *Timaeus* sentence).

Festugière is certainly right that, given the state of the text, the *Timaeus* sentence could have been displaced in the archetype behind F and P. There are problems, however that suggest first that if the sentence should be transposed, it should not be transposed to this place, and second that the topics of the *Timaeus* sentence and those here are different enough that no transposition should take place.

First, the problem in the placement of the sentence: Iamblichus could not be contrasting the view of the ancients with that of Plato. Whatever conclusion Iamblichus reached about the ancients in the mutilated first sentence, he could not have thought that Plato disagreed with them. The whole thrust of his philosophy is that Plato preserves the truths of the ancient tradition (hence his attacks on Platonists, such as Plotinus and Porphyry, who "misunderstand" Plato). Since Iamblichus' topic changes after the sentence about Plotinus (457.13-14 W) to the soul's properties, there are only two possibilities for the position of the *Timaeus* sentence: either after the first sentence (where Festugière places it) or after the sentence about Plotinus. The latter possibility is preferable for two reasons. First, the *Timaeus* sentence forms a better contrast with the Plotinus' views than with the ancients'. Plotinus does not keep the soul in its own τάξις, but Plato does. An even stronger case could be made if the reading of FP, οἱ παλαιότεροι ("the ancients"), were changed to ἄλλοι Πλατωνικοὶ ("other Platonists"), as Wachsmuth suggested but did not print in his text. (We do not believe, however, that the text should be altered.) Second, the *Timaeus* sentence has a crux that is easily solved if it follows the sentence about Plotinus. In the *Timaeus* sentence, concerning the soul's appropriate boundaries (i.e., τάξις), the manuscripts have: τὸν ὅρον τῆς οἰκείας ("the boundary of its own . . ."), where the feminine τῆς οἰκείας has no identifiable noun to which it can refer. Festugière suggests changing it to τὸν ὅρον τῆς οἰκίας ("the boundary of the abode"). The phrase ἐπὶ τῆς οἰκείας τάξεως ("in its proper order") appears in the sentence before the one about Plotinus (457.11 W) and τάξεων is clearly the understood referent of πάντων τούτων in the sentence about Plotinus (457.13 W). If we place the *Timaeus* sentence after these, then τῆς οἰκείας in that sentence has a referent (τάξεως).

There remains a major obstacle to allowing the transposition even to this place. The topic of the *Timaeus* sentence is not the same as that of the other sentences under consideration. The mutilated sentence about the view of the ancients that souls go "to angels and angelic souls" and the following two sentences about whether the soul remains in its own τάξις concern the question of whether the human soul can ever break out of its own rank and become something greater than a human soul. Thus, its τάξις is its defined rank or order, and for a soul to "preserve its τάξις" is for it to remain the kind of soul it is and not become a greater (e.g., angelic) or lesser (animal) soul. For Iamblichus' doctrine that each kind of soul remains separately what it is, see above, section 6 (365.22-366.11 W). In the *Timaeus* sentence, however, it is no longer a question of the human soul remaining what it is but of the human soul's ascent to another τάξις. The soul may ascend to the soul of a visible god and be united with it, but it does not become that god. Thus, we do not believe that the *Timaeus* sentence should be transposed.

As to the present sentence itself, Festugière (246 note 3) can find no passage in Plutarch to support Iamblichus' thesis that the Chaeronean philosopher preserved the human soul in its rank. Indeed, the case seems to be just the opposite, as the passage cited by Festugière proves (*def. or.* 415b), where humans can turn into heroes and heroes into daemons. See also Dillon (1977) 216-219. On the other hand, Iamblichus may be referring to a lost work of Plutarch on the soul, in

which the latter adopts a more restrictive view.[89] On Iamblichus'
hesitancy over Porphyry and the status he gave to the human soul,
see above, sections 5 (365.17-19 W) and 18 (372.9-14), where he
distinguishes Porphyry's view on the soul's τάξις from Plotinus', and
section 24 (374.21-24), where he links them. See also Finamore
(1985) 21-23. For Plotinus, see his treatise 3.4, "On the Daemon
Allotted to Us," where our guardian daemon is our higher soul. Such
statements as "What is a daemon? The one here. What is god? The
one here." (Τίς οὖν δαίμων; ὁ καὶ ἐνταῦθα. Τίς δὲ θεός; ἢ ὁ ἐνταῦθα,
3.4.3.1-2) could easily have led Iamblichus to the conclusion that
Plotinus identified daemons with human souls.

48

Οἱ δ᾽ ἀρχαιότεροι παραπλησίαν τοῖς θεοῖς κατὰ νοῦν διάθεσιν
ἀγαθοειδῆ . . . The topic changes from the soul remaining in its τάξις
to the question of what properly belongs to the soul. The first
sentence of this section concerns the soul's intellect, the following
sentence the soul's reasoning element, and the third sentence the
soul's irrational powers.

Iamblichus held that the Intellect and the human soul were
separate entities, existing at different levels of reality (above, section
6, 365.22-26W): "But the opinion opposed to this [i.e., that of Numenius, Plotinus, Amelius, and Porphyry] separates the soul, on the
grounds that it comes into being second after Intellect at a different
level of being; explains the aspect of it that is with Intellect as
dependent on Intellect but with the power to subsist independently
on its own." Here Iamblichus calls the intellect-in-us a disposition
(διάθεσις), thus carefully preserving the soul's separation from the
Intellect itself. This intellectual disposition is also called "good in
form" (ἀγαθοειδής). This term suggests that this highest faculty in the
soul also has some relation to the Good. In his typical scholastic
fashion, Iamblichus wants to incorporate into the soul the faculties
necessary for the soul's ascent beyond the visible gods. In *In Phdr.*

---

[89] Frs. 173-178 Sandbach. There is admittedly nothing in the surviving
fragments to confirm or deny such a conjecture, except that in Fr. 178 (= Stob.
5.1089.14-1090.1 Hense) the disembodied soul is portrayed as entering the afterlife
still as a soul.

Fr. 6, he distinguished the soul's intellect, which he equated with the soul's charioteer in the *Phaedrus* myth, and the "one of the soul," which he equated with the helmsman. In *De Myst.* 1.15, as here, he is less careful and calls this highest element τὸ θεῖον ἐν ἡμῖν καὶ νοερὸν καὶ ἕν, ἢ εἰ νοητὸν αὐτὸ καλεῖν ἐθέλοις ("the divine, intellectual, and one in us — or if you wish to call it so, the intelligible" 46.13-14). Whether two separate faculties or a single highest faculty with two aspects, Iamblichus here clearly houses the principle in the human soul. On this topic, see Finamore (1997) 166-173. For a similar use of the word ἀγαθοειδής, see Plotinus *Enn.* 1.2.4.13, where he differentiates being good (ἀγαθός) and hence not being in need of purification at all and being ἀγαθοειδής and thereby being capable of doing wrong and needing purification.

καὶ προστασίαν τῶν τῇδε αὐτῇ ἀπονέμουσι καλῶς . . . The concept that soul cares for ἄψυχα is common Platonic doctrine. (See below, section 52, 458.16-17 W.) For the concept in relation to Intellect, see Proclus, *ET* 57, where "what soul gives to secondary natures, Intellect also gives in a greater degree" (56.10-11). Whereas for Proclus, Intellect has an effect further down the scale than soul, Iamblichus holds that the power of both extends as far as ἄψυχα but that Intellect's is "more piercing" (δριμύτερος); see Iamblichus, *In Alc.* Fr. 8 and Dillon's note (236). Here in the *De Anima*, a soul after it is purified is concerned with the good of souls and objects below. Compare the souls that descend for "the salvation, purification, and perfection of this realm" and "for the exercise and correction of its own character," in section 29 (380.7-12).

Πορφύριος δὲ καὶ τοῦτο ἀπ᾽ αὐτῆς ἀφαιρεῖ. . . . What does Porphyry remove? The manuscripts have τούτους (masculine plural), but there are no masculine nouns in this sentence. Heeren suggested τοῦτο (neuter singular), and he was followed by Wachsmuth and Festugière. We have adopted this change as well. According to this reading, Iamblichus has nothing to say about Porphyry's opinion about the soul's relation to Intellect, but says only that Porphyry rejects the idea of a soul, after it has been purified, having a superintendence over this lower realm. Since in section 5 (365.17-19 W) Iamblichus says that Porphyry is of two minds about distinguishing soul from Intellect, this reading is probably correct. For Porphyry's doctrine that the soul of the philosopher was removed from the lower realm after death and escaped the cycle of birth, see *De Regressu* Fr. 11 and Finamore (1985) 26-27, especially note 35.

Τῶν δὲ πρεσβυτέρων τινὲς ὑπερέχειν μὲν αὐτὴν λογισμοῦ φασι . . . The word for "it" (αὐτὴν) refers here to the human soul after it has been purified, i.e., to the rational soul in itself. Compare "On the Acts of the Soul," above, sections 18-25 (370.14-375.28 W), where Iamblichus distinguishes between the acts of embodied and disembodied souls. Those of the disembodied soul are, as here, superior to and more pure than those of the embodied.

Although Plotinus, *Enn.* 4.3.18, believes that the reasoning element (λογισμός) is a faculty of the lower soul, as Festugière points out (247 note 1), the doctrine is Iamblichean as well. In *De Myst.* 1.21, Iamblichus discusses errors that occur when human beings reason inappropriately about the divine because they try to use λογισμός to attain γνῶσις:

> For human beings, because they are unable to grasp knowledge of them [i.e., the gods] through reasoning but think that they are able, are completely carried headlong to their own appropriate human passions and make guesses about the divine from their own [human] point of view. (Ἀδύνατοι γὰρ ὄντες αὐτῶν οἱ ἄνθρωποι λογισμῷ τὴν γνῶσιν ἐπιλαβεῖν νομίζοντες δ' εἶναι δυνατὸν φέρονται ὅλοι πρὸς τὰ οἰκεῖα ἑαυτῶν τὰ ἀνθρώπινα πάθη, καὶ ἀπὸ τῶν παρ' ἑαυτοῖς τὰ θεῖα τεκμαίρονται, 65.16-66.2)

In *De Myst.* 10.3, Iamblichus disassociates true divination (which he elucidates in 10.4) from a kind of sympathy that depends on λογισμός:

> If anyone by human reasoning or systematic observation makes guesses from signs concerning matters that these signs reveal (just as doctors foretell that someone will have a fever from a chill or shivering), this person seems to me to possess nothing honorable or good. (οὔτε εἴ τις κατὰ λογισμὸν ἀνθρώπινον ἢ τεχνικὴν παρατήρησιν ἀπὸ σημείων τεκμηριοῦται ἐκεῖνα ὧν ἐστι τὰ σημεῖα δηλωτικά (ὡς ἀπὸ συστολῆς ἢ φρίκης τὸν μέλλοντα πυρετὸν προγιγνώσκουσιν οἱ ἰατροί), οὐδὲν οὐδὲ οὗτος μοι δοκεῖ τίμιον ἔχειν καὶ ἀγαθόν, 288.7-12)

Thus, Iamblichus associates λογισμός with lower-order human thinking, not with true knowledge and intellection that the gods provide. Compare *De Myst* 5.18, where Iamblichus divides humanity into three classes, the lowest of which "always uses λογισμός" and the highest class uses "some supernatural power of intellect" (223.10-224.1). On this last passage, see the notes to section 30, above.

ὡς οὐκ ἂν ἐξεύροι τῶν λογισμῶν ὁ καθαρὸς καὶ τελειότατος < . . . >
Πορφύριος δὲ αὐτὰς ἀφαιρεῖ παντάπασιν ἀπὸ τῆς ἀδεσπότου ζωῆς . . .
Festugière (245 note 1) first saw that there was a lacuna here, arguing
that αὐτὰς in the next sentence could not refer to "souls," for Iamblichus could not have believed that Porphyry would remove souls from
the soul's independent life. The "independent life" (ἡ ἀδέσποτος
ζωή) is the life of the soul independent of body. See section 44
(456.17 W), where it is the highest class of purified souls that are
called "independent;" cf. ἀδέσποτος βίος, Sallustius 21. Thus, the
pronoun αὐτὰς refers not to "souls" but to something separable from
the disembodied soul, viz., the soul's lower, irrational powers.

As Festugière says, Iamblichus has already drawn a distinction
between Porphyry and "the most ancient of priests" on this topic in
section 37 (384.19-28 W). Porphyry believed that the irrational
faculties were gathered from the various celestial bodies in the soul's
descent and then sloughed off and returned to those bodies during
its re-ascent. Iamblichus believes that the irrational faculties continue
to exist as a whole after the soul's ascent. For details, see the notes to
section 37.

Since here in the present passage Iamblichus is presenting first the
doctrine of the ancients and then that of Porphyry, Festugière fills
the lacuna as follows: "Les anciens (sc. Jamblique) ont admis que les
δυνάμεις (ou ἐνέργειαι) inférieures de l'ame sont immortelles."

The problem with Festugière's suggestion is that it allows neither
for an expression of Porphyry's doctrine on the purified rational
soul, i.e., how Porphyry differentiates it from the reasoning element
(λογισμός), nor for the doctrine of the ancients on the afterlife of the
soul's irrational elements. In other words, instead of the two topics in
section 48 that Festugière posits, there are actually three. Each topic
would have been divided into two parts. The first part would have
described what the ancients thought; the second what Porphyry
thought.[90] The three topics that would have appeared in this section
are as follows:

(1) The ancients rightly attribute to the soul a disposition, good in
form, similar to that of the gods in intellect and a superintendence
over things in this realm; Porphyry, however, removes from it this
latter characteristic.

---

[90] For what follows, see Finamore (1985) 20-24.

(2) Some of the ancients furthermore claim that it is superior to the reasoning element, and define its acts so precisely that not even the pure and most perfect reasoning element could attain them. < . . . >

(3) < . . . > Porphyry removes them completely from the independent life, on the grounds that they belong naturally to generation and were given as an aid to composite living beings.

Thus, we are missing both Porphyry's position on the relation of the pure soul to λογισμός in (2) and the ancients' doctrine concerning the separation of the irrational powers from the rational soul after death in (3). If this hypothesis is correct, it helps to explain the cause of the lacuna, for the scribe's eye would have wandered from the first (now missing) Πορφύριος δὲ in (2) to that in the MSS at the beginning of the next sentence (3).

It is possible too to reconstruct what is missing in the lacuna. With regard to (2), Iamblichus does differentiate Porphyry's doctrine from what he sees as Plotinus' doctrine that the soul is the same as intellect. He says that Porphyry "is in doubt" (ἐνδοιάζει) whether or not soul is separate from intellect (section 5, 365.17-19 W), that Porphyry differentiates the acts (ἐνεργήματα) of the Universal and individual souls (section 18, 372.9-14 W), and that he preserves souls in their proper τάξις (section 47, 457.11-12). Iamblichus nonetheless associates Porphyry with Plotinus as combining different acts (ἐνεργήματα) of soul into a single co-arrangement and form (εἰς μίαν σύνταξιν καὶ μίαν ἰδέαν, section 24, 374.21-24 W) and probably includes him with the Platonists (in section 14, 318.12-15 W) who "do not completely differentiate the soul from its intellect." Thus, in the lacuna, Iamblichus would have probably differentiated Porphyry's position from that of the ancients by claiming that Porphyry had not sufficiently distinguished intellect and reasoning.

With regard to (3), Iamblichus holds that Porphyry removed the irrational faculties from the soul after it has been separated from the body and that the separated soul lives as a pure soul. For Porphyry's doctrine, see also section 12 (370.5-11 W), where we are told that Plotinus and Porphyry "maintain that the soul projects its own powers to each part of the universe and that the lives, howsoever they have been projected, are dissolved and cease to exist." Iamblichus, on the other hand, believes that "these powers continue to exist in the universe and do not perish." See also section 37 (384.19-28 W), where it is given as Porphyry's opinion that "each irrational power is freed into the whole life of the universe from which it was separated, where each remains as far as possible unchanged;" Iamblichus believes that "the whole irrational life continues to exist, separated from the discursive reasoning and preserved in the cosmos." See notes there and Finamore (1985) 17-19.

The doctrine of Porphyry here is that these irrational faculties have no place in the life of a soul after it has been purified. Rather, they are appropriate to an embodied soul living in the realm of generation. Since they are not needed, they are removed and perish (i.e., return to their source in the cosmos). Iamblichus however, although he agrees that the irrational powers are not used by the disembodied soul, argues that they remain intact, presumably in the intact vehicle, ready to be actualized when the soul descends again. It is this latter doctrine that would have appeared in the lacuna.

We therefore fill the lacuna as follows (exempli gratia):

> Porphyry does not carefully distinguish the rational functions of the embodied soul from the intellectual functions of the disembodied soul. The ancients separate and preserve the soul's irrational powers intact.[91]

ὡς οὔσας συμφυεῖς τῇ γενέσει καὶ πρὸς ἐπικουρίαν δοθείσας τοῖς συνθέτοις ζῴοις . . . For the term "composite" (σύνθετος), see section 9 (367.22-368.11 W), where we are told that Plato and Pythagoras (and therefore Iamblichus) believe that the soul leads a double life, one in body and one outside of it, but others "think that there is a single life of the soul, that of the composite (συνθέτου)." Thus the "composite living being" is the compound of body and soul. For Porphyry, the irrational powers properly belong to the composite, not to the disembodied soul.

49

Ὁ δὲ παρὰ Πλάτωνι Τίμαιος . . . We have argued above (in the notes to section 47) that Festugière was wrong to transpose this sentence. As it now stands, however, there is no logical place for it. It does not belong in section 47 because it does not concern the soul remaining in its own τάξις. It does not belong in section 48 because it does not concern the question of which parts of the soul belong properly to

---

[91] See Finamore (1985) 24.

the disembodied, purified soul. It is therefore a fragment without a home. It does, however, belong to a discussion of the soul's post-mortem reward. For what follows, cf. Finamore (1985) 131-132.

Iamblichus returns to the hierarchy established in his interpretation of Plato's *Timaeus*, the topic of the second paragraph of section 26 (377.16-29 W). There he argued that the soul's descent into the realm of generation began from the heavenly region into which the Demiurge first sowed the soul: the heavenly gods, sublunar gods, and their entourage of superior classes (angels, heroes, daemons). Here Iamblichus states that in their re-ascent souls follow the same path in reverse. Thus, the human soul after it has undergone judgment, punishment, and purification, would ascend back to the divinities into which it had been sown. (This is Iamblichus' response to the question of where purified souls go, a question to which, as we have seen, Plato presented no definite answer.)

Iamblichus mentions only the Sun and Earth here. Plato, *Tim.* 41e4-42a1, says that the Demiurge sowed the souls "into the organs of time appropriate for each;" at *Tim.* 42d4-5, he says that the Demiurge "sowed some into the earth, some into the Moon, and others into the other organs of time." Neoplatonists interpreted this to mean all the heavenly bodies and used the passage as a basis for their belief in astrology, since one's appropriate god imparted its own influence. See further, Damascius, *In Phd.* 1.509.2-3, who claims that the *Timaeus* mentions Sun, Moon, and Earth; and Finamore (1985) 84-85. For Iamblichus, then, the demiurgic sowing provided each soul with its leader-god to which it would re-ascend. There, following the *Phaedrus* myth, the soul would follow in the entourage of its god.

Since the topic of the nature of the soul's union with the gods seems naturally to follow upon the topic of the soul's goal in its re-ascent, it is possible that this sentence is placed correctly before section 50. If so, there is another lacuna at the opening of section 49. In it, perhaps, Iamblichus considered the views of various philosophers concerning the place to which purified souls go, possibly those of the Platonists in section 26 (378.1-18 W), whom Iamblichus discusses immediately following his earlier discussion of the *Timaeus*. These Platonists thought that souls descended into bodies from various places above the earth: the Milky Way, the heavenly spheres, or the Moon. Since souls descend from these places, it is logical to suppose that they ascend to them after death and to the subsequent judgment, punishment, and purification. (See notes to section 26.)

ταύτῃ καὶ τὴν ἄνοδον αὐτὰς ἀνάγει, μὴ ὑπερβαίνουσαν τὸν ὅρον τῆς οἰκίας ἑκάστην πρὸς τῆς δημιουργικῆς καταβολῆς . . . There are some textual matters to consider at the end of this sentence as well. As Festugière (245 note 1) says, the pronoun αὐτὰς refers to "souls" here.

Festugière (246 note 2) is also correct to keep the reading of the manuscripts, ὑπερβαίνουσαν ("overstepping," in the singular). Wachsmuth followed Usener and printed ὑπερβαίνουσας (plural). Although the antecedent is plural (αὐτὰς, i.e. "souls"), Iamblichus switches to the singular here to refer to each soul individually.

It is also best, therefore, to keep Heeren's suggested ἑκάστην (feminine, "each [soul]") in place of FP's ἕκαστον (masculine, with ὅρον, "each boundary").

We also hesitantly adopt Festugière's alteration (246 note 2) of FP's οἰκείας ("one's own," with no referent) to οἰκίας ("abode"). For οἴκησις used in this sense, see Damascius, *in Phd.* 1.505.4-5: οἴκησις εὐδαιμόνων ψυχῶν, "abode of happy souls."[92] Although it is possible that the noun τάξεως could be understood after οἰκείας ("of its own level," i.e., the level from which its descent originated), this seems to us most unlikely. Whenever Iamblichus uses the phrase ἡ οἰκεία τάξις, it refers not to an entity's specific location at one time (in contrast to its location at another), but rather to the entity's rank or assigned place in the universe. See the use of the phrase in section 47, above, where Iamblichus is discussing the soul's assigned rank and place in the universe.

Some examples from the *De Mysteriis* will help prove this point. In 1.5 Iamblichus is discussing the role of the Good in creating and preserving the rank of various divinities from visible gods through souls. He says that the Good "preserves their appropriate distribution and rank" (τηροῦν μὲν αὐτῶν τὴν οἰκείαν διανομὴν καὶ τάξιν, 15.9-10), that is, the appropriate and permanent ranking of each individual class of divinities (gods, angels, heroes, and souls). In 2.7, Iamblichus discusses the different way each of the superior classes appears in their epiphanies. A purified soul, Iamblichus tells us, "exhibits a pure and unmixed fire" (ἄχραντον καὶ ἀμιγὲς τὸ πῦρ, 84.11-12), "follows its own leader god as he elevates it" (μετὰ τοῦ ἀναγωγοῦ ἡγεμόνος

---

[92] Although οἶκος appears in the sense of "house" of a given planet, neither οἰκία nor οἴκησις appear to be used in this way. On the other hand, the meaning here is not strictly astrological.

ἀκολουθεῖ, 84.13-14), and "itself manifests the rank proper to itself in its works" (αὐτὴ τὴν οἰκείαν ἑαυτῇ τάξιν ἐπὶ τῶν ἔργων ἐκφαίνουσα, 84.14-15). Then, a little later in the same chapter, Iamblichus sums up his remarks on the epiphanies as follows: "And in sum, all these classes manifest their own proper ranks along with themselves" (καὶ συλλήβδην φάναι, πάντα τὰ γένη ταῦτα τὰς οἰκείας τάξεις ἐπιδείκνυσιν ἅμα μεθ' ἑαυτῶν, 85.1-2). Thus, in all of these instances, the phrase ἡ οἰκεία τάξις refers to the permanent order or rank of one or more of the superior classes, not to some place in the cosmos that they may temporarily inhabit. Cf. 1.14, where Necessity among the gods (as opposed to a lower-order human necessity) "is disposed in the same, permanent fashion in the proper rank of the gods" (τάξει τε οἰκείᾳ θεῶν ἔχει τὸ ταὐτὸν καὶ ἄτρεπτον, 45.1), and 3.9, where sounds and songs that are consecrated to the gods form a kinship "appropriately in accordance with the ranks and powers proper to each" (προσφόρως κατὰ τὰς οἰκείας ἑκάστων τάξεις καὶ δυνάμεις, 119.1-2).

Finally, with Festugière (246 note 2), we keep FP's πρὸς τῆς ("in the") in place of πρόσθεν ("before"), which was suggested by Wachsmuth.

50

Ἕνωσιν μὲν οὖν καὶ ταυτότητα ἀδιάκριτον τῆς ψυχῆς πρὸς τὰς ἑαυτῆς ἀρχὰς πρεσβεύειν φαίνεται Νουμήνιος . . . Iamblichus now turns to the union of the soul with the gods and other divine principles. Festugière (247 note 5) says that this section concerns "the posthumous condition of the intellective soul, of νοῦς itself released from the sensible world and attached to its principles." More precisely, it concerns the intellectual component of the rational soul housed in the ethereal vehicle. As we have seen, the soul undergoes judgment, punishment, and purification in its vehicle. The soul then ascends in its vehicle via the ethereal rays of the divine bodies and links with those gods, vehicle to vehicle and soul to soul. See Finamore (1985) 144-151. Iamblichus must now explain how the soul, once in this state, can be said to be "united" with the gods.

Iamblichus again proceeds in this section by dichotomy, isolating Numenius and (it seems) others in one camp and "the ancients" in the other. Before we consider what is at issue between them, we should consider whether Stobaeus has again excerpted this material from a longer passage in the *De Anima*. The paragraph consists of three balanced sentences, each indicating the views of the antagonists. Each sentence contains two clauses, introduced by μέν or δέ. The final sentence is not a dichotomy but introduces an explanation of the final clause of the third sentence. Although the section begins neatly enough with a μέν clause, the reader is plunged immediately into the discussion of the topic with no indication as to what the topic may be. Thus it seems that an introductory sentence has been lost, for example: "After the soul has ascended, there is a question about its union with the gods." Furthermore, we begin with the only μέν clause that gives the opinion of Numenius. The other two μέν clauses give opinions of unnamed thinkers (in the plural). This leads us to believe that Numenius is one of a set of philosophers ("Platonists and Pythagoreans," as in sections 42-44 above?) whom Iamblichus is opposing to the ancients and that there was an earlier sentence in which Iamblichus specifically named this set of philosophers. If so, it probably would have been another dichotomy, with the philosophers opposed to the ancients. We therefore mark an ellipsis at the beginning of this paragraph.

Iamblichus is opposing two alternative ways in which a soul can be said to be united with the gods. The point at issue is whether the soul becomes fully mixed with the divine soul or forms a kind of separated unity in which the soul retains its own substance. The latter view is that of the ancients and Iamblichus. On the Neoplatonic view of individuality among immaterial, incorporeal entities, see Proclus, *E.T.* 176 (on Forms) and Dodds' note (291-292); cf. Iamblichus, *In Tim.* Fr. 42 and Dillon's note (315).

The vocabulary used in this section is precise. Iamblichus' opponents, of whom only Numenius is named, see the union as "undifferentiated" (ἀδιάκριτος); the process is like "dissolving" (ἀνάλυσις), that is, the human soul becomes fused and blended with the divine; and the resulting union is "without individuation" (ἀδιόριστος), that is, total and complete: the human soul becomes part of the divine. The ancients, however, preserve the soul in its own τάξις. It cannot become divine but only attached to the divine. It is permanently inferior. Iamblichus uses compounds of συν- (σύμφυσις, "coalescence," and σύνταξις, "co-arrangement") to emphasize the shared aspect of this union. He also says that the union occurs "with individuation" (διωρισμένη). The individuality and separateness of the soul remain even in divine union. This is a direct result of its inferior essence. The soul may unite with higher entities, but it must remain what it is. (See section 34 above and notes.)

Οὐ μέντοι κρατεῖται ὁ διορισμὸς αὐτῶν ὑπὸ τοῦ κόσμου ἢ κατέχεται ὑπὸ τῆς φύσεως . . . The final sentence of this section raises another problem. The subject of the sentence is ὁ διορισμὸς αὐτῶν (literally, "their individuation"). Festugière (247 note 6) understands ὁ διορισμὸς αὐτῶν as αὐταὶ (αἱ ψυχαὶ) διωρισμέναι and translates "les âmes ainsi distinguées (de leurs principes)." This is the correct interpretation. Iamblichus is using an abstract noun for the concrete. We have tried to follow Iamblichus' example, rendering the abstract "individuation" concretely as "individuated existence." The point is that the soul, once it has achieved union with the gods, is no longer subject to the world of generation or therefore Fate. On this topic, see Finamore (1985) 125-133, where it is shown that freedom from generation and Fate follows after the soul's purification and ascent; once the soul (in its vehicle) is attached to its god, it is once again separated from nature and free.

Once the soul has achieved this union with the gods — a union marked by both attachment and separateness — the soul attains its highest essence. The soul as a mean changes in its very essence in its ascent. In the realm of generation its essence is divided, but when with the gods it is undivided and pure. See Pseudo-Simplicius, *De An.* 89.33-90.27. Compare Damascius, *in Phd.* 1.93: "Just as the soul when it is joined with sensation seems to be corporeal and unseparated, so also when it accompanies entities intelligible and immaterial one could not think it anything but separated." The concept is based in part on Aristotle, *De An.* 430a22-23: "Only after it has been separated (χωρισθείς) is it [i.e., the active intellect] that which it is, and this alone is immortal and eternal." For Iamblichus, Aristotle's words mean that the soul only attains its highest essence when it is separated from body and joined to the gods. It is then free from all influences emanating from the realm of generation.

It is difficult to ascertain the identity of the "Platonists" who believe that the soul in its disembodied state is still "governed by the cosmos or controlled by nature." Festugière is silent on the issue. Iamblichus perhaps has in mind Platonists such as Eratosthenes and Ptolemy (mentioned in section 26, above) who held that the soul was always in a body. Such souls would never be free from the influences of the sensible realm and of Fate, but it is hard to see how permanently embodied souls could be unified with the gods. The point for Iamblichus is that the human soul, once purified from its body and ascended to the gods, escapes Fate and lives a life as close to the divine as possible.

ἀνεῖται δὲ πάντῃ ἀφ᾽ ὅλων, ὥσπερ ἐπὶ τῶν χωριστῶν οὐσιῶν τουτὶ νοοῦμεν . . . The final clause of the last sentence is also problematic. Both manuscripts have ἀχωρίστων ("unseparated"), which Wachsmuth prints. The term "unseparated" normally means "unseparated from body" in Neoplatonic writings, in the way that "snubness" is inseparable from a nose. (See Aristotle, *De An.* 431b12-16.) This presents difficulties for adopting the MSS. reading. Festugière (248) considers replacing it with χωριστῶν ("separated"), but decides to keep the reading of the MSS. and translate it as equivalent to ἀμερίστων ("indivisible"). Festugière cites Proclus' use of the term in *E.T.*, but even there "separated" means "separated from body." See especially Propositions 16: "Everything that can revert upon itself has an essence that is separated from body (χωριστὴν . . . παντὸς σώματος), for if anything is unseparated from body (ἀχώριστον . . . σώματος), it will not have any activity separated from the body (σώματος χωριστήν)." Cf. Proposition 186. And this is how Iamblichus uses χωριστός in the *De Anima*. See section 15 (371.5-6 W): χωριστὴ τοῦ σώματος ("separated from body") and compare sections 21 (373.9-21 W, esp. lines 12 and 18-21) and 22 (373.24-25 W). Since Iamblichus could not have written that separated disembodied souls are released from Fate just as unseparated embodied souls are, we emend ἀχωρίστων to χωριστῶν.

51-52

These two sections also present difficulties. There are two points that suggest emendation of some sort is needed. First, there is not the usual dichotomy of views in these sections. Indeed the ancients are not mentioned at all. Second, the contrast that exists (if one does at all) is between Porphyry (in section 51) and "the Platonists" (in section 52), which would be odd because, of course, Porphyry is a Platonist.

Οἱ δὲ περὶ Πορφύριον ἄχρι τῶν ἀνθρωπίνων βίων . . . Wachsmuth follows Heeren in marking a lacuna after these words ("Porphyry and his school, as far as human lives"). Festugière (248 note 1) argues that the phrase "human lives" refers to the rational life of the soul; he cites section 24 (375.18-20 W): "According to Aristotle, these [i.e., "irregular movements" of 375.2-3 W, i.e., irrational ones; see Festugière 211 note 2 and 209 note 1] are distinguished from human [movements, i.e., rational ones] by their forms of life and other properties." Festugière then fills the lacuna by adding <τὴν ἀθανασίαν διατείνεσθαι λέγουσι> after Οἱ δὲ περὶ Πορφύριον ἄχρι τῶν ἀνθρωπίνων βίων. The complete sentence would then be translated: "Porphyry and his school <say that immortality extends> as far as human lives." That is, Porphyry grants immortality only to the rational soul and not to the irrational. As Festugière says, this is in accord with 384.23-25 W: "each irrational faculty is freed into the whole life of the universe from which it was separated, where each remains as far as possible unchanged, as Porphyry thinks." See section 37 and notes; cf. section 12 (370.5-11 W) and notes there.

The problem with Festugière's suggestion is not with its meaning (for this is certainly the view of Porphyry that Iamblichus is considering) but with the location of the lacuna. As we have argued, this long chapter on the soul's reward is riddled with lacunae but also shows evidence of the editing of Stobaeus. This paragraph, like the previous one, begins abruptly. This abruptness again suggests that Stobaeus is editing a longer passage in such a way as to concentrate on those parts of the passage that are of most concern to him. We believe, therefore, that Stobaeus has omitted both an introductory sentence (e.g., "What happens to the disembodied soul after it has been purified?") and a partial sentence that would have given the opinion of the ancients (e.g., "The ancients extend immortality to the irrational soul;"). For a similar phraseology, see Damascius, *in Phd.* 1.177.1-2: οἱ μὲν . . . ἄχρι . . . ἀπαθανατίζουσιν ("Some extend immortality as far as . . ."). Damascius says (lines 3-5) that Iamblichus extends it μέχρι τῆς ἀλογίας ("as far as the irrational soul").

Ἔτι τοίνυν Πορφύριος μὲν ἀφομοιοῖ τὴν ψυχὴν τοῖς πᾶσι, μένουσαν καθ᾽ ἑαυτὴν ἥτις ἐστίν . . . This sentence also presents a problem. Festugière (248 note 3) rightly states that after the clause, "Porphyry assimilates the soul to the universe," Iamblichus cannot write "According to the Platonists, they care for inanimate things." The latter does not correspond to the former. He suggests therefore that the words οὐ μὴν τῶν τῇδε ἀξιοῖ τὰς ψυχὰς προϊστάναι be added in between, producing the following translation: "Further, Porphyry assimilates the soul to the universe, although it remains what it is in itself, <but he does not think that souls preside over things of this realm>. According to the Platonists, they care for inanimate things."

The problem with this is that the sentence, "According to the Platonists, they care for inanimate things," introduces a new topic (what the disembodied soul does) not specifically related to the earlier one of the extent of immortality. It seems to us that we have the beginning of a new section, and we have divided it as such. We also suspect that it should be directly attached to the following section, since it shares its topic. (Note as well that in section 53, the ancients are compared to the "Platonists" throughout.) In that case, what is missing is the first half of the dichotomy, which (like those in section 53) would concern the ancients.

Section 51 therefore ends as abruptly as it begins. Stobaeus seems to have been interested only in the views of Porphyry. We know from elsewhere that Porphyry held that the irrational soul and vehicle were gathered from the celestial bodies in the soul's descent and then sloughed off again during its re-ascent. The irrational soul and vehicle were then returned to their sources. The rational soul, the only immortal part, escaped this fate. See section 12 (370.5-11 W), section 37 (384.19-25 W), and Proclus, *In Tim.* 3.234.8-32. We also know from section 48 (457.15-16 W) that Porphyry did not allow the soul any further role in the universe after its ascent. In his *De Regressu*, Fr. 11, Porphyry states that the soul, "after it has been purified from all evils and has been established with the Father, will never again endure the evils of this world" and "will never return to the evils of this world." Now, in section 51, Iamblichus explains what Porphyry thought happened to the separated rational soul. Iamblichus is, however, less than clear. Porphyry "assimilates the soul to the universe." This seems to be opposed to the normal Neoplatonic goal of assimilation to god (ὁμοίωσις θεῷ, Plato, *Tht.* 176b1) and may suggest that Iamblichus saw Porphyry's view of immortality as inferior to his own. For Porphyry's use of the phrase τῷ παντὶ ὁμοιωθῆναι, see with Festugière (248 note 2) *Sent.* 40, p. 48.12-17 Lamberz.

Κατὰ δὲ τοὺς Πλατωνικοὺς ἐπιμελοῦνται τῶν ἀψύχων . . . For this doctrine, see Plato, *Phdr.* 246b6: ψυχὴ πᾶσα παντὸς ἐπιμελεῖται τοῦ ἀψύχου. Iamblichus would not, of course, be disagreeing with Plato. Rather, he would have probably thought that the "ancients" added a more elevated role for disembodied souls to play in the universe. See the following section.

53

In this final paragraph, Iamblichus considers what the role of these disembodied human souls may be. He again contrasts his view ("the ancients'") with that of other Platonists. Originally in Iamblichus' *De Anima*, this section may have followed directly after section 52, where the "Platonists" held that disembodied souls merely "care for inanimate things" (ἐπιμελοῦνται τῶν ἀψύχων). In section 53, Iamblichus makes two contrasts between the ancients and Platonists concerning the soul's post-bodily activities. In each case, the view of the ancients precedes that of the Platonists (κατὰ μὲν τοὺς παλαιοὺς . . . κατὰ δὲ τοὺς Πλατωνικοὺς . . . κατ᾽ ἐκείνους μὲν . . . κατὰ δὲ τούτους). This order suggests that the missing beginning of section 52 would have contained a clause concerning the ancients' views on the soul's activities as well. Thus, we can again see the heavy editorial hand of Stobaeus at work. All three sentences (sections 52 and 53) concern the role of the human soul after it has been separated from its body.

As to the contrast between the ancients and Platonists in section 53, Iamblichus again (as in section 50) uses compounds of συν- (συνδιοικοῦσι, "administer the universe together," and συνδημιουρ-γοῦσι "help with the creation of the universe") to emphasize the shared experience of human and divine. This time, however, the emphasis is on the fact that human souls are more actively involved along with higher divinities (gods and angels) in actually governing and controlling the universe below them. Human souls, as it were, have a more "hands on" role according to the ancients than they do according to Platonists.

The first contrast is between the more active συνδιοικοῦσι τοῖς θεοῖς and the more passive θεωροῦσιν αὐτῶν τὴν τάξιν. Both verbs derive from Plato's *Phaedrus* (πάντα τὸν κόσμον διοικεῖ, "[the winged soul] administers all the cosmos," 246c1-2; and αἱ δὲ θεωροῦσι τὰ ἔξω τοῦ οὐρανοῦ, "[the souls] contemplate what is outside heaven," 247c1-2; cf. 247d4). The point behind Iamblichus' use of θεωροῦσιν is that the Platonists consider the separated soul to observe the gods passively, just as Plato has souls observing the Forms. The term συνδιοικοῦσι, on the other hand, emphasizes the soul's actions that are carried out along with the gods. The term is found regularly in Neoplatonic contexts for the soul's sharing in the world's governance.[93] Sallustius in *De Deis et Mundo*, 21.1.1-4 writes:

Αἱ δὲ κατ' ἀρετὴν ζήσασαι ψυχαὶ τά τε ἄλλα εὐδαιμονοῦσαι καὶ τῆς ἀλόγου χωρισθεῖσαι καὶ καθαραὶ παντὸς γενόμεναι σώματος θεοῖς τε συνάπτονται, καὶ τὸν ὅλον κόσμον συνδιοικοῦσιν ἐκείνοις. ("Souls that have lived in accordance with virtue and are blessed in other respects, since they are separated from the irrational soul and are pure, attach themselves to the gods and administer the whole cosmos with them")

In the next sentence, Iamblichus again contrasts active and passive roles for the disembodied souls. According to the ancients souls "help the angels with the creation of the universe" (καὶ ἀγγέλοις ὡσαύτως κατ' ἐκείνους μὲν συνδημιουργοῦσι τὰ ὅλα); according to the Platonists souls merely "accompany them" (κατὰ δὲ τούτους συμπεριπολοῦσιν). More literally, συμπεριπολοῦσιν means simply "revolve with" or "go around with." In this sense it too is found (without its συν- prefix) in *Phdr.* 246b6-7: πάντα δὲ οὐρανὸν περιπολεῖ, "[the winged soul] revolves around all of heaven." The term συμπεριπολοῦσιν becomes common in Neoplatonism in the context of souls following along with divinities, but it usually has "gods" (or some god) as its dative object, not "angels."[94]

The term συνδημιουργεῖν is found much less often among the later Neoplatonists. Of Sallustius, Proclus, Damascius, and Olympiodorus, only Proclus uses the verb (four times), but never of souls. In *In Tim.* 3.65.22-25 (= Iamblichus, *In Tim.* Fr. 70.18-19), Proclus uses it (in an Iamblichean context) of the planets Venus and Mercury, which assist the Sun in the creation of the universe. In *In Tim.* 3.248.2-5, where Proclus is giving Syrianus' explanation of the mixing bowl of *Timaeus* 41d, he says that the mixing bowl, as the source of life for souls, creates the universe with the Demiurge. In *Theol. Plat.*

---

[93] See also Proclus, *In Remp.* 1.52.10-13; 2.99.6-10; 2.177.26-29; *In Alc.* 1.149.1-5 (where Proclus uses vocabulary from and refers explicitly to Plato's *Phaedrus* 246bc); *In Tim.* 1.70.30-71.5 (esp. 71.2-3: εἰθισμέναι γὰρ ἐκεῖ συμπεριπολεῖν τοῖς θεοῖς καὶ συνδιοικεῖν τὸ πᾶν, "souls accustomed to accompany the gods and administer the universe with them"); 1.111.14-17; 3.284.19-21 (esp. lines 20-21 συμπεριπολοῦσι μετὰ τῶν θεῶν καὶ συνδιοικοῦσι τὸν ὅλον κόσμον); 3.296.25-26; and Olympiodorus, *In Alc.* 60.5-7 (φησὶν ὁ Πλάτων ὅτι αἱ μὲν τελειότεραι ψυχαὶ συνεπιτροπεύουσι τὰ τῇδε τῷ θεῷ καὶ συνδιοικοῦσιν, αἱ δὲ ἀτελέστεραι ὡς ὄργανόν εἰσι καὶ οὕτως χρῆται αὐταῖς ὁ θεὸς πρὸς τὰ ἐνταῦθα).
[94] Proclus. *In Remp.* 2.160.19-20; 2.161.27-28; *In Alc.* 1.72.19-20; 1.137.7-8; *In Crat.* 174.48-49; *In Tim.* 1.71.1-2; 1.115.23-25; 3.129.14-15; 3.131.6-7; 3.245.31-32; 3.284.20; 3.348.30-349.1; and Damascius, *In Phd.* 1.509.4-5.

66.18-20 and 71.10-15, the younger gods of the *Timaeus* create along with the Demiurge. This fact suggests strongly that Iamblichus is creating the term here and using it deliberately to contrast his own conception of the active involvement of separated souls in the administration and creation of the world below. (The verb appears nowhere else in Iamblichus' writings.)

That the verb is coupled with angels may mean that Iamblichus is thinking of *Chald. Or.* Fr. 138, "in the angelic space" (ἀγγελικῷ ἐνὶ χώρῳ). According to Olympiodorus, this oracle concerns the descent of the purified souls of theurgists (see section 47, above). Iamblichus may believe that such pure souls descend to the τάξις of angels and aid them in ministering to the universe. In *De Myst.* 2.6, Iamblichus situates purified souls at this angelic level (ἐν ἀγγέλων τάξει, 83.3) and gives them the role of raising mortal souls upwards toward the gods. This is not quite a demiurgic role, but one can see how angels and purified souls, by their very proximity to the gods, would come to be seen as "syndemiurgic" in Iamblichus' philosophy.

For Iamblichus, then, the disembodied life involves more than following in the god's train, as suggested by Plato's *Phaedrus*. The soul is actively involved in the divine activities of governance and creation. This new, active role is the final reward for souls of theurgists.

Here Stobaeus' extracts from the *De Anima* end. Although the final reward of the soul is a fitting place to end a treatise on the soul, it is doubtful that Iamblichus ended his work here. He may have had more to say about the role of purified souls in the cosmos. It seems likely that he would have gone on to discuss the higher reward of union with the One. As in the *De Mysteriis*, Iamblichus may have concluded with a prayer to the gods.

Fragmenta Incertae Sedis
54

These final two fragments (54 and 55) come from book 2 of Stobaeus' *Anthologium*. Neither appeared in Festugière's text. Their exact place in Iamblichus' *De Anima* is uncertain. There is little reason to doubt that both fragments derive from Iamblichus' work since both are explicitly attributed to it. Neither fragment, however, concerns the soul itself. Rather, they both seem to be either introductory comments or simply asides in what may have been longer psychological passages.

Πόσῳ δὴ οὖν βέλτιον Ἡράκλειτος . . . Iamblichus is our only source for this fragment of Heraclitus' writings (Fr. 70 D-K). Heraclitus' meaning is clear enough. It is one of a string of his pronouncements directed against the pretensions of those who dare to claim wisdom.[95] Here human wisdom is compared to children's toys (παίδων ἀθύρματα).

In Stobaeus, the fragment appears in the context of several fragments which downplay the possibility of complete human wisdom. The fragments include short quotations from Didymus, Bion, Pindar, and others, as well as two quotations from Plato's *Timaeus* (28c3-5 and 29c4-d3).

The subject is a *topos* in philosophy, and one to which Iamblichus himself is no stranger. In *In Tim.* Fr. 88, he says

> . . . it is not possible to conclude this either, how on the one hand the gods create body, and how the life in the body, and how then they combine with each other. For these things are by nature incomprehensible to us. That everything takes its existence from the Gods, we firmly maintain, looking to their goodness and power, but how things proceed from them, we are not competent to comprehend.[96]

The sentiment expressed in the *Timaeus* commentary is an extension of that given in the *De Anima*. In both passages Iamblichus sees a necessary limitation to human understanding. Human beings are not gods and cannot know all that gods know. Thus human wisdom compared to divine wisdom is like children's toys compared to the real object they represent.

The passage seems to us introductory in nature, perhaps occurring very near the beginning of the *De Anima*. One could imagine, for example, Iamblichus first claiming that not all the truths about the human soul are comprehensible to philosophers, and then bringing Heraclitus in to support his claim about the limitation of human knowledge. Nonetheless, the exact place of the fragment in the *De Anima* must remain uncertain.

---

[95] See W. K. C. Guthrie, *A History of Greek Philosophy*, Vol. 1 (Cambridge 1962) 412, who quotes Frr. 1, 17, 19, 29, 34, 70, 104.
[96] The translation is Dillon's (1973) 203.

55

This is a short fragment on the proper role of students, who should pay close attention to their teachers. The issue is of general concern, but a search of the term for "listening" (ἀκρόασις) shows that Iamblichus uses the term only in Pythagorean contexts.[97] This suggests that the proper kind of student-teacher relationship is that which existed between Pythagoras and his best students, who faithfully learned and repeated their master's teachings.[98] Thus, this short fragment may have formed part of a criticism against philosophers who did not follow the "correct" teaching of Pythagoras or Plato. The fragment may have formed part of Iamblichus' introduction, in which case he may have begun by admonishing what he saw as wrong-headed philosophers, or it may be part of an attack on (probably Platonist) philosophers in the course of some particular discussion in the body of the *De Anima*.

---

[97] The term occurs seven times in the *Pyth Vit.* (6.30.3; 18.80.11; 19.90.8; 19.90.10; 29.158.8; 29.164.9; 34.246.10), once in the Pseudo-Iamblichean *Th. Ar.* (82.13, Πυθαγορικῶν ἀκροάσεων) and nowhere else in any text of Iamblichus.

[98] On Iamblichus' view of Pythagoras' educational system, see *Vit. Pyth.* 17.71-18.92.

APPENDIX

Extracts relating to Iamblichus' *De Anima* from
Pseudo-Simplicius, *In De Anima*

and

Priscianus, *Metaphrasis in Theophrastum*

Extracts from Pseudo-Simplicius, In De Anima
and Priscianus, Metaphrasis in Theophrastum

A. Pseudo-Simplicius, *In De Anima* 1.1-20

1, 1   Περισπούδαστον μὲν προηγουμένως ἡ περὶ αὐτῶν τῶν πραγμάτων τῶν
       τε ἄλλων καὶ ἡ περὶ ψυχῆς ἀλήθεια, αὐτίκα οἰκειοτάτη πασῶν ἡμῖν
5   ὑπάρχουσα· δευτέρως δὲ καὶ ἡ τῶν δοκούντων τοῖς εἰς ἄκρον
       ἐπιστήμης ἥκουσι κατάληψις. διὸ καὶ τῆς Περὶ ψυχῆς Ἀριστοτέλους
       πεφροντισμένως ἄγαν ἀντέχεσθαι ἡγοῦμαι δεῖν πραγματείας. πολλὰ
       μὲν οὖν καὶ μακάρια θεωρήματα περὶ αὐτῆς καὶ ὑπὸ Πλάτωνος
10   παραδέδοται, ἀλλ' ἐκεῖνα καὶ ἱκανῶς καὶ συμφώνως ἀλλήλοις τοῖς
       Πλάτωνος ἐξηγηταῖς ἐπεξείργασταί τε καὶ σεσαφήνισται. τελεωσαμέ-
       νου δὲ τὴν Περὶ ψυχῆς πραγματείαν τοῦ Ἀριστοτέλους, ὡς τῷ ἀρίστῳ
       τῆς ἀληθείας κριτῇ δοκεῖ τῷ Ἰαμβλίχῳ, πολλὴ ἡ τῶν τὰ ἐκείνου
       σαφηνιζόντων πρὸς ἀλλήλους διαφωνία οὐ περὶ τὴν τῆς Ἀριστοτελικῆς
       λέξεως μόνον ἑρμηνείαν, ἀλλὰ καὶ περὶ αὐτὰ τὰ πράγματα μάλιστα.
15   διὸ καὶ αὐτῷ μοι ἔδοξε ζητῆσαί τε καὶ γράψαι τὴν αὐτοῦ τε πρὸς
       ἑαυτὸν τοῦ φιλοσόφου καὶ τὴν πρὸς τὴν ἀλήθειαν συμφωνίαν, τὰς μὲν
       πρὸς τοὺς ἄλλους ἀντιρρήσεις φυλαττομένῳ, πιστουμένῳ δὲ τὰ
       δοκοῦντα ἐν τοῖς ἀμφιβόλοις ἐκ τῶν Ἀριστοτέλους ἐναργῶν δογμάτων
       τε καὶ ῥητῶν, πανταχοῦ δὲ κατὰ δύναμιν τῆς τῶν πραγμάτων
       ἀντεχομένῳ ἀληθείας κατὰ τὴν Ἰαμβλίχου ἐν τοῖς ἰδίοις αὐτοῦ περὶ
20   ψυχῆς συγγράμμασιν ὑφήγησιν.

1: 3 περισπούδαστον] Prooemii p. 1. 2 desunt in Aa: explevit Hayduck ex AᵃD,
passim inspectus C.   **4** δευτέρως AᵃD: δεύτερον C.   **10** τελεωσαμένου AᵃC:
πλεοσαμένου D τοῦ AᵃC: τῆς D.   **12** δοκεῖ post κριτῇ AᵃD: post ᾽Ιαμβλίχῳ C.   **19**τε D:
om. AᵃC.

Extracts from Pseudo-Simplicius, In De Anima
and Priscianus, Metaphrasis in Theophrastum

A. Pseudo-Simplicius, *In De Anima* 1.1-20

First, we are seeking the truth concerning both other metaphysical
realities and the soul, since of all realities it is immediately most
appropriate to us; secondarily, [we seek] the opinions of those who
have reached the pinnacle of knowledge. I therefore believe that it is
necessary to give a careful examination to Aristotle's treatise *On the
Soul.* Plato has handed down many blessed doctrines on the soul, but
interpreters of Plato have investigated and explained them sufficiently and in harmony with one another. After Aristotle had completed
his treatise *On the Soul,* as Iamblichus who is the best judge of the
truth thought, a great deal of controversy arose among those
explicating Aristotle's doctrine not only concerning the interpretation of Aristotle's text but especially also concerning the soul itself.

I have therefore decided to investigate and record the coherence
of the philosopher both with himself and with the truth, avoiding
controversies with others, while seeking confirmation for his opinions
on doubtful points from Aristotle's clear doctrines and words. And in
every way and to the best of my ability I will adhere to the truth about
the metaphysical realities under the guidance of Iamblichus in his
own writings on the soul.

B. Pseudo-Simplicius, *In De Anima* 5.38-6.17

5, 38 Ἔτι ἐν τῷ τρίτῳ κατ' αὐτὸ τὸ λογικὸν τὴν ἡμετέραν ψυχὴν ἐν μεσότητι
40 τῶν ἄκρων ὁρῶν ζῴων, ποτὲ μὲν ἀπεικάζει τῇ αἰσθητικῇ ποτὲ δὲ τῇ
νοερᾷ· καὶ ποτὲ μὲν εἰς τὴν αἰσθητικὴν ὑποβαίνουσαν, ποτὲ δὲ εἰς
6 τὴν | νοερὰν ἀνιοῦσαν μίμησιν· καὶ ποτὲ μὲν εἰς τὸ ἀμέριστον ὡς οἷόν
τε αὐτῇ συναιρουμένην καὶ ὅλην ἐν ἑαυτῇ μένουσαν, ὅτε καὶ τὸν
ὑπερέχοντα αὐτῆς μιμεῖται νοῦν, ποτὲ δὲ ἀφισταμένην πως ἑαυτῆς ἐν
τῇ ἔξω ῥοπῇ καὶ κατὰ προβολὴν ἐνεργοῦσαν καὶ εἰς μερισμὸν
5 προϊοῦσαν· οὐ μὴν ὡς πάντῃ τῶν ἀντικειμένων ἀφισταμένην. καὶ γὰρ
ὁ μερισμὸς αὐτῆς μετὰ τῆς εἰς τὸ ἀμέριστον συναιρέσεως, καὶ ἡ
προβολὴ μετὰ τῆς εἰς ἑαυτὴν ἐπιστροφῆς, καὶ ἡ ἑαυτῆς ἀπόστασις μετὰ
τῆς ἐν ἑαυτῇ μονῆς, ἀμυδρουμένης ὅτε εἰς τὸ ἔξω ῥέπει· ἵνα καὶ μένῃ
ἅμα καὶ μεταβάλλῃ διὰ τὴν τῶν μόνως τε μενόντων καὶ πάντῃ
10 μεταβαλλομένων μεσότητα ἡ ἡμετέρα ψυχὴ ἑκατέρῳ πως ἐπικοι-
νωνοῦσα τῶν ἄκρων, ὥσπερ καὶ μερίζεταί πως καὶ οἷον ἀμέριστος [τε]
ἅμα γίνεταί τε καὶ ἀγένητος ὑπάρχει, φθείρεταί τε τρόπον τινὰ καὶ
ἄφθαρτος διασῴζεται. διὸ οὔτε μένειν τι αὐτῆς θησόμεθα κατὰ τὸν
Πλωτῖνον ἀεὶ ὡσαύτως καὶ καθαρῶς οὔτε παντελῶς προϊέναι ἐν τῇ εἰς
γένεσιν ῥοπῇ, ἀλλ' ὅλη πρόεισι καὶ μένει εἰλικρινῶς ἐν τῇ πρὸς τὰ
15 δεύτερα ῥοπῇ. ἀλλὰ ταῦτα μὲν σαφέστερον καὶ ἡ ὅλη τῶν λόγων
ἐπιδείξει διέξοδος ὡς καὶ Ἀριστοτέλει δοκοῦντα καὶ ὑπὸ τοῦ
Ἰαμβλίχου ἐναργέστερον ἐκπεφασμένα.

6: 7 ἑαυτὸν a. **8** μόνης a. **11** τε (ante ἅμα) expunxit Hayduck γίνεται τε D: τε om.
Aa.

B. Pseudo-Simplicius, *In De Anima* 5.38-6.17

Further, in the third book he sees that our soul in accordance with the rational element itself is a mean between the extreme lives. Sometimes he likens it to the sensible life, at other times to the intellectual. Sometimes [he portrays it] descending into the sensible; at other times rising to the imitation of the intellectual. Sometimes when it has gathered itself together into partlessness as much as is possible for it and when it remains whole in itself, it imitates the Intellect that transcends it; at other times it somehow departs from itself in its inclination toward what is external to it, actualizing in accordance with its projection and proceeding into partedness, yet not in such a way as completely to depart from what is opposite to this. For what is partial in it exists together with a coalescence into partlessness, its projection with a return to itself, and its departure from itself with an abiding in itself, which is weakened when it declines toward what is external to it. Wherefore our soul simultaneously abides and changes because it is a mean between what is permanently abiding and in every way changing, and yet it shares somehow in each of the extremes, just as it is somehow both divided and as it were undivided, and simultaneously comes into existence but is ungenerated, and is destroyed in some way yet is preserved indestructible. Therefore we will not agree with Plotinus that any of it remains always the same and pure or that it processes completely in its declination toward generation. Rather, it processes as a whole and remains pure in its declination toward what is secondary to it. As to these matters, a complete examination of the arguments will demonstrate both that this is Aristotle's doctrine and that it has been set out more perspicuously by Iamblichus.

C. Pseudo-Simplicius, *In De Anima* 89.33-90.25

89, 33   εἰ δέ, ὡς τῷ Ἰαμβλίχῳ δοκεῖ, οὐκ ἂν ἐξ ἀπαθοῦς καὶ τελείας οὐσίας
35   διεστραμμένη καὶ ἀτελὴς προΐοι ἐνέργεια, εἴη ἂν παθαινομένη πως
καὶ κατ' οὐσίαν· ὡς καὶ ταύτη εἶναι μέση οὐ τῶν μεριστῶν μόνον καὶ
ἀμερίστων οὐδὲ τῶν μενόντων καὶ προεληλυθότων οὐδὲ τῶν νοερῶν
καὶ ἀλόγων, ἀλλὰ καὶ τῶν ἀγενήτων καὶ γενητῶν, κατὰ μὲν τὸ μόνιμον
ἑαυτῆς καὶ νοερὸν καὶ ἀμέριστον ἀγένητος οὖσα, κατὰ δὲ τὴν πρόοδον
90   καὶ τὸ μεριστὸν καὶ τὴν πρὸς τὸ ἄλογον κοινωνίαν γινομένη, | οὐδὲ τὸ
ἀγένητον εἰλικρινὲς ἔχουσα, οἷον τὸ νοερόν, ἐπειδὴ οὐδὲ τὸ ἀμέριστον ἢ τὸ μόνιμον, οὐδὲ τὸ γενητὸν τοῖς ἐσχάτοις ὅμοιον, τοῖς ὅλως ποτὲ
μὴ οὖσιν· ἀλλὰ τὸ μὲν οἷον ἐξίστασθαί πως ἑαυτοῦ ποτε τῇ πρὸς τὴν
γένεσιν κοινωνίᾳ καὶ οὐχ ἁπλῶς ἔτι μένειν, ἀλλὰ τὸ συναμφότερον
5   ὁμοῦ μένειν τε ὅπερ ἐστὶ καὶ γίνεσθαι, τὸ δὲ οὐδέποτε τοῦ ἀγενήτου
ἀπολειπόμενον, ἀλλ' ἀεὶ αὐτῷ συνηρτημένον καὶ ἔνδοθεν ἔχον τὸ
διαμένειν καὶ οἷον ἐπιρρέον καὶ ἀναπληρωματικὸν τοῦ ἀπογινομένου.
ἀλλὰ τὸ μὲν γενητὸν αὐτῆς καὶ προϊὸν οὐδέποτε ἄνευ τοῦ μονίμου καὶ
ἀγενήτου, τὸ δὲ ἀγένητον αὐτῆς ποτε πάσης ἀπαλλάσσεται τῆς πρὸς
10   γένεσιν κοινωνίας ἐν τῇ χωριστῇ ἀπὸ σωμάτων ζωῇ. διὸ καὶ ἀθάνατος
ἡ ψυχὴ καὶ μόνιμος, ἀεὶ μὲν τῆς νοερᾶς ζωῆς ὑφειμένην ἔχουσα τὴν
ἀθανασίαν καὶ μονιμότητα, καὶ πρὸς ἑαυτὴν δὲ ἡ ἡμετέρα διαφο-
ρουμένη· καὶ ἀκραιφνὲς μέν, ὅσον αὐτῇ προσήκει, τὸ ἀθάνατον καὶ
μόνιμον καὶ ἀμέριστον ἀπολαμβάνουσα ἐν τῇ χωριστῇ καὶ νοερᾷ ζωῇ·
15   χωρισθεῖσα γάρ, ὡς ἐρεῖ, ἔστιν ὅπερ ἐστίν· ἐν δὲ τῇ πρὸς τὰ ἔξω ῥοπῇ
οὐ παντελῶς μὲν ἀπολείπουσα ἑαυτὴν μένει, (δηλοῖ δὲ πᾶσα λογικὴ
ἐνέργεια, οὐκ ἄνευ τῆς πρὸς ἑαυτὴν γινομένη ἐπιστροφῆς, ὅθεν καὶ ἡ
πίστις μετὰ τὴν συγκατάθεσιν, τὸ γνωσθὲν ὅτι ἀληθὲς ἐπικρινούσης
καὶ τότε συγκατατιθεμένης· τοῦτο γὰρ ἡ πίστις· δηλοῖ δὲ καὶ ἡ ἔνδοθεν αὖθις ἐπὶ τὸ κρεῖττον ἀνάκλησις καὶ ἡ ὑφ' ἑαυτῆς τελείωσις), οὐ
20   μὴν καθαρὸν τὸ ἑαυτῆς σώζουσα μόνιμον. διὰ γὰρ τὴν ἔξω ῥοπὴν ὁμοῦ
ὅλη καὶ μένει καὶ πρόεισι, καὶ οὐδέτερον ἔχει παντελῶς οὐδὲ ἀπηλλαγμένον τοῦ λοιποῦ (ὅθεν καὶ τὸ ἀθάνατον αὐτῆς τότε ἀναπίμπλαται
τοῦ θνητοῦ κατὰ πᾶν ἑαυτό, καὶ οὐ μένει μόνον ἀθάνατον, καὶ τὸ
ἀγένητον γινόμενόν πως τυγχάνει ὄν, ὡς καὶ τὸ ἀμέριστον αὐτῆς
25   μεριζόμενον), οὐκέτι τῇ οὐσίᾳ οὖσα ἐνέργεια, καθ' ὅσον αὐτῇ θέμις.

90: 2 ἐπειδὴ οὐ a. **6** ἀεὶ] εἰ a. **9** ἀγέννητου Α. **15** ἐρεῖ] v. Γ 5. **16** μένειν a. **21/22** παντελῶς – λοιποῦ] τοῦ λοιποῦ ἀπηλλαγμένον παντελῶς a. **23** θνητοῦ] λοιποῦ a.

C. Pseudo-Simplicius, *In De Anima* 89.33-90.25

But if, as Iamblichus thinks, a distorted and imperfect activity cannot proceed from an impassible and perfect substance, the soul would be affected somehow even in its essence. Thus also in this way it is a mean not only between the divisible and the indivisible, or what remains and what proceeds, or the intellective and the irrational, but also between the ungenerated and the generated. It is ungenerated in accordance with its permanent, intellectual, and indivisible aspect, while it is generated in accordance with its procession, divisibility, and association with the irrational. It possesses neither its ungenerated aspect purely, as an intellectual entity does, since it is not indivisible or permanent, nor its generated aspect as the lowest entities do, since these never completely exist. But in its association with generation, it sometimes in some way abandons itself as it were, and it does not simply remain but simultaneously both remains what it is and becomes; it never leaves what is ungenerated but is always joined to it and holds permanence within and as it were flows onward replenishing what is lost. The generated aspect of it, however, also never proceeds without the stable and ungenerated, while the ungenerated aspect of it is sometimes removed from all association with generation in the life separated from body. Therefore the soul is both immortal and permanent, always having its immortality and permanency inferior to the intellectual life. But our soul is differentiated in itself. It is pure, on the one hand, insofar as is appropriate for it, receiving immortality, permanence, and indivisibility from the separated and intellectual life; for once it has been separated, as he will say, "it is what it is." In its declension toward the outside, on the other hand, it remains without completely abandoning itself. (This is evident from every rational activity since such activity does not come into being without reversion to itself, whence also there is belief after assent, when it judges that the thing known is true and then assents. For this is belief. It is evident also from its restoration from within itself toward what is superior and its perfection by itself.) But it does not preserve its permanence pure. For because of its declension outside, as a whole it simultaneously both remains and proceeds, and it has neither completely without the other. Whence, its immortality is at that time filled with mortality in its whole self, and it does not remain immortal only. Its ungeneratedness somehow happens to

κατὰ τὸ γενητὸν οὖν ἑαυτῆς ἡ πρώτη ἐστὶν ἐντελέχεια διὰ τὸν ἀπὸ τῆς οὐσίας τῆς ἐνεργείας μερισμόν, καὶ οὐ κατὰ τὸ ἐπιστάμενον (οὐ γὰρ ἦν τὸ σύνθετον), ἀλλ' ὡς ἡ ἐπιστήμη ἤτοι ὡς τὸ εἶδος.

D. Pseudo-Simplicius, *In De Anima* 240.33-241.26

240,33 εἰ μὲν οὖν παντελῶς ἡ αὐτὴ μένοι ἡ τῆς ψυχῆς ἀκροτάτη οὐσία, ἡ
35 ἐνέργεια οὐχ ἡ αὐτὴ μένουσα οὐκ ἂν εἴη ὅπερ ἡ οὐσία, εἴ γε ὁτὲ μὲν
νοεῖ, ὁτὲ δὲ οὐ νοεῖ. εἰ δὲ καὶ αὐτὴ ἡ ἄκρα αὐτῆς οὐσία οὐ μένει ἐν
τῇ πρὸς τὰ δεύτερα ῥοπῇ εἰλικρινής, ἵνα καὶ ταύτῃ ᾖ μέση, ὡς καὶ τῷ
Ἰαμβλίχῳ ἐν τῇ ἰδίᾳ Περὶ ψυχῆς πραγματείᾳ δοκεῖ, οὐ μεριστῶν
μόνον καὶ ἀμερίστων, ἀλλὰ καὶ γενητῶν καὶ ἀγενήτων καὶ φθαρτῶν
241 καὶ ἀφθάρτων, καὶ ἵνα καὶ αὐτὸ τοῦτο ὁτὲ μὲν | νοῇ ὁτὲ δὲ μὴ (ἀφ'
ἑαυτῆς γὰρ ἐνεργοῦσα ἡ αὐτὴ ἀπαράλλακτος μένουσα καὶ ἐνήργει ἂν
ὡσαύτως ἀεί, ἀλλ' οὐδ' ἂν ποτὲ μὲν προβαλλομένη δευτέρας ζωὰς καὶ
ταύταις συμπλεκομένη ἐν τῇ συμπλοκῇ ἔμενεν αὐτῶν ἀχώριστος, ποτὲ
5 δὲ ἐχωρίζετο· ἴσως γὰρ καὶ αὐτὸ τοῦτο ἐστιν ὁ χωρισμός, ἡ τῆς οὐσίας
ἀδιάφθορος εἰλικρίνεια, ὅπερ καὶ ὁ Ἀριστοτέλης ἐμφαίνει γράφων
"χωρισθεὶς δέ ἐστιν ὅπερ ἐστίν," ὡς τῆς ἔτι τῶν δευτέρων ἀχωρίστου
ζωῆς οὐκ οὔσης ὅπερ ἐστίν), εὔλογον ἄρα μᾶλλον δὲ ἀναγκαῖον οὐ τὴν
ἐνέργειαν μόνην, ἀλλὰ καὶ τὴν οὐσίαν τῆς ψυχῆς καὶ αὐτὴν τὴν
ἀκροτάτην, τῆς ἡμετέρας φημί, διαφορεῖσθαί πως καὶ χαλᾶσθαι καὶ
10 οἷον ὑφιζάνειν ἐν τῇ πρὸς τὰ δεύτερα νεύσει, οὐ παντελῶς ἑαυτῆς
ἐξισταμένην (οὐδὲ γὰρ ἂν ἔμενεν ἔτι ψυχή), ἀλλὰ τὸ ἀκραιφνὲς οὐκέτι
σώζουσα, ὡς ἅμα τὴν αὐτήν τε καὶ οὐ τὴν αὐτὴν φυλάττεσθαι, οὔτε τῆς
ἑτερότητος ἑαυτὴν ἐξαλλαττούσης παντελῶς οὔτε τῆς ταυτότητος
καθαρᾶς καὶ ἀνεξαλλάκτου μενούσης, καὶ οὕτω μερισθεῖσα ὁπωσοῦν
15 τῇ ἐξαλλαγῇ καὶ οὐ μείνασα ὅπερ ἦν, ὑπομένει καὶ τὸν τῆς ἐνεργείας
ἀπὸ τῆς οὐσίας μερισμόν, ὡς καὶ ποτὲ μὴ ἐνεργεῖν. εἰς δὲ τὴν ἑαυτῆς
εἰλικρινῶς ἀναδραμοῦσα οὐσίαν, ἀφιεῖσα μὲν πᾶσαν τὴν ἔξω προβολήν, τῇ δὲ πρὸς ἑαυτὴν ῥωσθεῖσα στροφῇ καὶ ἀναλαβοῦσα τὸ προσῆκον
αὐτῇ μέτρον ἔστι τε ὅπερ ἐστὶ καὶ τῇ ἄκρᾳ εἰς ἑαυτὴν στροφῇ ἀμερῶς
συναιρουμένη καὶ τὴν ἐνέργειαν τῇ οὐσίᾳ ἑνοῖ. καὶ αὕτη μὲν ἡ`

240: 34 ἀκροτάτη] πικροτάτη Aⁱ. **241: 1** νοῇ Hayduck: νοεῖ Aa. **241: 5** γράφων p. 430ᵃ22. **12. 13** οὔτε – οὔτε Hayduck οὐδὲ – οὐδὲ Aa. **12:** ἑαυτὴν (post ἑτερότητος) Aa αὐτὴν Hayduck.

come to be, and its indivisibility is divided. It is no longer activity in essence, insofar as is right for it. In accordance with its generated aspect, it is first entelechy because of the division of its activity from its essence, and not as a knower (for it is not a composite) but as knowledge or as form.

D. Pseudo-Simplicius, *In De Anima* 240.33-241.26

If, then, the highest essence of the soul should completely remain the same, its activity, which does not remain the same, would not be the same as its essence, since it sometimes intelligizes and sometimes does not. Again, even its highest essence does not itself remain pure in its inclination toward what is secondary — so that even in this, as is the view of Iamblichus in his own treatise *On the Soul*, it is a mean not only between the divisible and indivisible but also between the generated and ungenerated and the perishable and imperishable and so that it itself sometimes intelligizes and sometimes does not (for a thing that remains the same and unaltered in generating activities from itself would always act in the same way, but would not, when it projects secondary lives and is interwoven with them, some-times remain unseparated from them in the interwoven compound and sometimes not). For perhaps separation is this, uncorrupted purity of essence, as Aristotle also indicates when he writes, "after it is separated, it is what it is," implying that the life unseparated from what is secondary is not "what it is.") It is reasonable then, or rather, necessary that not the soul's activity alone but also its essence and the highest part itself — of *our* soul, I mean — is somehow dissipated and slackened and as it were sinks down in the inclination toward what is secondary. It does not entirely abandon itself (for then it would no longer remain soul), but it no longer preserves its own purity, with the result that it keeps itself simultaneously the same and not the same. Its otherness does not alter itself completely, nor does its same-ness remain pure and unaltered. The soul, since it was thus divided in some way by the alteration and does not remain what it was, even abides the division of its activity from its essence so that it sometimes does not act. But when it returns in purity to its own essence, aban-dons every external projection, is strengthened by its reversion to itself, and regains its due measure, it is what it is; when it is gathered

20   ἀκροτάτη τῆς ψυχῆς τελειότης ἐν τῷ παντελεῖ τῶν δευτέρων ζῴων
      χωρισμῷ· ἐν δὲ τῇ ἀχωρίστῳ πρὸς αὐτὰς συμπλοκῇ τελειοῦται καὶ
      ἔστι τελεία δευτέρως, καὶ ἡ ἤδη τελειοῦν τὴν προβληθεῖσαν ζωὴν
      ἱκανὴ εἴτε πρακτικῶς εἴτε θεωρητικῶς οὐκ οὖσα δηλαδὴ ἀτελὴς αὐτὴ
      ἐτελείου ἄν, ἀλλ' οὔπω κατὰ ἄκρα μέτρα τελεία, ὡς καὶ ἑαυτῆς εἶναι
25   μόνης· κατὰ δὲ τά [τε] τῶν ἄλλων τελειωτικά, καθ' ἅ ἐστι, προάγει
      ἑαυτὴν καὶ ἄνεισιν εἰς τὴν ἄκραν ἑαυτῆς τελειότητα.

      E. Priscianus, *Metaphrasis in Theophrastum* 31.27-32.19

31,27 Ἐπεὶ οὖν ἀπὸ τῆς οὐσίας αἵ τε ἕξεις καὶ ἐνέργειαι, ἀδύνατον
      ὑποτίθεσθαι τὴν οὐσίαν μένουσαν πάντη ἀμετάβλητον καὶ ἀεὶ
30   ὡσαύτως ἔχουσαν, ποτὲ μὲν τελείων καὶ ἀγαθοειδῶν ἐνεργειῶν εἶναι
      ἀποδοτικήν, ποτὲ δὲ ἀτελῶν καὶ διεστραμμένων. αἱ γὰρ οὐσίαι τῶν
      ἐνεργειῶν αἴτιαι, καὶ ὁποῖαι ἂν ὦσιν αἱ ἐνέργειαι τοιοῦτον ἡμῖν καὶ
      τῆς δυνάμεως καὶ τῆς οὐσίας τὸ εἶδος συλλογίζεσθαι παρέχονται. εἰ
      δὲ διττὴν ἐν ἡμῖν οὐσίαν νοοῖτό τις καὶ διττὰς δυνάμεις τε καὶ
32   ἐνεργείας, καὶ τὰς μὲν ἀεὶ τελείας, | τὰς δὲ ποτὲ μὲν ἀτελεῖς ποτὲ δὲ
      τελείας οἰηθείη, εἰ μὲν διεσπασμένας, πολλὰ ζῷα τὸ ἓν ποιήσει καὶ
      παντελῶς ἀποστήσει τὴν κρείττονα οὐσίαν, ὡς μήτε ἄρχουσαν τῆς
      ζωῆς μήτε κοινόν τι ἔχουσαν, εἴ γε κατὰ τὴν δευτέραν τὸ παρὰ μέρος
5   ἀτελές τε καὶ τέλειον, ἐν ᾧ ἡ ἀνθρωπεία ὁρίζεται ζωή. εἰ δὲ σχέσεις
      λέγων διττὰς ἢ λόγους ἢ ζωὰς τὴν ἕνωσιν τοῖν δυοῖν μὴ ἀναιροίη, ἵνα
      μὴ χορῷ ἢ ἄλλῳ πλήθει προσεοίκῃ τὸ ἡμέτερον, συνέρχηται δὲ εἰς ἓν
      πάντα καὶ πρὸς μίαν συμφύηται ἀρχήν, τὸ ἓν τοῦτο ζητήσωμεν,
      πότερον μονοειδές ἐστι καὶ ἀκήρατον πάντη καὶ ἀμετάβλητον. ἀλλ'
      οὕτω πάλιν οὐδεμία ἔσται ποτὲ ἐν ταῖς ψυχαῖς ἢ κατ' οὐσίαν ἢ κατ'
10   ἐνέργειαν ἀτέλεια ἢ κακία ἢ πάθος· ἀκολουθοῦσι γὰρ τῇ οὐσίᾳ καὶ αἱ
      ἐνέργειαι. ἀλλ' οὐδὲ πάντη μεταβαλλόμενον οἷόν τε συγχωρεῖν·
      διαμένει γὰρ ἡ ζωὴ ἐν ταῖς μεταβολαῖς.
         Ἄμφω ἄρα κατὰ τὸν Ἰάμβλιχον ἡ μερικὴ ψυχὴ ἐξ ἴσου συνείληφε,
      καὶ τὸ μόνιμον καὶ τὸ μεταβαλλόμενον, ἵνα καὶ ταύτῃ ἡ

240: 25 τελεία Hayduck: τέλεια Aa τε delevit Hayduck.   31: 30 ὡσαύτως]
ἀμεταβλήτως w. 3 1 ἀποδεικτικὴν B¹L¹. 33 ἐνεργείαι L¹. 32: 3 οἰηθεὶς HMPb
διεσπασμέναις LMPQ. 6 μὴ om. w 7 προσεοίκῃ BL¹: προσεοίκοι HL²MPQV:
προσέοικε b: προσεοικὸς w συνέχηται bw. δὲ om. bw 8 συμφύεται codd. b.
ζητήσωμεν Pbw 9 οὕτω] οὔτε L¹.

together without parts at the summit of its own reversion to itself, it unites its activity with its essence. And this is the highest perfection of the soul in its complete separation from secondary lives. In its unseparated interweaving with them, on the other hand, it is perfected and is perfect in a secondary way. The means sufficient to perfect the projected life, whether through actions or through contemplation, although it is clearly not imperfect, would itself perfect the soul, but it would not be perfect in the highest measures in such a way that the soul would also belong to itself alone. But after the fashion of things that perfect other things, inasmuch as the soul is such, it leads itself forward and ascends to its own supreme perfection.

E. Priscianus, *Metaphrasis in Theophrastum* 31.27-32.19

Since states and activities arise from essence, it is impossible to suppose that the essence remains completely unchanging and always the same, producing activities perfect and good in form at one time and imperfect and distorted at another. For essences are the causes of activities, and as are the activities, such also they induce us to conclude is the kind of potency and essence.

If someone should conceive of a double essence in us and a double set of potencies and activities and should think that some are always perfect while others are sometimes imperfect and sometimes perfect, then (if they are torn asunder) he will make the single entity many living things and will cause the complete separation of its superior essence, as neither ruling its life nor having anything in common with it, if that is to say we consider it in the second way, as partly perfect and imperfect, which is the definition of human life.

But if someone, by speaking of two relations or reason principles or lives, should not destroy the unity of the two, so that our case may not resemble that of a chorus or any other multiplicity but so that all things may come together into one and be fused into one principle, then let us inquire about this one entity whether it is uniform and completely pure and unchanging. But in that case once again there will never be in souls either in essence or in activity any imperfection, evil, or passibility. For activities follow essence. But neither can one accept that it is changed in every respect. For life endures through the changes.

15 μεσότης σώζηται. τὰ μὲν γὰρ κρείττω μόνιμα μόνως, τὰ δὲ θνητὰ πάντη
μεταβλητά. ἡ δὲ μερικὴ ψυχή, ὡς μέση πᾶσι τοῖς περικοσμίοις γένεσι
συμμεριζομένη τε καὶ συμπληθυνομένη, οὐ μόνον μένει ἀλλὰ καὶ
μεταβάλλει τοσαύτας διαζῶσα μεριστὰς ζωάς. καὶ οὐ κατὰ τὰς ἕξεις
μόνας ἀλλὰ καὶ κατὰ τὴν οὐσίαν μεταβάλλεται πη.

F. Priscianus, *Metaphrasis in Theophrastum* 23.13-24.20

23, 13 προσθετέον δὲ καὶ τὰ Ἰαμβλίχεια, ὡς πάσαις ταῖς δυνάμεσι τῆς ψυχῆς
παραπέφυκεν ἡ φαντασία καὶ πάσας ἀποτυποῦται καὶ ἐκμάττεται τὰς
15 τῶν εἰδῶν ὁμοιότητας καὶ τὰς τῶν ἑτέρων δυνάμεων ἐμφάσεις εἰς τὰς
ἑτέρας διαπέμπει, τὰς μὲν ἀπὸ τῆς αἰσθήσεως εἰς δόξαν ἀνεγείρουσα,
τὰς δὲ ἀπὸ νοῦ δευτέρας τῇ δόξῃ προτείνουσα, ἐν ἑαυτῇ δὲ ἀπὸ τῶν
ὅλων τὰ φαντάσματα παραδεχομένη· καὶ ὡς ἰδίως κατὰ τὴν ἀφομοίωσιν
χαρακτηρίζεται ἔν τε τῷ ποιεῖν καὶ ἐν τῷ δέχεσθαι τὰ προσεοικότα ἢ
20 τοῖς νοεροῖς ἢ τοῖς γενεσιουργοῖς ἢ τοῖς μέσοις ἐνεργήμασιν, ἀπο-
τυπουμένη τε τὰς πάσας τῆς ψυχῆς ἐνεργείας καὶ συναρμόζουσα τὰς
ἐκτὸς πρὸς τὰς εἴσω καὶ ἐπιτιθεῖσα ταῖς περὶ τὸ σῶμα κατα-
τεινομέναις ζωαῖς τὰς ἀπὸ τοῦ νοῦ κατιούσας ἐμφάσεις. καθ' ἑαυτὴν
ἄρα ἡ φαντασία δύναμις οὖσα τοῦ ἀφομοιοῦν αὐτὰ πρὸς ἑαυτὴν
ἐντεῦθεν καὶ ταῖς ἄλλαις συνάπτεται δυνάμεσι, προκατάρχουσα
25 αὐτῶν ταῖς ἐνεργείαις, οὐκ οὖσα πάθος οὐδὲ κίνησις ἀλλ' ἀμέριστος
καὶ ὡρισμένη ἐνέργεια, καὶ οὐ κατὰ παραδοχὴν ἔξωθεν ὡς ὁ κηρὸς
διαπλαττομένη ἀλλ' ἔνδοθεν καὶ κατὰ ⟨τὴν⟩ λόγων τῶν ἀφομοιωτικῶν
24 προβολὴν | εἰς τὴν τῶν φαντασμάτων ἐγειρομένη ἐπίκρισιν. Ἀλλ' εἰ
καὶ τὰς ἄλλας ἀποτυποῦται ζωὰς κατὰ τὸν Ἰάμβλιχον καὶ αὐτὰς τὰς
5 λογικάς τε καὶ νοερὰς ἐνεργείας, πῶς ἔτι ἀληθὲς τὸ Ἀριστοτελικόν,
τὸ ὑπὸ τῶν αἰσθητικῶν εἰδῶν κινεῖσθαι τὴν φαντασίαν; ἢ εἰ καὶ τὰς
κρείττους ἀποτυποῦται ἐνεργείας πάσας, ὅμως κατὰ τὰ αἰσθητικὰ
ἀπεικονίζεται εἴδη μορφωτικῶς καὶ μεριστῶς καὶ κατὰ τὴν πρὸς τὰ
αἰσθητὰ ἀναφοράν, ὥστε καὶ τὰς κρείττους ἀποτυποῦται ἐνεργείας ἢ
ὑπὸ τῶν αἰσθητικῶν κινεῖται εἰδῶν. πῶς οὖν καὶ μὴ παρόντων τῶν

240: 16 γάρ om. L¹ μόνως] μόνον w. **19** μεταβάλλει w. **23: 14** πάσαις b ἐκμμάττεται
(sic) L. **15** τὰς τῶν ἑτέρων δυνάμεων w (cum Ficino), ταῖς τῶν ἑτέρων δυνάμεσιν
Bywater. **17** νοῦ] τοῦ νοῦ Hw δευτέρως w αὐτῇ b: αὐτῇ w. **20/21** ἢ τοῖς νοεροῖς] ἐν
τοῖς νοεροῖς HMPbw. **22** fort. πάσας τὰς Bywater **24** καθ' ἑαυτὰ codd. αὐτὰ] τἆλλα
bw: fort. ἄττα Bywater **27** ἡ κηρὸς bw. **28** τὴν addidit Bywater λόγων Bywater: λόγον
vulg. προβολῶν w. **24: 3** ἀληθὲς ἔτι w. **8** ᾗ bw: ἢ codd. **10** post αἰσθητικῶν excidit
fort. εἰδῶν Bywater.

So then, according to Iamblichus, the individual soul partakes equally of both permanence and change, so that also in this way its median role is preserved. For the superior classes are permanent *simpliciter*, but the mortal classes are completely changeable. The individual soul, as a mean that is divided and multiplied among all the classes in the cosmos, not only remains permanent but also changes by living through so many individual lives. And it changes somehow not in regard to its states alone but also in accordance with its essence.

F. Priscianus, *Metaphrasis in Theophrastum* 23.13-24.20

One must also add the teachings of Iamblichus that the imagination is produced alongside all the faculties of the soul and receives an impression and stamp from all the likenesses of forms and transmits the appearances of some to other faculties, rousing some from sense perception to opinion and offering a second set from intellect to opinion, since it receives images from all of these in itself; and that it is appropriately characterized in accordance with assimilation, in making and receiving what belongs to intellectual or generative or median operations, receiving impressions from all the activities of the soul, combining external with internal activities, and bestowing on lives extended around bodies the appearances descending from the Intellect.

Imagination, then, is in itself a power of assimilating them from there to itself and conjoining them with other faculties, beginning their activities. It is neither a passion nor a motion but an indivisible and determinate activity. Unlike wax it is not molded by receiving something from outside, but it is roused to select images internally and through the projection of its assimilative reason-principles.

But if, as Iamblichus says, it receives impressions both from the other lives and from the rational and intellectual activities themselves, how is what Aristotle says still true, that imagination is moved by sensible forms?

Now, if it receives impressions from all superior activities, nevertheless it represents them in images and divisibly in accordance with the sensible forms and in accordance with their reference to sensible objects so that it receives impressions even from superior activities

αἰσθητῶν κινεῖται ἡ φαντασία; καὶ γὰρ εἰ ὑπὸ τῶν αἰσθητικῶν
10   κινεῖται, ἀλλὰ καὶ ταῦτα παρόντων τῶν αἰσθητῶν προβάλλεται καὶ
ἀπόντων ἀπολείπει. ἢ οὐχ ὡς ἡ αἴσθησις παρόντων μόνον κινεῖται τῶν
αἰσθητῶν, οὕτω καὶ ἡ φαντασία, ἀλλ' ἐπειδὰν ἅπαξ κινηθῇ, δύναται ἀφ'
ἑαυτῆς ἐγείρεσθαι καὶ προβάλλειν τὰ φαντάσματα κατὰ τὴν πρὸς τὰ
εἴδη ‹τὰ› κινήσαντα ἀναφοράν. ἐνίοτε δὲ οὐχ ἅπαξ ἢ δὶς ἀλλὰ
πλεονάκις κινηθῆναι δεῖται πρὸς τὸ ἀφ' ἑαυτῆς ὅμοια τοῖς κινήσασι
15   προτείνειν. καὶ τῷ μὲν μορφωτικῷ καὶ μεριστῷ κοινωνεῖ πρὸς τὴν
αἴσθησιν· τῷ δὲ καὶ ἀφ' ἑαυτῆς προτείνειν τὰ φαντάσματα καὶ μὴ
παρόντων ἔτι τῶν κινούντων ἐξῄρηται τῆς αἰσθήσεως· τῷ δὲ εἰς ἕτερα
ἀναφέρειν ἀεὶ καὶ ἀφομοιοῦσθαι πρὸς τὰς διαφόρους ἐνεργείας τῆς
ψυχῆς, ταύτῃ πρὸς πάσας τε τῆς ψυχῆς παραπέφυκε τὰς δυνάμεις καὶ
20   κατὰ τὸ ἀφομοιωτικὸν τῆς ψυχῆς ἵσταται ἰδίωμα.

G. Pseudo-Simplicius, *In De Anima* 213.23-214.26

213, 23 Διὰ τῶν προειρημένων ὅτι διώρισται τῶν ἄλλων γνωστικῶν δυνάμεων
ἡ φαντασία ἐπιδείξας, ἐφεξῆς τίς ποτέ ἐστιν αὕτη παραδίδωσιν, ἀπὸ
25   τῶν ἐνεργειῶν αὐτῆς τὴν οὐσίαν τεκμαιρόμενος. κινεῖται μὲν οὖν
προσεχῶς ὑπὸ τῶν αἰσθητῶν τὸ αἰσθητήριον, οὐ πάσχον μόνον ἀλλὰ
καὶ ἐνεργοῦν διὰ τὸ ζωτικόν, ἐγειρομένης δὲ ἐπὶ τῷ ἐνεργητικῷ τούτῳ
πάθει τῆς αἰσθητικῆς καθαρᾶς ἐνεργείας καὶ κρίσεως, κατὰ τὸ τοῦ
αἰσθητοῦ ἑστώσης εἶδος, οὐκ ἔξωθεν οὐδὲ κατὰ πάθος, ἀλλ' ἔνδοθεν
30   τῆς αἰσθητικῆς οὐσίας κατὰ τοὺς οἰκείους λόγους αὐτὸ προβαλλούσης
συμφώνως τῇ ἐν τῷ αἰσθητηρίῳ ἐγγινομένῃ παθητικῇ ἐνεργείᾳ· ὡς
κίνησιν μὲν εἶναι τὴν ἐν τῷ αἰσθητηρίῳ ὑπὸ τοῦ αἰσθητοῦ γεγονυῖαν
πάθην, τὴν δὲ τοῦ λόγου προβολὴν καὶ τὴν καθαρὰν τῆς αἰσθητικῆς
ζωῆς κρίσιν καὶ τὸν κατὰ τὸ εἶδος τοῦ αἰσθητοῦ ὅρον οὐ κίνησιν, ἀλλ'
35   ἀμέριστον ἐνέργειαν. ἐφ' ᾗ προσεχῶς αὐτῇ συνημμένη ἡ φανταστικὴ
ἐγείρεται ζωή, ὀργάνῳ μὲν τῷ αὐτῷ χρωμένη, ἀλλ' οὐχ ὡς αἰσθητικῷ
καὶ ἔξωθέν τι παθαινομένῳ, ὡς δὲ φανταστικῷ καὶ ὑπὸ τῆς φανταστ-
ικῆς ζωῆς τυπουμένῳ καὶ μορφουμένῳ.
καὶ οὐ θαυμαστὸν εἰ τὸ αὐτὸ ὄχημα ταῖς διαφόροις ἡμῶν
214   ὑπέστρωται ζωαῖς, ὅπου γε καὶ τῇ λογικῇ ἡμῶν | ζωῇ· συνδιατίθεται
γοῦν ταῖς λογικαῖς ἡμῶν ἐνεργείαις οὐ τὸ πνεῦμα μόνον, ἀλλὰ καὶ τὸ
στερεὸν τοῦτο ὄργανον. προηγουμένως δ' οὖν ὡς αἰσθητικὸν παθὸν τὸ

24: 13 κινηθῇς Bywater: κινῇ vulg. 15 τὰ addidit Bywater. 18 προτείνειν bis L¹. 19
τῷ Hw: τὸ L cet. 213: 28 τοῦ om. a.

just as it is moved by sensible forms. How then is the imagination moved also when sensible objects are not present? For indeed if it is moved by sensible forms, nevertheless it projects these when sensible objects are present and stops when they are absent. Now unlike sense perception the imagination is not moved only when sensible objects are present, but when once it is moved, it can be roused in itself and can project images in accordance with their reference to the forms that moved it. Sometimes it must be moved not once or twice but often in order to bring forth from itself [images] similar to those that moved it. And with sense perception it shares in what is in images and divisible, but it transcends sense perception by bringing forth from itself images even when what moves them is no longer present. Since it always has reference to other things and is assimilated to different activities, in this way it is produced alongside all the faculties of the soul and is established as a special property of the soul in its assimilative [ability].

G. *In De Anima* 213.23-214.26

Having shown through what he [i.e., Aristotle] said earlier that imagination is distinct from the other cognitive faculties, next he shows what it is, using its activities as evidence for its essence. Now the sense organ is immediately moved by sense objects and not only is affected but also acts because it has life, but when the pure sensible activity and judgment is roused in accordance with this active affection, it is established in accordance with the form of the sense object, not externally or as an affection, but internally with its sensible essence projecting it in accordance with appropriate reason-principles, in harmony with the passive activity existing in the sense organ. Now the affection arising in the sense organ from the sense object is a motion, but the projection of the reason-principle and the pure judgment of the sensible life and the limiting in accordance with the form of the sense object is not a motion but an indivisible activity.

Since it is immediately connected with it [i.e., with the sensible faculty], the imaginative life is aroused by it, using the same body, but not as sensible and externally affected in some way but as imaginative and imprinted and shaped by the imaginative life. And it is not

πνεῦμα, καὶ τῆς αἰσθήσεως εἰς τὴν κατὰ τὸ εἶδος στάσης ἐνέργειαν,
καὶ τὸ πνεῦμα ἐπιτήδειον γίνεται πρὸς τὴν τῶν φανταστῶν τύπων
ὑποδοχήν, καὶ αὐτὴ ἡ φαντασία ἐγείρεται πρὸς τὴν κατ' οἰκείους
λόγους τῶν φανταστικῶν τύπων προβολὴν οἰκείως τοῖς αἰσθητικοῖς
εἴδεσιν, οὐχ ἅπαξ ἢ δὶς ἐνίοτε μόνον τῶν αἰσθητικῶν δεηθεῖσα τύπων
ἀλλὰ καὶ πλεονάκις πρὸς τὴν τῶν ὁμοίων προβολήν. ἐγερθεῖσα δ' οὖν
καὶ ἀφ' ἑαυτῆς προβάλλει τὰ φαντάσματα καὶ τυποῖ καὶ διαμορφοῖ τὸ
σχῆμα ἀφ' ἑαυτῆς ἢ ὁμοίως τοῖς εἴδεσι τῶν αἰσθητῶν ἢ καὶ τὸ ἀκριβὲς
προστιθεῖσα, ὡς καὶ τὴν ἁπλατῆ προτείνουσα εὐθεῖαν καὶ σχήματα τὰ
ἀκριβέστατα, καὶ ἀοριστaίνουσα δὲ ἐνίοτε καὶ ποικίλλουσα
πολυτρόπως τοὺς τύπους. καὶ τὸ μὲν τῆς αἰσθήσεως δεῖσθαι πρὸς τὴν
ἐξ ἀρχῆς ἔγερσιν κοινὸν ἔχουσα καὶ ταῖς λογικαῖς ἡμῶν ζωαῖς (καὶ
γὰρ αὗται διὰ τὴν ὅλην ἔξω τῆς ψυχῆς στροφὴν τῆς ὑπὸ τῶν ἔξωθεν
οἷον πληγῆς τοῦ αἰσθητηρίου τὴν ἀρχὴν ἐδεήθησαν πρὸς τὴν τῶν
οἰκείων γνωστῶν ἀντίληψιν), ἀλλὰ τούτων μεταβαινουσῶν ἐπὶ τὸ
ἀσώματον καὶ ἀτύπωτον καὶ ἀμέριστον γνωστὸν ἡ φαντασία ἐν τῷ
σωματοειδεῖ καὶ τυπωτικῷ καὶ μεριστῷ κατέχεται. καὶ γὰρ εἰ καὶ τὰς
λογικὰς ἡμῶν, ὡς ὁ Ἰάμβλιχος βούλεται, ἀποτυποῦται ἐνεργείας
πάσας, ὅμως κατὰ τὰ αἰσθητὰ ἀπεικονίζεται εἴδη μορφωτικῶς καὶ
μεριστῶς. διὸ καὶ προσεχής ἐστι τῇ αἰσθήσει, ὑπερέχουσα ὅμως τῷ
μετὰ τὴν ἐξ ἀρχῆς ἔγερσιν καὶ ἀφ' ἑαυτῆς ἐνεργεῖν καὶ οὐκ ἀεὶ
παρόντων δεῖσθαι τῶν αἰσθητῶν, καὶ τῷ τὴν ἀκρίβειαν προστιθέναι,
ὅπερ ἴσως οὐ πᾶσα ἀλλ' ἡ τῶν λογικῶν ἕξει φαντασία. ἅπασα δὲ τὸ
ἡγεμονικὸν καὶ κινητικὸν τῶν ζῴων, τῶν μὲν ἄλλων ὡς πρώτη ἐν
αὐτοῖς οὖσα γνωστικὴ ζωή, ἐν δὲ τοῖς ἀνθρώποις, ὅταν δι' ἥντινά ποτε
αἰτίαν ἐπικαλύπτηται ὁ λόγος.

214: **4** τῶν– **5** τὴν om. A. **10** καὶ τὸ] κατὰ τὸ a.

surprising if the same vehicle is subject to our different lives, since it is also subject to our rational life. For indeed not only the pneuma but also this solid body are affected by our rational activities. So previously the pneuma was like a sensitive affection, when sensation was established with regard to the activity in accordance with the form, and the pneuma becomes adapted to the reception of impressions connected with imagination, and imagination itself is aroused to project imaginative impressions in accordance with appropriate reason-principles appropriately to the sensible forms, often not only requiring the sensitive impressions once or twice but even many times in order to the project similar ones. And so having been aroused, it also projects the images from itself and molds and shapes the figure from itself either in a way similar to the forms of the sense object or even imposing an accurate one, such as presenting a straight line without breadth or the most accurate figures, and sometimes producing indeterminate impressions and embellishing them in many ways.

Now its need for sensation for its initial arousal it shares also with our rational lives (for because the whole process is outside of the soul, these also require a beginning from the outside as if from a blow from the sense organ in order to apprehend the appropriate objects of knowledge), but when these become immaterial, formless, and indivisible objects of knowledge, the imagination is restricted to what is bodily, has form, and is divisible. For even if it receives impressions from all our rational activities, as Iamblichus thinks, nevertheless it represents them in forms and divisibly in accordance with the sensible forms. Therefore it is next to [the faculty of] sensation but nevertheless transcends it by acting from itself after its initial arousal, by not always requiring the presence of sense objects, and by imposing accuracy, which [last] perhaps will not be a trait of every sort of imagination but only of that associated with rational [creatures]. Now every [imaginative faculty] is the ruling element and the element which moves the animal, but of some animals this will be the primary cognitive life in them and in human beings, whenever reason is veiled for any reason.

H. Priscianus, *Metaphrasis in Theophrastum* 9.7-9.31

9, 7 πρῶτον μὲν οὖν ἐκεῖνο ἀξιῶ διορίζεσθαι ὡς ἕτερον μὲν τὸ αἰτιατὸν
φῶς ἕτερον δὲ τὸ τούτου αἴτιον, οἷον τὸ ἐν ἡλίῳ ἢ ἐν πυρί· καὶ οὐ περὶ
10 τοῦ αἰτίου ὁ λόγος ἐν τῇ περὶ τοῦ τί τὸ φῶς ζητήσει, ἀλλὰ περὶ τοῦ ἀπ'
αὐτοῦ προϊόντος, ὃ δὴ ἐνέργεια εἶναι λέγεται τοῦ διαφανοῦς τοῦ ἐν
ἀέρι καὶ ὕδατι καὶ ἐν τοῖς παρὰ μέρος φωτὸς καὶ σκότους δεκτικοῖς.
Ἔπειτα δὲ τῷ Ἰαμβλίχῳ ἑπόμενος οὔτε σῶμα τοῦτο εἶναι ἀξιῶ, ὥσπερ
οἱ Περιπατητικοί, οὔτε μὴν πάθος ἢ ποιότητα σώματος ὁτουοῦν· οὐ
15 γὰρ ἐν τῷ ἀέρι ἔχει τὸ εἶναι φῶς· κινουμένου γοῦν ἐκείνου ἕστηκεν
αὐτὸ καὶ τρεπομένου πολυειδῶς αὐτὸ χωριστῶς ἀποτέτμηται καὶ
σῴζει τὴν πρὸς τὸ αἴτιον ἀδιαίρετον συνέχειαν. ἀλλὰ καὶ ἡ ἀθρόα
αὐτοῦ παρουσία ἐπὶ πάντα τὰ δέχεσθαι αὐτὸ δυνάμενα παρόντος τοῦ
ἐλλάμποντος, καὶ αὖθις ἀπελθόντος ἡ ἀθρόα ἀπόλειψις, μηδὲν ἴχνος
ἑαυτοῦ καταλείποντος, σημεῖον τοῦ μὴ πάθημα εἶναι τοῦ ἀέρος τὸ φῶς.
20 τὰ γὰρ πάθη οἷον ἡ θερμότης οὔτε ἀθρόως ἐγγίνεται, καὶ τοῦ πυρὸς
ἀπελθόντος ἀμυδρόν τι ἐγκαταλείπει ἑαυτῆς εἶδος τῷ πεπονθότι. καὶ
τὸ μὴ κατὰ διάδοσιν δὲ μηδὲ κατὰ τροπὴν ἐγγίνεσθαι, καὶ τὸ μὴ
περιγράφεσθαι μέχρι τινός, προϊέναι δὲ ἄχρι παντὸς τοῦ δυναμένου
αὐτὸ δέχεσθαι, καὶ τὸ μὴ συγκεῖσθαι ἐν ἀλλήλοις τὰ φῶτα, δηλοῖ
25 ἅπαντα ταῦτα χωριστὴν εἶναι σωμάτων τὴν τοῦ φωτὸς ἐνέργειαν. πῶς
οὖν ἐνέργεια λέγεται τοῦ διαφανοῦς; οὐχ ὡς πάθος, φήσω, οὐδὲ ὡς
τελειότης αὐτοῦ ἐν ὑποκειμένῳ αὐτῷ γενομένη, ἀλλ' ὡς χωριστῶς
αὐτὸ τελειοῦσα, οὐκ αὐτὴ ἐκείνου ἀλλ' ἑαυτῆς ἐκεῖνο ποιουμένη,
μένουσα συνεχὴς αὐτὴ τῷ ἐλλάμποντι καὶ ἐκείνῳ συμπεριαγομένη.
τοῦτο μὲν οὖν ὧδε συντόμως ὑπεμνήσθην, ἵνα μὴ ὁμοίως ὡς ἐν τοῖς
30 ἄλλοις τοῖς πάσχουσι καὶ τὸ φῶς ἐγγίνεσθαι ὑποπτεύσωμεν.

9: 8 τὸ] τῷ LMPb. 13 οὔτε] οὔποτε vulg. 13/14 ὥσπερ οἱ περιπατητικοί post
ὁτουοῦν M²Pbw (cum Ficino): om. HM¹ fort. recte (Bywater). 16 αὐτοχειριστῶς
HMPbw (Ficinus *suo in se impetu*). 18 αὐτῷ L¹ (et sic passim). 19 τοῦ μὴ Bywater: τὸ
μὴ vulg. 20 ἀθρόα w. 22 διδόασιν L¹. 29 ἐλλάμποντι L ἐκεῖνο L¹ συνπεριαγομένη
LM. 30 ὑπεμνήσθην Bywater: ὑπεμνήσθω (sic) codd. b: ὑπεμνήσθη w.

H. Priscianus, *Metaphrasis in Theophrastum*, 9.7-31

First, then, I think it proper to draw the distinction that the caused light is one thing but its cause is another, as for instance the light in the sun or in a fire. The argument in the investigation concerning what light is does not concern the cause but what proceeds from it, namely what is called "the actualization of the transparent," which exists in air, in water, and in what is partially receptive of light and darkness.

Second, following Iamblichus, I do not maintain that this is a body, as do the Peripatetics, or indeed an affection or quality of any body whatsoever, for light does not have its essence by being in the air. Indeed, while the air is moving, light remains still, and while the air changes in various ways, light is set off apart and preserves its undivided connection with its cause. And it is also a sign that light is not an affection of air that it is present all at once in everything capable of receiving it when a source of light is present, and again that it immediately departs leaving no trace of itself when the source of light has withdrawn. For affections, such as heat, do not come to be in the air all at once, and when fire has departed, it leaves behind some faint form of itself in what it has affected. And all of the following make clear that the actualization of light is separate from bodies: light does not come to exist in something by distributing or changing itself, it is not limited by anything else but continues on to everything capable of receiving it, and lights are not combined with one another.

How, then, is it called "an actualization of the transparent?" Not as an affection, I will say, nor as a perfection of it coming about in the substrate itself, but as perfecting it in a transcendent way, not itself belonging to the transparent, but rather making the transparent belong to itself, while it itself remains continuous with the source of light and is carried round together with it. I have then touched on this matter briefly in this way, so that we may not imagine that light comes to be in the transparent in the same way as it does in other affected things.

I. Pseudo-Simplicius, *In De Anima* 131.16-132.17

131, 16 ἀλλ' ἐπεὶ τὸ φῶς τοῦ διαφανοῦς ἐστι τελειότης, προληπτέον τί τὸ διαφανές. οὐ γάρ ἐστι τὸ φῶς, ὡς ἡ νόησις, ἐμμένουσα τῇ προαγούσῃ αὐτὴν οὐσίᾳ καὶ ἡ αὐτὴ οὖσα τῇ οὐσίᾳ· ἀλλ' ἐνέργεια μὲν καὶ τὸ φῶς, οὔτε δὲ ἡ αὐτὴ τῷ ἐνεργοῦντι οὔτε μένουσα ἐν αὐτῷ, οὐ μὴν οὐδὲ

20 ἀπεσπασμένη, ἀλλ' ἅμα τε τοῦ προϊόντος αὐτὴ ἐχομένη καὶ ἑτέρῳ ἐνδιδομένη, οὐ κατὰ πάθος ἀλλὰ κατὰ ἀθρόαν τελειότητα, οἰκειότητος πανταχοῦ θεωρουμένης τῷ δεκτικῷ πρὸς τὸ ἐγγινόμενον, ὡς ἀφ' ἑκατέρου τὸ λοιπὸν γνωρίζεσθαι. δυνάμει γοῦν ἐστι τὸ δεκτικὸν τοῦτο, ὅπερ ἐνεργείᾳ τὸ δεδεγμένον· ἐνέργεια δὲ καὶ ὅρος καὶ

25 τελειότης ἡ καθ' ἣν τὸ δεδεγμένον ὁρίζεται φύσις, τοῦτο μὲν ἐνεργείᾳ, δυνάμει δὲ τὸ δεκτικόν, οἷον ἡ ὑγίεια, καθ' ἣν καὶ τὸ ὑγιαῖνον καὶ τὸ ὑγιασθῆναι δυνάμενον, τοῦτο μὲν ἀτελῶς ἐκεῖνο δὲ τελείως, ὡς καὶ τὸ δεκτικὸν καὶ τὸ δεδεγμένον τῇ ἐνδοθείσῃ ἐνεργείᾳ ὁρίζεσθαι. καὶ ἡ μὲν ἐπιστήμη ἀκολούθως τῇ φύσει ἐκ τοῦ ὅρου καὶ τὰ ἐνεργείᾳ

30 ὁριζόμενα γινώσκει καὶ τὰ δεκτικὰ ὡς κατὰ ἀτελὲς αὐτοῦ ἴχνος χαρακτηριζόμενα· ὁ δὲ ζητῶν ἔτι ἀπὸ τῶν αἰτιατῶν καὶ ὡς πρὸς ἡμᾶς πρώτων ἐπὶ τὰ φύσει πρῶτα καὶ αἴτια ἀνιὼν καὶ ἐκ τῶν ἀτελῶν ἐπὶ τὰ τέλεια, ἀπὸ τούτων γνωρίζει τὴν τελειότητα. ἐκ δὴ τοῦ διαφανοῦς ὡς ὕλης ὑπεστρωμένου τῷ φωτὶ καὶ κατ' αὐτὸ τελειουμένου, ὅτε καὶ ἐνεργείᾳ γίνεται διαφανές, ὁποῖον τὸ φῶς γινώσκομεν, ὅτι τῷ

35 πεφωτισμένῳ ἀλλ' οὐ τῷ εἴδει προηγουμένως προσβάλλει ἡ αἴσθησις. ἐρεῖ δὲ καὶ αὐτὸ τὸ εἶδος ἐναργέστατα· τί γὰρ ἂν εἴη φωτὸς ἐναργέστερον; ἡ μὲν οὖν ἁπλῆ τοῦ φωτὸς ἰδιότης καὶ τῇ νοήσει ἡμῶν κατὰ ἁπλὴν ἐπιβολὴν ἐκ τῆς αἰσθήσεως γίνεται γνώριμος· ὅτι δὲ

132 ἀσώματον καὶ ὅτι οὐ πάθος ἀλλ' ἐνέργεια, | συλλογιζόμεθα, τὸ μὲν δι' ὅλου τοῦ διαφανοῦς ἰὸν αὐτὸ ὁρῶντες, τὸ δὲ διὰ τὴν ἄχρονον ἀπουσίαν καὶ παρουσίαν. τὰ γὰρ πάθη ἐν χρόνῳ παραγίνεταί τε καὶ ἀπογίνεται, καὶ τὰ σώματα δι' ἀλλήλων οὐ χωρεῖ τά γε ἔνυλα· ἔνυλον δέ, εἴπερ σῶμα, τὸ ἀπὸ τοῦ φωτὸς πῦρ, ἀλλὰ καὶ τὸ δεκτικὸν αὐτοῦ ὁ ἀήρ.

I. Pseudo-Simplicius, *In De Anima*, 131.16-132.17

Since light is the perfection of the transparent, one must first grasp what the transparent is. For light is not like intellection, which remains in the essence which produces it and is the same as its essence. But light is an actualization. It is neither the same as nor does it remain in what brings it into actuality, but nonetheless it is not severed from it either. Rather it simultaneously holds onto that which emits it and gives itself to something else, not as an affection but as an instantaneous perfection. The affinity of that which arises in the receptive medium to that medium is everywhere apparent, so that one is known from the other. For this receptive medium is potentially what that same medium, after it has received, is actually. The nature through which the medium that has received light is determined is its actuality, definition, and perfection. This medium possesses these actually; the receptive potentially. Just as health is that in accordance with which both being healthy and being able to be healthy exist (the latter imperfectly and the former perfectly), so also the receptive and that which has received are determined by the actuality given to them.

Also science, consistently with nature, comes to know from the paradigm both that which is actually determined and that which is receptive, as though it were stamped by an imperfect trace. One who is still investigating, however, ascending from the caused (which is primary in regard to us) to the cause (which is primary in nature), and from the imperfect to the perfect, from these comes to know perfection. It is from the transparent — matter as it were underlying the light and being perfected by it, when, that is, the transparent comes to be actually — that we will come to know what sort of thing light is, since sense perception focuses on what is illuminated and not principally on the form. He will also speak most clearly about the form itself, for what could be clearer than light? Consequently, the simple character of light comes to be known also by our own thought processes through a simple application from sense perception.

We conclude that it is incorporeal (since we see it traveling through all the transparent) and that it is not an affection but an actualization (because of its instantaneous absence and presence). For affections become present and depart in time, and bodies do not travel through one another when they are material. Fire that

ἆρα οὖν οὐσία ὡς ἡ ἀπὸ τῆς ψυχῆς τῷ σώματι ἐνδιδομένη ζωή; ἀλλ' εἰ
καὶ ἡ ζωὴ ἀθρόως ἐγγίνεταί τε καὶ αὐτὴ τῷ σώματι καὶ αὖ ἀπογίνεται,
προηγεῖσθαι ὅμως ἀνάγκη τὴν διεξοδικὴν τοῦ συνθέτου γένεσιν, καὶ
τῇ ἀπουσίᾳ ἕπεσθαι τὴν φθοράν. ἀλλὰ καὶ τῶν ἐναντίων δεκτικὴ ἡ
ζωή· καὶ ἐναργῶς δὲ τὸ ζῷον οὐσία, ὥστε καὶ τὸ ὁριστικὸν αὐτοῦ
εἶδος ἡ ζωή. οὔτε δὲ ὁ πεφωτισμένος ἀὴρ ὡς πεφωτισμένος οὐσία,
καθάπερ οὐδὲ ὁ ἐπικτήτως θερμανθείς, οὐδὲ τῶν ἐναντίων ἢ αὐτὸς
δεκτικὸς ἢ τὸ φῶς, οὐδὲ προηγεῖταί τις τῆς παρουσίας αὐτοῦ μεταβολὴ
ἢ τῇ ἀπουσίᾳ ἐπακολουθεῖ. ἀλλ' ἔστιν αὐτὸ τοῦτο ἐνέργεια, οὐχ ὡς ἐν
ὑποκειμένῳ ἐγγινομένη τῷ διαφανεῖ, χωριστῶς δὲ αὐτῷ παροῦσα καὶ
τελειοῦσα αὐτό, οὐδέποτε τοῦ προάγοντος αὐτὴν χωριζομένη, ἀλλ'
ἐκείνῳ ἐνιδρυμένη, καὶ ἐκείνου ἐχομένη. διὸ καὶ τούτῳ μὲν
μεθισταμένῳ συμμεθίσταται, οὐκέτι δὲ τῷ δεχομένῳ ὁπωσοῦν
μεταβαλλομένῳ συμμεταβάλλεται.

132: 6 τῷ σώματι καὶ αὐτὴ ἀθρόως ἐγγίνεταί τε a. **17** τοῦτο A.

proceeds from light, however, is material since it is a body, but so is the air that is capable of receiving it.

Is it the case then that light is a substance like the life bestowed upon the body from the soul? Although life comes to be in the body and departs from it again all at once, nevertheless the gradual generation of the composite must precede, and its destruction must follow its departure. But life is also capable of receiving opposites, and clearly the animal is a substance so that the determinate form of it, life, is also substance. Now, the illuminated air is not substance *qua* illuminated, just as it is not after it has been heated adventitiously, and neither it nor light is capable of receiving opposites, and no change precedes its presence or follows upon its departure. It itself is an actualization. It does not come to be in the transparent as though in a substrate, but is present to it in a transcendent way and perfects it, never separated from what produces it but established in it and holding on to it. Therefore light changes along with its source when it changes, but it does not change in any way whatsoever when what receives it changes.

A. *In De Anima* 1.1-20

We present the opening of the commentary not because it contains an important Iamblichean interpretation of Aristotle or the soul but because it shows the high esteem in which the commentator holds Iamblichus. Although it is safe to conclude that the commentator usually follows Iamblichus in his interpretations, there is at least one point of disagreement between them, on the interpretation of Aristotle's active and passive Intellect. Iamblichus believes that these are the unparticipated and participated Intellects and are, therefore, above the soul in rank. The commentator, on the other hand, believes that they are in the soul, although he attempts to argue that he and Iamblichus are not at odds but only looking at the same issue from different perspectives. See 313-314 and Steel 142-145 and 153-154.

ἡ περὶ αὐτῶν τῶν πραγμάτων τῶν τε ἄλλων . . . The Greek term for "metaphysical realities" is αὐτὰ τὰ πράγματα, literally "the facts themselves" or "the actual circumstances" or "the matters of importance." The commentator repeats the term below (1.13-14), where it is contrasted with the text (λέξις) of Aristotle. There it seems to be the soul itself, i.e., the metaphysical principle at issue in the *De Anima*. The noun is used again in line 18, where it refers to external realities including the soul. Urmson (15) translates the first instance as "things themselves," the second as "the subject-matter itself," and the third as "things."

Another difference between Urmson's translation and ours concerns the number of conjuncts in the first clause. Urmson (15) translates: "The primary and most important object of concern is the truth about things themselves, both about other things and concerning the soul." He therefore separates ἡ περὶ αὐτῶν τῶν πραγμάτων from τῶν τε ἄλλων. This cannot be right. The commentator is distinguishing two conjuncts, marked both by the repeated article ἡ and the use of τε . . . καί ("both . . . and"). Thus τε does not separate πραγμάτων from τῶν ἄλλων, but rather conjoins them: "both the truth about other πράγματα and the (truth) about the soul."

ὡς τῷ ἀρίστῳ τῆς ἀληθείας κριτῇ δοκεῖ τῷ' Ιαμβλίχου . . . As we have seen, various passages from Iamblichus' own *De Anima* support the statement that Iamblichus believed both that Plato and Aristotle's theory of the soul was compatible and that later Peripatetics misinterpreted what Aristotle meant.

We agree with Blumenthal that Iamblichus did not write a separate commentary on Aristotle's *De Anima*. See H. Blumenthal, "Did Iamblichus write a Commentary on the *De Anima?*," *Hermes* 102 (1974) 540-556. The references to Iamblichus' "writings on the soul" are therefore to his own *De Anima*.

B. *In De An.* 5.38-6.17

Festugière gives a French translation (254). This passage concerns Iamblichus' doctrine that the soul is a mean between the realm of generation and the Intelligible realm. See Iamblichus, *De An.* section 7 (365.22-366.11 W). This passage, however, exhibits a doctrine stronger than any of the surviving passages in Iamblichus' *De Anima*. For in the *De Anima*, Iamblichus says that the soul is indeed a mean between unchanging realities and the world of generation, but he does not anywhere state the almost contradictory tension inherent in the human soul. Here, however, the tension is introduced and startlingly articulated. The soul is somehow both divided and undivided, departing and returning, *simultaneously* abiding and changing, generated and ungenerated, and destroyed and preserved. Iamblichus, as it seems, argues that the soul is neither undescended (as he thinks Plotinus held) nor completely descended. It is a mean, and as such is in tension with itself, never fully at either extreme. (Possibly Iamblichus has Heraclitean notions in mind here.) He says: "it is a mean between what is permanently abiding and in every way changing." Thus the soul cannot be either extreme, but an ever-changing mean. This explains his statement: "when it has gathered itself together into partlessness *as much as is possible for it*." For the soul cannot be completely indivisible, or it would not be a mean. It would become Intellect rather than "imitate" it.

The statement that the soul "remains pure in its declination toward what is secondary to it" requires further explanation. For, as we have seen, the soul does not strictly remain "pure" (or indeed remain in any state). Rather what Iamblichus must have in mind is that the soul *qua* soul remains exactly what it is, a mean term, neither here nor there, as it were, but always in between. This is the changeable essence of the soul. Even when it is most stable, it is declining.

Ἔτι ἐν τῷ τρίτῳ . . . The subject of this sentence ("he") is Aristotle. For the phrase "extreme lives" (τῶν ἄκρων ζωῶν) and the associated idea of the soul's "double life," one in the body and the other separated from it, see section 10 and notes.

κατὰ προβολὴν ἐνεργοῦσαν . . . Projection (ἡ προβολή) is a technical term in Neoplatonism. (Iamblichus uses the term in section 13. See notes there and to section 38. Cf. Passage D below.) A soul projects various lives in its descent to the sensible from the Intelligible. Here these lives are those of the lower aspects of the soul and therefore are akin to what Iamblichus calls the inclination toward the external (ἡ ἔξω ῥοπή) and procession into partedness (εἰς μερισμὸν προιοῦσα). The soul in its descent becomes less and less unified, and hence becomes more "partial" and develops different kinds of life (nutritive, sensitive, imaginative, etc.).

διὸ οὔτε μένειν τι αὐτῆς θησόμεθα κατὰ τὸν Πλωτῖνον . . . For Iamblichus' interpretation of the "undescended soul" in Plotinus, see *In Tim.* Fr. 87; cf. above, sections 6, 17, 19, and 26 of the *De Anima* and notes there.

C. *In De An.* 89.33-90.25

Festugière gives a French translation (254-255). Steel (53-55) discusses this passage as well.

εἰ δέ, ὡς τῷ Ἰαμβλίχῳ δόκει . . . The entire passage is in the form of an indirect statement dependent on the phrase ὡς τῷ Ἰαμβλίχῳ δοκεῖ ("as Iamblichus thinks"). It therefore represents Iamblichus' view throughout.

The passage provides the clearest account of Iamblichus idiosyncratic view of the soul: that it is a mean in the strongest possible sense. It is neither completely Intelligible nor completely a generated entity. It is in between the two extremes, yet somehow nevertheless embraces both these extremes as its own property. It is *both* divided and undivided, generated and ungenerated, permanent and changing. Thus, the soul's essence is double, just as its acts are. In fact, the souls' acts, which are varying and contrary to one another at different times, lead us to the true nature and essence of the soul. When the soul is involved in the Intelligible Realm, it is just that: Intelligible, but not permanently (for it is not Intellect). The soul cannot act on the Intelligible level always, but will descend again to lower-order thinking and to sensation and to all the other activities of the embodied soul. When in this latter state, the soul takes on this role essentially. The soul therefore has two essences, enacting each at different times, but holding both natures in itself permanently.

ἀλλὰ τὸ μὲν οἷον ἐξίστασθαί πως ἑαυτοῦ ποτε . . . The subject changes from the feminine ψυχή ("soul") to the neuter τό. In the previous sentence, the neuter singular was used for the different aspects of soul, the ungenerated and the generated. If the commentator is following Iamblichus in this usage, then Iamblichus has slipped into language that allows him to distinguish the aspects within the soul as he discusses its descent to and joining with generation. Indeed, the use of τὸ μέν here in line 3 seems to indicate that Iamblichus had the higher aspect in mind, while τὸ δέ in line 5 ("it" after the semicolon) that he had the lower. The commentator continues this usage of τό in the next sentence, but adds the adjectives for "generated" or "ungenerated" to the article as well as the feminine pronoun αὐτῆς ("of it," i.e., the soul).

χωρισθεῖσα γάρ, ὡς ἐρεῖ, ἔστιν ὅπερ ἐστίν . . . This is a reference to Aristotle, De An. 430a22-23: "Only after it has been separated (χωρισθείς) is it [i.e., the active intellect] what it is, and this alone is immortal and eternal."

ἐν δὲ τῇ πρὸς τὰ ἔξω ῥοπῇ . . . On the term "declension" (ῥοπή), see Iamblichus' De Anima, section 33 (382.7 W) and note there.

ἡ πίστις μετὰ τὴν συγκατάθεσιν . . . For the Stoic term συγκατάθεσις, the assent the mind gives to the body's perceptions, see Iamblichus, De Anima section 11 (368.19-20 W) and note there. Cf. section 12 (369.8 W).

δηλοῖ δὲ πᾶσα λογικὴ ἐνέργεια . . . The higher aspect of soul is not completely submerged when the soul is embodied. Iamblichus (if the commentator is still quoting him in the parenthesis) gives two proofs.

The first is that whenever the soul makes a rational judgment on and assents to data taken from the body (as, for example, that this torch is hot). The second seems to concern some kind of ritual ascent in which the soul restores itself to the divine beings above it. Here again the higher soul must do the recognizing.

D. *In De An.* 240.33-241.26

Festugière (253) gives a French translation of part of this passage (240.33-241.15). Steel also discusses the passage (58).

εἰ δὲ καὶ αὐτὴ ἡ ἄκρα αὐτῆς οὐσία . . . This is the start of a long and intricate sentence (240.35-241.15), which we have translated as six sentences. It begins with an unanswered protasis: "Again, even if its highest essence does not itself remain pure in its inclination toward what is secondary." The author seems to have forgotten this dangling protasis as he works his way through the Iamblichean theory of the descent of the soul. For ease of understanding as well as for correct grammar and syntax, we have not translated the "if."

Iamblichus' position is that the human soul is a mean between divine souls (which always engage in intellection) and irrational souls (which never do). The latter are divisible, generated, and perishable. Now, if a soul sometimes intelligizes and sometimes does not then its activity varies. As we have seen before, Iamblichus insists that if the activities of the soul vary so too must its essence. The soul, once separated from "what is secondary," i.e. its lower nature, attains its pure essence. (Iamblichus evidently cited Aristotle, *De An.* 430a22-23, arguing that the soul "is what it is" after it is thus separated.) But this separated state is always temporary for the human soul. It is, Iamblichus says, "dissipated and slackened" and thus it sinks, becomes associated with secondary natures, and intelligizes only intermittently. This is the nature of the soul. It both is and is not like divine souls. Iamblichus seems to rely on Plato's *Timaeus* for corroboration. There the soul was made up of three constituents: sameness, difference, and existence. The divine souls were concocted of an exceptionally pure compound of these ingredients. Human souls were however combined from a mixture that was less pure. The otherness and sameness in the human soul, Iamblichus suggests, alter somewhat. As a result of this alteration in the soul's constituents, the soul descends and cannot intelligize at all times. Its activity below differs from its essence above.

ἀλλ' οὐδ' ἂν ποτὲ μὲν προβαλλομένη δευτέρας ζωὰς . . . These secondary lives are the various powers (both rational and irrational) of the soul that are contained in embryo in the pure intellectual soul and that the soul produces or "projects" in its descent into body. For the Iamblichean origin of the phrase, see Steel 62 note 33. For "projection," see our note in section C, above.

ὅπερ καὶ ὁ Ἀριστοτέλης ἐμφαίνει γράφων "χωρισθεὶς δὲ ἐστιν ὅπερ ἐστίν" . . . Aristotle, *De An.* 430a22-23. See note in section C, above.

διαφορεῖσθαί πως καὶ χαλᾶσθαι . . . Iamblichus' doctrine is extreme. As the soul falls into generation, it changes in its very essence. Just as its activities are diluted by the addition of sense perception, passions, etc., so to it is weakened in itself. Again, however, Iamblichus would stress that the soul is not destroyed. It is *weakened* but not to the point that it ceases to be soul, just as when it was engaged in intellection, it did not cease to be soul and become pure Intellect. For the Greek verb χαλᾶσθαι ("weakened"), see Steel 66 note 53.

οὔτε τῆς ἑτερότητος ἑαυτὴν ἐξαλλαττούσας . . . We retain ἑαυτὴν with the MSS. Hayduck corrects to αὐτὴν, "it" (= "the soul").

καὶ ἡ ἤδη τελειοῦν τὴν προβληθεῖσαν ζωὴν ἱκανὴ . . . The Greek has the feminine article alone (ἡ), referring to the noun τελειότης ("perfection"), two lines above. Here it must mean "perfection" in the sense of the means by which that perfection is achieved, and we accordingly supply the English word "means.".

ἀλλ' οὔπω κατὰ ἄκρα μέτρα τελεία . . . With Hayduck, we read τελεία (nominative, singular, feminine, in agreement with the understood subject "[means of] perfection). If with the MSS we keep τέλεια (accusative, plural, neuter, in agreement with μέτρα), the translation would be: "would itself perfect the soul, but not in the highest perfect measures in such a way that that the soul would also belong to itself."

Iamblichus' point is that the soul has two perfections. One, its highest (ἡ ἀκροτάτη τῆς ψυχῆς τελειότης, 241.19-20), occurs when the soul is at its highest state (when it "is what it is," i.e., when it is actually intelligizing). There is a second and secondary kind of perfection as well, when the soul is enmeshed in the realm of generation. This perfection is not imperfect (οὐκ οὖσα δηλαδὴ ἀτελής, 23) but it is not of the same high level of perfection as the first sort (ἀλλ' οὔπω κατὰ ἄκρα μέτρα τελεία, 23-24) and so the soul in this case "does not belong to itself" (ἑαυτῆς εἶναι μόνης, 24). The soul, whether through theurgic rites or philosophy (εἴτε πρακτικῶς εἴτε θεωρητικῶς , 22-23), attains secondary perfection and only then can ascend higher "to its supreme perfection (εἰς τὴν ἄκραν ἑαυτῆς τελειότητα, 25-26).

There seems to be a distinction here between the soul-in-Nature being brought to perfection (along with its secondary lives) by something else and the soul-separated-from-Nature bringing itself to perfection. If so, this suggests a limit to the role of theurgy. Theurgy would suffice to bring the soul-in-Nature back to the brink of its true self, at which point the soul itself would perfect itself again. One would, however, expect that an individual must undergo much theurgical training before being ready to intelligize.

E. Priscianus, *Metaphrasis in Theophrastum* 31.27-32.19

Festugière (257) gives a French translation of part of this passage (32.13-19). Steel also discusses the passage (55-58). Huby (in Blumenthal and Clark) examines the passage in the larger context of 29.6-32.19 (10-12, cf. 8).

We again have the Iamblichean doctrine that the human soul's essence and activities must not differ from one another. If the soul's activities vary between permanence and change, then so too must the soul's essence. Priscianus lays out this doctrine in the first paragraph. The second paragraph posits a double set of essences and activities for the soul, but this concept leads to a problem: the human soul's higher essence will have nothing to do with its lower instantiations. In the third paragraph, Priscianus suggests that an opponent may try to solve the dilemma by positing not two essences in one soul but rather two relations or reason principles or lives. But this attempted solution does not solve the problem. For either the proposed single soul with an internal duality will be "uniform and completely pure and unchanging," in which case there can be no change or passibility in the soul (cp. *In Tim.* Fr. 87) or it will be constantly changing, in which case there would be no permanence in the soul at all. Finally, in the fourth paragraph, we read Iamblichus' solution. The soul is truly a mean in that it partakes of both permanence and change. Unlike divine souls (which never vary) and souls of animals (which have no permanence), the human soul is both permanent (inasmuch as it remains alive forever) and changeable (inasmuch as it leads various different lives).

τελείων καὶ ἀγαθοειδῶν . . . The adjective ἀγαθοειδής ("good in form") is Iamblichean. See *De Anima* section 48 and notes.

εἰ δὲ διττὴν ἐν ἡμῖν οὐσίαν . . . Huby (68 note 386) points out that the position that Priscianus attacks (that of a double soul) is reminiscent of Pseudo-Simplicius' view that the human intellect (i.e., the psychic intellect) is double in *In De An.* 240.8-10. As she says, if this is so, then this passage is evidence that Pseudo-Simplicius and Priscianus are not the same person. She refers to H. Blumenthal, "Neoplatonic Elements in the *De Anima* Commentaries," *Phronesis* 21 (1976) 79-81, reprinted in R. Sorabji, *Aristotle Transformed* 317-319. See also H. Blumenthal, *Aristotle and Neoplatonism in Late Antiquity* 169.

εἰ μὲν διεσπασμένας . . . That is, if the double set of essences, potencies, and/or activities is separated into one that is always perfect and another that is sometimes perfect and sometimes not.

F. Priscianus, *Metaphrasis in Theophrastum* 23.13-24.20

Passages F and G both refer directly to Iamblichus on the topic of the faculty of imagination. They therefore represent (at least in part) what Iamblichus would have written concerning imagination in his *De Anima*, probably in the section on the "powers of the soul" (see sections 10-15, above). Discussion of the faculty of imagination would have immediately preceded section 14 "On Memory."

There are two problems that confront the reader of these two passages: how much of the material is by Iamblichus and are the authors of the two passages the same? We begin with the second question. Steel (in Huby and Steel, 133-134) argues that the similarity of these two passages is an argument for their authors being the same person, Priscianus. He points out that both passages show "a remarkable influence from Iamblichus," although the parallels "are not so literal" as others he has found (and which he discusses on pages 127-133). Steel also claims that Priscianus wrote passage G with passage F "before his eyes" (133). Huby (also in Huby and Steel, 62 note 277) agrees that both passages are similar "but not very close." As Huby also notes, Blumenthal (1982, 87) briefly discusses the passage. At the beginning and end of this paper (73-75 and 92-93), Blumenthal rehearses reasons for doubting that the authors of the two works are the same.[1]

As we shall see, there are differences between the two passages that suggest that we are dealing with two authors, both of whom are consulting the same text (Iamblichus' *De Anima*). First, passage G makes greater use of the pneumatic vehicle of the soul as the place in which the images are projected from the imagination for the use of the soul (τὸ ὄχημα, 213.38; τὸ πνεῦμα, 214.1, 3, 4) than does passage F, which refers to the vehicle only once (τὸ πνεῦμα, 25.11). We know that Iamblichus laid great stress on the soul's vehicle as the place of images, both in earthly activities and in the theurgical ritual of ascent,[2] and we would therefore expect that he would stress its use in imagination in the *De Anima*. Thus, it looks as if Priscianus downplays its role (as he does throughout the *Metaphrasis*) whereas the Pseudo-Simplicius does not, which again is characteristic of him in his *In De Anima*.[3]

Another difference between the two passages concerns the way the imagination can affect its own images. Whereas both passages state that imagination starts from a received sensible object but later can project the image without a sensible form being present, only passage G makes the further point that the faculty of imagination can make its image "more exact." That is to say, imagination can take a sensible

---

[1] See also Blumenthal (1996) 65-71, where he admits that the *De Anima* commentary may not be by Simplicius but still denies that it is by Priscianus. In addition, it is worth noting another difference here between the two authors. The Pseudo-Simplicius prefers the feminine (πάθη) to the neuter (πάθος); Priscianus uses the feminine once and the neuter seven times.

[2] For a history of and background to the soul's vehicle, see Finamore (1985) 1-6. For its role in theurgy, see 125-155, esp. 128-131 and 145-146. The vehicle is the place where images appear. These images may be formed in the natural course of human life, set off initially by sensible forms and then retained in the imagination for future use. (This function of the vehicle and imagination is discussed below.) In ritual ascent, the gods take over the human vehicle and project their own images, so necessary for the ascent, into the individual's vehicle. See *De Myst.* 3.14 (132.11-17) and 3.6 (113.7-114.2).

[3] See the indices to both works.

form of, say, a straight line and improve on it so that it approaches, as much as possible, a geometrically straight line. Again, this difference indicates different interests in the two authors, especially since the context in both works (Aristotle's theory of imagination in the *De Anima*) is the same.

Huby (in Blumenthal and Clark) discusses passage F, attempting to distinguish the aspects that are clearly Iamblichus' from those that are Priscianus' (6-7). As always, it is a difficult task to differentiate an author's own views from those of another writer with whom the author agrees. How far does Priscianus elaborate on Iamblichus' doctrines and how much of the discussion is truly Iamblichus? Huby accepts only the lines in which Iamblichus is mentioned by name as Iamblichus himself (23.13-23 and 24.1-4, the first and third paragraphs of our translation). The rest of the passage is, Huby thinks, Priscianus elaborating on Iamblichus' doctrine. In passage G, Iamblichus is mentioned only once (214.19). Taking these references together, the only doctrine that is certifiably Iamblichean is that imagination receives images from sensation and from thought and passes these images along to other faculties of the soul. We very much doubt that this is all that remains of Iamblichus' thoughts on imagination. First, imagination clearly plays an important role in the soul's activities, since it is intermediary between other functions. Second, the importance of the imagination in Aristotle's philosophy by itself would suggest that Iamblichus would have developed his own interpretation of what Aristotle said. Third, passages F and G have much in common, and that commonality is best explained (we think) by positing a third text to which the two authors had access. Since both authors cite Iamblichus in the course of their examination of the imagination, it is most likely that their source was Iamblichus' work on the soul.

Coming now to passage F, we agree that the first and third paragraphs, in which Iamblichus is specifically named, represent Iamblichus' doctrine of the faculty of imagination. We also believe, however, that the second paragraph is substantially Iamblichus as well. Huby (7) thinks it is Priscianus here because "he refers to Peripatetic matters: he says that *phantasia* is not a *pathos* or a *kinêsis* and it is not moulded from the outside like wax (23.25-6)." The concept of the imaginative faculty is, however, at its core Aristotelian. If Iamblichus were going to speak of the imagination at all, he would naturally fall into Aristotelian language. Further, as we shall see below, the comparison of imagination to wax is in Plato as well as in Aristotle. Thus, the doctrine expounded in the second paragraph seems to be Neoplatonic in interweaving Plato and Aristotle, and it also continues Iamblichus' doctrine in the first paragraph in such a way that one expects that it too is Iamblichean. We therefore see the second paragraph as essentially Iamblichus.

The fourth paragraph also seems Iamblichean. As Huby says (7), Priscianus is using Iamblichus' doctrine of the imagination to construct his own argument. But there is nothing in the paragraph with which Iamblichus would disagree. Indeed the way the argument unfolds seems to us to suggest Priscianus is working through Iamblichus' own arguments, which explain how the faculty of imagination makes use of both sensible and intellective forms.

In sum, in both the second and fourth paragraphs, Priscianus is led to a discussion of the role of imagination because of some statement of Aristotle's in the *De Anima*, but this fact does not force us to conclude that Iamblichus was not concerned with the same problems. Indeed, the matters examined and the resulting doctrine (that imagination is a mediatory faculty that connects the various lower powers of the soul with intellect and that thereby has as its own special property the power to bring forth images from itself with no external stimulus) are matters which Iamblichus would necessarily have considered. They go to the heart of what the imagination is.

ἀποτυποῦται καὶ ἐκμάττεται . . . There is an echo of Plato's discussion of memory in *Tht.* 191c-e. Plato is discussing how one comes to know something that was not known before. He posits a wax imprint-receptacle in the soul (ἐν ταῖς ψυχαῖς ἡμῶν ἐνὸν κήρινον ἐκμαγεῖον, 191c8-9). Concerning this faculty, Plato says (191d2-e1):

> We say that this is a gift of Memory, the mother of the Muses, and whatever we wish to remember of those things which we ourselves saw or heard or thought (ἐννοήσωμεν), we lay this [faculty of memory] under the sense perceptions and thoughts and we make an impression (ἀποτυποῦσθαι), as if taking impressions from rings. What is stamped (ἐκμαγῇ), we remember and know as long as the image of it exists in [the memory]. Whatever is erased or was unable to be stamped (ἐκμαγῆναι), we forget and do not remember.

Iamblichus takes over this description of Memory for the faculty of Imagination (which, of course, is responsible for memory as well as other "imaging"). Imagination comes into being along with all the other lower powers of the soul (that is, it is equally a psychic προβολή) and receives imprints from those powers as well as from Intellect above. Iamblichus may have found evidence for this part of his belief in the *Theaetetus* passage, where Plato states that we recall past thoughts as well as perceptions.[4] Once the imagination has taken the imprint from one faculty, it not only stores the image but can also pass the image along to another faculty. Thus, we can form opinions about things on the basis of stored images of perceptions, thoughts, etc. As the next part of the sentence will make clear, the faculty of imagination again makes soul a mean between Intellect above and life in Nature below.

τὰς τῶν ἑτέρων δυνάμεων . . . This is Wimmer's reading, supported by Ficino. The MSS. have ταῖς τῶν ἑτέρων δυνάμεσιν ἐμφάσεις, which is adopted by Bywater and Huby. Although the MSS. reading is possible, it is strained. One would have to translate: "and transmits the appearances from the faculties of other [aspects of soul?] to other [faculties? aspects of soul?]." Iamblichus point is simply that the imaginative power transfers the appearances from one *faculty* to another *faculty*, and the MSS. reading muddies the parallelism. We therefore adopt the emended text.

δύναμις οὖσα τοῦ ἀφομοιοῦν αὖτα . . . Huby (62 note 283) points out that αὖτα ("them") has no antecedent agreeing with it in gender and number. As she says, Wimmer suggests τἆλλα ("other things") and Bywater considers ἄττα ("some things"), but retains the MSS. reading. This is a case of using the neuter plural instead of the expected feminine plural for "appearances" or "likenesses." Alternatively, Priscianus may already be thinking of the neuter plural "images" (φαντάσματα), which he will write shortly below at 24.1, rather than the feminine "appearances" (ἐμφάσεις), which he used above at 23.22-23. There is no need to emend the text. Imagination receives appearances/images from different faculties, assimilates these to itself, and then transmits them to other faculties, thereby being the first cause of these faculties' activities.

---

[4] The distinction between αἰσθητικὴ and βουλευτικὴ φαντασία is, of course, Aristotelian (*De An.* 434a5-7), and the latter belongs solely to rational creatures (ἐν τοῖς λογιστικοῖς, 7). Cf. *De An.* 433a9-12, where imagination is "a kind of thinking" (νόησίν τινα, 10), and 433b29-30.

οὐ κατὰ παραδοχὴν ἔξωθεν ὡς ὁ κηρὸς διαπλαττομένη . . . Iamblichus engages in some fine-tuning of Plato's doctrine at *Tht.* 191c-e, on which see above. The imagination is like wax in some ways, but we must not be misled by the analogy.[5] It differs in important respects. Wax receives an impression from the outside, but the imagination is affected internally (ἔνδοθεν). Below, this will become an important distinction between the faculties of sense perception and imagination. Sense perception, like wax, is affected from without. Imagination works from within the soul. It is, Iamblichus tells us, neither a πάθος nor a κίνησις, but rather a ἀμέριστος καὶ ὡρισμένη ἐνέργεια. Thus, imagination is an ongoing activity in the soul.[6] Its role is to produce images from itself (ἔνδοθεν) and project these images appropriately for the other faculties so that the images will produce motions in them. In this way, imagination sets other faculties in motion.

κατὰ <τὴν> λόγων τῶν ἀφομοιωτικῶν προβολὴν . . . The text is corrupt. We have adopted the suggestion of Bywater, but with some misgivings. The MSS. have κατὰ λόγον τῶν ἀφομοιωτικῶν προβολὴν, which yields no good sense. Wimmer suggested κατὰ λόγον τῶν ἀφομοιωτικῶν προβολῶν, "analogously with its assimilative projections," which may well be correct. Huby accepts Bywater's emendation without comment. Iamblichus' point is that imagination is a kind of engine continuously in activity that possesses a store of images that it brings forth as reason-principles from itself. These reason-principles are adapted appropriately to other images that had once moved the sense organs but are now absent. Thus, the image can now substitute for the original sensible form and can move the soul to recall the original through the stored image.

ὅμως κατὰ τὰ αἰσθητικὰ ἀπεικονίζεται εἴδη μορφωτικῶς καὶ μεριστῶς καὶ κατὰ τὴν πρὸς τὰ αἰσθητὰ ἀναφοράν . . . For the term μορφωτικῶς

---

[5] As Huby (62 note 284) points out, Aristotle too uses the image of wax (in this case, for the faculty of perception). Aristotle says that the faculty "is receptive of perceptible forms without matter" (τὸ δεκτικὸν τῶν αἰσθητῶν εἰδῶν ἄνευ τῆς ὕλης, 424a18-19), thus also making a distinction between wax and psychic faculty.

[6] This is Iamblichus' interpretation of Aristotle (428b10-17), who says that imagination is a kind of motion (κίνησίς τις, 11) and arises from the activity of sensation (ὑπὸ τῆς ἐνεργείας τῆς αἰσθήσεως, 13-14). For Iamblichus, the use of τις shows that it is not a motion at all.

("in images") and its relation to images, see our commentary to *De Anima*, section 39, above. Compare passage G, 214.19- 20: ὅμως κατὰ τὰ αἰσθητὰ ἀπεικονίζεται εἴδη μορφωτικῶς καὶ μεριστῶς.

ἢ ὑπὸ τῶν αἰσθητικῶν κινεῖται εἰδῶν . . . This is a problematic phrase in a difficult sentence (24.4-7). Priscianus (and probably Iamblichus before him) is wondering how it can be true both that the imagination takes images from superior activities, such as intellection, and that it is moved by sensible forms, for intellections have no sensible form. Priscianus here suggests that the imagination receives superior activities but appropriately to its lower status, in images and partially.

On this interpretation, the reading of the MSS. ἢ ("or it is moved by sensible forms ") makes no sense. We therefore adopt Bywater's emendation ᾗ. Huby (62 note 287) also adopts this emendation, but says that "Bywater's reading is also difficult." She translates the clause "by the fact that it is moved by the sensible forms" (33). But ᾗ carries the sense of "as" here. The point is that the imagination receives impressions from the intellect in the way that it receives them from sensible forms (viz., in images and divisibly). Thus an image of a thought is necessarily different from the thought itself, which need have no image.

πῶς οὖν καὶ μὴ παρόντων τῶν αἰσθητῶν κινεῖται ἡ φαντασία; . . . Priscianus moves to the next point. Imagination, we have seen, differs from intellection in that it uses images. But it also differs from sense perception, for sense perception is moved only when a sensible object is present. Imagination is moved even when a sensible object is absent. It is then moved from itself (ἀφ' ἑαυτῆς, 24.12) and projects images (προβάλλειν τὰ φαντάσματα, 12) that are like those that originally moved it. This is how memory works. The imagination receives sensible forms once, say of Socrates. Later, when Socrates is not present, the imagination can raise the image of the sensible form again from within itself. Themistius, *In De An.* 28.5-17, is similar: sense perceptions occur when the sense organ is moved by a sensible image, but in an act of memory (ἀνάμνησις) the images come from the soul itself; memory is the projection of images from the soul.

G. *In De Anima* 213.23-214.26

This passage is a commentary on Aristotle, *De Anima* 428b10-13: Ἀλλ' ἐπειδή ἔστι κινηθέντος τουδὶ κινεῖσθαι ἕτερον ὑπὸ τούτου, ἡ δὲ φαντασία κίνησίς τις δοκεῖ εἶναι καὶ οὐκ ἄνευ αἰσθήσεως γίγνεσθαι ἀλλ' αἰσθανομένοις καὶ ὧν αἴσθησίς ἐστιν. ("But since when one thing is moved another thing is able to be moved by it, imagination seems to be some kind of movement and seems not to occur without sense perception but in creatures that perceive and of things that are perceived."). Thus this passage is closely related to passage F, above. About this passage, Blumenthal says that the author sees the two faculties (sense perception and imagination) as "different cognitive faculties" and that "[w]hile *phantasia* adjoins *aisthêsis*, it is nevertheless above it" (87). Blumenthal's words about *phantasia* in the *De Anima* commentary should also be read (84-90).

διὰ τῶν προειρημένων . . . In *De An.* 3.3, Aristotle distinguishes imagination from sensation (428a5-15), from knowledge and intellect (428a15-18), and from opinion (428a18-428b1).

κινεῖται μὲν οὖν προσεχῶς ὑπὸ τῶν αἰσθητῶν τὸ αἰσθητήριον . . . The author is differentiating what happens in the sense organ from what happens in the soul. The sense organ is in an intermediate position. It is affected by the sense object but in turn registers what it sees and therefore acts. This is possible because the organ has life, which is of course given to it by the soul, which enlivens it along with the whole body. Thus, the sense organ is both passive and active (οὐ πάσχον μόνον ἀλλὰ καὶ ἐνεργοῦν, 213.26; ἐπὶ τῷ ἐνεργητικῷ τούτῳ πάθει, 27; ἐν τῷ αἰσθητηρίῳ ἐγγινομένη παθητική, 30-31). The soul itself (here termed τῆς αἰσθητικῆς καθαρᾶς ἐνεργείας καὶ κρίσεως, 27-28, that is, the highest facet of the sensible activity, that which judges, the soul) is activated by the actualized sense organ and projects from itself a sensible form in accordance with the sensible form in the actualized organ. The affection arising in the sense organ when it is affected by the sense object is a motion (31-32).

οὐ κίνησιν, ἀλλ' ἀμέριστον ἐνέργειαν . . . In passage F, Priscianus had said that imagination was "neither a passion nor a motion but an indivisible and determinate activity" (οὐκ οὖσα πάθος οὐδὲ κίνησις ἀλλ' ἀμέριστος καὶ ὡρισμένη ἐνέργεια, 23.25-26). The author of passage G makes a related point, that the soul in its sensitive capacity (that is, soul *qua* sensitive faculty) acts in a similar way when presented with a sensible form from the sense organ. If both authors are following Iamblichus, it would seem that both aspects of soul (sensitive and imaginative) are so closely connected as to have similar powers: projection of λόγοι, making judgments about the sensitive forms, and being restricted to the sensible form when it judges. Further, these are activities brought forth from the soul (in either aspect) in itself; they are not motions caused externally, as by a sense object.[7] Unlike Priscianus in passage F, the author of passage G does not discuss imagination using higher forms from Intellect.

In the next sentence, our author appeals directly to the imaginative faculty. It is aroused by the sensitive faculty, as we have seen, and in fact makes use of the same body. But there is a difference. Whereas the sensitive faculty uses the body by being externally affected by it, the imagination uses the body without the external affection. As Priscianus said in passage F, it brings these images forth from itself.

Next, the author brings in the vehicle. As the ethereal body connecting the soul to the body, the vehicle is the place where images are projected. It is subject to both sensible and imaginative images, just as it is subject (as indeed is the material body) to the rational soul.[8] The author's point, as Blumenthal (1982) 87 sees, is

---

[7] See Priscianus, *Metaphrasis* 24.24-25.1, which follows shortly after passage F. There Priscianus says that imagination is next to (προσεχῆ, 24.25) the faculty of sensation and makes use of sensible forms. Further, the sense organ receives sense images from the imagination (images that imagination has taken in from sensible forms from previous sense objects, to be sure). When this occurs, the images in the sense organ are not caused externally (i.e., by sense objects) but rather come from the faculty of imagination.

[8] Cf. Priscianus, *Metaphrasis* 25.1-3: "And this is not surprising [viz., that the body is affected by images from the imaginative faculty] since some appearances of our rational activity also descend into the body, as the rolling of the eyes and the furrowing of the brow in study make evident." (καὶ οὐ θαυμαστόν· ἐπεὶ καὶ τῆς λογικῆς ἡμῶν ἐνεργείας ἐμφάσεις τινὲς εἰς τὸ σῶμα καθήκουσιν, ὡς αἱ συστροφαὶ δηλοῦσι τῶν ὀμμάτων καὶ αἱ τῶν ὀφρύων συναγωγαὶ ἐν ταῖς ζητήσεσι.) Steel (in Huby and Steel, 133-134) says that this passage from Priscianus is needed to explain the sentence in passage G: "For indeed not only the pneuma but also this solid body is affected by our rational activities." But such is clearly not the case. Although both passages are discussing the effect of the rational soul upon the body, the passage from Priscianus is much more precise, giving rolled eyes and furrowed brow as examples. Passage G, on the other hand, is simply more general. Any rational activity will have (unspecified) effects upon the body — and indeed the vehicle as well.

that although sensation and imagination inhere in a single sub-stratum, the vehicle, they are two separate faculties.

προηγουμένως δ' οὖν ὡς αἰσθητικὸν παθὸν τὸ πνεῦμα . . . Some light may be cast on this long sentence (214.2-8) by what Priscianus says in passage F (24.10-14). Priscianus was concerned with the distinction between sense perception and imagination, viz., that imagination is moved in both the presence and the absence of a sense object. The author of passage G, though not interested in precisely that topic, does use similar material. The pneumatic vehicle of the soul, like the faculty of imagination in Priscianus, is moved first like a "sensitive affection," i.e., in the presence of a sense object. The vehicle itself is specifically adapted to receive forms from the imagination (214.4). The faculty of imagination may take on an image of a sensible form without an object being present. In some cases, the faculty must be moved more than once (οὐχ ἅπαξ ἢ δὶς ἐνίοτε μόνον . . . ἀλλὰ καὶ πλεονάκις, 214.6-7), as was the case in the Priscianus passage (ἐνίοτε δὲ οὐχ ἅπαξ ἢ δὶς ἀλλὰ πλεονάκις, 24.13-14), before it can project the appropriate images without the sense object being present. Thus, in this passage, there are three objects of comparison: sensation, the vehicle, and imagination.

It is puzzling why Priscianus does not mention the vehicle in passage F. If our hypothesis that both he and the author of passage G are following Iamblichus is correct, then Iamblichus certainly discussed the vehicle in the context of the comparison between the faculties of sensation and imagination. That Iamblichus would discuss the vehicle here of course makes sense, since the vehicle is the seat of the images projected from the soul. It may be that in the context in which Priscianus was working (Theophrastus' *Physics*), there was no need to raise the vehicle at this moment. All that was required was to show how the two *faculties* differed, wherever the images might be projected. Priscianus does mention the vehicle (τὸ πνεῦμα) at 25.11, when discussing how we can have false beliefs about true perceptions and *vice versa*. He says (25.10-13):

> And just as we are simultaneously able when we perceive true [sensible objects] to project false images concerning them, so conse-quently the pneuma, being on the one hand able to perceive, receives true appearances from sense objects, and being on the other able to imagine, it receives false ones from the sense object and true ones from the imagination.

This excerpt is interesting because it shows the vehicle as straddling both the realm of sensations and that of images. This is very similar to what our author says here (214.2-8), though of course from a slightly different perspective. It is probable, therefore, that Iamblichus, in his *De Anima*, made greater use of the vehicle than either passage F or G would suggest. If so, each author for reasons of his own decided to excise certain references to the vehicle. From both passages, it is clear that Iamblichus saw the vehicle itself as intermediary between not only soul and body but also between the faculties of sensation and imagination, being as it were a place where through images both faculties could come together.

ἐγερθεῖσα δ' οὖν καὶ ἀφ' ἑαυτῆς προβάλλει τὰ φαντάσματα . . . The point here (214.8-12) is that once the faculty of imagination is primed, as it were, by previous sensible forms, it can then either faithfully reproduce these sensible forms in its projected images or embellish the sensible form, correcting a false one or altering the form in some way so as to make it more precise (for example, re-adjusting the appearance of the size of the sun; cf. Priscianus, *Metaphrasis* 24.24-29 and 25.10-15). For the term "embroider" (ποικίλλουσα, 214.12), compare Priscianus, *Metaphrasis* 24.28, where the same verb is used. In this passage, however, the author adds that the faculty of imagination can make its image accurate (ἀκριβές, 214.10) in a way that the original sensible form was not. Thus, it can project an image of a line that has no breadth, even though there can exist no such sensible form. Later (214.20-23), the author summarizes three ways in which imagination is superior to sense perception: "by acting from itself after its initial arousal, by not always requiring the presence of sense objects, and by imposing accuracy." The first two ways are found in the Priscianus passage (24.10-13), but the third is not. It is likely, therefore, that Iamblichus had all three differences, and that Priscianus decided to omit the third for reasons of his own.

καὶ τὸ μὲν τῆς αἰσθήσεως δεῖσθαι . . . Imagination, like rational thinking requires an external stimulus to get it started. This is the view of Aristotle, *De An.* 431a14-17: "To the thinking soul images are like sensations. And whenever it affirms or denies good or evil, it avoids or pursues (on which account the soul never thinks without an image)." (τῇ δὲ διανοητικῇ ψυχῇ τὰ φαντάσματα οἷον αἰσθήματα ὑπάρχει. ὅταν δὲ ἀγαθὸν ἢ κακὸν φήσῃ ἢ ἀποφήσῃ, φεύγει ἢ διώκει (διὸ οὐδέποτε νοεῖ ἄνευ φαντάσματος ἡ ψυχή).) Since every image arises from a sensible form, thinking starts from external sensible forms. Even when the imagination projects forms of immaterial, formless, indivisible objects, it does so with images that are bodily, have form, and are divisible. Compare passage F, 24.4-7.

καὶ γὰρ εἰ καὶ τὰς λογικὰς ἡμῶν, ὡς ὁ Ἰάμβλιχος βούλεται, ἀποτυποῦται ἐνεργείας πάσας . . . Compare Priscianus in passage F, 24.1-7.

ἅπασα δὲ τὸ ἡγεμονικὸν καὶ κινητικὸν τῶν ζῴων . . . For the "ruling element," see above, *De Anima* section 11 (368.14) and notes. The ruling element in human beings is normally the rational soul, but when reason is "veiled" (ἐπικαλύπτηται, 214.26) (that is, presumably, when it is overpowered by the irrational soul, as is the case in children), irrational impulses do the leading. At such times, human beings differ little from other animals when they make choices.

H. Priscianus, *Metaphrasis in Theophrastum* 9.7-31

In Passages H and I, we find a discussion of light and the transparent. Iamblichus is mentioned only in the first passage (by Priscianus), but the topic is introduced in Passage I as well, a passage which also contains Iamblichus' doctrine. Once again, there are similarities and differences between the two passages, which we will explore in the notes below.

The concept of the transparent is Aristotle's (*De An.* 2.7, 418a26-419b3). In order for colors to be perceived, they must appear to the sense organ through a medium. This medium is transparent, e.g., air, water, or some translucent solid like glass. But, Aristotle argues, in order for the perceptible object to be visible in the medium another entity must be present actualizing the medium. This entity is light. Thus, in any act of vision, there will be a perceptible object, the organ of sight, a transparent medium between the object and organ, and some light source actualizing the transparent medium allowing the object to be visible to the organ.

Priscianus began discussion of light and the transparent at 7.25. He looks into Theophrastus' discussion of the transparent, and then gives his own view (8.9-14):

I say that the transparent is neither an affection nor a disposition brought into existence from something but that it is a form that unites bodies in [the realm of] generation with the perfection of light and makes them suitable for receiving light and dark. These bodies either partake essentially of one of these [i.e., either of light or dark], or partially of both, or of a mixture of the two. (λέγω δὴ οὐ πάθος οὐδὲ διάθεσιν ὑπό τινος ἐγγενομένην εἶναι τὸ διαφανὲς ἀλλ' εἶδος ὑπάρχειν συναρμοτικὸν τῶν ἐν γενέσει σωμάτων πρὸς τὴν τοῦ φωτὸς τελειότητα καὶ ἐπιτηδειότητα αὐτοῖς πρός τε τὴν τοῦ φωτὸς καὶ πρὸς τὴν τοῦ σκότους ὑποδοχὴν παρεχόμενον, ἢ οὐσιώδως θατέρου μετέχουσιν ἢ παρὰ μέρος ἀμφοτέρων ἢ κατά τινα μῖξιν.)

This doctrine is probably Iamblichean since it mirrors Iamblichus' view of light (Passage H, 9.12-14), where Priscianus substitutes "quality" (ποιότης) for "disposition" (διάθεσις). Neither light nor the transparent, then, belong to bodies but are separate entities in their own right. The transparent is the form that is perfected or actualized by light — or indeed, as it turns out, by darkness, since it too is an actuality (8.16).

It is no surprise, therefore, to find both Priscianus (8.15-16) and the Pseudo-Simplicius (133.11-13) stating that darkness is not the privation of light (as Aristotle would have it 418b18-19) but is an actuality (ἐνέργεια). Steel[9] sees this as evidence that Priscianus and the Pseudo-Simplicius are the same person: "the only reason to insert this heterodox view on light in this section of the commentary is that he [i.e., Pseudo-Simplicius] must have adhered to it, as is clear from the *Metaphrasis*, perhaps following Iamblichus' views" (Huby and Steel, 133). It is true that this doctrine is heterodox, but no matter how unusual the doctrine may be there is no *a priori* reason to deny that two philosophers could hold it. In fact, the possibility is increased when we realize that the doctrine in question is most probably Iamblichean, from his *De Anima*. Further, as Huby points out,[10] the subsequent passage in the Pseudo-Simplicius "has a different account of earth and darkness/light" from that in Priscianus. This suggests that each writer accepted the unorthodox Iamblichean doctrine that darkness is an actuality but then went on to discuss the view in different terms.[11]

---

[9] Huby and Steel, 132-133. Cf. 218, notes 80 and 81).

[10] Huby and Steel, 54 note 94.

[11] Huby discusses one other point of difference between the texts of Priscianus and the Pseudo-Simplicius on light (in Huby and Steel, 55 note 123). The latter author (135.25-136.2), while discussing Aristotle's statement that luminous objects are not seen in the dark but rather cause perception there (*De An.* 419a2-3), says

Priscianus in passage G discusses the nature of light but stresses its transcendent nature. In this, he is almost certainly following Iamblichus, who stressed the transcendence of divine light in theurgic matters. (See notes below.)[12]

πρῶτον μὲν οὖν ἐκεῖνο ἀξιῶ διορίζεσθαι . . . Priscianus begins with a distinction between the light source and the light itself. Although it is true that light is emitted by bright objects, like the sun or a fire, our discussion concerns the nature of light, not of the light-emitting object. Light, Priscianus reminds us, has been defined as ἐνέργεια τοῦ διαφανοῦς ("the actualization of the transparent") and the transparent is what exists in translucent media, such as air, water, and certain solids that are partially clear.

Ἔπειτα δὲ τῷ Ἰαμβλίχου ἑπόμενος . . . Priscianus brings in Iamblichus as the source of the doctrine that light is neither a body nor a quality of body. As we have seen above, this Iamblichean doctrine dovetails with the doctrine that the transparent itself is not a disposition of body but rather a form that unites bodies with light (8.9-14). The Iamblichean doctrine of visibility of objects, therefore, is that an object becomes visible only when it takes on the form of visibility that the transparent provides. The transparent can provide this form only when it is itself actualized by light. When the transparent remains dark, however, it is still actualized but by darkness rather than by light. Light itself, as an activator of a form, is not bodily. This point Priscianus takes as straightforward, for he spends the remainder of this passage arguing that light is not an affection or quality of body.

ὥσπερ οἱ Περιπατητικοί . . . As Huby (in Huby and Steel, 54 note 103) points out, this phrase is odd since Peripatetics do not tend to think that light is a body, although (Huby also says) Strato of Lampsacus did. Bywater is tempted to delete the phrase, which is

---

that "light and the bright object that is productive of light are what are primarily seen" (διὰ γὰρ τὸ προηγουμένως ὁρατὸν εἶναι τὸ φῶς καὶ τὸ τοῦ φωτὸς ἀποδοτικὸν λαμπρόν. 135.26-27). Priscianus, however, first states that position hypothetically: "Perhaps someone might say that what are primarily seen are the bright object and light itself" (Μή ποτε δὲ εἴπῃ τις καὶ τὸ προηγουμένως ὁρατὸν τὸ λαμπρὸν εἶναι καὶ αὐτὸ τὸ φῶς, 10.30-32). But he then goes on to criticize this position on the grounds that it would require that light blot out colors rather than illuminate them (11.1-5).

[12] Huby (in Blumenthal and Clark 9-10) briefly considers this passage and concludes that Priscianus is summarizing Iamblichus although she questions "whether the rejected theories are brought in by Priscian himself" (10).

absent from H and M[1]. Huby also suggests that the phrase may be interpreted to mean "like the Peripatetics I want it not to be a body," but this interpretation stretches the Greek too much. Another possible solution is to move the phrase after the word σώματος ότουοῦν ("of any body whatsoever"), with M[2]Pbw and Ficino. This may well be the best solution, especially since it is against this point (that light is an affection or quality of body) that Priscianus wishes to bring arguments.

κινουμένου γοῦν ἐκείνου ἔστηκεν αὐτὸ . . . Priscianus proceeds to lay out five indications that light is not an affection of the body. (1) Light is not moved by perturbations in the air. (2) Light comes to exist in the transparent and departs from it all at once, unlike true affections of bodies, such as heat, which build up gradually and leave a faint trace of themselves behind as they withdraw. (3) Light does not insert itself into a medium by distributing itself throughout or by changing the medium as it goes. (4) The medium does not limit the extent to which light can progress. (5) Light does not form a compound with another light.

αὐτὸ χωριστῶς ἀποτέτμηται . . . Priscianus emphasizes that light is completely separate (χωριστῶς) from body. Cf. lines 25-26, χωριστὴν εἶναι σωμάτων τὴν τοῦ φωτὸς ἐνέργειαν ("the actualization of light is separate from the body") and 27-28, χωριστῶς αὐτὸ τελειοῦσα (light "perfects it [i.e., the transparent] in a transcendent way"). This notion that light is completely separated mirrors the Iamblichean doctrine of divine illumination in theurgy. The gods are completely separated from the realm of matter and do not descend here themselves but rather shine their incorporeal light on the theurgist or on physical objects that have been made suitable to receive the light. See De Myst. 3.16, 188.12-15; 1.8, 28.16-29.3; 1.9, 30.13-19; cf. J. F. Finamore (1999) 58-60 and (in Blumenthal and Clark) 63 note 17. This is a good example of how Iamblichus' metaphysics supports his religious doctrines. Cp. Finamore (in Blumenthal and Clark) 60-61. In this connection, note that Priscianus calls light "a more divine Form" (10.25).

πῶς οὖν ἐνέργεια λέγεται τοῦ διαφανοῦς; . . . If light is as transcendent as Priscianus (following Iamblichus) has implied, how can it ever actualize the transparent? It cannot be in the usual way, for when the Form Heat (say) actualizes an object (so that it is hot), heat somehow is present to the object. Light , however, cannot be present; it must be separate. Thus, Priscianus concludes, light actualizes the transparent not by becoming part of the transparent but by "making the transparent belong to itself." Light itself remains aloof, at one with its source, transcendentally actualizing the medium without descending to its level.[13] Cf. Priscianus' discussion of color and the transparent at 12.17-28.

μένουσα συνεχὴς αὐτὴ τῷ ἐλλάμποντι καὶ ἐκείνῳ συμπεριαγομένη . . . For συνεχὴς, see line 16: σῴζει τὴν πρὸς τὸ αἴτιον ἀδιαίρετον συνέχειαν (light "preserves its undivided connection with its cause"). The use of συμπεριαγομένη is odd. It is the verb used of souls revolving around the realm of the Forms as they follow along with their leader gods.[14] Here it emphasizes the transcendence of light, which remains in the orbit of the light source (as it were) and not directly involved with lower objects.

I. *In De Anima* 131.13-132.17

The commentator is discussing Aristotle, *De Anima* 418b3: "Therefore one must first grasp concerning light" (διὸ περὶ φωτὸς πρῶτον ληπτέον[15]). He distinguishes light and the transparent, and then goes on to discuss light. There are reminiscences of Priscianus in Passage H, and these common areas are probably due to Iamblichus.

ἀλλ' ἐπεὶ τὸ φῶς τοῦ διαφανοῦς ἐστι τελειότης . . . Priscianus also used the term "perfection" (τελειότης, 9.27; cf. τελειοῦσα, 9.28) of light in the transparent.

ἀλλ' ἐνέργεια μὲν καὶ τὸ φῶς . . . For light as actualization (ἐνέργεια), see Priscianus 9.11 and 26. Our commentator, like Priscianus, wishes

---

[13] See J. F. Finamore's discussion of Iamblichus' *De Myst.* 3.11 (the oracle of Apollo at Claros) in Blumenthal and Clark, 58-59.

[14] See, for example, Proclus, *In Rem Publicam* 2.162.2; 2.300.21; *Theol. Plat.* 4.21.7; 4.32.10; 4.44.9; *In Tim.* 3.306.24. The term occurs only here in Priscianus and never in the Pseudo-Simplicius or in Iamblichus. It does appear in Simplicius, *In De Caelo* (36.34; 51.5; 151.31; 154.22; 155.32; 380.22; 462.27; 492.19; 493.13; 500.19; 507.2; 508.1; 508.28) and *In Phys.* (589.22). This furnishes further proof, if more were needed, that the author of the *De Anima* commentary is not Simplicius.

[15] Our texts of the *De Anima* have λεκτέον. See Steel (in Huby and Steel) 218 note 73.

to emphasize that light is a special kind of actualizer, one that remains aloof while it imparts itself. Thus, he says that light both remains in its source and gives itself to the transparent. This is similar to what Priscianus says, but not quite the same. For Priscianus stresses light's lack of involvement with the transparent medium: "not itself belonging to the transparent, but rather making the transparent belong to itself, while it itself remains continuous with the source of light and is carried round together with it" (9.28-29), while our commentator stresses that light is involved *both* with the light source and with the transparent medium. This is, of course, a difference in emphasis rather than a difference in doctrine. One should further note that whereas Priscianus compared this sort of actualization to that of heat in the air (which is an actualization taking place in the substrate), our commentator compares it to intellection (which is an actualization that remains above a substrate). What we seem to have is two authors, each emphasizing a different aspect of Iamblichus' doctrine on light: that it is an actualization of the transparent that differs from both kinds described (heat and intellection). But see below on 132.13-17, where the commentator is much closer to Priscianus.

ἀλλ' ἅμα τε τοῦ προϊέντος αὐτὴ ἐχομένη καὶ ἑτέρῳ ἐνδιδομένη . . . We adopt the conjecture of Steel, προϊέντος for προϊόντος. The sense requires that we contrast the light source with the transparent that receives the light from the light source.

ἐνέργεια δὲ καὶ ὅρος καὶ τελειότης . . . The writer turns now to the Aristotelian distinction between a potential and actual medium. This string of synonyms has an Iamblichean ring.

οὐ κατὰ πάθος ἀλλὰ κατὰ ἀθρόαν τελειότητα . . . According to the doctrine that Priscianus explicitly referred to Iamblichus (9.13-14) light is not "an affection or quality of any body whatsoever" (οὔτε μὴν πάθος ἢ ποιότητα σώματος ὁτουοῦν). Cf. 9.19 (σημεῖον τοῦ μὴ πάθημα εἶναι τοῦ ἀέρος τὸ φῶς) and 9.26 (πῶς οὖν ἐνέργεια λέγεται τοῦ διαφανοῦς; οὐχ ὡς πάθος, φήσω). For light occurring all at once (ἀθρόως), see 9.16-18 (ἀλλὰ καὶ ἡ ἀθρόα αὐτοῦ παρουσία ἐπὶ πάντα τὰ δέχεσθαι αὐτὸ δυνάμενα παρόντος τοῦ ἐλλάμποντος, καὶ αὖθις ἀπελθόντος ἡ ἀθρόα ἀπόλειψις) and 9.20 (τὰ γὰρ πάθη οἷον ἡ θερμότης οὔτε ἀθρόως ἐγγίνεται).

καὶ ἡ μὲν ἐπιστήμη . . . Knowledge of light is compared to scientific knowledge. In the latter, one knows by comparing the natural object to the paradigm or Platonic Form. When the Form is actualized in the object, it is easily known; when it is not yet present but potentially present, one knows that object is capable of having the Form by the Form's "faint trace," as perhaps we can tell that a green bell pepper will be a sweet red pepper by faint traces of red pigment on parts of it. So too we come to know what light is not by direct perception of the form of light (which is impossible) but through perceiving its effects in the transparent. See Steel (in Huby and Steel) 218 note 76.

ὡς κατὰ ἀτελὲς αὐτοῦ ἴχνος χαρακτηριζόμενα . . . For ἴχνος, see Priscianus 9.18-19: μηδὲν ἴχνος ἑαυτοῦ καταλείποντος (light "does not leave a trace of itself behind"). Our commentator, however, is making a different point. For Priscianus, light comes to be and leaves all at once; it leaves without a trace. For the commentator, objects and entities that possess a Form only potentially still have a trace of that Form; thus light can be known through its trace (as it were) in the transparent.

ὁ δὲ ζητῶν ἔτι ἀπὸ τῶν αἰτιατῶν καὶ ὡς πρὸς ἡμᾶς πρώτων . . . The commentator makes an analogy from the normal procedure of investigation in the sciences to the present inquiry into light. Just as one knows what the Form is by first seeing it in the material substrate, so too one comes to recognize what light is by seeing it instantiated in the transparent. Indeed, the commentator puns on the clarity of light (τί γὰρ ἂν εἴη φωτὸς ἐναργέστερον;), making the point that if one can come to know a Form in matter, a fortiori one can know light in the transparent.

ὅτι δὲ ἀσώματον καὶ ὅτι οὐ πάθος ἀλλ᾿ ἐνέργεια . . . This is Iamblichus' doctrine, as given by Priscianus (9.13-14). Our commentator explains what Priscianus did not, that light is incorporeal because it travels freely through the transparent. Like Priscianus, he argues that it is an actualization and not an affection because it comes and goes all at once with no interval of time.

ἔνυλον δέ, εἴπερ σῶμα, τὸ ἀπὸ τοῦ φωτὸς πῦρ . . . The distinction between corporeal fire and incorporeal light is Iamblichean. See Finamore (in Blumenthal and Clark) 58-61.

ἆρα οὖν οὐσία ὡς ἡ ἀπὸ τῆς ψυχῆς τῷ σώματι ἐνδιδομένη ζωή; Having stated that light is incorporeal and not an affection of a body, the commentator must say how light is an actualization of the transparent. Cp. Priscianus 9.26-31. The commentator raises a question not raised by Priscianus: is light present in the transparent as life is present in the body? There is a similarity, he says, in that both light and life become present and depart all at once (ἀθρόως, 132.6). There are differences too. The organic body must gradually come into existence before life can enter it, but the transparent (which for Iamblichus is Form) always exists as it is (although sometimes actualized by light and sometimes by darkness). It undergoes no such gradual change. Further, when the Form of Life leaves, the body perishes and decays. When light leaves, the transparent does neither. Finally, life, the Form which determines the living creature, is itself a substance and receptive of opposites. Light is not a substance but an actualization.

οὔτε δὲ ὁ πεφωτισμένος ἀὴρ ὡς πεφωτισμένος οὐσία . . . These words begin a difficult sentence. Having argued that Life is a substance and receptive of opposites, the commentator now goes on to say that light is neither. Illuminated air is not a substance because it is illuminated, just as heated air is not a substance because it is heated.[16] Then follows a disjunction: "neither it (αὐτός) nor light is receptive of opposites." To what does "it" refer? The only masculine noun in the sentence is "air," but certainly air is receptive of opposites. The flow of the argument seems to require "heat" (τὸ θερμόν), but that is neuter as well. The commentator must then be thinking not of air unqualified but of "illuminated air" and "heated air." Heated air cannot admit of cold, or it would cease to be heated; illuminated air cannot admit of darkness or it would cease to be illuminated. Just so, light cannot admit of darkness and remain what it is. Thus, the commentator says, "no change precedes its presence or follows upon its departure." That is to say, no change in light (not in the medium). Light remains what it is.

---

[16] This is clearly the meaning of the Greek. Steel (in Huby and Steel, 162) translates: "But neither is the illuminated air substance *qua* illuminated, just as the adventitiously warmed is not." But "the adventitiously warmed" would require the neuter (τὸ ἐπικτήτως θερμανθέν) not the masculine (ὁ ἐπικτήτως θερμανθείς), which must refer to ἀήρ.

καθάπερ οὐδὲ ὁ ἐπικτήτως θερμανθείς . . . The adverb ἐπικτήτως appears only once in Priscianus (21.15, in a different context), eighteen times in the present text,[17] and nowhere else. This variation offers further proof that Priscianus and the Pseudo-Simplicius are different authors.

ἀλλ' ἔστιν αὐτὸ τοῦτο ἐνέργεια . . . For the remainder of the argument, see also Priscianus 9.25-31. Both writers make similar points, which argues for a common Iamblichean source. For οὐχ ὡς ἐν ὑποκειμένῳ ἐγγινομένη τῷ διαφανεῖ, χωριστῶς δὲ αὐτῷ παροῦσα καὶ τελειοῦσα αὐτό, see Priscianus 9.26-27: οὐχ ὡς πάθος, φήσω, οὐδὲ ὡς τελειότης αὐτοῦ ἐν ὑποκειμένῳ αὐτῷ γενομένη, ἀλλ' ὡς χωριστῶς αὐτὸ τελειοῦσα. For οὐδέποτε τοῦ προάγοντος αὐτὴν χωριζομένη, ἀλλ' ἐκείνῳ ἐνιδρυμένη, καὶ ἐκείνου ἐχομένη, see Priscianus 9.28-29: οὐκ αὐτὴ ἐκείνου ἀλλ' ἑαυτῆς ἐκεῖνο ποιουμένη, μένουσα συνεχὴς αὐτὴ τῷ ἐλλάμποντι καὶ ἐκείνῳ συμπεριαγομένη.

---

[17]   49.3; 59.28; 59.30; 68.19; 87.8; 129.5; 132.29; 219.19; 219.20; 228.2; 236.27; 239.7; 316.18; 316.19; 316.24; 316.37; 318.12; 318.27.

BIBLIOGRAPHY

Primary Sources

ALCINOUS. *Alcinoou Didaskalikos tôn Platônos Dogmatôn,* in *Platonis Dialogi Secundum Thrasylli Tetralogias Dispositi.* Ed. C.F. Hermann. Vol. 6. 3rd ed. Leipzig 1907.

ALEXANDER OF APHRODISIAS. *De Anima.* In *Supplementum Aristotelicum,* vol. 2, pt. 1. Ed. I Bruns. Berlin 1887.

ARISTOTLE. *Ethica Nicomachea.* Ed. I. Bywater. Oxford 1894, rpt. 1962.
Metaphysica. 2 Vols. Ed. W. D. Ross. Oxford 1924, rpt. 1970.
Physica. Ed. W. D. Ross. Oxford 1950, rpt. 1966.
De Anima. Ed. and tr. R. D. Hicks. Cambridge 1907.
De Anima. Ed. W. D. Ross. Oxford 1961, rpt. 1967.

CHALDAEAN ORACLES. *The Chaldaean Oracles.* Ed. and Tr. R. Majercik. Leiden 1989.
Oracles Chaldaïques. Tr. and ed. E. Des Places. Paris 1971.

CICERO. *Academica.* Ed. J. S. Reid. London 1885.
De Finibus Bonorum et Malorum. Ed. T. Schiche. Stuttgart 1915.
Tusculan Disputations. Ed. T. W. Dougan and R. M. Henry. Oxford 1905-1934.

CLEMENT OF ALEXANDRIA. *Stromata.* Ed. O. Stählin, L. Früchtel, and U. Treu. Berlin 1960 and 1970.

Corpus Hermeticum. Hermès Trismégiste. 4 vols. Ed. A. D. Nock and tr. A. J. Festugière. Paris 1954-1960.

DAMASCIUS. *In Platonis Phaedonem Commentaria.* Ed. and tr. L. G. Westerink. Amsterdam 1977.

EPICURUS. *Epicurea.* Ed. H. Usener. Leipzig 1887; rpt. Stuttgart 1966.

GALEN. *De Placitis Hippocratis et Platonis.* Ed. I. Mueller. Leipzig 1874.

HERMIAS. *In Platonis Phaedrum Scholia.* Ed. P. Couvreur. Paris 1901; rpt. Hildesheim 1971.

IAMBLICHUS. *De Communi Mathematica Scientia.* Ed. U. Klein. Leipzig 1894, rpt. Stuttgart 1975.
De Mysteriis. Ed. and tr. É. Des Places. Paris 1966.
De Vita Pythagorica. Ed. U. Klein. Leipzig 1937, rpt. Stuttgart 1975.
In Nicomachi Arithmeticam Introductionem. Ed. H. Pistelli and U. Klein. Stuttgart 1975.
Protrepticus. Ed. H. Pistelli. Stuttgart and Leipzig 1888; rpt. 1996

JULIAN. *Oeuvres Completès.* 3 vols. Tr. and ed. Bidez-Cumont-Rochefort-Lacombrade. Paris 1932-1964.

LUCRETIUS. *De Rerum Natura.* Tr. and ed. C. Bailey. Oxford 1947.

NEMESIUS. *De Natura Hominis.* Ed. M. Morani. Leipzig 1987.
De Natura Hominis. Ed. C. Matthaei. Magdeburg 1802.

NUMENIUS. *Fragments.* Tr. and ed. E. Des Places. Paris 1973.

OLYMPIODORUS. *In Platonis Phaedonem Commentaria.* Ed. and tr. L. G. Westerink. Amsterdam 1976.
On the Alcibiades. Ed. L. G. Westerink. Amsterdam 1966.

ORPHICA. *Orphicorum Fragmenta.* Ed. O. Kern. Berlin 1922.

PHILOPONUS. *In Aristotelis De Anima Commentaria,* in *Commentaria in Aristotelem Graeca.* Vol. 15. Ed. M. Hayduck. Berlin 1897.

PHOTIUS. *Bibliotèque.* Ed. R. Henry. 8 vols. Paris 1959-1977.

PLATO. *Platonis Opera.* Ed. J. Burnet. 5 vols. Oxford 1900-1907.

PLOTINUS. *Les Ennéades de Plotin.* 3 vols. Ed. and tr. M. H. Bouillet. Paris 1857-1861; rep. Frankfurt 1968.
Opera. 3 vols. Ed. P. Henry and H. R. Schwyzer. Oxford 1964-1982.
Plotinus. 7 vols. Tr. and ed. H. Armstrong. Cambridge 1966-1995.

PLUTARCH. *Moralia.* Various eds. 7 vols. Leipzig 1959.

PORPHYRY. *Porphyre: De l'abstinence.* 2 vols. Ed. and tr. J. Bouffartigue and M. Patillon. Paris 1977.
Porphyrii Philosophi Fragmenta. Ed. A. Smith. Leipzig1993.
Porphyrii: Sententiae Ad Intelligibilia Ducentes. Ed. E. Lamberz. Leipzig 1975.
Pros Gauron Peri tou Pôs Empsuchoutai ta Embrua (Ad Gaurum), in *Abhandl. d. Preuss. Akad. d. Wiss.* Ed. K. Kalbfleisch 1895.

PRESOCRATIC PHILOSOPHERS. *Die Fragmente der Vorsokratiker.* 6th ed. 3 Vols. Ed. H. Diels and W. Kranz. Berlin 1951-1952.

PRISCIANUS. *Metaphrasis in Theophrastum,* in *Commentaria in Aristotelem Graeca.* Suppl. 1.2. Ed. I. Bywater. Berlin 1886.

PROCLUS. *Commentarium in Platonis Parmenidem.* 2nd ed. Ed. V. Cousin. Paris 1864; rpt. Hildesheim 1961.
Commentary on the First Alcibiades of Plato. Ed. L. G. Westerink. Amsterdam 1954.
The Elements of Theology. 2nd ed. Ed. and tr. E. R. Dodds. Oxford 1963.
In Platonis Cratylum Commentaria. Ed. G. Pasquali. Leipzig 1908.
In Platonis Rempublicam Commentaria. 2 vols. Ed. W. Kroll. Leipzig 1899-1901; rpt. Amsterdam 1965.

In Platonis Timaeum Commentaria. 3 vols. Ed. E. Diehl. Leipzig 1903-1906; rpt. Amsterdam 1965.

Théologie Platonicienne. 6 vols. Tr. and ed. H. D. Saffrey and L. G. Westerink. Paris 1968-1997.

PSEUDO-SIMPLICIUS. *Simplicii in Libros Aristotelis De Anima Commentaria,* in *Commentaria in Aristotelem Graeca.* Vol. 11. Ed. M. Hayduck. Berlin 1882.

SALLUSTIUS. *Concerning the Gods and the Universe.* Tr. and ed. A. D. Nock. Hildesheim 1966.

Saloustios, des Dieux et du Monde, Ed. G. Rocheford. Paris 1983.

SIMPLICIUS. *In Aristotelis Categorias Commentarium,* in *Commentaria in Aristotelem Graeca.* Vol. 8. Ed. K. Kalbfleisch. Berlin 1907.

In Aristotelis De Caelo Commentaria, in *Commentaria in Aristotelem Graeca.* Vol. 7. Ed. J. L. Heiberg. Berlin 1894.

In Aristotelis Physicorum Octo Commentaria, in *Commentaria in Aristotelem Graeca.* Vols. 9-10. Ed. H. Diels. Berlin 1882-1895.

STOBAEUS, IOANNIS. *Anthologii Libri Duo Priores Qui Inscribi Solent Eclogae Physicae et Ethicae.* 2 vols. Ed. C. Wachsmuth. Berlin 1884; rpt. 1958.

Anthologii Libri Duo Posteriores. 3 vols. Ed. O. Hense. Berlin 1894-1923; rpt. 1958.

Stoicorum Veterum Fragmenta. 3 vols. Ed. J. von Arnim. Leipzig 1903-1905. Vol. 4, indices by M. Adler. Leipzig 1924.

THEMISTIUS. *In Libros Aristotelis De Anima Paraphrasis,* in *Commentaria in Aristotelem Graeca.* Vol. 5.6. Ed. R. Heinze. Berlin 1903.

Secondary Sources

ARMSTRONG, A. H. *Plotinus.* 7 vols. Cambridge 1966-1995.

ATHANASSIADI, P. *Damascius, The Philosophical History.* Athens 1999.

BAZÁN, F. "Jámblicho y el Descenso del Alma: Síntesis de Doctrinas y Relectura Neoplatónica," in Blumenthal and Finamore, 129-147.

BIDEZ, J. *Vie de Porphyre.* Ghent and Leipzig 1913.

BLUMENTHAL, H. J. *Aristotle and Neoplatonism in Late Antiquity: Interpretations of the* De Anima. Ithaca 1996.

——, "Did Iamblichus write a Commentary on the *De Anima?*" *Hermes* 102 (1974) 540-556.

——, "Neoplatonic Elements in the *De Anima* Commentaries," *Phronesis* 21 (1976) 64-87, reprinted in R. SORABJI, *Aristotle Transformed* 305-324.

——, "The Psychology of (?) Simplicius' Commentary on the *De Anima*," in BLUMENTHAL and LLOYD, 73-93.

——, "Simplicius(?) on the First Book of Aristotle's *De Anima* ," in I. HADOT (ed.), *Simplicius: sa vie, son oeuvre, sa survie*, Berlin-New York, 1987, 91-112.

——, "Soul, world-soul, and individual soul in Plotinus," in *Le Néoplatonisme, Colloques internationaux du CNRS*, Paris, 1971, 55-63 (rpt. in his collected essays, *Soul and Intellect*, Aldershot (1993).

BLUMENTHAL, H. J. and CLARK, E. G. *The Divine Iamblichus: Philosopher and Man of Gods*. Bristol 1993.

BLUMENTHAL, H. J. and FINAMORE, J. F. *Iamblichus: The Philosopher. Syllecta Classica* 8 (1997).

BLUMENTHAL, H. J. and A. C. LLOYD. *Soul and the Structure of Being in Late Platonism: Syrianus, Proclus, Simplicius*. Liverpool 1982.

BRISSON, L. "'Amélius: sa vie, son oeuvre, sa doctrine, son style." *ANRW* 2.36.2 (1987) 836-47.

——, "Démocritus," in *Dictionnaire des Philosophes Antiques* II, R. GOULET (ed.), Paris (1994) 716-717.

BURKERT, W. *Lore and Science in Ancient Pythagoreanism*. Translated by E. L. Minar, Jr. Cambridge 1972.

——, "Plotin, Plutarch und die Platonisierende Interpretation von Heraklit und Empedokles," in J. MANSFELD and L. M. DE RIJK (edd.), *Kephalaion: Studies in Greek Philosophy and its Continuation, Offered to Professor C. J. De Vogel*, Assen (1975) 137-146.

CAMERON, A. "The Date of Iamblichus' Birth." *Hermes* 96 (1969), 374-6.

CUMONT, F. *After Life in Roman Paganism*. New Haven 1922.

DES PLACES, E. *Numénius: Fragments*. Paris 1973.

DEUSE, W. *Theodoros von Asine: Sammlung der Testimonien und Kommentar*. Wiesbaden 1973.

DIHLE, A. "Der Platoniker Ptolemaios," *Hermes* 85 (1957) 315-325.

DILLON, J. M. *Alcinous: The Handbook of Platonism*. Oxford 1993.

——, "*Asomatos*: Nuances of Incorporeality in Philo," in. C. LÉVY (ed.) *Philon D'Alexandrie et Le Langage De La Philosophie* (Brepols 1998) 99-110.

——, "Harpocration's Commentary on Plato...", *CSCA* 4 (1971), 125-7 (repr. in *The Golden Chain*, Aldershot, 1990, Essay XIV).

——, *Iamblichi Chalcidensis in Platonis Dialogos Commentariorum Fragmenta*. Edited with translation and commentary. Philosophia Antiqua 23. Leiden, 1973.

——, "Iamblichus of Chalcis (ca. AD 240-325)," in *Aufstieg und Nieder-gang der römischen Welt* II, 36.2 Berlin and New York 1987, 862-909.

——, *The Middle Platonists. A Study of Platonism 80 B.C. to A.D. 220.* London 1977.

——, "The Theory of the Three Classes of Men in Plotinus and Philo," in R. LINK-SALINGER (ed.), *Scholars, Savants, and their Texts: Studies in Philosophy and Religious Thought in Honor of Arthur Hyman* (New York 1989) 69-76, reprinted in J. M. DILLON, *The Golden Chain* (Aldershot 1990) 69-76.

FESTUGIÈRE, A.J. *Commentaire sur le Timée.* 5 vols. Paris 1966-1968.

——, *La Révélation d'Hermès Trismégiste,* Vol. 3. Paris 1953.

FINAMORE, J. F. *Iamblichus and the Theory of the Vehicle of the Soul.* Chico 1985.

——, "Iamblichus on Light and the Transparent," in BLUMENTHAL and CLARK, 55-64.

——, "Julian and the Descent of Asclepius." *Journal of Neoplatonic Studies* (forthcoming).

——, "The Rational Soul in Iamblichus' Philosophy," in BLUMEN-THAL and FINAMORE, (1997) 163-176.

——, "What the Hades? Iamblichus and Proclus on Judges and Judgment in the Afterlife." *Mediterranean Perspectives: Philosophy, Literature, and History* 1 (1998) 45-59.

GOTTSCHALK, H. B. *Heraclides of Pontus.* Oxford 1980.

GUTHRIE, W. K. C. *A History of Greek Philosophy.* 6 Vols. Cambridge 1962-1981.

——, *Orpheus and Greek Religion.* 2nd ed. Princeton 1993.

HADOT, I. "The Life and Work of Simplicius in Arabic Sources," in R. SORABJI, *Aristotle Transformed* 275-303.

HUBY, P. "Priscian of Lydia as Evidence for Iamblichus, "in BLUMEN-THAL and CLARK, 5-12.

HUBY, P. and STEEL, C. *Priscian On Theophrastus' On Sense Perception and "Simplicius" On Aristotle's On the Soul 2.5-12.* Ithaca 1997.

INWOOD, B. *Ethics and Human Action in Early Stoicism.* Oxford 1985.

LAKS, A. *Diogène d'Apollonie.* Lille 1983.

LEWY, H. *The Chaldaean Oracles and Theurgy.* Paris 1978.

LONG, A. A. "Soul and Body in Stoicism." *Phronesis* 27 (1982) 49-51.

LONG, A. A. and D. N. SEDLEY. *The Hellenistic Philosophers.* 2 vols. Cambridge 1987.

MANSFELD, J. "Doxography and Dialectic: The *Sitz im Leben* of the 'Placita.'" *ANRW* 2.36.4 (1990) 3056-3215.

——, "Heraclitus, Empedocles, and Others in a Middle Platonic Cento in Philo of Alexandria." *Vigiliae Christianae* 39 (1985) 131-156. Rpt. in J. MANSFELD, *Studies in Later Greek Philosophy and Gnosticism* (London 1989).

——, *Heresiology in Context: Hippolytus' Elenchos as a Source for Greek Philosophy.* Leiden 1992.

MANSFELD, J. and RUNIA, D. T. *Aëtiana: The Method and Intellectual Context of a Doxographer.* Vol. 1. Leiden 1997.

O'MEARA, D. J. *Pythagoras Revived: Mathematics and Philosophy in Late Antiquity.* Oxford 1989.

PICCIONE, R. M. "Caratterizzazione di lemmi nell' *Anthologion* di Giovanni Stobeo." *Rivista di Filologia e di Instruzione Classica.* 127 (1999) 139-175.

RIST, J.M. 'The Problem of 'Otherness' in the *Enneads'*, in *le Néo-platonisme: Colloques internationaux de la C.N.R.S.*, Paris, 1971, 77-87, repr. in *Platonism and its Christian Heritage*, Aldershot, 1985

ROBINSON, T. M. *Plato's Psychology.* 2nd ed. Toronto 1995.

SMITH, A. *Porphyry's Place in the Neoplatonic Tradition.* The Hague 1974.

SOLMSEN, F. "Eratosthenes as Platonist and Poet," *TAPA* 73 (1942) 192-213.

SORABJI, R. *Aristotle Transformed: The Ancient Commentators and their Influence.* Ithaca 1990.

STEEL, C. *The Changing Self, A Study on the Soul in Later Neoplatonism: Iamblichus, Damascius, and Priscianus.* Brussels1978.

STEEL, C. and BOISSIER F. "Priscianus Lydus en de *in De Anima* van Pseudo (?)-Simplicius." *Tijdschrift voor filosofie* 34 (1972), 761-822.

TARÁN, L. *Speusippus of Athens: A Critical Study with a Collection of the Related Texts and Commentary.* Leiden 1981.

THEILER, W. 'Ein vergessenes Aristoteleszeugnis', *JHS* 77 (1957), 127-131.

THESLEFF, H., *The Pythagorean Texts of the Hellenistic Period.* Abo Akademi 1965.

TODD, R. B. *Themistius on Aristotle's On the Soul.* Ithaca 1996.

URMSON, J. O. *Simplicius: On Aristotle's On The Soul 1.1-2.4.* Ithaca 1995.

VANDERSPOEL, J. "Themistios and the Origin of Iamblichos." *Hermes* 116 (1988), 125-33.

WEHRLI, F. *Die Schule des Aristoteles; Texte und Kommentar.* 10 vols. Basel 1944-1959.

Westerink, L. G. *Anonymous Prolegomena to Platonic Philosophy.* Amsterdam 1962.

——, *The Greek Commentaries on Plato's Phaedo.* 2 vols. Ed. and tr. L. G. Westerink. Amsterdam 1976-1977.

INDEX LOCORUM

Aesarus of Lucania
"On the Nature of Man"   113

Aetius
Placita
4.2, 1, p. 386b   83
4.3, 6, p. 388   96
5.24, 2   178

Alcinous (Albinus)
Didaskalikos
178.16-23   167
178, 34ff.   136
178.34-39   164
178.35   165
178.37-39   167
178.39   136 note #63

Alexander of Aphrodisias
1.29   169
17.11-15   102
20.26-21.13   102
21.4-5   120
21.13-21   102
21.22-24.17   120
22.7-10   120
22.23-23.5   120
23.29-24.1   120
27.4-7   109
30.26-31.6   110
30.29-31.1   106
31.1-4   104, 106
31.4-6   104
39.8   120
80.16-81.22   118
81.13-15   118
108.22-109.1   106
115.5   79
118.6-9   109

Aristotle
De Anima
402b1-5   105
403a25   189
403b25ff.   76
403b31ff.   78
404a3-4   180
404b18-24   85
404b28   76
404b29   82 note #6
405a6ff   76
405a18   76
405a21ff.   76

405a24   76
405b2   94
405b11-12   76
405b13   76
405b23ff.   95
405b30-b25   119
406b24-25   120
408b32 ff.   82 note #6
409a9-10   147
410b27-30   144
411a26-b3   105
411b5   105
411b5-30   105
411b7   105
411b8-9   105
411b9-14   105
411b14-19   105
411b19-24   105
411b19-30   147
412a6-22   170
412a19-21   179
412a19   78
412a27   101
412a27-29   168
412b5   95
412b16-17   168
413a8-9   169
413a23-25   114
413b11-13   114
413b13-32   105
413b16-19   147
413b16-24   105
413b24-27   105
413b27-32   105
414a12-14   179
414a29-32   114
414b29   102
415a14-22   119
418a26-419b3   270
418b3   274
418b18-19   271
419a2-3   271 note #11
428a5-15   266
428a15-18   266
424a18-19   264 note #5
428a18-428b1   266
428b10-13   266
428b10-17   264 note #6
428b11   264 note #6
428b13-14   264 note #6
420b29   178
430a3-5   189
431a16-17   77

(ARISTOTLE, *De Anima*, cont.)
430a22-23   220, 255, 256, 257
431a14-17   269
431b2   77
431b12-16   221
432a22-b3   105
432a22-b7   105, 114
432b3-7   105
433a9-10   120
433a10   263 note #4
433a9-12   263 note #4
433b1-5   114
433b29-30   263 note #4
434a5-7   263 note #4
434a7   263 note #4
434a16-21   120
439a17   118

1.2   76, 82 note #6, 85
1.4   82 note #6
2.5   119
3.3   266
3.5   93, 118
3.10-11   120

De generatione et corruptione
736b28   118

De Memoria
451a14   117

Metaphysica
986a6   192
985b26ff.   82
1020a33ff.   79
1028b15-27   80
1065b14ff.   77
1090b20ff   86 note #10

Nicomachean Ethics.
1102b28-1103a1   110
1131a24-33   196
1132b21-1133a5   196
1133a5   222
1140b26   190
1177b26ff.   174

1.13   114
5.3   196
5.4   196
5.5   196
6.5   190

Peri Philosophias   85 note #11

Politeia
1301b26-1302a1   196

Physica
201a8ff.   77

ATTICUS
247.12-14   127 note #51

AURELIUS, MARCUS
10.38   185
11.12   131 note#57

CHALDAEAN ORACLES
Fr. 138   173, 206, 226
Fr. 163   197

CHRYSIPPUS
3.181   118

CICERO
Tusculan Disputations
1.10   97, 99

Lucullus (= *Academica* book 2)
129-131   173
129   174
130   174
131   175

De Finibus
2.34-35   173
5.16-23   173
5.20   175

CLEMENT
Stromateis
2.133.4   175
4.45   180

Corpus Hermeticum
10.7   95 note #32
10.17   185

CRONIUS
Fr. 43   137
Fr. 52, ll. 64ff   134

DAMASCIUS
In Parm.
2.137.18   84 note #9

In Phaed.
1.93   220
1.177   116, 222
1.177.1-2   222
1.481   191, 203
1.481.1   194
1.481.4-7; 2.99   194
1.482   191, 194
1.503.3   115
1.505.4-5   217

(DAMASCIUS, *In Parm.* cont.)
1.509.2-3   216
1.509.4-5   225 note #92
1.543   204
1.547   200
1.551   204
2.146   204
2.99   191, 194
2.147   200
2.542   194

DIOGENES OF APOLLONIA
64B4 D-K = Fr. 8   178
64B5 = Fr. 9   178
64A19 D-K   178
64A29 D-K   178

EMPEDOCLES
Fr. 155.13   20 note #52

EPICHARMUS
23B10 D-K   180

EPICURUS
Epistola Ad Menoeceum
62,12   175

*Epistola ad Herodotus*m 63   180

EUNAPIUS
Vitae Sophistarum
457   1, 2, 3
458   8
458-459   6
459   7

EUSEBIUS
Praep. Evang
15.15   173

GALEN
De Placitis Hippocratis et Platonis
643   157

HERACLITUS
Fr. 84a   21 note #52

HERMEIAS
In Phaedrum
104.7   166
104.9   166
104.15   166
157.5-159.3   160
160.18-20   189
162.29-163.19   200

HIPPOCRATES
Nat. Puer. 18   163

HIPPOLYTUS
Refutation of All Heresies
I 15, 2   82

IAMBLICHUS
De Communi Mathemetica Scientia
9   80
15.40   101
17.38   101

De Mysteriis
1.5   217
1.5 (15.9-10)   217
1.5-7   126
1.6, (19.13)   143
1.7 (21.8)   121
1.7 (21.7-10)   121
1.7 (22.1-8)   121
1.8   157
1.8: 23   143
1.8, (25.9)   165
1.8 (28.16-29.3)   273
1.9 (30.13-19)   273
1.12 (41.18-42.1) 198
1.14 (45.1)   218
1.15 (46.13-14)   211
1.20 (64.8)   171
1.21 (65.16-66.2) 212
1.39.28-40.4   188
2.1   193
2.2   172, 206, 207
2.5 (79.7-11)   193
2.5 (80.6-7)   91 note #24
2.6 (83.3)   226
2.7 (84.16)   171
2.7 (84.11-15)   217-218
2.7 (85.1-2)   218
3.6 (113.7-114.2) 260 note 2
3.9 (119.1-2)   218
3.14 (132.11-17)   260 note #2
3.16 (188.12-15)   273
3.21   127 note #48
3.3   102
3.31 (178.3-179.12) 198
3.31 (180.12)   101
4.5   188 note #84
4.5 (187.13)   101
4.6   112
5.15 (219.7-12)   198
5.18 (223.10-224.2) 161, 212
5.18 (225.1-5)   162
5.18   159, 161
5.18-19   198
5.20   204
5.22   204
6.3   189
8.3 (264.14)   101
8.4 (267.5)   101
8.5 (268.14)   112

(IAMBLICHUS, *De Mysteriis* cont.)
8.6 (269.1-12)   116
10.3 (288.7-12)   212
10.3 (288.12-15)   188 note #84
10.4   212
10.6   198
10.7   204

In Alcibiadem
Fr. 8   211

In Nicomachi Intr. Arith.
10.20   84

*In Phaedo*nem
Fr. 5   162, 192, 200

In Phaedrum
Fr. 2   166
Fr. 6   169, 204, 210-211
Fr. 7   162

In Philebum
Fr. 6   201

In Sophistam
Fr. 1.1-2   193

In Timaeum
Fr. 7   81
Fr. 10   189
Fr. 16.9   171
Fr. 22   171
Fr. 39   89
Fr. 42   219
Fr. 49.51   171
Fr. 50   145
Fr. 53   87
Fr. 54-56   145
Fr. 54.8-11   150
Fr. 56   145
Fr. 57   128 note #54
Fr. 62-63   21 note #54
Fr. 67-68   21 note #54
Fr. 70.18-19   225
Fr. 81   98, 116, 182, 184
Fr. 81.6-10   186
Fr. 82   126, 151
Fr. 84   98, 184
Fr. 84.4-7   186
Fr. 87   90, 168, 254, 258
Fr. 88   227
Fr. 89   21 note #54
Fr. 90   21 note #54

Protrepticus
70.9ff   198
108.3-4   197
122.22-123.2   197

Vita Pythagorica
6.30.3   228 note #97
17.71-18.92   228 note #96
18.80.11   228 note #97
19.90.8   228 note #97
19.90.10   228 note #97
29.158.8   228 note #97
29.164.9   228 note #97
34.246.10   228 note #97
35.266   113

JULIAN
Epistulae
181   8 note #18
183-187   8 note #18

Hymn to the Mother of the Gods
5, 162C   139

LUCRETIUS
2.114-115   180

LYDUS, JOHN
De Mensibus 167.21 ff. 202

MACROBIUS
In Somnium Scipionis
1, 14, 20   98 note #34
2.3.15   88

NEMESIUS OF EMESA
De Natura Hominis
51   141-142

NUMENIUS
Frs. 11-16   89
fr. 36   163
Fr. 41   89 note #20
Fr. 43   137
Fr. 44   116, 134
Fr. 52   134, 137

ORPHICA
Fr. 27   94
Fr. 32   145
Fr. 228ab   145
Fr. 228 cd   145

OLYMPIODORUS
In Alc.
60.5-7   225 note #93
70   115

In Phd.
10.14.1-8   206
10.14.8-10   206

ORIGEN
Com. In Joh. 1.5.   76 note #1

PHILO OF ALEXANDRIA
Somn
1.30   97

PHILOPONUS

In De Anima
35.12   109

De Anima
224.10-225.31   169
224.28-37   169-170

PLATO
Cratylus,
399E   94

Gorgias
482c4   128 note #52
523a-524a   187
523a-526d   174, 191
524a   191
524a-525d   200
525a   191
525a7   200
525ab   196
525b   199
526c5   201
526cd   203
526b7   201

Laws
854d   196
894b-895b   166
904c-e   201
904c-905c   191
904de   204

Phaedo
69e6-72e2   206
72b1-3   206
78b   101
80c-81e   174
84a   189
85e ff.   86
91d1-2   123
91d-92e   123
107d   177
107de   194
113d-114c   191
113d8-e1   196
113de   200, 201
113e6   200
114ab   191
114bc   201, 203,
                       204
114c2   191
114c2-4   203

Phaedrus
245c5   166
246ab   101, 107
246b6   223
246b6-7   225
246bc   225 note #93
246c1-2   224
247b1   192
247c1-2   224
247c-e   160
247c7   169
247d4   224
248a   127 note #50,
                       160
248a-d   200
248ab   161
248b   189
248b4   160
248b5   189
248c   161, 162
248c-249d   191
248c3   160
248c3-5   200
248c3-8   200
248c4   200,
248cd   161
248c-e   161
248e-249c   161
249a   200
249a5   200
249a5-6   201
249a6-7   191, 200, 201
249a7-8   191
249a7-9   200
249a7-b1   204
249ab   203
250c1-3   160
250c5-6   153
250e1   160
251a2   160
253c-e   101
256b1   201

Politicus
297a   33

Republic
435a-442d   101
436ab   105
440e-441a   107
464a9   157
488a-489a   168
546b3-4   148
554e4   201
580de   101
614b-616c   187
614b-621b   191
614c3-6   203
614cd   191, 200
614c-e   203

(PHILOPONUS, *Republic,* cont.)

614d7-e4	203
614e5-6	201
615a-616b	174
615a2	201
615ab	196
615b7-c1	196
615e-616a	191
616a4	201
617d-620d	175
617e4-5	192
618b6-c6	175
618e2-3	176
620de	177
611a4-9	148

Theaetetus

176ab	187
176b1	223
191c8-9	262
191c-e	262, 264
191d2-e1	262
194a8-b6	197
194b2-4	197

Timaeus

18cd	144
30a4	158
31b-32c	86
33c	132
35a	80, 83, 91 note #26, 92
35a-36d	86
35bc	87, 144
37.4-6	110
39d2-7	148
39e3-40a2	155
41a3-5	193
41b7-c2	155
41d	127, 127 note #49, 128, 129, 225
41d1-2	182
41d-42a	150
41d4-7	151
41d8-e1	148
41e	127, 170
41e4-42a1	216
42a-d	187
42d4-5	216
43a-44d	163
43d-44a	118
43d	86
44d7	118
44de	184
47-49	155
69b-71a	101
69c	170
69c-71a	184
69d-70e	107

70d1	178
77b5	180
77e1	180
78c6	178
86bff.	138 note #67
89e	101
91b7-c7	165
93.33-94.2	110
Not Specified	

PLOTINUS
Enneads

1.1.2	114
1.1.2.25-26	114
1.1.3.20-24	169
1.1.3.21-26	202
1.1.6-9	114
1.1.7	114
1.2.4	190, 202
1.2.4.5-7	187
1.2.4.13	211
1.2.4.16	190
1.2.4.17	190
1.2.4.18	190
1.2.4.19-20	190
1.2.4.20-23	190
1.2.5	198
1.2.5.6-7	198
1.2.5.7-8	198
1.2.5.22-32	198
1.2	187
1.2.1.1-6	187
1.2.3.11-19	187
1.2.3.19-21	187
1,2.3.20	187
1.2.4.5-7	187, 198
1.2.5	198
1.3.1.28ff.	87
1.6.3.28ff.	87
1.6.5.49	131
1.8	138, 139
1.8.8	138
2.9	131, 136
2.9.4.6-8	171
2.9.10-12	136
2.9.10.19	171
3.4.3.1-2	210
3.4.3.22ff.	89
3.4.5	177
3.6.1-5	134
3.6.4.41-52	87
3.6.5.14-30	190
3.6.5.24	190
3.6.5.23ff.	131
3.6.5.25	131
4.1.1.41ff	91 note #26
4.2	128
4.3.1-8	90
4.3.3	167
4.3.3.8-9	168

(PLOTINUS, *Enneads*, cont.)
4.3.4.14ff.	124
4.3.4.22ff.	131
4.3.4.26ff.	125
4.3.9	157, 163
4.3.9.1-8	134, 151
4.3.9.8	165
4.3.9.9-10	157
4.3.9.37-8	157
4.3.15.1-5	184
4.3.18	114, 212
4.3.20.30-34	171
4.3.21	169
4.3.21.5-8	169
4.3.21.9-11	169
4.3.21.11-12	169
4.3.21.11-21	171
4.3.22.12-18	168
4.3.23	167
4.3.26-32	114
4.3.23.33	168
4.4.1-7	114
4.4.44.31ff.	139
4.4.8.54	131
4.7.8	86, 87
4.7.9-13	87 note #18
4.7.10	187
4.7.10.11-20	187
4.7.10.41-47	187
4.7.14	181
4.8.1	21 note #52, 135, 154
4.8.1.11-23	135
4.8.1.12-17	154
4.8.1.40-50	155
4.8.5	154, 156
4.8, 5.5-8	135 note #61
4.8.6.1ff.	93
4.9	90, 125
5.1	90, 135
5.1.1,.2	136
5.1.1.2-6	135
5.1.1.5	20 note #52
5.1.12.1-10	129
6.4.4.	126
6.4.4.37ff.	126

PLUTARCH
Proc. An.
1012DE	82 note #6, 83, 158
1014BC	134

Isis et Osiris
369E	137 #64
371B	137 #64
370EF	137 #64

Def. Or.
415B	209

428E	137 #64

PORPHYRY
De Abst.
1.47.8	92 note #30
2.47.14	92 note #30
3.2-6	142 note #76
3.7	142 note #76
3.27	139
4.20	139

Ad Aneb.
2.3a	92 note #30

Ad Gaurum
35.9ff	165
35.11	165
35.16	165

Concerning the Powers of the Soul
253F.1-122	108, 110
253F.11-18	110,
253F.14-15	113
253F.15-18	113
253F.32-33	110
253F.33-36	108
253F.37-42	108
253F.48	109
253F. 63-76	108
253F.68-70	104
253F.77-87	110
253F.88-109	111
253F.100-107	111
253F.100-109	111
253F.107-109	111
253F.110-122	111
253F.116-117	111
253F.120-122	111
255F	117

De Regressu
Fr. 11	212, 223

Letter to Anebo	143

On the Soul: Against Boethus
	125

Sententiae
3-4	171
7	131
10	89, 90
18	87
28	171
30	90
37	125-126, 134
37.16-19	116
40	223

Vit. Plot.
3   88
9   1
      20.31 and 60
      114-115

PRISCIANUS
Metaphrasis in Theophrastum
8.1-15.5   23 note #60
8.9-14   270-271
8.15-16   271
8.16   271
10.30-32   272 note #11
10.31-11.14   22
11.1-5   272 note #11
12.17-28   274
23.25-26   261
24.24-29   269
24.24-25.1   267 note #7
24.28   269
25.1-3   267 note #8
25.11   268
25.10-13   268
25.10-15   269
31.32-33   22

PROCLUS
Elem. Theol.
16   221
20   166
57   211
103   89
146   171
176   219
177   92
184-85   124
186   221
195   190
196   122
199-200   148
209.1-4   189

In Alcibiadem
1.60.5-7   225 note #93
1.72.19-20   225 note #94
1.121.2   205
1.137.7-8   225 note #94
1.149.1-5   225 note #93
1.245.15-246.3   188 note #83
1.264.15-18   188 note #83
1.325.8-12   195 note #87

In Cratylum
129.7-10   188 note #83
174.48-49   225 note #94

In Euclidem
46.1-9   188 note #83
49.10.   76 note #1
51.17-52.3   188 note #83

55.20-23   188 note #83
94.19-21   188 note #83

In Parm.
679.24-30   188 note #83
804.1-11   188 note #83
946.37-947.2   188 note #83
994.32-42   188 note #83
1025.9-11   188 note #83
1049.20   76 note #1

In Remp.
1.39.28-40.4   188
1.52.10-13   225 note #93
1.74.24-30   188
1. 74, 27   77 note #2
1.111.19-23   188
1.111, 22   77 note #2
1.120.25-121.3   188
1.121, 2-3   77 note #2
1.152.1-2   205
1.172.7   205
1.175.17-18.   205
1.235, 18-19   77 note #2
1.235.18-21   188
2.97.22   205
2.99.6-10   225 note #93
2.100   194
2.107.21-22   188 note #83
2.128.3-140.25   191
2.132.5-133.20   194
2.128.3-140.25   191
2.160.19-20   225 note #94
2.161.27-28   225 note #94
2.162.2   274 note #14
2.177.26-29   225 note #93
2.300.1   274 note #14

In Timaeum
1.33.20   76 note#1
1.49, 29ff.   144
1.70.30-71.5   225 note #93
1.71.1-2   225 note #94
1.71.2-3   225 note #93
1.111.14-17   225 note #93
1.115.23-25   225 note #94
1.352.16-19   188 note #83
1.362.9   84 note #9
1. 380, 26   124
1.381.26ff   158
1. 381, 26 - 382, 12   134
2.20, 4-9   144
2.33.13ff.   115
2.81, 21ff   132
2.152.26ff.   153
2.153.21ff.   80
2.153.17-25   89
2.153.25ff.   158
2.160.17   84 note #9
2.195.1ff   193

(PROCLUS, *In Timaeum*, cont.)
2.212.3 - 213.7	88
2.213.8 -215.28	87
2.213.13-15	91
2.213.9ff.	148, note #80
2.232.16	84 note #9
2.263.17	84 note #9
2 277.26ff.	128 note #54
2.285, 12-15	144
2.299.18	190
3.25.2	141
3.65.22-25	225
3.68.14ff.	193
3.93.22ff	148
3.129.14-15	225 note #94
3.131.6-7	225 note #94
3.198.16ff	193
3.234.8ff.	158
3.234.8-32	223
3.234.9-18	182
3.234.9-237.1	182
3.234.18-26	184
3.234.18-32	182
3.234.18	116
3.236.31-238.26	204
3.245.31-32	225 note #94
3.322.18-31	164
3.245.19-246.4	126
3.246.23-28	128
3.248.2-5	225
3.284.19-21	225 note #93
3.284.20-21	225 note #93
3.284.20	225 note #94
3.289.8-9	195 note #87
3.296.25-26	225 note #93
3.306.24	274 note #14
3.333.28ff.	128 note #54
3.348.6-21	118
3.348.19	118
3.348.30-349.1	225 note #94

Theologia Platonica
1.14	166
1.57.15	76 note #1
4.21.7	274 note # 14
4.32.10	274 note # 14
4.44.9	274 note # 14

PSELLUS
De Omniafaria Doctrina
115	164

PSEUDO-PLATO
Definitiones
411d	195

PSEUDO-PLUTARCH
Epitome (De Placitis Philosophorum)
877A	82

PSEUDO-SIMPLICIUS
In De Anima
17.2-5	188 note #83
89, 33ff. (Extract 3)	91 note #28
89.33-90.27	220
96.1-10	169
133.11-13	271
133.31-35	21 note #54
135.25-136.2	271 note #11
135.26-27	272 note #11
136.29	23
214.16-21	188 note #83
215.15-25	188 note #83
221, 29ff	97
240.8-10	22, 259
240, 33ff.	91 note #28

SALLUSTIUS
De Deis et Mundo
21	213
21.1.1-4	225

SEXTUS EMPIRICUS
IV 6	82, 82 note #5

SIMPLICIUS
In Categorias
2.9	4 note #14
18, 26ff.	78
135.8ff.	81
301.20	80
374-75	185

In De Cael.
36.34	274 note #14
51.5	274 note #14
151.31	274 note #14
154.22	274 note #14
155.32	274 note #14
380.22	274 note #14
462.27	274 note #14
469.7	132 note #57
492.19	274 note #14
493.13	274 note #14
500.19	274 note #14
507.2	274 note #14
508.1	274 note #14
508.28	274 note #14

In Phys.
589.22	274 note #14
620.3	76 note #1

SPEUSIPPUS
Fr. 28	84
Fr. 29	80
Fr. 54	80

STOBAEUS
1.350.8-354.18	108

1.355.1-357.22	113
1.350.19-25	113
1. 448.17-454.9	187
3.605.12	117
3.608.25-609.2	117
5.1089.14-1090.1	210 note #89

STOICORUM VETERUM FRAGMENTA
1.143	112
1.145	99
1.149	118
1.179	174
1.764	118
2.52	104
2.74	104
2.83	118
2.119	121
2. 471a	117
2.528	173, 174
2.473	99
2. 633	124
2.714ff	140
2.720	140
2.806	164
2.823	109
2.824	109
2.826	101
2.827	103, 112
2.828	103, 112
2.830	103, 112
2.832	103, 112
2.836	103, 112
2.837	104
2.841	117
2.879	103, 112

2.879.28-37	113
3.17	118
3.177	104
3.169-177	104
3.181	118

SYRIANUS
In Met.
81, 38ff.	89
123.8	84 note #9
142.23	84 note #9

TERTULLIAN
De Anima
| 5. 1 | 96 note #34 |

THEMISTIUS
In De Anima
3.7-16	108
3.14-16	109-110
25.23ff.	94
28.5-17	265
37.4-6	110
93.33-94.2	110

THEOPHRASTUS
Met.
| 6a19ff | 82 note #4 |

TIMAEUS LOCRUS
| 95E-96C | 86 |
| 99d-100a | 118 |

VETIUS VALENS
| 309.12 | 80 |

INDEX NOMINUM

Aeacus 191, 203
Aesarus of Lucania 113
Aetius 82 note #6, 83, 96, 104, 172, 178
Ahriman 137 note #65
Albinus 7, 136, 182
Alcinous 136, 136 note #63, 164, 165, 167, 184
Alexander of Aphrodisias 79, 82, 102, 104, 106, 109, 110, 118, 120, 169, 171,
Amelius 6, 10, 14, 29, 31, 45, 51, 53, 87, 88, 91, 119, 124, 124 note #47, 128, 128 note #54, 129, 141 note #72, 142, 143, 144, 145, 146, 147, 148, 148 note #79. 148 note #80, 149, 150, 151, 177, 210
Ammonius 108
Antiochus of Ascalon 95, 97, 103
Archytas 37, 82 note #4, 92, 113, 114
Aresas 113
Ariston of Chios 63, 174
Aristotle 4, 6, 8, 9, 10, 12, 12 note #26, 13, 14, 14 note #52, 18, 19, 22 note #55, 23, 27, 29, 31, 33, 35, 37, 41, 51, 76, 77, 78, 80, 81, 82, 85, 93, 94, 95, 96, 97, 99, 100, 101, 102, 104, 105, 106, 108, 110, 112, 113, 114, 117, 118, 119, 120, 139, 140, 144, 145, 147, 166, 168, 169, 170, 174, 178, 179, 180, 189, 190, 192, 196, 220, 221, 222, 231, 233, 237, 241, 243, 252, 253, 254, 255, 256, 257, 261, 262, 264, 266, 269, 270, 271, 274
Arius Didymus 173
Armstrong, A. H. 89-90, 91 note #26, 93, 125, 129, 131, 138, 184
Athanassiadi, P. 2 note #6
Athenodorus 78
Atomists 76, 78, 109, 112, 142, 146, 180, 181
Atticus 49, 57, 88, 127 note #51, 134, 135, 137, 156, 158-159, 182
Aurelius, Marcus 131 note #57, 185

Bazán, F. 185 note #182
Bidez, J. 4, 8 note #18
Blumenthal, H. J. 12 note #26, 19 note #45, 19 note #46, 19 note #47, 19 note #48, 23, 23 note #61, 125, 253, 259, 260, 266, 267

Brisson, L. 115, 124 note #47
Burkert, W. 21 note #52, 82 note #5
Bywater, I. 18 note #42, 263, 264, 265, 272

Calcidius 113, 134, 137
Cameron, A. 1
Carneades 96
Cebes 180
Chaldaean Oracles 7, 173, 182, 185 note #82, 197, 206, 226
Christianity 4, 7, 92
Chrysippus 35, 117-118
Cicero 97, 99, 100, 173, 174, 175
Clement 21 note #52, 175, 180
Cornutus, L. Annaeus 65, 78, 178
Corpus Hermeticum 95 note #32, 177, 182, 184
Critolaus 96, 98
Cronius 49, 57, 137, 138, 141, 160
Cumont, F. 8 note #18, 151

Damascius 2, 3, 9, 84 note #9, 92, 115, 116, 143, 181-182, 191, 194, 200, 202, 204, 216, 217, 220, 222, 225
Democritus of Abdera 51, 63, 65, 77, 78, 109, 111, 174, 180
Democritus the Platonist 39, 115
Dicaearchus 33, 99-100, 123
Dihle, A. 153
Dillon, J. M. 1 note #1, 3 note #11, 21 note #53, 21 note #54, 78 note #3, 81, 84 note #7, 87, 97 note #40, 116, 126-127, 137 note #64, 145, 153, 155, 158, 159, 160, 162 note #81, 164, 166, 167, 182, 183, 184, 189, 193, 204, 209, 211, 219, 227
Diogenes of Apollonia 76, 178
Diogenes Laertius 104

Ecphantus 82
Empedocles 20-21 note #52, 49, 94, 135-136, 178
Epicharmus 180
Epicurus 51, 65, 175
Er, Myth of 174, 175, 176, 191, 205
Eratosthenes 55, 152-153, 184, 220
Eunapius 1, 2, 3, 4, 5, 6, 7, 8, 141
Eusebius 4, 173
Festugière, A. J. 11 note #25, 24, 79, 81, 83, 86, 87, 92, 93, 95 note #32, 96 note #37, 100 note #43, 101,

Festugière, A. J (cont.) 102, 103, 106, 112, 113, 115, 116, 117, 119, 122, 123, 124. 126, 134, 139, 140, 143, 145, 146, 147, 149, 150, 152, 153, 154, 155, 156, 157, 158, 160, 163, 164, 165, 166, 167, 168, 170, 171, 172, 173, 175, 177, 179, 180, 181, 183, 184, 185, 186, 187, 188, 189, 190, 192, 193, 195, 196, 198, 199, 202, 203, 205, 208, 209, 211, 212. 213, 215, 217, 218, 220, 221, 222, 223, 226, 253, 254, 256, 258

Ficino 9, 263, 273,

Finamore, J. F. 99 note #41, 116, 119, 150, 151, 152, 153, 155, 159, 160, 172, 182, 183, 184, 185, 186, 191 note #86, 193, 195, 201, 204, 207, 210, 211, 212, 214 note #90, 215, 216, 218, 260 note #2, 273, 274 note #13, 276

Galen 23, 117, 157, 164
Gellius, Aulus 155
Gnostics 49, 92, 136, 162 note #81, 171
Gottschalk, H. B. 153
Guthrie, W. K. C. 109, 145, 227 note #95

Hadot, I. 12 note #26, 19, 19 note #94
Harpocration of Argos 49, 57, 88, 137-138, 158, 160
Hayduck, M. 18 note #41, 257
Hense 11, 24 note #63
Heraclides of Pontus 96, 153
Heraclitus 20-21 note #52, 49, 55, 75, 94, 135-136, 154-155, 156, 227
Herillus of Carthage 63, 174
Hermias 160, 166, 189, 200
Hieronymus of Rhodes 63, 174
Hippasus 29, 80, 82, 83, 84,
Hippolytus 154
Hippon 94
Huby, P. 22, 23 note #61, 258, 259, 260, 261, 262, 263, 264, 265, 271, 272, 273

Inwood, B. 104

Julian 2 note #8, 3, 7, 8, 141, 193

Leucippus 78,
Lewy, H. 197 note #88
Long, A. A. 104, 109
Longinus 108-112, 115
Lucan 178
Lucretius 180
John Lydus 19 note #44, 202

Macrobius 88, 96 note #34
Majercik, R. 206
Mansfeld, J. 10 note #22, 11 note #23 and 24, 13 note #28, 21 note #52, 24 note #63, 64, and 65
Middle Platonists 10, 13, 88, 110-112, 115, 133, 138, 167
Moderatus 29, 80, 82, 83, 84, 86
Minos 191, 203

Nemesius of Emesa 141
Nicolaus 110, 111, 112
Nicomachus of Gerasa 6, 9, 88
Numenius 6, 14, 31, 49, 73, 88, 89, 116, 119, 128 note #54, 133, 134, 137, 138, 158, 160, 163, 164, 172, 181, 218, 219

Olympiodorus 9, 115, 206, 225 note #93, 226
O'Meara, D. J. 9
Orpheus 10, 33, 94-95, 144-146, 147, 165
Orphics 33, 51, 94-95, 142, 143, 144-145, 145-146, 147, 165

Peripatetics 10, 14, 78, 79, 94, 96, 98, 99, 100, 101, 102, 106, 107-108, 112, 118, 119, 120, 121, 122, 133, 175, 179, 182, 253, 261, 272-273
Philo of Alexandria 21 note #52, 77 note #2, 84, 97, 153, 162 note #81
Philoponus 109, 155, 169, 170
Piccione, R. M. 11 note #23
Plato 3, 6, 10, 13, 14, 16, 17, 21 note #52 and 54,29, 31, 35, 37, 39, 43, 47, 49, 53, 63, 73, 81, 82, 83, 84, 85, 86, 92, 94, 95, 101, 102, 103, 105, 106, 107, 108, 110, 111, 112, 113, 114, 115, 116, 118, 119, 121, 122, 123, 127, 128, 132. 133, 134, 137, 138, 140, 145, 148, 149, 152, 153, 155, 156, 160, 161, 162, 163, 164, 165, 166, 168, 169, 173, 174, 175, 176, 177, 178, 179, 180, 182, 184, 187, 189, 191, 192, 193, 194, 195, 196, 197, 199, 200, 201, 203, 204, 206, 208, 209, 215, 216, 223, 224, 225, 226, 227, 228, 231, 253, 256, 262, 263, 264
Plotinus 1, 4, 5, 6, 10, 13, 14, 15, 20, 21, 29, 31, 39, 45, 49, 53, 57, 61, 67, 71, 73, 86, 87, 88, 89, 90, 91, 92, 93, 114, 115, 119, 120, 124, 125, 126, 127, 128, 129, 130, 131, 136, 137, 138, 139, 143, 148, 149, 150, 151, 152, 154, 155, 157, 162, 165, 167, 168, 169, 171, 177, 181, 182, 184, 186, 187, 190, 198, 202, 208, 209, 210, 211, 212, 214, 233, 253, 254

Plutarch of Athens 141 note #72, 182
Plutarch of Chaeronea 21, 49, 73, 82
   note #6, 83, 134, 137, 158, 209
Porphyry 1, 2, 4, 5, 6, 8, 10, 14, 15,
   29, 31, 39, 45, 49, 51, 53, 59, 67, 73,
   75, 86, 87, 88, 89, 90, 91, 92, 93,
   98104, 108, 109, 110, 111, 112, 113,
   114, 115, 116, 117, 119, 124, 125,
   126, 127, 130, 131, 133, 134, 137,
   138, 139, 140, 141, 142, 143, 144,
   148, 149, 150, 151, 163, 164, 165,
   166, 171, 177, 182, 184, 208, 210,
   211, 213, 214, 215, 221, 222, 223
Presocratics 135, 140
Priscianus 9, 13, 18, 19, 20, 22, 23,
   91, 108, 111, 258, 259, 260, 261,
   262, 263, 265, 266, 267, 268, 269,
   270, 271, 272, 273, 274, 275, 276,
   277, 278
Proclus 3, 7, 9, 10, 20, 21, 76, 77, 80,
   84, 87, 88, 89, 91, 92, 99, 115, 116,
   118, 120, 122, 124, 126, 127, 128,
   132, 141, 143, 144, 148, 153, 158,
   164, 166, 171, 182, 184, 188, 189,
   190, 191, 193, 194, 195, 200, 204,
   205, 211, 219, 221, 223, 225, 274
Psellus 9, 164, 185 note #3
Pseudo-Simplicius 12, 13, 15, 18, 19-
   24, 97, 108, 111, 117, 169, 170, 188
   note #83, 220, 252-278, 259, 260,
   271, 274 note #14, 278
Pythagoras 9, 14, 17, 31, 35, 39, 49,
   83, 95, 101, 102, 118, 133, 135, 156,
   162, 215, 228
Pythagoreans 6, 9-10, 18, 29, 37, 69,
   71, 80, 82, 83, 86, 92, 113, 137, 140,
   187, 192, 194, 196, 197, 198, 219,
   228

Rhadamanthus 191, 203
Rist, J. M. 135 note #60
Robinson, T. M. 166
Ryle, G. 100

Sallustius 9, 213, 225
Seneca 178
Septimius Severus 1
Seth-Typhon 137 note #65
Severus 29, 80, 81
Sextus Empiricus 82
Simplicius 4, 9, 76 note #1, 78, 81,
   131 note #57, 185, 260 note #1,
   274 note #14
Smith, A. 110, 114, 183
Simmias 86, 123, 180
Socrates 123, 143, 176, 180
Solmsen, F. 152-153
Solon 189
Speusippus 29, 79, 80-81, 84, 175, 182

Steel, C. 19-24, 119, 252, 254, 256,
   257, 258, 259-260, 267 note #8,
   271, 272, 274 note #15, 275, 276,
   277 note #16
Stobaeus 9, 10-13, 14, 24, 94, 108,
   113, 116, 117, 119, 123, 135, 139,
   142 note #77, 143, 149, 157, 163,
   172, 175, 177, 181, 187, 203, 205,
   218, 222, 223, 224, 226, 227
Stoics 10, 14, 33, 35, 37, 39, 43, 45,
   47, 51, 63, 77 note #3, 78, 84, 95
   note #32, 99, 101, 102, 103, 104,
   107, 109, 110, 111, 112, 113, 117,
   119, 121, 123, 124, 130, 140, 141,
   147, 150, 157, 163, 164, 170, 171,
   173, 174, 175, 178, 255
Strato of Lampsacus 78, 95
Syrianus 3, 9, 85 note #9, 89, 99, 160,
   200, 204, 225

Tarán, L. 80-81
Taurus, Calvenus 55, 155, 156, 167
Tertullian 96 note #34, 172
Theiler, W. 96 note #35
Themistius 23, 94, 108, 109-110, 265
Theodorus of Asine 8, 128, 141, 141
   note #72
Theophrastus 18, 19, 23. 82 note #4,
   96, 96 note #57, 97, 270
Thesleff, H. 84 note #8, 113 note #45
Timaeus Locrus 86, 118
Todd, R. B. 110 note #44

Urmson, J. O. 19, 252
Usener, H. 89 note #19, 92 note #20,
   93 note #31, 95 note #33, 101, 106-
   107, 112, 124 note #46, 133, 140,
   140 note #70, 167, 171, 175, 196,
   205, 217

Vanderspoel, J. 1 note #3

Wachsmuth, C. 11, 24-25, 100 note
   #10, 101, 103, 106-107, 113, 122,
   133, 137 note #62, 149, 152, 158,
   160, 164, 167, 167, 171, 172, 173,
   179, 180, 183, 184, 186, 195, 196,
   205, 207, 209, 211, 217, 218, 221,
   221
Wehrli, F. 96 note #34
Westerink, L. G. 7 note #17, 182,
   200, 204
Wyttenbach 101

Xenocrates 79, 80, 81, 82-83, 85, 89,
   182

Zeno of Citium 174

INDEX RERUM

[*We list here only significant discussions or mentions of important concepts dealt with in the introduction or commentary*]

Aether, 96-9,153
Angel, 16, 172, 193, 205-7, 216-17, 224-6

Body, 95-100, 102, 130-2, 138, 149-53, 168-71,175, 177, 184, 215, 221, 277

Contemplation, 190, 224

Demiurge, 16, 127, 148, 150, 155, 216, 226
  sublunar, 193
Daemon, 16, 126, 144, 150, 172, 191, 193, 200, 206, 216
Dyad, 89,137

Fate, 220-1

God, gods, 16, 18, 126, 144, 150, 156-8, 166, 171-3, 188, 191, 194, 200, 216-18, 220, 224, 273
  planetary gods, 157-8, 193

Hero,16, 126, 150, 172, 191, 193, 200, 206, 216-18

Imagination (*phantasia*), 77, 59-65
Immortality, *see under* Soul
Intellect, 90-3, 118-22, 129, 185, 187, 189, 192-3, 201, 210-11, 254
  Intellection, 119-20, 124
  Intelligible realm, 162-3, 202

Light, 96, 270
Logos, 84, 92

Materialism, materialists, 95-100
Matter, 137-9, 189
Memory, 117, 262

One, 81, 90, 135, 187, 193, 226
  'one in us', 211
Opinion (*doxa*), 189-90, 263

Planet, 88, 150, 225
Pneuma, 103-4, 140, 177-8

pneumatic vehicle (*okhêma*), 131-2, 150, 152, 183-6, 194, 204, 218, 223, 260, 267-9

Reason (*logos*), 117-18, 212
Reincarnation, 141-2, 192, 200
Reversion (*epistrophê*), 130-1

Sensation, 134, 220, 257, 265-7
  sense object, 265
  sense organ, 265, 267
Soul
  act (*ergon, energêma*) of, 123-133, 214
  activity (*energeia*) of, 111, 119-23
  as attunement (*harmonia*), 86-8
  as entelechy, 79, 95-8
  as mathematical, 79-84
  as mean, 14-16, 92, 253-6, 259
  ascent of, 172, 260
  descent of, 135-9, 149-56, 167, 186, 216, 255
  ensoulment, moment of, 163-8
  immortality of, 222
  irrational, 114-17, 134, 158, 182-3, 213-15, 222-3, 256, 270
  judgment of, 194-200
  number of, 142-9
  parts of, 104, 114
  power, faculty (*dynamis*) of, 100-17, 213
  pure, 16-17, 108, 126, 129, 159-60, 198-9, 201
  purification of, 173-4, 186-204
  rational, 134, 168-70, 181-2, 212, 222
  rewards of, 203-7, 216, 226
  theory of two souls, 134.
  three types of, 159-63
  world-soul (All-Soul), 95, 124-6, 131, 145, 157, 166, 192

Theurgy, 16, 172, 176, 206, 226, 258, 260, 273

Vehicle, *see* Pneuma
Virtue, 187

CPSIA information can be obtained
at www.ICGtesting.com
Printed in the USA
LVHW112131020720
659622LV00001B/24

9 781589 834682